Interior Lighting for

Environmental Designers

James L. Nuckolls

Interior Lighting for Environmental Designers

Second Edition

A WILEY-INTERSCIENCE PUBLICATION

JOHN WILEY & SONS
New York • Chichester • Brisbane • Toronto • Singapore

Library of Congress Cataloging in Publication Data:

Nuckolls, James L.
  Interior lighting for environmental designers.

  "A Wiley-Interscience publication."
  Includes index.
  1. Electric lighting. 2. Lighting, Architectural and
decorative. I. Title.
TK4175.N82   1983   729'.28   83-1382
ISBN 0-471-87381-0

Printed in the United States of America

10 9 8 7 6 5 4 3 2

To

Bernard Braverman

Preface

The American Association of the Blind estimates that seven-eighths of all our perceptions are through sight. Obviously, there is no sight without light, so the way structures and objects in our world are illuminated makes a tremendous difference in the way they look to us and how we respond to them. It stands to reason, then, that lighting is an essential design and building element. Yet detailed knowledge of lighting—its capacities for expanding or minimizing interior and exterior space, its effects on colors and textures, and its atmospheric potentials—is one of the least developed professional areas.

Once confined to chandeliers and wall-mounted lanterns lighting now includes wall-wide projections, finite control of light intensities and focus, the exquisite subtleties of light sculpturing, and decorative fixtures that present a flexibility of illumination never before possible. Artistic and practical knowledge of the effective uses of these new systems has not kept pace with technological advances.

Because it presents so many new challenges, lighting design is a dynamic, exciting field. It is the purpose of this book to define these challenges and describe the creative fundamentals of designed lighting in a way that will bring a more complete understanding of its potential to those who can utilize its strength.

There are some who would tell you that lighting is a fantastically complex, technical subject that must be approached mathematically. Lighting *is* based on technology, and it *does* have its mathematical and scientific sides, but it should be applied with as much aesthetic awareness as mechanical proficiency. It is important to remember that lighting is a design medium as well as a technical process. The goal of this book is to provide a background in design and an understanding of, and an appreciation for, the technical matters that are necessary to execute a design.

This book is divided into three parts. Part One, An Introduction to Lighting, includes a brief introduction to electric light, the seeing process, electric power, color, light sources, measurement of light, control of light, and brightness relationships. Part Two, A Review of Lighting Techniques, contains chapters on calculations, typical luminaires, control of electricity, and the layout and specification of equipment. Part Three, A Survey of Lighting Design, covers theater and photographic design theory, architectural lighting design, lighting and the human condition, and architectural lighting and associated phenomena.

I accept the responsibility for omissive errors in this complex undertaking, and I sincerely thank its many contributors. My deep appreciation goes to Jeffrey Milham for his creative primary editing of the first edition, as well as for most of the illustrations that grace these pages. Robert Newell developed the second edition's additional drawings.

The concern demonstrated by members of the International Association of Lighting Designers was essential to this book's development. In particular, I am indebted to Jules Horton, P.E., for his meticulous criticism of the first edition. The factual data available from the Illuminating Engineering Society have been invaluable. And, most important, the book continues to be inspired by New York's Parsons School of Design (New School for Social Research) Environmental Design and Continuing Education departments.

In its second edition, many topics have benefited from the help of interested individuals. Special thanks must go to: William A. Thornton of the Westinghouse Electric Corporation (*Color*); Thomas Lemons of TLA Lighting Consultants and Frank LaGuisa of General Electric (*Light Sources*); the late Monroe Hirsch of the University of California at Berkeley (*The Aging Eye*); John Spofford of the Shaw-Walker Co., Nancy Carlson of Mohasco Corporation Carpet Division, and writer Donald Wheeler (*Furniture Integrated Lighting*—portions reprinted by permission of Shaw-Walker); Beverly Russell of *Interiors* (*Lighting Design*—portions reprinted by permission); Jo Standley of Urbahn Associates (*Brightness Relationships*); Paul Smester (*Recommendations for Standard Interior Luminaires Based on Data Sheet Information*). The text has received the constant support and flow of information provided by my professional associates: Carroll Cline, Francesca Bettridge, Worth Young, and Melvin Schrier.

JAMES L. NUCKOLLS, I.A.L.D.

New York, New York
September 1983

Contents

PART TWO   A REVIEW OF LIGHTING TECHNIQUES

PART THREE   A SURVEY OF LIGHTING DESIGN

Interior Lighting for
Environmental Designers

Part One

An Introduction to Lighting

Chapter One

A Brief History of and Introduction to Electric Light

A review of the entire history of light, from the first uses of sunlight, to the development of candles, down through the oil burner and gas jet, and then to the incandescent lamp, would be a book in itself. However, since we are concerned with the use of artificial light as a modern and flexible design medium, we shall limit our discussion in this chapter to the development of electric light.

Several terms used during the course of this chapter should be defined before we go any further.

DEFINITIONS

LAMP: An assembly consisting of the glass bulb, metal or ceramic base, and internal elements that produce light. Many people incorrectly use the term "light bulb" when referring to a lamp (the bulb is simply a glass envelope surrounding a light source).

Incandescent Lamp. A source that produces light by heating a tungsten wire to incandescence. The most familiar incandescent lamp is pear-shaped and screws into a common socket. (see Figure 1.1).

Figure 1.1. Typical incandescent lamp. (Reproduced, by permission, from Westinghouse Electric Corporation, Lamp Divisions.)

Fluorescent Lamp. A lamp that produces light by means of an electric arc that excites a phosphor coating deposited on the inside of the glass bulb; it does not contain wire as the basic light generator. Long, tubular fluorescent lamps are often used in lighting fixtures (see Figure 1.2).

HID Lamp. HID, or "high intensity discharge," lamps consist of small tubes containing electric arcs that generate useful quantities of light within the arc itself, but they may employ phosphors for additional light output or color enrichment. These lamps were traditionally used to light roadways or floodlight buildings, but more recently they have been used for interior illumination (see Figure 1.3).

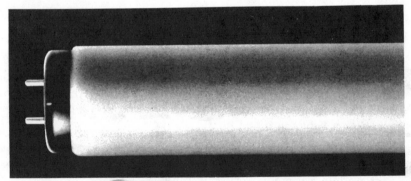

Figure 1.2. Typical fluorescent lamp. (Reproduced, by permission, from Westinghouse Electric Corporation, Lamp Divisions.)

Figure 1.3. Typical HID lamp. (Reproduced, by permission, from General Electric, 220-1611R2.)

LUMINAIRE: The more proper term for the total lighting device, including lamps, reflectors, lenses, wiring, and sockets. Synonyms are lighting fixture or lighting device (see Figure 1.4).

FOOTCANDLE: A footcandle is a measure of the amount of light that reaches a surface (see Figure 1.5).

THE FIRST AGE OF LIGHT

Although the development of lighting sources, hardware, and their application has been a continuous process, for convenience, we divide our historical

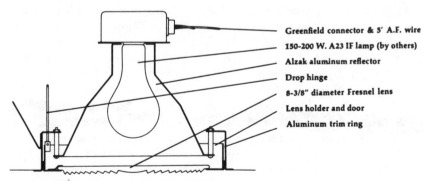

Greenfield connector & 5' A.F. wire
150-200 W. A23 IF lamp (by others)
Alzak aluminum reflector
Drop hinge
8-3/8" diameter Fresnel lens
Lens holder and door
Aluminum trim ring

Figure 1.4. Typical recessed incandescent luminaire. (Reprinted, by permission, from *Lighting and Electronics*, D-2.)

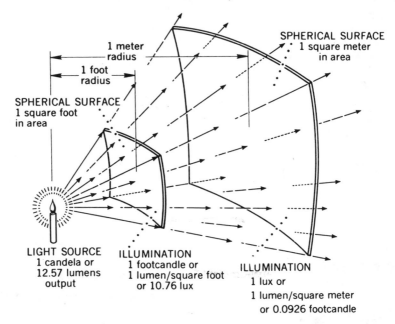

Figure 1.5.   Relationship of candelas or lumens to footcandles or lux. One footcandle is the illumination on a surface 1 square foot in area that is 1 foot from a "standard" candle. (Reprinted, by permission, from General Electric, TP-118.)

commentary into four "ages" or periods of development. The year 1881 marks the first age of light. In that year, Sir Joseph W. Swan in England and Thomas A. Edison in the United States almost simultaneously produced the first practical incandescent source of light. Edison marketed his first commercial lamp 9 years later.

The first lamp consisted of a glass bulb containing a bamboo fiber that had been reduced to carbon. To prevent this fiber or filament of bamboo from oxidizing too rapidly when electrically heated, a partial vacuum was created by exhausting most of the air inside the bulb. The first lamp was rather inefficient; the bamboo fiber produced a very weak light and had a short life.

In 1907, with the production of the first tungsten filament lamp, the efficiency of the lamp was more than doubled. The electric current passing through the tungsten heats the filament, creating a bright incandescence. Today tungsten is used almost universally as the filament material.

At first, the bare lamp was considered only as a source of light for interiors. Once electric lamps were established as an alternative to gas lighting, however, designers began to adapt it decoratively. At first, they merely designed new holders, then they moved to enclosing lamps in globes

Figure 1.6. Typical silver-bowl lamp. (Reproduced, by permission, from General Electric, TP-110.)

and eventually to indirect lighting using lamps with integral reflectors called "silverbowls." (see Figure 1.6).

In this first age of light, lamps were considered from a purely pragmatic standpoint; they were used to simply dispel darkness in interiors. For this reason, one writer has called this the "age of necessity." The lamp did, however, often find application as a means of decoration on the exteriors of buildings. In 1901, for example, bare lamps were used at the Pan American Exposition in Buffalo to outline buildings with light.

THE SECOND AGE OF LIGHT

During 1939 and 1940, the fluorescent lamp was introduced at the two world's fairs that ran simultaneously in eastern and western United States. This introduction revolutionized the field of lighting when it was demonstrated that the fluorescent lamp produced more light at a lower cost than did the incandescent lamp. The fluorescent lamp has four other important advantages: It has a relatively low surface brightness, its life is comparatively long, it can produce shadowless lighting, and it does not produce as much heat per unit of light as its incandescent counterpart.

We know that in 1939 the industrial 500-watt incandescent lamp provided about 20 lumens per watt. (The phrase "lumens per watt" is used to compare the efficiency of lamps.) The first 40-watt fluorescent source, on the other hand, delivered about 40 lumens per watt. Improvements in the fluorescent lamp came quickly: In 1945, the 40-watt lamp was producing about 2000 lumens; by 1955, the figure was close to 2500; and in 1965 the simple 40-watt source could boast an output of about 3200 lumens. Note that today the 40-watt incandescent lamp produces an average of only 455 lumens, although efficiency does increase as wattage increases.

The efficiency of fluorescent lamps can be demonstrated in another way. We estimate that approximately 50 footcandles of light falling on a work surface is a necessary minimum if we wish to perform an easy task with comfort. Using typical luminaires in an average room measuring 25 by 17 feet with a work surface 8 feet from the luminaire, we would need over 87 incandescent 40-watt lamps to provide 50 footcandles of light, yet only 13 fluorescent lamps would deliver the same amount of light.

It is clear that on the basis of intensity alone, the fluorescent lamp was a great improvement over its incandescent predecessor. In a short time, the 40-watt tube became the workhorse of industry. In the year 1965, this source provided nearly 75% of the world's light.

However, all good things also have their limitations, and fluorescent lighting is no exception. First of all, because of its diffuse nature, fluorescent lighting is difficult to control (unlike the point source provided by many incandescent lamps—we learn more about this in Chapter Twelve). A space illuminated only with fluorescent sources may look bland—it lacks sparkle. The fluorescent method of producing light is also somewhat handicapped when it comes to revealing balanced color, and this is important when color perception is critical.

However, the introduction of the fluorescent lamp, with its increased efficiency, heralded the "age of abundance." Abundance not only in lamp output, however, but also in the use of electric light. Using 1940 as the base year, the use of all types of lamps had increased over 16 times by 1965.

With higher output and increased application, it became desirable to accurately predict the amount of light in a space. Since quantity was of prime importance, engineers followed four simple steps in their application of lighting:

1. Determine the desired level of illumination (usually based on a published recommendation).
2. Select a luminaire that will produce this level.
3. Calculate the required number of luminaires.
4. Lay out the installation for uniformity of illumination.

With the exception of Step 2, little in this approach has to do with design— at least from an aesthetic standpoint. With a few modifications, this approach is still used today.

THE THIRD AGE OF LIGHT

In the mid-1960s, the approach to lighting began to change. We entered a period that has been called the "age of refinement." There were several new trends in lighting application:

1. Architects and interior designers demanded solutions to their lighting problems that required an inventiveness not solely connected with the quantity of light.
2. New sources became popular. HID lamps were particularly promising. They were considered for indoor use as well as for the outdoor applications that led to their development.
3. New professionals entered lighting design—traditionally an engineering field. They approached lighting from the standpoint of its *use* rather than its technical production. Lighting design and lighting design professionals were no longer limited to the theatre; they became prominent in architecture.
4. There was a dramatic increase in the flexibility of lighting materials. Modular instrumentation was now a fact, and luminal art influenced all other areas of the industry.
5. Engineering advances, largely supported by the Illuminating Engineering Society, N.A., allowed a flexibility permitting aesthetic demands to be realized. In addition, recommendations and models were developed against which we could check the validity of design results.

These advances demanded change in our approach to lighting design. The Illuminating Engineering Society suggested the following broad outline:

1. Determine composition. Think about a space in three dimensions, evaluating the parameters of line, form, texture, and color. Spaces must be related to each other.
2. Analyze the appearance of objects. Visibility should be reviewed in terms of glare (or sparkle), shadow factor, modeling, and so on.
3. Select luminaires.
4. Lay out and evaluate the lighting system. The I.E.S. recommends that a design be evaluated for visual comfort, glare, maintenance, and heat control.

THE FOURTH AGE OF LIGHT

About 1974, we all had cause to reexamine our approach to lighting. That was the year of the oil embargo in the United States, and electric energy available for lighting started to escalate in price. At the start of this period, there were also predictions that certain basic materials might be running out; these included silver, mercury, and copper. It was doubtful whether the small amounts of these materials actually used in luminaire or lamp manufacture would severely limit lighting manufacture, but it might drive up the price. Inflated prices led to a fresh consideration of initial versus operating costs.

Comfort and efficiency became issues at the start of this period. Visual Comfort Probability (VCP), the Illuminating Engineering Society NA metric used to evaluate discomfort glare caused by luminaires directly in the field of view, was proposed in the 1960s and found regular use by the mid-1970s. Although difficult to evaluate, evidence seemed to suggest that the comfortable employee would be both stable and productive. The federal government was also populariziing barrier-free design. This suggested that the elderly and infirm should have equal use of facilities. Since an otherwise healthy eye is considered old around age 50, and seeing parameters change at this age and thereafter, it is reasonable to design building lighting design systems to accommodate this country's increasing quantity of active and productive senior citizens.

In other areas of consultation, architectural and interior design considerations were balanced against engineering requirements. The occurences in this period suggested that the balance now applied to a previously technically-dominated lighting profession.

For want of better words, we might use the terms "production" and "consumption" to differentiate the approaches to architectural lighting defined during this fourth age of light. The older production approach started out with electric power, determined how it reached luminaires, selected the appropriate lamp, and wound up with a specification of footcandles. The newly popularized consumption approach began with the observer (his/her physiology and—very definitely—psychology) and progressed to the seeing task, its environment, footlambert evaluations, and then footcandles, lamps, luminaires, wiring, and so on. This was not a poor political stance either, since it avoided nervous confrontations on sensitive issues. One was not talking about an exclusivity of information, suggesting the superiority of either approach, or labeling all engineers as technicians and all architects as aestheticians. The consumption approach stressed the validity of both approaches and suggested that different educational backgrounds were appropriate. The consumption approach, however, is very much the issue herein.

In previous periods, a *general* lighting level was often recommended for design areas. In this period, a *task/ambient* approach gained popularity. "Task/ambient" does not describe a particular type of lighting equipment; it does suggest that we should illuminate the task in an appropriate manner while balancing the illumination of surrounding areas. For example, typing tasks require more light than passageways in offices; kitchen conters need different illumination than do dinette areas in homes. Since many parts of an installation may not require higher task lighting, this technique of variable intensities can save equipment, maintenance, and fuel costs.

BIBLIOGRAPHY

Dorsey, R. T., "Design Approach, The New Thrust in Lighting Practice," *Lighting Design and Application* 1 (1971): 13.

General Electric, *Incandescent Lamps*, TP-110 (Nela Park, Cleveland, no date).

————, "Unity with Variety," unpublished paper (Nela Park, Cleveland, revised 1970).

McCandless, Stanley, *A Syllabus of Stage Lighting* (New Haven, Conn., 1958), p. 8

Sylvania, *Incandescent Lamps*, Engineering Bulletin 0-324 (Danvers, Mass., revised June 15, 1971).

Chapter Two

The Seeing Process

THE HUMAN EYE

Roughly speaking, the human eye can be compared to a camera. Each has a light-sensitive plane—in the eye it is called the retina and in the camera it is the film—on which a lens focuses an inverted image. In each, the amount of light passing through the lens can be controlled—by an iris in the eye and by the iris diaphragm in the camera. The camera's shutter and the eyelid further control the entrance of light (see Figure 2.1).

This analogy is limited, however, because the human eye is a living organ with a built-in adaptability that would make any camera manufacturer envious. All the changes required for everyday seeing are made continuously and automatically by the eye. When compared to the eye, cameras are very restricted in their illumination ranges since the eye can rapidly adapt to radical changes in lighting levels.

The various parts of the eye work together to provide a stimulus that the brain interprets as the sense of sight (see Figure 2.2). We now discuss each of these parts.

The *retina* is the thin, light-sensitive inner surface of the back of the eye. This surface is composed of a fine mosaic of photoreceptors that are connected to the brain through a network of nerves. There are two types of photoreceptors: rods and cones. Their concentration varies over the retinal area.

Rods are found only outside of the main vision point in the outer portions of the retina. They do not afford distinct vision nor do they respond to color,

12

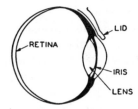

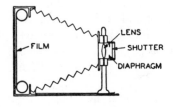

Figure 2.1. Comparison of the eye and the camera. (Reprinted, by permission, from Westinghouse Electric Corporation, Lamp Divisions.)

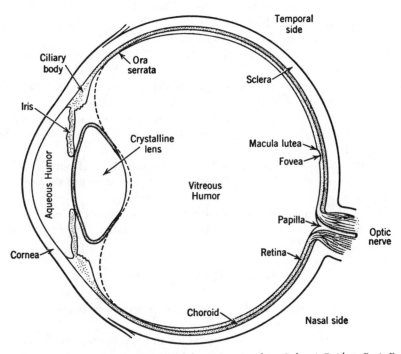

Figure 2.2. Section of the eye. (Reprinted, by permission, from *Color: A Guide to Basic Facts and Concepts*, John Wiley & Sons, 1963.)

but they are more sensitive to light than are cones and respond to movement and flicker. The rods are much slower in their response to stimuli than are the cones and are also notably slower in their recovery. A light-sensitive substance called visual purple is found in the rods. This substance bleaches rapidly when exposed to light. The regeneration of visual purple is important for dark adaptation.

Cones are found principally near the center of the retina; the central vision point is composed only of cones in great concentration. Although the rods are connected to a nerve system in groups, it is assumed that each cone is individually connected to a single nerve ending and is thus capable of transmitting very sharp and detailed images to the brain. The cones perceive color but are not as sensitive to low levels of light as the rods are. The cones are much faster in action than the rods are and the cones are faster in their recovery after changes in stimulus.

The greatest concentration of cones is found in the *fovea*, near the center of the retinal area. In section, the fovea would look like a tiny pit in the surface of the retina. It is here that the eye involuntarily focuses any object that must be examined in great detail.

The *optic nerve* carries light impulses to the brain. It enters the retina at a point called the *papilla* (blind spot). In this small area, there are no rods or cones and therefore no visual sensations.

The *lens* is a transparent capsule that focuses visual images on the retina. The shape of the lens is controlled by the *ciliary muscle*, which is attached to the lens by suspensary ligaments. The ring-shaped ciliary muscle actually changes the curvature of the lens by adjusting tension on it.

The *iris* functions as a variable diaphragm that controls the amount of light admitted to the eye. In the middle of the colored iris area is the opening (*pupil*) through which light enters the eye.

The *sclera* is the tough outer coating that protects the back portions of the eye, and the *cornea* is the clear front covering. The spherical shape of the eye is maintained by both the sclera and cornea.

The *aqueous humor* is a limpid fluid found between the lens and the cornea. All other spaces inside the eyeball are also filled with clear liquids.

PHYSIOLOGICAL FACTORS

The physiological factors of the seeing process are those that concern the organism's healthy or normal functions.

Accommodation is the process by which the eye locates and focuses on objects within the visual field (see Figure 2.3). The nearer an object is to the

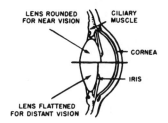

Figure 2.3. Accommodation. (Reprinted, by permission, from Westinghouse Electric Corporation, Lamp Divisions.)

eye, the greater the convexity of the lens must be. To achieve this convexity, the ciliary muscle contracts, permitting the lens to assume a more spherical shape. When objects are far away (greater than 20 feet), the ciliary muscle relaxes, and the lens flattens. When the lens is at its flattest, the eye is focused at infinity. The accommodation process causes changes in the form and, to a lesser extent, in the position of the lens inside the eye. However, accommodation also involves changes in the diameter of the *pupil;* its diameter is comparatively large for distant objects and small for near objects.

Adaptation is a two-part process involving the *size of the pupil opening* and the *sensitivity of the retina.* The pupil dilates, or opens, when light is low and contracts in bright light. The corresponding retinal changes are in the regeneration rate of the reina's photochemical substances. Whenever there is a change of illumination, there is a photochemical change, and this change requires time. It takes the eye longer to adapt to a change from light to dark, as a general rule, than to a change from dark to light. For example, when one enters a dark theater on a sunny day, it will take about 2 minutes to "adapt" to the lower illumination; however, complete adaptation may require a full 30 minutes.

Visual field is what the eye can see in horizontal and vertical directions (see Figure 2.4). The normal total visual field is approximately 130° vertically and 180° horizontally. Toward the outside of this field, details become very indistinct, although it is possible to readily detect movement or changes in brightness. The binocular field is the area seen by both eyes when they focus on a single object. The fovea sees only a small fraction of the total visual field—less than 1° at the center—but in this area, one can recognize the greatest detail.

The exact nature of the *photochemical process* by which the eye converts light energy into impulses that are recognized by the brain is not fully understood. However, it is generally assumed that upon exposure to light, there is a chemical reaction in the retinal receptors that results in a train of impulses which pass through the retina to the optic nerve and then on to the

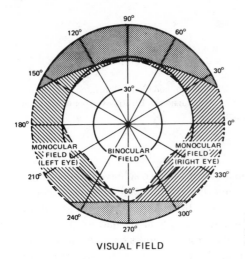

VISUAL FIELD

Figure 2.4. Visual field. (Reprinted, by permission, from Westinghouse Electric Corporation, Lamp Divisions.)

brain. The intensity of the stimulus is thought to determine the frequency of the impulses.

Color has a great deal to do with seeing, and color processes are studied in detail in a later chapter.

STRUCTURAL DEFECTS

There are four common structural eye defects that affect vision. The two most common defects are illustrated in Figure 2.5.

Presbyopia is the inability of the lens to accommodate easily. It is frequently a result of the normal aging process; the lens becomes progressively less elastic, resulting in a condition similar to nearsightedness.

Myopia occurs when the focal length of the lens is too short. Light rays then focus in front of the retina rather than on it. A person with this condition, known as "nearsightedness," cannot see distant objects clearly.

Hypermetropia is just the opposite of myopia. The focal point of light rays entering the eye is beyond the retina because the focal length of the eye is too great. A person with "farsightedness" has difficulty seeing close objects clearly.

Astigmatism is found when there are irregularities in the curvature of the cornea and the lens. In this case, the focal length of the eye is different in two planes at right angles to each other. A person with this condition cannot bring horizontal and vertical lines into focus at the same time.

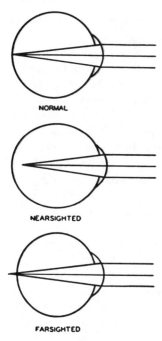

NORMAL

NEARSIGHTED

FARSIGHTED

Figure 2.5. Structural eye defects. (Reprinted, by permission, from Westinghouse Electric Corporation, Lamp Divisions.)

PHYSICAL FACTORS

Although they are thoroughly interrelated, it is convenient to separate the elements of a visual task in terms of size, luminance, contrast, and time.

The Illuminating Engineering Society states the "visual size of any detail that needs to be seen is a function of its physical size and its distance from the point of observation." Therefore, the size of any object *as it appears to the eye* is more important than its actual physical size. Visual size is usually expressed by combining the elements of actual size and distance into an expression of *visual angle*. The visual angle is the angle subtended by (or included within) lines drawn from the eye to the outside edges of the object being observed. *Visual acuity* is another way of expressing the size threshold of the eye; it is a measure of the smallest detail that can be seen (it is the reciprocal of the visual angle).

Luminance is the proper term for what is often called brightness or, more properly, "photometric brightness." Luminance is also composed of two elements, the intensity of light striking an object and the amount of that light reflected toward the eye. The illumination falling on an object is measured in *footcandles*, as defined earlier, and the reflected light is measured in *footlamberts*. Luminance is measured in footlamberts.

It might be interesting to review the history of these terms. The earliest sources of artificial illumination were relatively small in terms of the source itself (candles, oil lamps, gas mantles, etc.). Therefore, early measurements of lighting intensity were built around the concept of a very small (or "point") source of light. The "candle" (actually a candle of a specified size and burning rate) became the basic unit of intensity. The quantity of light cast by a standard candle on a 1-foot square was, quite naturally, called a footcandle. A footcandle is, therefore, the amount of incident light on an object. This measurement is to be differentiated from the amount of light returned from, or passed through, a surface. The amount of reflected or transmitted light is measured in footlamberts. We can review this distinction with the aid of Table 2.1.

It is important to remember that the darker the task, the more light will be needed on it to create a luminance equal to that reflected from a light surface. Let us take an example using two surfaces. One surface has a reflectance of 100%, and the other has a 40% reflectance. If 100 footcandles fall on both surfaces, then the luminance of the first surface will be 100 footlamberts and the luminance of the second will be 40 footlamberts. For the second surface:

$$100 \text{ fc} \times 40\% \text{ reflectance} = 40 \text{ fL}$$
$$\text{or}$$
$$100 \times 0.40 = 40 \text{ fL}$$

Since, as we stated earlier, the eye needs a certain amount of light to see

Table 2.1.

Incident Light	Reflected Light
Light falling on an object	Light reflected from an object or transmitted through an object
A measure of illumination	A measure of luminance (or photometric brightness)
Symbol: fc	Symbol: fL
Definition: The quantity of light cast by a "standard candle," or standard luminous unit, on a 1-square-foot surface that is foot away from the source	*Definition:* The footcandles striking a diffuse reflecting surface times the reflective ability of that surface, or the footcandles transmitted through a surface times the transmission ability of that surface

easily and with full color perception, the problem of adequate luminance is a very real one.

Contrast given in terms of color and luminance is as important as luminance level in the seeing process. Simple black-and-white contrast can be defined as "percentage brightness difference" and depends on the relative reflectances of two or more adjoining surfaces or of an object and its background.

Another example will help to explain how contrast is expressed. A pure white object on a pure black background will have a contrast of 100% and will be very easy to see. On the other hand, a gray object with a reflectance of 40% against an evenly illuminated gray background reflecting 80% will have a contrast of only 50%. This gray object will be more difficult to see, unless one substitutes a different color (note that color can influence contrast as can the amount of illumination).

Time is another factor in vision. The lower the illumination, the longer it will take to distinguish fine detail. The same can be said for low contrast and low luminance. Time becomes a vital factor when objects are in motion; under low light levels, an object appears to move slower than under high levels of illumination.

BIBLIOGRAPHY

Eastman, Arthur A., "Seeing Parameters" (Nela Park, Cleveland).

Kaufman, John E., et. al., eds., *J. E. S. Lighting Handbook* (New York, 1966), pp. 2-5–2-12.

Westinghouse Electric Corporation, *Lighting Handbook* (Bloomfield, N.J., revised 1969), pp. 1-1–1-7.

Chapter Three

Basic Principles of Electricity for the Lighting Designer

Although electrical theory is an interesting study in itself, we must limit our discussion to its application in lighting. Therefore, we will review only those principles that the designer or environmentalist must understand if he or she wishes to speak intelligently to an engineer, installing electrician, equipment supplier, or other electrical specialist.

One of the basic theories of physics suggests that everything in the universe is made up of electricity. The hypothesis, called the *electron theory*, states that all matter is composed of small units called molecules. Molecules, in turn, are made up of atoms (see Figure 3.1). Atoms are composed of two types of electrical matter: negatively charged electrons that are normally held in place by attraction to a positively charged electrical center called the nucleus. This is easily visualized if we think of the nucleus as the planet Saturn and the electrons as Saturn's moons.

It is believed that the electrons in an atom are constantly revolving about the atom's nucleus at great speeds. In the neutral atom, the amount of negative energy of the moving electrons is exactly equal to the amount of positive energy found in the nucleus. Since the positive and negative charges exactly counteract one another, the normal atom outwardly exhibits no sign of electrification; it may be considered to be at rest. The electrons can, however, be forced from the atom. (Except under unusual conditions involving disruption of the atom, the nucleus cannot be moved from the

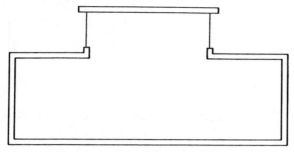

Figure 5.3.   Roof monitor section.

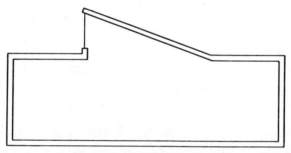

Figure 5.4.   Clerestory section.

same direction as the main window, tends to extend room-thrust limitations. So does the *sawtooth* section (Figure 5.5), which is suitable for low-roofed structures extending over a considerable area.

Skylights. (Figure 5.6). Horizontal roof openings are reminiscent of primitive roof holes used by our ancestors to let the light in and the smoke out. Flat skylights have both drainage and dirt-accumulation problems.

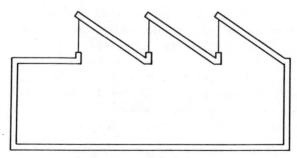

Figure 5.5.   Sawtooth section.

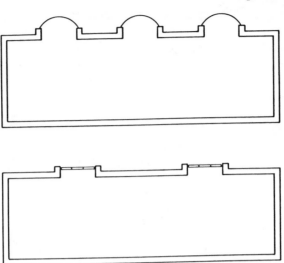

Figure 5.6.   Skylight sections.

Curved or slanted skylights slightly improve these negative conditions. Both kinds of skylights often cause considerable glare and heat buildup since they are most apt to allow the entrance of direct glare. Thus some form of brightness control is desirable. The practical lighting value of skylights is questionable, although they may have positive decorative importance.

DAYLIGHT CONTROLLING ELEMENTS

Designs can incorporate numerous materials and architectural configurations or finishes to control natural light, starting with the landscaping and moving in and throughout a building.

Landscaping.   Deciduous trees provide shade and protect against glare from the sky during the warm months. When they lose their foliage, they allow the sun to warm a building during cold months.

Reflective ground covers (e.g., white gravel) direct light into the lower stories of windowed structures. They can also be used to color the interior illumination with interesting or alarming effects, as with green light reflected from grass. Interior planners should be aware of the potential glare problems resulting from specular water surfaces.

Overhangs.   These structures are properly designed when they shade windows from direct sunlight while reducing brightness on the upper parts of windows. However, they also reduce the amount of light that can enter a space by increasing its thrust. In fact, the optimal depth of the interior space should be measured from the start of the overhang rather than the fenestration plane for vertical windows. Unfortunately, practical overhangs cannot provide complete shading at all times, so another treatment is necessary. Slatted horizontal overhangs are a partial answer to these problems.

Exterior Louvering and Shading. Horizontal louvers covering vertical windows (exterior blinds, slatted sun screens, and the like) offer several advantages; (1) They prevent entry of direct light. A portion of sunlight and skylight is reflected to the ceiling, where it is again reflected down to the horizontal work surface. Light reflected from the ground is permitted to enter interior spaces. (2) They limit the direct glare of large vertical window masses. (3) Heat buildup that is radiated by the louver blades can dissipate outside the interior fenestrated space. (4) If the windows can be opened or removed, louvers permit simultaneous light control and ventillation. (5) If the louver blades can be moved (a process that can be manual or automated), there are additional refinements to light control. Vertical blinds are not as acceptable, since the sun travels in a mostly vertical arc; they are mostly decorative.

Exterior louvers have disadvantages. (1) Their horizontal surfaces collect dirt causing both unsightly conditions and a reduction in louver reflectivity and light control. (2) They may obscure exterior views. (3) Unless permanently positioned or mechanically coordinated, varying louver angles create inconsistencies in a building's visible exterior surface. (4) The mechanisms operating variably positioned exterior slats do not stand up very well under the onslaught of adverse weather.

Fabric or metal sun screens (not louvered) are translucent materials that reduce the quantity of light when they cover window areas. However, they do not offer the directional properties associated with louvers. They also depreciate through dirt and weathering. Their positions may be static as well as manually or automatically varied to accommodate natural light changes.

Glazing. There are two reasons for placing apertures in building walls or ceiling: the desire for exterior views and the need to admit natural lighting.

Windows are finished with either high- or low-transmission materials. The former are usually sheet glass, acrylic sheet, and formed shapes or glass block. Here, double glazing aids heat control. The latter consist of reflectorized or tinted glass and plastic. The lower the transmission, the greater the one-way effect: High exterior and low interior illumination means that you can see outside from inside, but not the other way around.

Spread or diffuse transmitting treatments are accomplished with glass or plastic that is patterned, surface treated, opalized, or otherwise diffused. Remember that the level of transmission and brightness decrease as diffusion increases.

Glazing can also transmit light selectively. (1) Spectrally selective colored media are typical for church windows, but they have other architectural possibilities. Heat filtration is possible through colored media as well as dichroic coatings, although the latter has proven too expensive and fragile for large-area application. (2) Directionally selective windows and skylights of glass or plastic sheet and glass block have been proposed to contain louvers or prisms that reject undesirable direct sunlight while admitting more diffuse light from the rest of the luminous exterior.

Light Control Inside the Glazing. Once again, horizontal louvers (venetian blinds) offer advantages similar to their exterior counterparts. However, they obviously do not dissipate radiated heat outside enclosed spaces. They are also subject to dirt and mechanical deterioration, although these problems are not as severe. One type of blind has been encased between two panels of window glass to reduce the dirt problem.

Shades and draperies behave like exterior fabric or metal sunscreens in that they usually reduce the quantity of light with some degree of diffusion and limited directional control. Generally speaking, they should not be black, but may offer varying levels of opacity with reflective surfaces on all visible sides appropriate to the interior finishes.

Interior Finishes. As with all forms of illumination, the appropriately reflective interior reuses available light. Highly reflective interior walls around glazing diminish the variation in intensity (glare) between the wall and its aperture. Reflective walls and ceilings tend to extend the effective thrust of rooms with vertical windows.

BUILDING ARRANGEMENTS

Orientations. In northern latitudes, the windows might face south for maximum daylight and maximum heat gain. However, it is useful to point windows north in southern latitudes to limit solar heat buildup.

Stories. Single or top stories offer great freedom for side or top lighting in any combination. Multiple wings, open corridors, atria, set-backs, light wells, and courts can approximate the same effect in tall structures. Highly reflective exterior walls help transfer daylight to lower stories where tall buildings are placed close to each other. Of course, sidewall illumination is typical for multiple-stories buildings.

BIBLIOGRAPHY

American Society for Testing and Materials, "Recommended Practice for Lighting Cotton Classing Rooms for Color Grading," *ASTM Standards* (Philadelphia, 1961), Part 10.

Illuminating Engineering Society, "Daylighting," *I.E.S. Lighting Handbook*, 5th ed. (New York, 1972), Section 7.

_____, "Recommended Lighting Practice for the Color Appraisal of Reflection-Type Materials in Graphic Arts" (New York, 1957).

Nayatani, Y., and Wyszecki, G., "Color of Daylight from North Sky," National Research Council of Canada, *Journal of the Optical Society of America* **53** (1963): 626.

Nickerson, D., "The Illuminant in Textile Color Matching: An Illuminant to Satisfy Preferred Conditions of Daylight-Match," *Illuminating Engineering* **43** (1948): 416–64.

Chapter Six

Light Sources—Incandescent Lamps

Basically the incandescent lamp is a very simple device—just a wire sealed in a glass enclosure (see Figure 6.1). Electric current, passing through the wire, heats it to incandescence and the wire emits light. Thousands of types are available; only the most typical will be reviewed herein.

PARTS

Filament

The filament is usually a length or coil of tungsten wire. It may be a straight wire, a coil, or a coil that is coiled back again on itself (called a coiled-coil). The straight-wire filament, formerly used in all types of lamps, required a great many supports because of its length. Each support tended to drain heat from the filament and thereby reduce its efficacy (effectiveness in producing light). A reduction in heat losses and an increase in efficacy can be gained by coiling. Double coiling results in an even greater concentration of heat and light.

All incandescent lamp filament designs are a compromise between lamp life and output. Unfortunately, lamp efficacy is directly related to the temperature of the filament, and the most efficient lamps have both the highest temperatures and the shortest lives. Conversely, standard lamps with extremely long lives are very inefficient. The largest lamp manufacturers have found that a lamp life of between 750 and 1000 hours is most

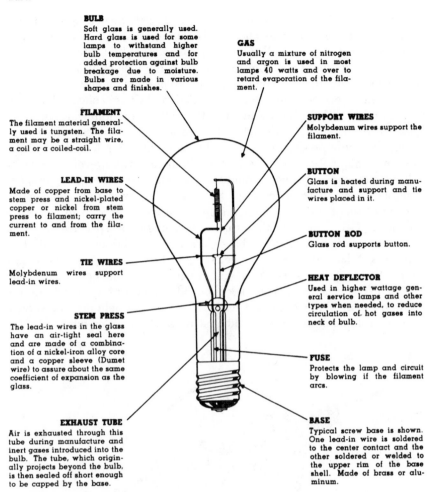

BULB
Soft glass is generally used. Hard glass is used for some lamps to withstand higher bulb temperatures and for added protection against bulb breakage due to moisture. Bulbs are made in various shapes and finishes.

GAS
Usually a mixture of nitrogen and argon is used in most lamps 40 watts and over to retard evaporation of the filament.

FILAMENT
The filament material generally used is tungsten. The filament may be a straight wire, a coil or a coiled-coil.

SUPPORT WIRES
Molybdenum wires support the filament.

LEAD-IN WIRES
Made of copper from base to stem press and nickel-plated copper or nickel from stem press to filament; carry the current to and from the filament.

BUTTON
Glass is heated during manufacture and support and tie wires placed in it.

BUTTON ROD
Glass rod supports button.

TIE WIRES
Molybdenum wires support lead-in wires.

HEAT DEFLECTOR
Used in higher wattage general service lamps and other types when needed, to reduce circulation of hot gases into neck of bulb.

STEM PRESS
The lead-in wires in the glass have an air-tight seal here and are made of a combination of a nickel-iron alloy core and a copper sleeve (Dumet wire) to assure about the same coefficient of expansion as the glass.

FUSE
Protects the lamp and circuit by blowing if the filament arcs.

EXHAUST TUBE
Air is exhausted through this tube during manufacture and inert gases introduced into the bulb. The tube, which originally projects beyond the bulb, is then sealed off short enough to be capped by the base.

BASE
Typical screw base is shown. One lead-in wire is soldered to the center contact and the other soldered or welded to the upper rim of the base shell. Made of brass or aluminum.

Figure 6.1. Parts of a typical incandescent lamp. (Reprinted, by permission, from GTE Sylvania Incorporated.)

economical for the greatest number of lighting installations, but many independent specialists insist that a good minimum should be at least 1000 hours. Although this means that some lamp efficacy is lost, one must remember that lamp cost is only a small part of the lighting problem. With today's high labor costs, lamp *changing* is nearly the most expensive part of illuminating installations with short source life.

Most filaments are made of tungsten and operate at temperatures of more than 4000°F (a higher temperature than almost any other encountered by

human beings). Since high temperature is so directly related to the efficacy
of the source, one tries to choose filament shapes that require as few
supports as possible. The filament shape is indicated by a two-part code.
This letter and number combination indicates the type of filament winding
and shape. The three common winding types are indicated by easily
recognized letters: S = straight, C = coiled, and CC = coiled-coil (shown
in Figure 6.2). The arbitrary number that follows the letter indicates the
shape of the filament. Although it is wise to remember what the letters
mean, it is only necessary to know that any number refers to a specific
filament configuration (see Figure 6.3). On occasion, however, a designer
will recommend a filament number. For example, when the designer
suggests a clear decorative lamp, he or she may wish to recommend a
specific filament, or if a complex filament shape is desired to add extra
sparkle, a C-1 filament rather than a C-8 might be specified. From a
technical standpoint, certain shapes are essential for use in projection
apparatus. Filament designs for precise optical control are usually compact
so that they emit the greatest amount of light in a certain optical area. The
glass bulb protects the filament, keeps outside air away from it and keeps the
vacuum and/or filling gases next to the filament. The bulb may aso serve a
decorative function or form an integral reflector, lens, or filter.

Figure 6.2.   Coiled-coil filament. (Reprinted, by permission, from GTE Sylvania Incorporated.)

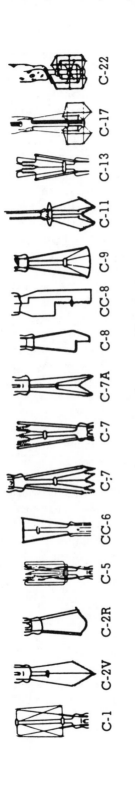

Figure 6.3. Typical incandescent lamp filament shapes. (Reprinted, by permission, from GTE Sylvania Incorporated.)

C-1   C-2V   C-2R   C-5   CC-6   C-7   C-7   C-7A   C-8   CC-8   C-9   C-11   C-13   C-17   C-22

C-23

57

The variations in bulb shape are designated by a standard two-part code: The first part, a letter, indicates the *shape* of the bulb; the second part is a number that indicates the maximum *diameter* of a bulb in eighths of an inch. For example, an R-40 bulb is a reflector shape with a maximum diameter of 5 inches (40 divided by 8 equals 5). Designers should know letter designations given in Table 6.1 and illustrated in Figure 6.4.

Bulb *glass* is usually common lime glass. Under special, but not uncommon, circumstances low-expansion, heat-resistant glass is required. In most cases, ordering codes distinguish bulbs made of special glass.

Bulb *finishes* are usually applied to spread the compact, high brightness of a concentrated filament when a softer light source is desired. (Bulb finishes should not be confused with bulb color coatings or bulb reflectors, which are discussed separately.) In standard-service lamps, the two most common bulb finishes are etched glass and applied silica powder. The interior silica powder treatment (called "soft white" by the major lamp manufacturers) produces the best diffusion, but cuts light output more than the acid-etched (known as "inside frosted") finish. An etched interior surface gives the impression of a glowing ball of light suspended inside the bulb, while the silica application makes the entire bulb glow evenly.

Four types of bulb *color coatings* are popular: sprayed lacquers, plastic coatings, ceramic enamels, and dichroic filters (special metal coatings).

The sprayed lacquers are applied to the exterior of completed lamps. Although their adhesion to the glass surface is good, they have a comparatively low resistance to scratches, scuffing, and the effects of weather. Sprayed lacquers are usually highly transparent, and they are therefore often used in displays where the sparkle of a clearly visible filament is desired. Plastic coatings, which have a similar effect, are an improvement on the sprayed lacquers. They have a higher resistance to abrasion and weather.

Transparent ceramic enamels are fused to the bulb by heat to form a hard surface that is essentially a part of the bulb itself. They are very resistant to abuse, but are not as brilliantly transparent as the lacquers or plastic coatings.

Dichroic filters are a relatively new system of color filtration. The filter is created by applying several thin coats of metallic film to the face of the lamp. Because the film passes wavelengths of one color band but reflects others, the system is called wavelength interference. It is more efficient than passing the light through conventional color-absorbing materials, and certain lighting experts judge the resulting colors to be particularly brilliant.

Bulb *silvering* can also be considered a lamp coating. When an application of specular aluminum is placed on the portion of a bulb that is shaped like a reflector, a total lighting system is produced, complete with a source, reflector, and lens. PAR lamps are an example of such a system.

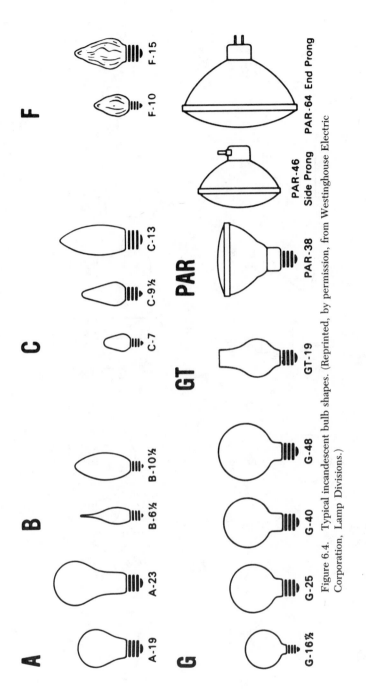

Figure 6.4. Typical incandescent bulb shapes. (Reprinted, by permission, from Westinghouse Electric Corporation, Lamp Divisions.)

59

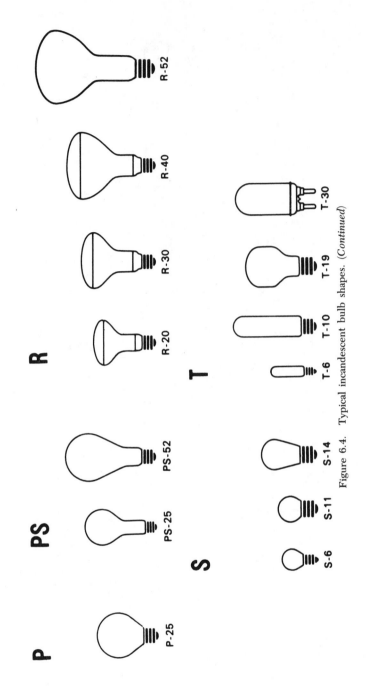

Figure 6.4. Typical incandescent bulb shapes. (*Continued*)

Table 6.1.

Code	Meaning
A and PS	A is an arbitrary bulb shape; PS stands for pear-shape. These are the most common shapes for general lighting.
PAR and R	These are bulbs with built-in reflectors. The PAR or parabolic aluminized reflector, offers good beam control, is relatively expensive, may be heavy, and can be used outdoors. The R lamp uses a reflector that is less accurate in its beam control, less expensive, lightweight, and generally restricted to interior use unless constructed of special glass.
ER	Ellipsoidal reflector lamps cross light rays at a point slightly in front of the bulb's lens thereby producing an efficient light distribution when these lamps are used in luminaires with small aperture openings or deep baffles (as shown in Figure 6.5).
T	Tubular
C	Conical
B	Flame-shaped (one of the few codes that does not relate to its meaning). B bulbs have smooth exteriors.
F	Flame-shaped
S	Straight-sided
P	Pear-shaped
G	Globe (round)
GT	Globe-tubular (also called chimney shape)

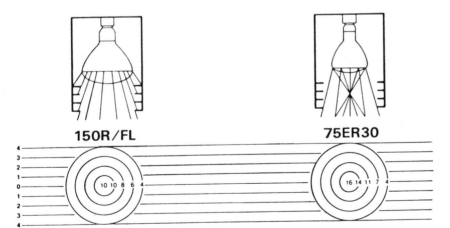

150R/FL   **75ER30**

Figure 6.5.   Comparative footcandle levels in typical direct down lights at 10-foot mounting heights using reflector and ellipsoidal reflector lamps. (Reproduced, by permission, from General Electric Company Lighting Business Group.)

Figure 6.6.   Dichroic reflector lamp. (Reproduced, by permission, from General Electric, TP-110).

A combination of the principles of silvering and dichroic filtration is used for incandescent spotlights that produce a light beam of relatively low temperature. These PAR-shaped spotlights are made with a dichroic coating on the reflector surface, which reflects most of the visible spectrum and transmits heat (see Figure 6.6). In this way, the useful light rays are projected from the front of the lamp, and the heat exits out of the back. (One manufacturer claims such lamps remove about 65% of the heat from the light beam.) These lamps were originally developed for use over grocery meat counters; they provided the richness of incandescent highlighting but, unlike hot PAR lamps, they did not cook the meat. Today, the lamps are used wherever the heat from spotlighting is not desired. Since the unwanted heat rays are released from the back of the lamp, the lamps must only be used in luminaires that are specially designed to dissipate the resulting temperatures.

Bases

The base for the incandescent lamp serves two purposes: (1) It carries electric power to the lead-in wires of the lamp and (2) it holds the lamp in its socket. Many types of bases are familiar, and the designer should know the popular types and their application (see Figure 6.7).

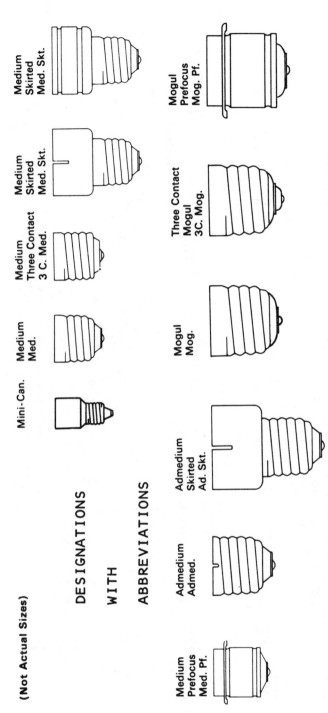

(Not Actual Sizes)

DESIGNATIONS

WITH

ABBREVIATIONS

Mini-Can.

Medium
Med.

Medium
Three Contact
3 C. Med.

Medium
Skirted
Med. Skt.

Medium
Skirted
Med. Skt.

Mogul
Mog.

Three Contact
Mogul
3C. Mog.

Mogul
Prefocus
Mog. Pf.

Medium
Prefocus
Med. Pf.

Admedium
Admed.

Admedium
Skirted
Ad. Skt.

Figure 6.7. Typical incandescent lamp bases. (Reprinted, by permission, from Westinghouse Electric Corporation, Lamp Divisions.)

63

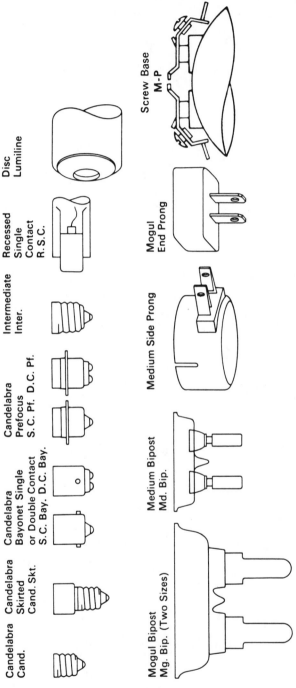

Figure 6.7. Typical incandescent lamp bases. (Continued)

Disc
Lumiline

Recessed
Single
Contact
R.S.C.

Intermediate
Inter.

Candelabra
Prefocus
S.C. Pf. D.C. Pf.

Candelabra
Bayonet Single
or Double Contact
S.C. Bay. D.C. Bay.

Candelabra Candelabra
Cand.   Skirted
            Cand. Skt.

Screw Base
M-P

Mogul
End Prong

Medium Side Prong

Medium Bipost
Md. Bip.

Mogul Bipost
Mg. Bip. (Two Sizes)

Screw Base Family

Mogul—a large base for lamps of 300 watts or more.

Ad medium—largely obsolete.

Medium—the most popular base.

Intermediate—a smaller base used for decorative lamps.

Candelabra—the smallest 120-volt socket size available. Used for decorative and indicator lamps.

Mini-candelabra—for high-wattage lamps of very small dimension. The socket is skirted.

Variations—(1) Skirted lamps have a cylinder of metal separating the lamp from the socket. They are used if the glass neck of the lamp is too large for the socket or to separate the lamp and the base to reduce heat at the socket. (2) Three-contact bases are used for lamps that have more than one filament—similar to those used in table lamps—and can be switched from high to medium to low light output.

Precise Positioning Bases

Also available in several sizes, these bases are used to precisely position the lamp filament in optical systems. Precision alignment is not possible with a screw base, because it can be turned a little more or less when it is inserted. Several types are common.

Bipost—has two cylindrical posts protruding through the bottom of the lamp. The base is commonly used in theatrical equipment.

Bayonet—has two small prongs extending from the sides of the base and is used on special lamps.

Prefocus—aligns the filament with flanges. It is used on theatrical spotlights, precise instruments, and so on.

Special-Purpose Bases

Side prong—appears to be a standard convenience plug mounted on the base of a PAR lamp. The side-prong base is used to shorten the lamp length.

End prong—the same as the side prong, but extends out the back of the lamp.

Recessed single contact—mounted on either end of special tubular lamps.

Disk—mounted on either end of a long incandescent tubular lamp called a lumiline.

Screw terminal—used where the lead-in wires are screwed to the lamp terminals. Screw terminals are common on low-voltage lamps.

Filling Gas

Lamp filaments burn either in a vacuum or in an atmosphere composed of special gases. Low-wattage lamps (below 40 watts) are vacuum pumped. The filaments in these lamps burn at such a low temperature that they show little signs of evaporation.

In lamps of more than 40 watts, bulb blackening (caused by evaporation of the filament) is a major problem because light output and color balance change as the bulb darkens. Blackening can be reduced by filling the bulb with an inert gas. The most common substance is a mixture of nitrogen and argon.

Bulbs filled with krypton have certain advantages over vacuum or nitrogen–argon bulbs. Since krypton has a lower heat conductivity than either nitrogen or argon, the efficacy of the lamp increases. (As you know, when heat is conducted away from the filament, there is a resulting reduction in lamp efficacy.)

The introduction of a gas type known as a halogen, used in the tungsten–halogen lamp, once revolutionized the incandescent lighting field (see Figure 6.8). Small amounts of the halogen (usually either iodine or bromine) are added to this lamp's small-diameter, tubular bulb. As the lamp reaches its full operating temperature, the iodine or bromine vapor acts as a barrier and prevents the tungsten particles expelled from the filament (because of evaporation) from depositing on the inner bulb wall. When the lamp cools, these particles return to the filament (see Figure 6.9). Therefore, the lamp is both kept clean and regenerated. The result is an increase in lamp life and operating efficiency.

GENERAL CLASSES

Lamps can be divided into general classes according to their uses and features.

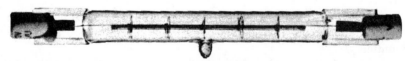

Figure 6.8. Typical tungsten–halogen lamp. (Reproduced, by permission, from GTE Sylvania Incorporated.)

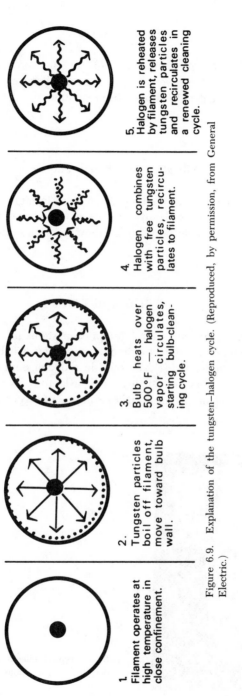

1.
Filament operates at high temperature in close confinement.

2.
Tungsten particles boil off filament, move toward bulb wall.

3.
Bulb heats over 500°F — halogen vapor circulates, starting bulb-cleaning cycle.

4.
Halogen combines with free tungsten particles, recirculates to filament.

5.
Halogen is reheated by filament, releases tungsten particles and recirculates in a renewed cleaning cycle.

Figure 6.9. Explanation of the tungsten–halogen cycle. (Reproduced, by permission, from General Electric.)

67

General Service

The A- and PS-shaped lamps are among the most common of the incandescent series. However, large lamp manufacturers have introduced other proprietary shapes; Westinghouse recommends a fat tubular shape, as an example.

Vibration and Rough Service

General service lamps are modified when used in high vibration or major shock areas. Because these lamps must have a number of filament supports than standard lamps to sustain shocks, they are not as efficient as standard lamps.

ER, R, and PAR

ER, R, and PAR lamps are complete optical systems in a single bulb. The bulb contains a filament, reflector, and lens (see Figure 6.10). There are four advantages to these lamps: (1) The built-in reflector eliminates the need to clean luminaires; every time you replace a lamp, you replace the entire optical system. (2) Compactness makes equipment less conspicuous in many

Figure 6.10.   Typical reflector lamp. (Reproduced, by permission, from Westinghouse Electric Corporation, Lamp Divisions.)

cases. (3) There is a lower initial equipment expense since there is no need for a luminaire with a separate reflector or lens. (4) They are famous for their long life. Their major disadvantage is their relatively high cost. See Table 6.1 for a description of each shape's characteristics.

Tungsten–Halogen

The tungsten–halogen (also called quartz or quartz-iodine) lamps use a halogen gas cycle to prevent rapid depreciation of the lamp filament and darkening of the transparent envelope, as described earlier. (The parts of the lamp are shown in Figure 6.11). Their advantages are: (1) The bulb does not blacken, (2) lamp life is very long, and (3) great amounts of light may be packed inside the small-diameter, transparent envelope. Because quartz (historically, the first bulb material) or other "hard" glass material is used in the bulb, the bulb will not crack when placed very close to the filament. One can actually take a hot tungsten–halogen lamp directly from a luminaire and drop it in a pail of cold water; the water will erupt with a roar, but the lamp enclosure will remain intact.

There are two disadvantages to this light source: (1) Because they are smaller than incandescent sources of comparable light output, users are tempted to place them in very small housings. Heat buildup can be critical in small, poorly constructed luminaires. (2) The typical linear shape of the filament may not always be the best shape for every optical requirement.

Tungsten–halogen lamps may be used as they are or enclosed in other bulbs (see Figure 6.12). This secondary enclosure (1) may allow a better optical placement, (2) will retain the temperature levels necessary for the operation of the halogen cycle, which is difficult in drafty installations, and (3) will keep greasy fingers away from the quartz wall. Gloves or other protective materials should always be used when installing bare quartz lamps. Oils from a human hand may cause the quartz surface to rupture or cloud and lose some of its transparency.

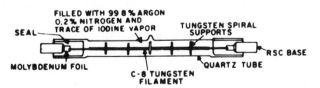

Figure 6.11.   Parts of a typical tungsten–halogen lamp. (Reprinted, by permission, from GTE Sylvania Incorporated.)

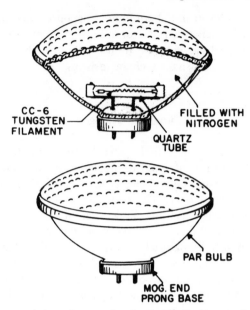

Figure 6.12.   Tungsten–halogen lamp enclosed in PAR bulb. (Reprinted, by permission from GTE Sylvania Incorporated.)

Low-Voltage

Lamps designed to operate within the range of 6–75 volts, rather than at the standard 120 volts, are classed as low-voltage lamps. The most popular low-voltage lamps designed for interior and exterior use operate on either 6 or 12 volts. Low voltage offers two main advantages: (1) Light output can be contained in a small area and tightly controlled because lamps can be constructed with smaller and tighter filaments. As a result, very small, low-voltage PAR lamps are available that project brilliant, pencil-thin beams of light over great distances. Because the light from the filament is easy to control, less elaborate luminaire shielding is required, and luminaires can be smaller. (2) Low-voltage electric service is safer than its 120-volt counterpart. Wiring requires less insulation, resulting in lower installation costs, and lighter and less expensive luminaire construction.

Unfortunately, there are also disadvantages to low-voltage lighting. Using the formula, amperes = watts/volts, one can see that the lower the voltage, the higher the amperage. Higher amperage means larger wire sizes and greater voltage drop over long wiring runs. As a result, low-voltage light sources must be kept as close as possible to their transformer sources of power. Since 120 volts is the standard lighting service in the United States, low-voltage lamps usually require transformers, which are heavy, and cannot be simply dimmed. However, despite these disadvantages, low-voltage lighting can be an excellent solution whenever space is limited or precise beam control is required. For example, low-voltage lighting is used in residences with low ceilings and inadequate space for recessed luminaires. Because low-voltage lighting is safer than standard sources, it is often used in exterior lighting or where light sources are placed near or under water.

Extended Service

Extended service lamps offer longer than normal lives at a sacrifice in efficacy. They are available from all major lamp manufacturers and should be limited to use where regular replacement schedules will result in high cost, unusual difficulty, or annoyance.

Silver-Bowl and White-Bowl Lamps

Both the silver- and white-bowl lamps are coated with reflective substances (see Figure 6.13). In most cases, the coating is applied to the globular part of standard A, G, or PS bulb shapes. The white-bowl uses a translucent white coating while the silver-coated bowl is opaque. Both lamps are used for various forms of decorative or indirect lighting.

Showcase and Lumiline Tubular Lamps

Two types of long, tubular, standard incandescent lamps are available in a variety of sizes. The so-called showcase lamp has a single screw base at one end; the lumiline uses one disk at each end. These lamps are used wherever a linear source of incandescent light is required. Unfortunately, they are rather fragile and are particularly susceptible to sagging and broken filaments. The improved use of fluorescent sources has tended to cut back the application of these incandescent lamps.

   Do not confuse this type of source with the typically tubular tungsten–halogen lamp. Showcase and lumiline sources are standard incandescent lamps and do not offer the tungsten–halogen advantages of long life, high light output, and lack of bulb blackening. Although tubular, tungsten–halogen lamps are comparatively short in length.

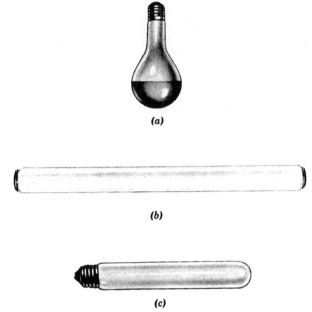

Figure 6.13.   (a) Silver-bowl lamp; (b) lumiline lamp; (c) showcase lamp. (Reproduced, by permission, from General Electric, TP-110.)

Impact Protective Bulbs

Also called "safety" or "safe-line" lamps, impact protective bulbs are coated with a clear silicone, rubber, or plastic. Since the coating absorbs impacts, the bulb may break but it will not shatter.

Multiple-Filament Lamps

Basically general service lamps, multiple filament sources contain two filaments that provide three intensities of illumination; either one or the other or both filaments are burned whenever a switch is turned to the appropriate setting. These lamps (usually used in table lamps) provide varied levels of light without the need for a dimmer. Unfortunately, the filament providing your most used light level usually burns out first, leaving you with a light level you do not desire. With the development of small, reliable and inexpensive dimmers, this comparatively expensive light source is becoming obsolete.

Precision Sources

Precision sources are used when accurate location of the light source is important. They usually feature a special base design (such as a prefocus, bayonet, or bipost base) and a detailed arrangement of the filament.

Decorative and Sign Lamps

Physical appearance, rather than efficient light production, is more important in decorative or sign lamps. Decorative lamps have distinctive bulb shapes or filament arrangements. Sign lamps are developed to provide incandescent sparkle to exterior or interior advertising as well as to provide long life. We will not review all the types of decorative lamps here because manufacturers change them frequently, and they are subject to the vagaries of fashion.

The lamps classes just discussed are of the greatest use to the designer, and one should become familiar with as many variations as possible by studying lamp catalogs and by visiting the showrooms of the major lamp manufacturers. Other classes of lamps, less often used by the designer, are *street lighting, appliance and indicator, signal, aviation, infrared and ultraviolet,* and *industrial service.*

SERVICING PROBLEMS

There are several reasons why incandescent lamps malfunction. The most common problems are discussed in this section.

Heat

Excessive heat *rarely* causes lamp failure, but early lamp outages are frequently blamed on either high temperature or poor luminaire ventilation. Remember that the filament is designed to operate at very high temperatures. However, the same is not true of the lamp base, and the bulbs may blister and bulge if overheated.

Loose Bases

Excessive temperatures concentrated near the lamp base may cause the cement fastening the metal base to the bulb to disintegrate and powder. If the base loosens, it may separate from the bulb when the lamp is removed from its socket.

Shock and Vibration

Since shock and vibration always affect lamp life, lamps designed to absorb shocks should be used when these problems are encountered.

Rattling

A slight rattle inside the bulb does *not* always indicate that the lamp is burned out. The noise may be caused by harmless loose materials.

Incorrect Burning Position

Some lamps must be burned only in a specified position (base up, base down, etc.). These lamps are rarely used in general lighting practice. If a particular burning position is mandated, the limitation will be noted on the lamp package or in lamp catalogs.

Seating and Corrosion

Most lamp bases are covered with a lubricant that retards corrosion of the base metal and facilitates lamp installation or removal. Despite this safeguard, corrosion may build up in the socket or on the lamp base and interfere with the flow of electricity, causing the lamp to sputter. Sputtering may also occur if the lamp is incorrectly seated in the socket (particularly important for precision or multiple filament sources), or if the electrical contacts are not making a connection with the base (the bottom contact may often be bent away from a screw base).

Leaks

If the bulb is cracked, outside air may seep into the lamp and eventually destroy the filament. Cracks can sometimes be very small and difficult to find. If the bulb suddenly develops an opaque interior coating, an air leak may be the cause.

Electrical Variations

If a lamp is operated on an electric circuit at a voltage exceeding its designed rating, lamp life will be shortened. On the other hand, lamp life is extended by underating the power to the lamp. Even a tiny change in the power supply will have a large effect on lamp life and output.

Table 6.2.

Code	Meaning
/A	Amber color
/B	Blue color
/BW	Blue-white color
/C	Clear
/CL	Clear
/DC	Double contact base
/FL	Flood (beam shape)
/G	Green color
/GO	Golden color
/IF	Inside frosted diffuser
/N+	Natural glass color when followed by a color code
/NSP	Narrow spot (beam shaped)
/O	Orange color
/PK	Pink color
/R	Red color
/R2	Rose color
/RS	Rough service
/RFL	Reflector (not a PAR- or R-shaped bulb)
/SB	Silver-bowl reflector
/SC	Single-contact base
/SP	Spot (beam shape)
/T	Transparent when followed by a color code
/VNSP	Very narrow spot (beam shape)
/VS	Vibration service
/VWFL	Very wide flood (beam shaped)
/W	White (a painted finish)
/WFL	Wide flood (beam shape)
/Y	Yellow color
/1Y	Bug light (yellow color)
/2	Low heat output with a dichroic filter
/3	Side prong lamps
/99	Long life

LAMP IDENTIFICATION

Manufacturers provide a code number that indicates lamp wattage, bulb shape, diameter (in eighths of an inch), and other information following a slash (/). Tungsten–halogen lamps are indicated by a Q before the wattage. The other information following the slash can be anything that the lamp manufacturer believes will help to define a lamp's characteristics. For example, a 60A21/B would be a 60-watt, arbitrary-shaped bulb, approximately 2½ inches in diameter that is colored blue. A few common abbreviations are listed in Table 6.2.

BIBLIOGRAPHY

General Electric, *Compact Quartzline Lamps*, Lamp Letter 70-5...4-70.

General Electric, *Incandescent Lamps*, TP-110, (Nela Park, Cleveland, no date).

Allphin, Willard, *Dichroic Filters*, Engineering Bulletin 0-298, Code 11571 (GTE Sylvania, Danvers, Mass., revised 1-15-71).

Sylvania, *Incandescent Lamps*, Engineering Bulletin 0-324, Code 61571 (Danvers, Mass., revised 6-15-71).

Westinghouse, *A Practical Guide to Westinghouse Incandescent Lamps*, A-8042 (Bloomfield, N.J., June 1968).

Chapter Seven

Light Sources—
Electric Discharge, Fluorescent

The fluorescent lamp is one member of a family of electric discharge sources. Its bulb contains a mercury-supported arc and is filled with an inert gas, kept at low pressure, which produces light by activating the thin film of phosphors (fluorescent material) that coat the glass tube (see Figure 7.1). *Low pressure* is important to this definition because it differentiates the fluorescent lamp from other electric discharge sources.

PARTS

Bulb

The fluorescent bulb is commonly tubular and ranges from a T5 (⅝ inch in diameter) to a T17 (2⅛ inches in diameter). The bulb holds the filling gas inside and excludes the outside air. The T12 is the most common bulb size and shape; it is approximately 1½ inches in diameter and may range from 15 inches to 8 feet in length. The T8 (1 in. in diameter) is enjoying a recently acquired popularity. Because of its smaller diameter, it offers increased optical control.

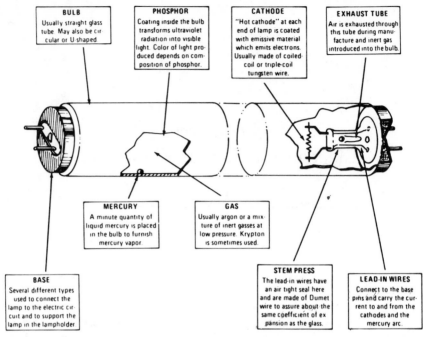

Figure 7.1. Parts of the standard fluorescent lamp. (Reprinted, by permission, from GTE Sylvania Incorporated.)

Bases

The fluorescent lamp base can have several possible configurations (see Figure 7.2). The most common, the *bi-pin base*, is available in several sizes: miniature, medium, and mogul. Of these, the medium bi-pin is most commonly used.

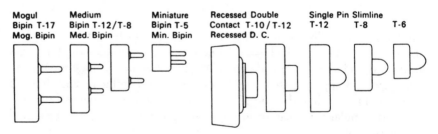

Figure 7.2. Typical fluorescent lamp bases. (Reprinted, by permission, from Westinghouse Electric Corporation, Lamp Divisions.)

Lamps that have a high light output may use a *recessed double-contact* base. Higher voltages are required for these lamps, and the recessed double contact affords better protection for the bulb structure and for the human installer.

Both the bi-pin and double-contact bases provide four electrical contacts to the lamp—two at each end. However, certain lamps only require one contact at each end; for example, the instant-start lamp commonly uses a *single-pin* base.

Electrodes

The electrodes (sometimes called "hot cathodes") resemble the filaments of an incandescent lamp (see Figure 7.3). However, instead of providing light, they serve as terminals for an electric arc and a source of electrons for lamp current. The electrodes are made of coiled-coil or triple-coiled tungsten wire. They may also be stick coiled (have a straight wire penetrating the coils). It should be noted that the space taken up by the two electrodes, which is the same regardless of lamp length, is not as luminous as the center section of the bulb. These dark lamp ends, therefore, tend to make the longer fluorescent lamps (3-, 4-, and 8-ft) more efficient than their shorter

Coiled Coil

Triple Coil

Stick Coil

Figure 7.3. Electrode Designs. (Reprinted, by permission, from General Electric, TP-111.)

counterparts (2-ft and below). For the same reason, several standard fluorescent lamps in a row will not produce a continuously high light level; unless lamp ends are overlapped, dark spots are often noticed in coves, perimeter lighting systems, and the like.

Mercury

Drops of lquid mercury placed in the fluorescent lamp bulb vaporize at a very low pressure when the lamp is operating. The current passing through this vapor causes it to radiate at a specific wavelength (253.7 nm) in the ultraviolet region of the electromagnetic spectrum. The mercury pressure created during lamp operation is important, because higher or lower than normal pressures tend to inhibit the production of ultraviolet energy. Since the pressure is regulated by the temperature of the bulb wall, drafts or ambient temperatures different from those for which the lamp is designed can alter the light output of the lamp.

Filling Gas

The fluorescent tube also contains a small quantity of argon, a combination of argon and neon, or, occasionally, krypton. These filling gases ionize readily when sufficient voltage is applied to the lamp. This allows the current to flow and the mercury to vaporize.

Phosphor Coating

Phosphor (a fluorescent material applied to the interior surface of the bulb) converts the 253.7-nanometer radiation produced by the mercury into visible light. The color of the light is determined by the chemical composition of the phosphor. Suitable phosphors are available for a variety of spectral mixes called "white" light and for a number of saturated colors. Because saturated colors, such as red or gold, are difficult to achieve with phosphor color alone, a subtractive pigment is applied to the inside of the bulb wall before the phosphor is applied.

The phosphor glow that produces most of the light from fluorescent lamps operates in much the same way as the light produced by "black light" or ultraviolet effects used in displays or discotheque decor. The phosphors absorb ultraviolet energy and reradiate it at wavelengths that can be seen as visible light. It is interesting to note that the unlighted fluorescent lamp may not appear to be the same color as the operating lamp (this is particularly true of the deeply colored fluorescent sources); a green lamp will appear white when it is off.

OPERATION

Light Production

When the lamp is first turned on, the passage of an electric current causes the electrodes at either end of the lamp to heat and thus expel electrons (see Figure 7.4). The electrons travel at high speeds from one electrode to the other, creating an arc (which is an electric discharge) through the mercury vapor. The heat from the lamp causes the pressure of the mercury vapor to increase to its most efficient level. Collision between the flowing electrons and the atoms of the mercury vapor knock electrons of the mercury atoms out of their normal position, thereby releasing ultraviolet radiation. The phosphors coating the inside of the lamp's tubular bulb absorb most of the ultraviolet energy and reradiate it as visible light.

Starting (Classes of Fluorescent Lamps)

A fluorescent lamp starts when the voltage difference between the electrodes is sufficient to strike an arc in the filling gas. There are three typical methods of starting a fluorescent lamp. It is important to know these

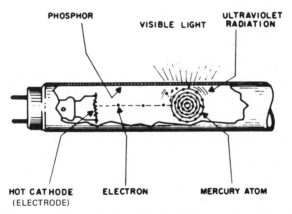

Figure 7.4. Fluorescent light production. (Reprinted, by permission, from GTE Sylvania Incorporated.)

methods, because fluorescent lamps are classified by starting method. Therefore, the starting methods and classes of fluorescent lamps are discussed together.

Preheat Lamps

Early fluorescent lamps were all of the preheat type. Less voltage is required to strike an arc between electrodes if they are first heated. In the preheat circuit, current is permitted to pass *through* each of the electrodes for several seconds to heat them before voltage is applied *between* the electrodes to strike the arc. Therefore, the electrodes are emitting electrons before the arc strikes. Once the electrodes reach the proper temperature, the preheat circuit is turned off, and the proper electrode operating temperature is maintained with the heat produced by the arc itself.

The preheating process takes a few seconds. An external switch is used to apply heating current through the electrodes and then remove this current and reapply it between the electrodes to strike the arc. In inexpensive or miniaturized systems, the preheating is accomplished by pressing down a manual starter button for a few seconds to heat the electrodes. When the button is released, the current is transferred to pass between the electrodes and the arc strikes. In most cases, however, the preheating process is accomplished by an automatic starter. For these reasons, this class is also called a *switch-start* or *starter-start* lamp.

In certain cases, the starter can be eliminated by using a device called a *trigger-start ballast*. The ballast serves a current-limiting function and provides an appropriate automatic starting system.

Instant-Start Lamps

To overcome the problems of slow starting and troublesome starters, the instant-start lamp was developed. When the lamp is first switched on, a sufficient voltage is applied *between* the electrode to strike the arc without preheating them. Once started, the arc quickly heats the fine wire of the electrodes that supply electrons to sustain the arc.

Instant-start lamps not only start as soon as current is turned on, but also eliminate the need for external starters. Therefore, they simplify the lighting system and eliminate one maintenace problem—that of replacing starters when they burn out.

As mentioned previously, only a single pin on each end of an instant-start lamp is required. Lamps with single-pin bases are sometimes called "slim-line" lamps. However, a few instant-start lamps are supplied with bi-pin bases. These specially marked lamps have pin orientations that keep them from damaging other circuits.

Rapid-Start Lamps

The rapid-start lamp is the most recent development and the one that is most widely used. Rapid-start lamps use low-resistance electrodes, which can be heated continuously with low current losses. These are the *only* fluorescent lamps that can be electrically dimmed or flashed.

Rapid-start lamps have several advantages over earlier types: (1) They start almost as quickly as instant-start lamps and in a much shorter time than preheat lamps—they are a compromise in starting speed; (2) no external starters are required; and (3) the current-limiting devices (ballasts) are smaller and more efficient than those in instant-start lamps of similar wattages.

SPECIAL LAMP DESIGNS

Special lamp designs usually differ either in output or in shape from those discussed previously (see Figure 7.5).

Shape

Many special shapes are available. The first is the *circle*. These lamps come in 8¼-, 12-, and 16-inch outside diameters. They are used whenever a circle

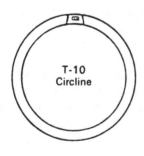

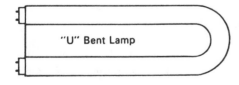

Figure 7.5. Special lamp designs. (Reprinted, by permission, from Westinghouse Electric Corporation, Lamp Divisions.)

of light is desired. However, designers must be aware that there is a black area where the electrodes and socket connect.

A second shape is the *U*. These lamps are all formed by bending or molding a straight tube into the U shape. When used to provide illumination within a confined space, U shapes have several advantages: (1) They produce slightly more light than two lamps placed side by side; (2) all wiring on the lampholders is at one end of the luminaire, thus reducing the number of system parts, the amount of wiring, and access problems; (3) they present a luminaire's optical system with a relatively compact light source.

U lamps come in a variety of sizes and widths. For ceiling-mounted general lighting luminaires, a standard 4-foot straight tube is bent or cast as a U shape. If the space between the lamp "legs" is 6 inches (one of two standard options), then the light source will occupy more space but provide a larger luminous area. If the second standard is used, providing a 3-inch lamp leg spacing, then the light source will be comparatively compact and more lamps can be placed in a single luminaire. For example, two lamps with 6-inch-spaced legs may be found in 2 foot × 2 foot fluorescent down lights; three lamps with 3-inch-spaced legs can occupy the same luminaire. The use of a few standard U lamps is preferred over multiples of straight shorter lamps. As the fluorescent lamp gets shorter (say, 2 foot long), the proportion of dark lamp ends to lighted area becomes greater (see the discussion of electrodes in this chapter), and the lamp becomes less efficient. By using three standard U lamps, instead of six 2-foot-long lamps, lamp light output is increased by 15%. Since the bent 4-foot lamp, even though it is then nominally 2 feet long, is still powered by efficient 40-watt ballasts, there are also ballast electrical efficiencies in favor of the U shape. Unfortunately, a single U lamp cost over three times as much as a single 4-foot straight lamp in 1982. Miniaturized U lamps are finding increased application for supplementary lighting, such as in the task luminaires mounted on desks with furniture integrated lighting systems.

Square lamps were also made, but this shape is not in favor at the moment. The square lamp is a solid—like a sandwich of light—and produces illumination from both side of the sandwich. For most applications, it does not offer an efficient or practical distribution of light. *Spirals, pelletized, snaked shapes,* and other unusual or proprietary lamp configurations are available, often through the sign industry.

Self-Ballasted Lamps

Circline and U lamps are sometimes supplied with ballast assemblies designed for use in standard, screw-base sockets operating at 120 volts.

When used as a replacement in a standard table lamp, one manufacturer claims its 44-watt circline adapter assembly generates as much light as the 100-watt A-shaped lamp it is designed to replace. The initial cost is, however, significantly higher. In circline lamp assemblies, the lamp can often be replaced separately from the ballast base.

One manufacturer produces a linear fluorescent lamp with integral resistance-type ballast, starting aid, electrical cord, and plug for direct attachment to 120-volt electrical service. The resulting thin lamp assembly is not as efficient as traditionally separate lamp-and-ballast combinations, but it does do away with bulky ballasts, boxy metal housings, and associated electrical hardware. This entire assembly is discarded when any component fails. It is intended mostly for the residential market.

OUTPUT

Quantity

A number of lamps are designed to produce more or less light than the standard fluorescent source (using 430 milliamperes).

Rapid-start fluorescent lamps with above average outputs may be 430-milliampere lamps with special filling gases and/or phosphors, or be called high output (800 milliamperes), and very high output (1500 milliamperes). Very high output lamps with special characterisitcs are marketed under several trade names, such as Power Groove (General Electric) and Super-Hi (Westinghouse). When recommending fluorescent lamps with high outputs, the specifier must be careful to weigh the possible negative factors, such as rapid light-output depreciation, high ballast noise, and decreased lamp life. These lamps may use special ballasts and can require special installation procedures. They are all listed and defined in the catalogs of major lamp manufacturers.

Low-output lamps can be used in existing installations where electrical energy consumption must be reduced and lower light output can be tolerated.

Temperature

Standard fluorescent lamps do not operate satisfactorily outdoors. As a result, a series of special lamps (with correspondingly special supportive equipment) have been developed and can be found in major lamp catalogs.

Direction

Two lamp styles have been developed to reinforce the light emitted on one side of the straight fluorescent tube (see Figure 7.6). The *reflector lamp* has an internal reflector applied to one side of the tube wall between the glass and the phosphor. As a result, approximately 60% more light passes through the uncovered side of the lamp. The *aperture lamp* is similar, but has a small clear area in the phosphor coating that extends the length of the tube. The aperture can have up to eight times the surface brightness of a standard tube. Directional fluorescent lamps are useful when tight light control is required.

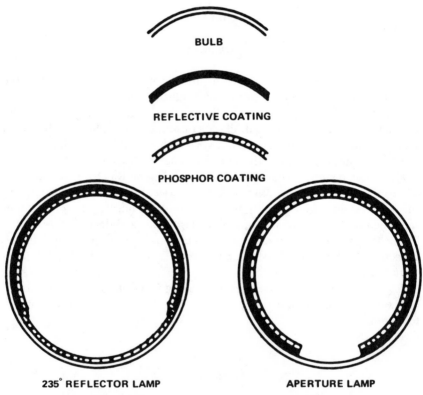

Figure 7.6.   Fluorescent reflector and aperture lamps. (Reprinted, by permission, from GTE Sylvania Incorporated.)

AUXILIARY EQUIPMENT—BALLASTS

Unfortunately, whenever you employ any electric discharge light source, you must be concerned with the auxiliary equipment necessary to make it function. The ballast limits the amount of current used by the lamp and provides the proper starting voltages (see Figure 7.7). As the current in an arc increases, the resistance of the arc decreases, thereby allowing the passage of still more current. If the current were not limited at an optimum point, the arc would eventually pass so much current that it would destroy the lamp. Therefore, current limitation is the most important function of a ballast, although it also supplies the correct starting voltage and provides circuit protection.

Each lamp uses a particular ballast. Class (preheat, instant start, or rapid start), wattage, ambient temperature, noise, and special factors are all important in determining the proper ballast.

Labels and Requirements

The USASI (U.S.A. Standards Institute) establishes standards of lamp performance. However, their specifications do not guarantee enforcement.

CBM (Certified Ballast Manufacturers) was formed by a group of ballast manufacturers to enforce certain of the USASI specifications. Ballasts carrying CBM certification either meet or exceed the minimum specifications that the industry has chosen to uphold.

UL (Underwriters Laboratories) is a company that tests all types of electrical equipment for safety. A ballast with a UL label has been tested by UL and has met their requirements for safe operation. CSA (Canadian Standards Association) is the Canadian counterpart of UL.

Class P is a further protective rating. Despite the CBM standards, there had been numerous complaints of excessive heat generated by ballasts. Overheating may lead to electrical failure, explosion of the ballast, or

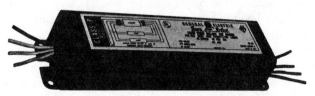

Figure 7.7.   Typical ballast. (Reproduced, by permission, from General Electric, 221-3067.)

Figure 7.8. Certifications and approvals. (Reprinted, by permission, from General Electric, GEC-983W.)

dangerous dripping of ballast contents on people or things located below the luminaire. As a result, the National Electrical Code was revised in 1968 to state that "fluorescent fixtures for indoor installations shall incorporate ballast protection." In compliance with the change in the code, the Underwriters' Laboratories created new standards and established a new ballast classification, Class P. The Class P ballast should now be specified for all interior applications. This ballast has an automatic thermal protector built into the ballast case that temporarily deactivates the ballast when it exceeds a permissible temperature.

Three examples of typical ballast certification labels are shown in Figure 7.8.

Multiple and Low Outputs

Ballasts may be required with special electrical outputs. Low-output ballasts produce electrical outputs that cause the lamps to operate with less light and reduced energy use. They can replace ballasts already in use where electrical energy must be conserved. They may also be applied where similar luminaires must provide differing light intensities; for example, aesthetics may dictate that all luminaires be the same, but pragmatism dictates that light levels vary according to task requirement.

Two-level ballasts are installed if on-site adjustment is required. One manufacturer produces ballasts with 100 and 55% light output, depending on the way that the ballast is connected to its lamps. Three-level ballasts offer further refinements. 100, 55, 38% light outputs are possible with one make of ballast. Two- and three-way ballasts are valuable when the same space has several uses. For example, the task locations may vary frequently in open or "landscaped" office layouts or in office spaces with movable partitions. Control of light output levels may be recommended when there are daily variations in occupancy or use.

Low Energy Consumption—Cool Operation

Ballasts use up some electrical power in normal operation and dissipate it as heat. For example, one 40-watt lamp attached to a standard ballast in a representative recessed luminaire may actually draw 52 watts (a 12-watt loss). Two 40-watt lamps attached to a single ballast may actually draw 84 watts (a 4-W loss). However, ballasts are now available with very low power losses. They are typically provided for 40-watt standard, 430-milliampere T12 lamps with either straight or U shapes in addition to slimline (T10) configurations. Using a single, standard 40-watt lamp in a representative recessed luminaire, one manufacturer claims that its low-loss ballast consumes only 45 watts (in contrast with 52 watts for a standard ballast). With a double lamp ballast, the same manufacturer suggests that only 74 watts will be consumed (versus 84); here the power consumption is *lower* than the lamp rating (you would expect two 40-watt lamps to consume at least 80 watts). For all these reasons, lamp wattages are considered only *nominal* (theoretical), and not actual, until the ballast electrical properties are computed.

Low temperature operation is a side benefit of most low energy consumption ballasts. Cool operation may extend ballast life and promote better lamp operation (if luminaire temperatures raise too high, lamp light output diminishes).

Exclusive combinations of lamp and ballast are also available. These are often proprietary and are said to offer improved light output with lower electric power consumption. Here, special phosphors and lamp shapes may be matched with special ballast types.

Until recently, ballasts have always been electromechanical devices (transformers connected with capacitors). However, ballasts using other electrical componetry have been recently introduced offering hertz outputs that are different from the usual 60 cycles with resulting lower energy consumption and cooler operation. These electronic ballasts may also feature simple remote dimming, switching, or photoelectric control. In 1982, their prices were significantly higher than those for standard ballasts.

Starters

There are three ways of starting a fluorescent lamp: The manual starter requires that a button be depressed and held (as explained previously); the automatic starter consists of a small canister installed next to the lamp; or the starting process is an integral part of the lamp design or a function of the ballast (as with "trigger start" ballasts).

OTHER ELECTRICAL CONSIDERATIONS

A *power factor* is frequently listed with each ballast description. Two choices are available. A low power factor ballast is cheap and inefficient; certain small fluorescent lamps require them. A high power factor ballast has superior electrical characteristics and high efficiency, but, unfortunately, usually a higher initial cost.

Lead-lag and *series-sequence* circuits help to stabilize light output for fluorescent lamps. An incandescent light appears to emit a constant light, although on alternating current circuits (AC), the power is not constantly on. Every time the current changes direction, the intensity of the power varies. The incandescent source appears to give off a constant light because the filament does not have time to cool off during each power dip (and the eye cannot detect a minute flicker). However, since incandescence is not a factor in electric discharge lamps, they experience a more severe drop in light output whenever the cycle changes. Fortunately, the fluorescent lamp phosphors have a slight "decay time" (the light fades quickly, it does not blink off), and the human eye is too slow to detect the change when looking directly at the light source. However, fluorescent lamps can produce stroboscopic (flickering) effects when the eye is trained on an object illuminated by a single lamp. The stroboscopic effect is eliminated when two lamps are used in a lead-lag or series-sequence circuit. These circuits ensure that one of the lamps is always on, thus covering up for the off cycle of the other lamp.

A *starting aid* consists of an electrically grounded strip of metal that extends the entire length of the lamp within 1 inch of the bulb wall. Without starting aids, rapid-start lamps are difficult to turn on. In most cases, the wiring channel or reflector of a fluorescent luminaire performs this function.

SPECIAL APPLICATIONS

Dimming

A fluorescent lamp cannot be dimmed as easily as an incandescent source. When fluorescent dimming is desired, consult an expert such as a lighting designer, engineer, luminaire manufacturer, dimmer manufacturer, or lamp company representative (see Chapter Twenty-one).

Flashing

Lamp flashing also requires specialized help. Lamp flashing and lamp dimming are handled in approximately the same manner.

High Frequency

Fluorescent light output and efficiency may increase at electrical frequencies above 60 cycles. Expert advice should be requested in planning these installations.

LAMP IDENTIFICATION

All fluorescent lamps begin with the letter "F" in their ordering codes. The preheat and rapid-start lamp families are then identified by wattage, bulb shape, bulb diameter (in eighths of an inch), and color (color follows a slash).

A special identification system is used for instant-start and high-output lamps, since they can be operated on more than one current and wattage. In this system, the number following the "F" is the nominal lamp length in inches rather than the lamp wattage, but the rest of the code is identical to that described earlier.

We have discussed fluorescent lamp colors previously. Here we will list only the standard color codes: CW = cool white, CWX = cool white deluxe, WW = warm white, WWX = warm white deluxe, W = white, D = daylight, and SW/N = soft white natural.

When the codes are known, translation is simple. For example, a F15T8/CW is a fluorescent preheat or rapid-start lamp drawing 15 watts (nominal) with a tubular (T) 1-inch bulb diameter and a cool white color. When the word "nominal" is used to describe either lamp length or wattage, it refers to the approximate total size or wattage. A 40-watt (nominal) lamp uses 40 watts before ballast current losses are considered. A 4-foot (nominal) length for a fluorescent tube refers to its length *in a fixture;* it includes the extra length added by the sockets. An F96T12/WW lamp is a fluorescent instant-start lamp, 96 inches long, with a tubular bulb 1½ inches in diameter and a warm wite color.

BIBLIOGRAPHY

General Electric, *Fluorescent Lamps,* TP-111 (Nela Park, Cleveland, February 1970).

Sylvania, *Fluorescent Lamps,* Engineering Bulletin 0-341 (Danvers, Mass. no date), Code No. 1071.

Chapter Eight

Light Sources—
High Intensity
Discharge Lamps

High intensity discharge (HID) lamps are members of the electric discharge family of light sources (as are fluorescent lamps). Three types are now commercially available: mercury vapor (shown in Figure 8.1), metal halide, and high-pressure sodium. Light is produced in all three when a high-pressure electric arc is passed through a gas vapor, rather than by a low-pressure arc as in fluorescent lamps.

PARTS

Bulb

The outer glass envelope is made of heat-resistant borosilicate glass. It has several functions: (1) It protects the inner parts. (2) It absorbs the ultraviolet radiation produced by the arc. (3) It maintains a nearly constant arc tube temperature (which is essential to efficient operation) by minimizing drafts from exterior cool air and by reducing the influence of ambient temperature. (4) It can be coated with phosphors to improve the color rendition of the often discontinuous arc-produced spectrum.

The outer bulbs are produced in several familiar shapes (see Figure 8.2).

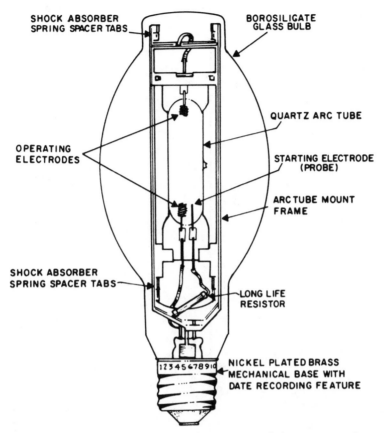

SHOCK ABSORBER
SPRING SPACER TABS

BOROSILICATE
GLASS BULB

OPERATING
ELECTRODES

QUARTZ ARC TUBE

STARTING ELECTRODE
(PROBE)

ARC TUBE MOUNT
FRAME

SHOCK ABSORBER
SPRING SPACER TABS

LONG LIFE
RESISTOR

NICKEL PLATED BRASS
MECHANICAL BASE WITH
DATE RECORDING FEATURE

Figure 8.1.   Parts of a typical mercury vapor lamp. (Reprinted, by permission, from GTE
Sylvania Incorporated.)

In addition, three shapes have been specially designed for HID service: E
(elliptical), B (bulged), and BT (bulged-tubular).

Arc Tube

The tube is constructed to withstand high temperatures. It contains the
vapors essential to the source's spectral characteristics as well as holding the
arc electrodes.

Electrodes

The electrodes are the terminals for the electric arc.

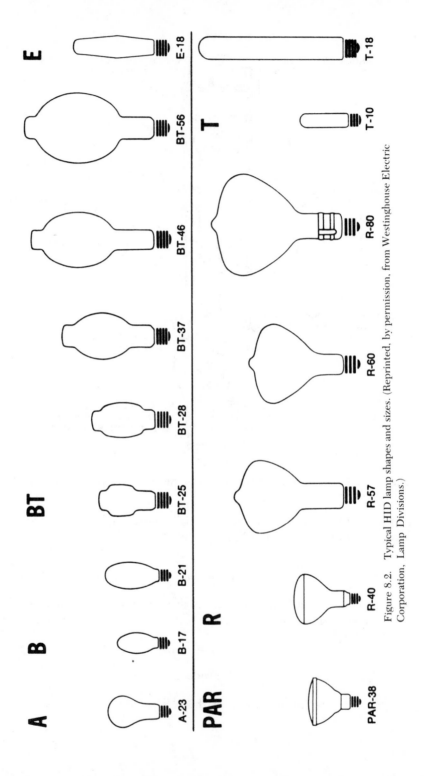

Figure 8.2. Typical HID lamp shapes and sizes. (Reprinted, by permission, from Westinghouse Electric Corporation, Lamp Divisions.)

Arc Tube Mount Structures

The mount structures hold the arc tube in place and protect it from vibration. They are made as thin as possible so that they will obstruct a minimum amount of light.

Base

Admedium-, medium-, and mogul-sized screw bases are most popular. These bases are usually connected mechanically to the lamp, because the high temperatures incurred in normal lamp operation will loosen most cements.

CLASSES

Mercury Vapor

Mercury lamps have four advantages over other light sources: (1) well-maintained light output, (2) high light output in relation to the energy used, (3) low cost, and (4) long life.

The mercury vapor is contained in a clear quartz arc tube. When electrically excited, the vapor produces visible light of a characteristically blue-green color. Since the blue-green color is discontinuous in its spectral composition, it is suitable only for limited industrial areas and certain outdoor applications.

Mercury lamps also produce a substantial amount of ultraviolet energy, but most of it is absorbed by the heat-resistant glass bulb. However, because ultraviolet energy is present, phosphors can be added to the interior of the glass bulb. These vastly improve the color properties and efficacy of the light. The most popular phosphor mixes available are named color improved (C), white (W), deluxe white (DX), and warm deluxe white (WDX). Many proprietary colors are also available. Color, particularly in the red end of the spectrum, may shift slightly during the life of the lamp.

Standard wattages for mercury lamps range from 40 to 1500 watts, however, 250 and 400 watts are the most common wattages for all major manufacturers.

Metal Halide

The metal halide lamp is, very simply, a modification of the mercury vapor lamp with an *arc* of improved color. In addition to mercury, the arc tube contains metallic vapors such as indium iodide, thallium iodide, or sodium iodide. Metal halide lamps have several advantages over mercury lamps: (1) increased light output, (2) improved color rendition without the use of phosphors, and (3) small source size. Since the color improvement is achieved through the use of additives, there is less need for a large phosphored bulb—an important point if precise optical control is required.

Unfortunately, metal halide lamps also have a few disadvantages when compared to mercury vapor: (1) shorter life, (2) lower lumen maintenance (which means that light output decreases faster), and (3) certain restrictions on the positions in which the lamps may be burned. In addition, color rendition varies from lamp to lamp and throughout the life cycle.

Metal halide lamps are available in wattages from 175 to 1500.

High-Pressure Sodium

The high-pressure sodium lamp is the newest addition to the HID field. Its arc tube is made of high-density polycrystalline alumina. The arc tube is very thin, and it contains a mixture composed primarily of sodium.

This lamp has two advantages: (1) The thin source provides excellent optical control and (2) light is produced with very high efficacy. However, there are two important disadvantages: (1) shorter life when compared with other HID sources and (2) severely distorted salmon-appearing color rendition.

High-pressure sodium lamps are commercially available in sizes from 50 through 1000 watts.

AUXILIARY EQUIPMENT—BALLASTS

Like fluorescent lamps, HID sources require a ballast between the power line and the lamp.

Ballast Types

Several types of ballasts are available. The following types are used for mercury vapor lamps.

Low Power Factor Reactor Ballast

This is the simplest, smallest, and least expensive type of ballast. Its only purpose is to limit the amount of current in the lamp, so that the lamp does not destroy itself (as outlined in the discussion of fluorescent ballasts).

High Power Factor Reactor Ballast

By adding a capacitor to the low power factor reactor ballast, the efficiency of the ballast is vastly improved. High power factor ballasts should be recommended whenever possible.

Low Power Factor Autotransformer Ballast

A transformer used in conjunction with the basic reactor increases the line voltage if it is too low to start the lamp.

High Power Factor Autotransformer Ballast

Once again, the addition of a capacitor improves the efficiency of the system.

Constant Wattage Autotransformer Ballast (CWA)

When the line voltage fluctuations are expected, a self-regulating ballast should be used. This ballast prevents the fluctuations from affecting lamp burning by providing a reasonable degree of correction to the current entering the lamp regardless of minor variations in the current entering the ballast. A Premium Constant Wattage Ballast (CW) can be used for very stable light output.

Two-Lamp Ballasts

When two lamps are operated within the same housing, a single ballast may supply both of them. Lead-lag and series-sequence models are available for this purpose.

Special ballasts are required for metal halide and high-pressure sodium lamps.

Interchanging Lamps Between Ballasts

Specific lamps must be used only with the ballasts that are designed for them. As a general rule, different HID lamps may not be interchanged with a single ballast.

Noise

In general, it can be said that HID ballasts are noisier than fluorescent ballasts. This problem has tended to limit their use in small, sound-sensitive interior spaces. However, the selection of encapsulated core and coil ballasts for indoor luminaires minimizes the sound problem. Transmitted vibration and its resultant sound are dampened by surrounding the core and coil in a potting material and floating this assembly in a metal case. The potting compound may also help to conduct heat away from the components, thereby leading to cooler operation and extended life.

Self-Ballasted Lamps

A few mercury vapor lamps contain a built-in ballast, which consists of an incandescent filament connected in series with a mercury arc tube. These lamps can be used in nonballasted equipment, but, unfortunately, only with some loss of lighting efficiency and lamp life. Self-ballasted lamps also tend to be very expensive.

SPECIAL APPLICATIONS AND CONDITIONS

Dimming

Several manufacturers produce a limited method of controlling 1000- and 400-watt sources. However, lamps cannot be dimmed to "full out" and the dimming response (time lag between moving the control and dimming the lamp) is slow.

Warm-up Time

HID sources require time to warm up (after they have been turned on) before they reach full light output. The warm-up time can approach 9 minutes to full output.

Blackout

HID sources are comparatively sensitive to current variations. If the variations are too great, the lamp will turn off. Once the lamp is off, it will not light again until it has cooled. This may be a problem if constant illumination must be provided for safety. Incandescent emergency lighting may be used to back up HID installations.

Stroboscopic Effect

With 60-cycle (Hz) alternating current, the lamp is completely extinguished 120 times a second. However, phosphor-coated lamps have some fluorescent afterglow, so they are not as stroboscopic (prone to flashing) as clear lamps. If this effect is a problem, two lamps should be recommended for use on a lead-lag ballast. Special wiring configurations will also reduce the phenomenon.

Temperature

The light output of HID sources is not as dependent on a stabilized ambient temperature as fluorescent lamps. However, severe low temperatures may effect starting; special low-temperature ballasts may be recommended to alleviate this problem.

Safety from Ultraviolet Radiation

Mercury vapor and metal halide light sources can cause serious skin burning and inflammation to the eyes due to their short wave ultraviolet radiation if the outer envelope of the lamp is broken or punctured, or if it falls away. These lamps may continue to operate for some time without their outer bulb walls. Sylvania states the following for its products, "Do not use where people will remain for more than a few minutes unless adequate shielding or other safety precautions are used. Certain types of lamps that automatically extinguish when the outer envelope is broken are commercially available." These safety lamps operate on one of two principles: Either removal of the outer bulb wall physically disconnects a switch, or air reaching a fuse element causes it to oxidize, thereby parting and interrupting power to the arc tube. If the lamps are used in luminaires with glass or plastic closures, the ultraviolet problem is minimized, and safety lamps are redundant.

OPERATING CHARACTERISTICS

Lamp Life

The life of HID sources is remarkably long, particularly when contrasted with incandescent lamps. For mercury vapor, more than 24,000 hours is not uncommon, and 20,000 hours are possible with some metal halide sources and high-pressure sodium lamps.

Light Output and Lumen Maintenance

HID sources are among the most efficient and practical light sources in regular use today. Their initial light output is very high in relation to the amount of electrical power they use, and this output decreases slightly in relation to their long rated lives.

Operating Voltages

Ballasts can be supplied to work with several voltages in addition to the 120-volt standard incandescent service.

LAMP IDENTIFICATION

Only mercury lamps have codes common throughout the industry, and these codes are authorized and administered by the American National Standards Institute (ANSI). All ANSI codes for mercury lamps start with the letter H (the first letter of the Greek word for mercury, *hydrargyrum*). The numbers following the "H" refer to the electrical characteristics of the lamp and ballast. The two following letters describe the bulb finish shape and size (excluding color). Any letters after the slash refer to the phosphor coating. For example, a H33-1GL/DX code is a mercury vapor lamp (H) that operates on a specific 400-watt ballast (33-1) and has an E-37 bulb (GL) that is coated with deluxe white phosphors (/DX).

BIBLIOGRAPHY

General Electric, *High Intensity Discharge Lamps*, TP-109 (Nela Park, Cleveland, October 1969).

Sylvania, *Mercury Lamps*, Engineering Bulletin 0-346 (Danvers, Mass. 1972).

———, *Metalarc Lamps*, Engineering Bulletin 0-344 (Danvers, Mass., no date).

———, *Troubleshooting Mercury-Metal Halide Lighting*, Engineering Bulletin 0-345 (Danvers, Mass., 1971).

Chapter Nine

Light Sources—Miscellaneous

In this chapter we briefly review light sources that are (1) infrequently used in architectural practice, (2) undeveloped, but offer future possibilities, and (3) interesting for the special effects that they may produce.

Black Light

"Black light" is a popular name for ultraviolet radiation between 320 and 380 nanometers. It is also called "near ultraviolet" (because it is nearest the visible spectrm) and "long wave ultraviolet" (to contrast it with "short wave ultraviolet," which is covered in ultraviolet radiation). This range of radiation effectively activates fluorescent materials such as paints and dyes. When activated, these materials become the producers or sources of visible light.

Four sources of black light are in common use. Since only about 1% of their energy is in the ultraviolet region, standard incandescent lamps are of little value in producing black-light effects. Tungsten–halogen lamps with ultraviolet-transmitting bulbs are more efficient generators of ultraviolet energy. As a by-product of their normal fluorescent operation, common fluorescent lamps produce a quantity of ultraviolet energy that is useful for black-light effects. The most efficient producers of black light, however, are special fluorescent lamps with UV-emitting phosphors. HID clear mercury lamps with ultraviolet transmitting glass or fused quartz bulbs are also very effective. Because of the "point source" characteristic of the arc tube, they offer beam control superior to fluorescent sources. Unfortunately, mercury sources cannot be switched on and off rapidly, so their use can result in control problems. Carbon arcs (see *Carbon-Arc Lamps* in this chapter) are also occasionally used, although they require constant attention.

Black light has many uses. We explore only a few uses here.

Detection. Certain natural materials fluoresce under black light. For example, when exposed to black light, bad eggs glow blue or green and can be separated from good stock. Oil stains on textiles and certain forms of mold can also be detected when irradiated with black light.

Display. Signs and decorative displays represent one of the earliest uses of black light.

Entertainment. Vivid effects can be produced with black light for psychedelic displays, stage effects, and costumes.

Identification. Marks that are invisible under standard illumination will fluoresce and thus identify objects or persons when exposed to black light.

Insect Attraction. Because certain insects are particularly attracted to ultraviolet light, they can be lured into traps for execution or study.

Inspection. Dyes sensitive to black light are used when checking for cracks on surfaces (the crack collects the dye, which then shows up as a bright line) and to detect leaks of liquid materials (oil leaking from an automotive braking system will be revealed).

Reprographics. Certain copying films are especially sensitive to black light.

Self-Luminous Objects or Areas. Designers have used fluorescent paints to create surfaces that produce their own light; the color and intensity of the surfaces can be either vivid or subtle. This technique is particularly useful with low-intensity general lighting if source brightness is a problem (the black-light radiator is invisible; only the object-produced light can be seen).

A surprisingly wide range of fluorescent colors are available in several commonly used materials such as bulletin paints, lacquers (usually transparent), water-soluble dyes, inks, crayons, chalk, powder, tracer paste, latex paint, water paint, and paper stocks. Three types of pigment are available:

1. *Invisible Fluorescent Colors.* The color of the pigment when seen under standard illumination is not the same as when it is irradiated with black light. These pigments are often buff-colored under standard light.
2. *Visible Fluorescent Colors.* The hue of the color is the same under both standard light and black light.
3. *"Daylight" Fluorescent Colors.* These pigments are activated by both invisible black light and the visible purple wavelengths and produce a

bright color under normal viewing conditions. Daylight colors tend to fade quickly.

See caution comments under *Ultraviolet Radiation*. Certain radiations can burn.

Carbon-Arc Lamps

Carbon-arc sources are electric discharge devices that produce an arc between two carbon electrodes. The electrodes are usually not enclosed in glass; as they burn up, they are physically moved closer together to maintain the appropriate gap between them. These sources are commonly used in theatre spotlights, searchlights, and 35mm motion picture projectors (used in commercial motion picture houses). Carbon arcs were the first practical sources of electric light. The light they produce is efficient, extremely bright, and develops a relatively even spectrum at a high Kelvin temperature. Carbon arcs require special auxiliary equipment and continuous attention; they must be specially ventilated and the strong ultraviolet radiations must be shielded from the human eye.

Chemical Light

The interaction of certain chemicals or the exposure of particular chemicals to gases can create light without electric power (e.g., the male firefly creates his bright and soft intermittent illumination through the oxidation of a substance called luciferin). A useful form of chemical light is now marketed. It is packaged in a plastic tube; the plastic outer envelope encloses a liquid and another vial made of thin glass. The glass vial contains a second liquid. When the plastic tube is bent, the glass vial breaks and allows the two liquids to combine. The result is a bright green glow that lasts for approximately 3 hours. This chemical light source is useful if electric sources are not available or are unreliable. This source produces light without heat, but can be used only once.

Flares also use the bright burning of chemicals to produce light without electric power. The chemical composition of the flare determines its burning color.

Cold-Cathode Lamps

"Neon," cold-cathode and instant-start fluorescent lamps all operate in an approximately similar way (See Chapter Seven). "Neon" uses a very thin glass tubular lamp. The lamp gasses may be varied to produce color without a phosphor. Although "neon" has become the generic name for all these lamps, neon actually refers to only one reddish gas among the many that may be used. "Neon" produces relatively little light, and their glow is most applicable to signage.

Cold cathode refers to a light source whose tubular bulb has a diameter larger than that used for "neon." There is greater bulb wall available for the application of efficient phosphors and, therefore, this lamp is more applicable to installations where fluorescent lamps are typical.

"Neon" and cold-cathode lamps are handmade in any length. They should be used whenever light must follow an unusual shape. These sources can be dimmed and flashed with relative simplicity, and they feature a very long life. Remember that these lamps are relatively expensive when originally purchased and when replaced. Ballasts are used to power them when they are within reach of their observers; more efficient high-voltage transformers are used when lamps will not come into casual human contact.

Few manufacturers produce true cold cathode light sources. The development of architectural installations should be guided by a specialist.

Electroluminescent Lamps

When light emitted by a phosphor is excited directly by a pulsating electromagnetic field, the phenomenon of electroluminescence occurs. Electroluminescent lamps are available as thin sheets and can be fabricated with flexible or stiff backings (see Figure 9.1). They are easily formed into simple or complex shapes.

The light output of electroluminescent lamps is low, but their life is very long, and they consume relatively little power. They do not fail catastrophi-

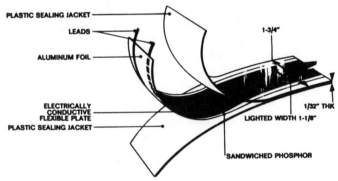

Figure 9.1. Typical electroluminescent lamp construction. (Reproduced, by permission, from Tau Electronic Products.)

cally (blow out quickly), but slowly dim with age. They can be used without ballasts directly on 120-volt electric service.

White, yellow, blue, and green lamps are available (the color is determined by the type of phosphor used). The green color offers the greatest luminance.

The applications of electroluminescent sources are limited only by the designer's imagination. They can be used wherever one may wish to paste on a sheet of light. At present, they are used mostly for digital readouts (clock faces, etc.).

Fiber Optics

A fiber optic bundle is not really a light source, but a light *transmitting* material (see Figure 9.2). However, the end result can be considered a source of specialized illumination. An optical fiber is a thin, flexible, cylindrical glass or plastic strand. To prevent light from leaking through the side of the bundle, each transparent fiber is coated with another transparent material of a reflective index lower than the fiber core. The fiber conducts light by a process of total internal reflection; light entering one end is transmitted to the other hand.

Optic fibers can be combined into two types of bundles. *Coherent bundles* contain fibers that are identically positioned at the point of light

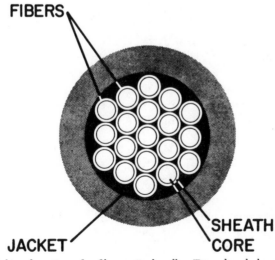

Figure 9.2.   Enlarged section of a fiber optic bundle. (Reproduced, by permission, from Dupont, A-76182.)

entrance and light exit. Since each fiber conducts a light pattern to the same point on the receiving end of a bundle, images may be transmitted through the fiber. *Incoherent bundles* contain a random set of fibers that mixes the image and, therefore, is used only to transmit illumination.

There are a great many uses for fiber optics. They can transmit images from inconvenient or dangerous locations or around corners, transmit light to locations where it is impossible to replace lamps, and create intricate lighting displays.

Fluorescence

See *Phosphorescence,* page 111.

Gaslight

The most efficient gaslights use incandescent mantles to produce a blue-green illumination. They are used decoratively and wherever electric power is not easy to obtain.

Germicidal Lamps

These sources are also called bactericidal lamps. They produce ultraviolet radiation in the far region of the spectrum (short wave) between 180 and 300 nanometers. This radiation has a lethal effect on bacteria, mold, virus, and yeast. Germicidal lamps are most frequently used to sterilize air and materials. They are also sometimes placed in air conditioning ducts to purify the air. (Ozone lamps are another type of germicidal lamp, see p. 110.)

Germicidal lamps produce dangerous levels of ultraviolet radiation and should never be used without shields to protect the user's skin and eyes.

Glow Lamps

The glow lamp is an electric discharge source that produces a low-level glow of soft light in the space close to the electrodes (see Figure 9.3). Most glow lamps emit either an orange or violet light, consume very little electric

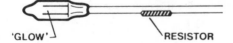

'GLOW'   RESISTOR

Figure 9.3. Typical glow lamp. (Reproduced, by permission, from General Electric, 3-6254.)

power, and have long lives. They are used primarily as indicator lamps in architectural lighting practice. They are also used as electrical testers. Glow lamps must be used in series with either an internal or external resistor when used on 120-volt service.

High-Frequency Activated Fluorescent Lamps

As we have already noted, it is not necessary to have ultraviolet radiation present in order to excite phosphors (see *Chemical Light* and *Electroluminescent Lamps*). An invisible, inaudible, high-frequency wave form has been commercially developed that excites miniature, nondeteriorating fluorescent glass capsules encased in a flexible, weatherproof, and transparent vinyl tube (see Figure 9.4). The capsules, measuring about 1 inch long and ½ inch in diameter, are held in place inside the tube by a network of hair-fine wires, which supply the high frequency to the capsules, causing them to glow. One manufacturer claimed that up to 196 feet of flexible tube could be powered from a generator connected to one end of the tube.

Hybrid Lamps

Mixed light sources are being introduced. One general family of hybrids is self-ballasted and may mix incandescent elements, small fluorescent U bulbs, or mercury tubes. They are designed to fit the standard screw socket and replace A- or PS-shaped general service lamps on either 120- or 240–277-volt power lines. Although their lives are extremely long in relation to the incandescents they are designed to replace, their costs are also high.

Infrared Lamps

Since incandescent lamps are very efficient producers of infrared radiation (from 75 to 85% of their electric power consumption is radiated at the invisible range of 780–5000 nm, they make excellent sources of heat. Lamps specifically designed for this service feature long life and low light output.

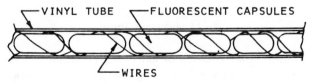

Figure 9.4. Section of a typical high-frequency activated fluorescent light tube.

Laser Lamps

The word "'laser" is an acronym for "light amplification by stimulated emission of radiation." While most sources emit light in a random fashion, the laser develops "coherent" light (the light waves are in phase with regard to space and time). Laser beams can be highly monochromatic.

Although special effects have been developed by using the pencil-thin beam of the laser as a source, they are not commonly used as architectural lighting devices.

Light Emitting Diodes (LED)

The light emitting diode is a semiconductor light source used in architectural lighting practice as an indicator lamp. The LED has a very low light level and an extremely long life. A range of wavelengths from green to far infrared is possible.

Low-Pressure Sodium Lamps

Producing nearly monochromatic light between 589.0 and 589.6 nanometers (yellow), these lamps have high efficacies. Both double- and single-ended types are available. They are rarely found in interior lighting applications. They are more often found in European exterior lighting than in the United States.

Metallic Iodide Vapor Arc Lamps

These arc lamps operate on direct current. They consist of a small arc tube with a very tiny source of light. Because of the compactness of the source, the lamps allow excellent beam control. Both this light control characteristic and their 5000°K color rating make them advantageous for use in small slide and motion picture projectors.

Miniature Lamps

"Miniature lamp" is an arbitrary designation developed by the industry to refer to light sources of small size and low power consumption.

Molecular Arc Lamps

Metal chloride (tin) is the basic additive to the arc tube of this experimental HID source. The light output of the first molecular arc lamp is claimed to be 60 lumens per watt, with a well-maintained output over an average life of 5000+ hours. The most exciting aspect of the source is its color rendering index (Ra) of 87 at a reference of 4900°K. The even spectrum is produced within the arc tube (no phosphors are used) so its light-control properties are superior to those of phosphor-coated lamps.

Open Mirror Lamps

To provide a very compact light source for use in display and architectural applications, a very small tungsten–halogen lamp is attached to a mirror with a surface composed of specular facets (see Figure 9.5) or a smooth plane. The mirror is generally ellipsoidal in shape, and the lamp's coiled filament is placed along its first focus (see Chapter Twelve and Figure 12.4). The resulting combination acts as a reflective condenser and does not need refractive optics (other lenses to control the light pattern). By changing the shape of the mirror and/or permanently relocating the light source

Figure 9.5.   Open mirror lamp.

within the reflector, the lamp manufacturer can produce a lamp with either a narrow or wide light beam distribution (from a 13° spot to a 39° flood). The lamp's power source is low voltage (11.8–13.8 V, with 12 V recommended) and they are currently offered in 20 watts (2500 hour rated average life), 50 watts (3000 h) and 75 watts (3500 h). They are 2½ in diameter, 2⅛ deep (not counting the socket) and may have a miniature bi-pin or bayonet base. They tend to be whiter in color (2950–3150°K) than standard incandescent sources (2800–2900°K). They have the combined advantages and disadvantages of reflectorized, low voltage, and tungsten–halogen lamps in a very compact envelope that can often be used without other optics (resulting in smaller, lighter, and less complex luminaires). Note that R and PAR reflectorized lamps have fully enclosed reflectors while these open reflectors are exposed to dust, dirt, and scratching, which may harm or dull their surfaces.

Neon Lamps

See *Cold-Cathode Lamps*, page 103.

Nuclear Lamps

Nuclear light sources consist of an internally phosphor-coated bulb filled with tritium gas. They require no external power supply and have a useful life of approximately 15 years. The glass wall of the lamp prevents radiation from escaping, and, therefore, there is no radiation hazard under normal circumstances. Light output averages about 0.5 footlamberts.

Nuclear lamps are currently monitored by a federal agency. Developers envision many future appllctions, including the illumination of instrument panels, locks, and other devices where an externally powered source is impractical. Tritium powered exit indicators have been introduced by several manufacturers in the United States. Their advantages include freedom from catastrophic (violent or sudden) light failure, independence from building wiring and electrical services, and relatively low maintenance. All three advantages have both economic and safety ramifications.

Ozone Lamps

Ozone lamps, which produce a majority of radiation at about 253 nanometers, are a form of bactericidal lamp. However, 184.9 nanometers is also produced in small quantities, and this forms ozone in the air. In addition to being a deodorant, ozone in the presence of water vapor is lethal to bacteria and fungus. Ozone lamps are used to disinfect the air in rooms and in the ducts of air-handling equipment. They may also be used to disinfect liquids and solid materials. Since the ultraviolet energy produced by ozone lamps is dangerous, they should always be used in equipment that shields them from the eyes and skin.

Phosphorescence

Phosphorescence is the ability of a material to retain a portion of the energy it receives and then to release it as light energy after the stimulator is removed. The phenomenon can be contrasted with fluorescence—a fluorescent material must be continuously stimulated in order to emit light. Most fluorescent materials are partly phosphorescent.

Short-Arc Lamps

The term "short-arc" refers to a family of lamps in which the length of the arc is smaller in size than the electrodes (see Figure 9.6). The *xenon lamp* is one of the most popular types. The arc color of this lamp closely approximates daylight at 6000°K, and its spectrum is continuous in the visible range.

Short-arc lamps are frequently used to replace carbon-arc sources when a relatively maintenance-free arc source is required. They are used in projectors of all types, searchlights, and similar equipment. Unfortunately, the complex auxiliary equipment required to run them (including water cooling devices in some instances) limits their use in general architectural lighting.

Stage and Studio Lamps

Stage and studio lamps are used primarily in photographic theatrical, television, and motion picture lighting equipment. Generally speaking, the

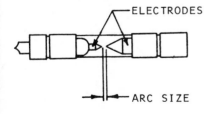

ELECTRODES

ARC SIZE

Figure 9.6. Typical short-arc lamp. (Reprinted, by permission, from ILC Technology Incorporated.)

sources are comparatively compact, very efficient, and tend to be short-lived.

Ultraviolet Radiation

The ultraviolet range exists between 380 and 10 nanometers. Although the divisions are not mutually exclusive, we frequently divide ultraviolet radiation as follows: 380 to 320 nanometers = black light, 320 to 280 = erythemal (capable of inflaming the skin), 300 to 220 = bactericidal (lethal to virus, bacteria, yeast, and mold), and 220 to 180 = ozone-producing. The ultraviolet range can also be divided into long wave or near ultraviolet (380 to 320 nm) and short wave or far ultraviolet (320 to 10 nm).

It is essential to protect the eyes from ultraviolet radiation. This precaution is particularly necessary for short wave ultraviolet. Special glasses should be used, or the source of the radiation should be opaquely shielded from the user. Wavelengths shorter than 340 nanometers are usually filtered out by ordinary window glass. However, precautions are still necessary in the presence of strong radiations.

BIBLIOGRAPHY

General Electric, *Black Light*, TP-125 (Nela Park, Cleveland, 1969).

_____, *Germicidal Lamps*, TP-122 (Nela Park, Cleveland, 1967).

_____, *Glow Lamps*, Catalog 3-6254 (Nela Park, Cleveland, 1970).

_____, *People Heating with Infrared Lamps*, TP-103 (Nela Park, Cleveland, 1966).

_____, *Product Heating with Infrared Lamps*, TP-116 (Nela Park, Cleveland, 1967).

Hile, E. J., *Fact Sheet on General Electric Developmental Molecular Arc Lamp* (Nela Park, Cleveland, 1970).

Illuminating Engineering Society, *I.E.S. Lighting Handbook*, 5th ed. (New York, 1972), Chapter 8.

Ultraviolet Products Inc., *Black-Ray Fluorescent Materials Catalog* (San Gabriel, Calif., no date).

Westinghouse, *Sterilamps* (Bloomfield, N.J., 1969).

Chapter Ten

Light Sources—Large Lamp Catalogs

By using the term "large" lamp catalog, we differentiate this reference material from other catalogs dealing with products infrequently used in architectural practice (e.g., miniature lamps, stage lamps, or photographic lamps). A typical catalog page is shown in Figure 10.1.

The catalogs published by most major lamp companies are roughly similar. They are first divided by type of light source, such as "Incandescent," "Fluorescent" and "High Intensity Discharge." There may be other subdivisions according to the specific manufacturers product policy (e.g., "Tungsten–Halogen" and "Street Lighting" may fall in the incandescent lamps section).

Within each section, lamps of similar *wattage ratings* are grouped in order of increasing wattage. Individual lamps are then defined through a series of columns.

A column is usually devoted to the *bulb characteristics* (both its shape and size). Another column contains an *ordering code*. (With the exception of the Duro-Test/Duro-Lite Company, the major manufacturers use self-explanatory standard codes. The Duro-Test/Duro-Lite Company prefers to use an arbitrary number.) In some cases, codes are abbreviated (thus F40T12/CW becomes F40/CW).

The *description* column contains a brief description of the lamp or its special features. The color of the lamp is frequently included in this column.

The *base* column gives information on the type and size of a lamp's base. If there can be a question about the number of electrical contacts on a

113

INCANDESCENT LAMPS

Burning Position—ANY, except as noted.

Bulb	Base	Lamp Ordering Code	Volts	DESCRIPTION (See Incandescent Lamp Footnotes—Page 38)	Std. Pkg. Qty.	Filament Design	M.O.L.	L.C.L.	Approx. Hours Life	Approx. Initial Lumens
150 WATTS (Continued)										
A-23	▲Medium	150A23/99CL	120	Clear—Extended Service (11)	60	CC-6	6 3/16	4 3/8	2500	2310
		150A23/99CL	130	Clear—Extended Service (11)	60	CC-6	6 3/16	4 3/8	2500	2310
	Medium	150A/RS 24PK	120	Inside Frosted—Rough Service. 24-Pack (11)	72	C-17	5 13/16	4 7/16	1000	. . .
		150A/RS 24PK	125-130	Inside Frosted—Rough Service. 24-Pack (11)	72	C-17	5 13/16	4 7/16	1000	. . .
PS-25 		150	120	Inside Frosted (11)	60	C-9	6 15/16	5 3/16	750	2680
		150	125	Inside Frosted (11)	60	C-9	6 15/16	5 3/16	750	2680
		150	130	Inside Frosted (11)	60	C-9	6 15/16	5 3/16	750	2680
	▲Medium	150PS25/TF	115-125	Clear —TUFF-SKIN (44)	60	C-9	6 15/16	. . .	1000	. . .
	Medium	150/CL	120	Clear (11)	60	C-9	6 15/16	5 3/16	750	2680
		150/CL	130	Clear (11)	60	C-9	6 15/16	5 3/16	750	2680
	▲Medium	150/99	120	Inside Frosted—Extended Service (11)	60	C-9	6 15/16	5 3/16	2500	2300
		150/99 24PK	120	Inside Frosted—Extended Service 24-Pack (11)	120	C-9	6 15/16	5 3/16	2500	2300
		150/99	130	Inside Frosted—Extended Service (11)	60	C-9	6 15/16	5 3/16	2500	2300
		150/99CL	120	Clear—Extended Service (11)	60	C-9	6 15/16	5 3/16	2500	2300
		150/99CL	130	Clear—Extended Service (11)	60	C-9	6 15/16	5 3/16	2500	2300
	Medium	150/RS	120	Inside Frosted—Rough Service (11)	60	C-17	6 15/16	5 3/16	1000	2160
		150/RS 24PK	120	I... Rough Service	72	C-17	[illegible]	5[illegible]	1000	2160

Figure 10.1. Typical lamp catalog page. (Reprinted, by permission, from General Electric, Form 9200.)

particular base, this is also indicated in the base column; for example, SC refers to single contact and DC to double contact (not direct current).

The column labeled *voltage* indicates the voltage for which the lamp was designed and on which the manufacturer will give a rated average life. If you want an incandescent lamp to burn for a long time (with lower light output and a drop in °K), then you can select a lamp designed for a voltage higher than prevails in your installation (e.g., 130-volt lamps are often used on 120-volt service to achieve longer life). Special lamps may be listed by amps and volts instead of by watts; lamps for marine, airport, railway, and other services are frequently treated in this way.

Three important dimensions are easily found in lamp catalogs. The incandescent and HID sections of the catalog have columns marked M.O.L. and L.C.L. M.O.L., or maximum overall length, is the maximum distance in inches from the top of the bulb to a point on the bottom of its base. L.C.L.—light center length—is the distance from the center of the light-producing element to some regularized point on the base. This dimension defines the position that a filament or arc tube will assume when placed in a luminaire using an external reflector. The maximum diameter of the bulb may be computed from the ordering code (in eighths of an inch) or from a special column (e.g., a 5-in.-diameter reflector bulb is an R-40). Note that both the M.O.L. and the diameter figures represent maximum dimensions; lamps are manufactured to certain tolerances and there may be slight variations in bulb dimensions.

Both the M.O.L. and L.C.L. are important for several reasons. If the optical properties of a certain luminaire are designed for a filament that is 2½ inches from the base, and a lamp is installed with a L.C.L. of 1⅞ inches, the beam shape produced by the luminaire will not be what the designer intended. Of course, if a luminaire is only 6 inches deep, a 9-inch M.O.L. lamp will not fit in it. The M.O.L., bulb diameter, and L.C.L. are also valuable if one wants to use a 100-watt incandescent lamp in a luminaire designed for a 150-watt lamp of established dimension. The designer will be able to tell if the lamp will fit into the luminaire and will be consistent with the luminaire's optical design.

The column marked *class and filament* contains a two-part code for incandescent lamps. The first part, frequently denoted B or C, indicates whether the lamp is gas filled (C) or features a filament burning in a simple vacuum (B). The code letters following the comma indicate the filament type: straight (S), coiled (C), or coiled-coil (CC). The number refers to the filament shape.

The column labeled *approximate initial lumens* describes the total light given out by a lamp in all directions at the beginning of its life. The measurement is given for the beginning of a lamp's life because output deteriorates during life. In certain parts of the catalog, *average lumens* or "Lumens at (some percentage) of Average Life" may be given. This is a measurement of light output after the lamp has been operated for a specified time.

The *average rated life* column must be interpreted carefully when comparing the products of different manufacturers. The number of times a lamp is turned on and off greatly decreases the life of many lamps, and this information should be clearly listed by any manufacturer. The longer the lamp is left on, the longer its total life. It is also important to understand that when an average life is listed, the manufacturer means that half the lamps will burn out before the rated time and half will burn out after the rated time. The concepts of average rated life and guaranteed minimum life should not be confused.

Throughout a catalog, the user will find marginal *numbers and symbols*. These are references to footnotes found at the bottom of the catalog page or elsewhere in the catalog. The footnotes provide information not easily represented in columnar form. Always read all footnotes—they contain information vital to the correct use of the light sources.

Since lamp catalogs are produced by independent companies, and each company has its own style, the information presented in this chapter must be general in nature. A specific manufacturer may alter, delete, or add to the basic descriptions we have presented.

Economic conditions have varied greatly within short periods of time during the last few years. For this reason, lamp manufacturers rarely provide price information in their expensively illustrated large lamp catalogs or other literature. Costs are now indicated on a separate nonillustrated price list. Note that costs frequently vary with the type of packaging and quantity per carton. The less fancy the package and the more units per carton, the less the price for each lamp. Easily obtainable price lists show only "list prices," the cost to the final user; these prices are useful to the environmental designer in establishing job costs. Bear in mind that discounted prices are always available to large users, lighting stores, distributors, contractors, and other volume buyers.

Chapter Eleven

The Measurement of Light

Four units of measurement for light are commonly used. They are lumens, candelas, footcandles, and footlamberts.

LUMENS (lm)

Definition

The Illuminating Engineering Society (I.E.S.) defines the lumen as the unit of the time rate of flow of light. We commonly use the lumen as a measure of the total light-producing output of a source.

Efficacy

Lumens are also used to determine the efficacy of a light source. Efficacy is expressed in terms of its lumens per watt. If a 40A19 lamp initially produces 460 lumens (as given in a lamp catalog), its efficacy is 11.5 (460 divided by 40 = 11.5). This might be contrasted with an F40T12/CW, which has 2770 initial lumens and, therefore, an efficacy of 69.25. The fluorescent source is obviously more efficient in producing light than its incandescent alternative.

Lumens are also used to calculate a source's contribution to the illumination of an area (other factors, e.g., the number of sources, the efficiency of the luminaire under specific conditions, maintenance, and the size and finishes of the space to be illuminated, are also important to the computation).

CANDELAS (cd)

Definition

Candlepower is the luminous intensity of a light source in a certain direction. The candela is its unit of measurement.

Although lumens might best express the light given out by a 40A19 lamp (since light issues from almost every side of the source), both lumens and candlepower are useful in describing the light production of a 150PAR38/SP or FL (because light issues from these lamps in a specific direction). Candlepower is also used to illustrate the light patterns produced by luminaires.

Diagrams

Two types of candlepower diagrams, the polar graph and the rectilinear graph, are in common use.

In the *polar graph,* all straight lines on the graph are related to a single point (see Figure 11.1). The candelas are read on the vertical scale of the graph, and the degrees are represented by lines radiating from the "polar" point. To determine the candlepower of the source at 15 degrees, simply find the appropriate angle from the lamp beam axis in Figure 11.1. Follow the radiating line of that angle up until it meets the curve. Then read the candlepower figure directly to the left on the vertical scale. For this example, a 150PAR38/FL lamp at 120 volts produces 2300 candelas at 15 degrees from the vertical.

If the light intensity of a source changes rapidly within a small angular area, values are difficult to read with the polar graph. Therefore, a *rectilinear graph* is sometimes used to illustrate candlepower. The term "rectilinear" refers to a series of straight lines that are at right angles to each other. In Figure 11.2, degrees from the beam axis are located on the horizontal axis, and candlepower is presented on the vertical axis. On this graph, approximately 3000 candelas are produced by the 150PAR38/FL source at 10° from the axis.

To save space, graphs are only drawn for a portion of a source's output. In our illustrations of the 150PAR38/FL lamp, the light source is symmetrical on all sides of the vertical axis, so it is sufficient to show the curve in one direction and to use only angles from 0 to 60°.

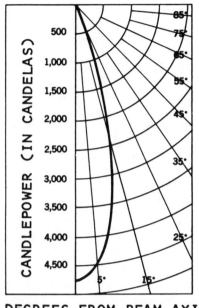

DEGREES FROM BEAM AXIS

Figure 11.1. Polar graph for the candlepower produced by a 150PAR38/FL lamp. (Reprinted, by permission, from Gotham Lighting.)

The luminous output from luminaires whose light output may vary in several planes, as illustrated by the polar graph for a fluorescent luminaire (Figure 11.3), may require readings in a number of planes. Typically, one set of figures is taken parallel to the lamps, another is taken perpendicular to the lamps, and a third is read on a plane at 45°. Also note that light passes through the top of the illustrated luminaire and is measured by candlepower curves above 90°. A luminaire that produces differing illumination patterns in several planes is said to be asymmetrical in its light distribution.

The candlepower curves not only give a measured value of the luminous intensity of a light source in certain directions, they also show a total picture of the light pattern produced by the source. Candlepower diagrams are used

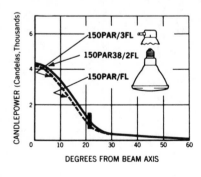

Figure 11.2. Rectilinear graph for the candlepower produced by various 150PAR38/FL lamps. (Reprinted, by permission, from General Electric, 212-399.)

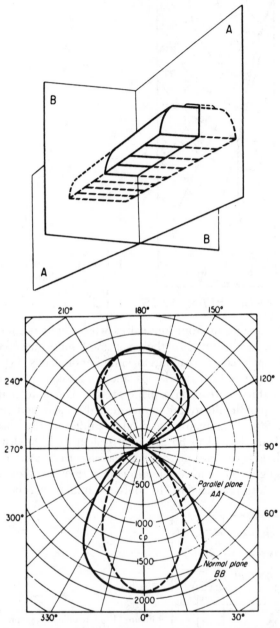

Figure 11.3. Polar graph showing the candlepower of a fluorescent luminaire. (Reprinted, by permission, from GTE Sylvania Incorporated.)

to represent graphically the way in which a light source (either a directional lamp or a luminaire) directs light. They are also the basis of direct calculations of light intensity.

FOOTCANDLES (fc)

Definition

The I.E.S. defines a footcandle as "the illumination produced on a surface all points of which are at a distance of one foot from a directionally uniform point source of one candela." We work with the footcandle as a measure of the amount of light falling on a surface. It is a measure of incident illumination, that is, the amount of light arriving on a surface.

Standards

The minimum footcandles recommended for many standard seeing tasks are prepared and recorded in the United States by the Illuminating Engineering Society. These data are available in I.E.S. handbooks and other lighting information publications (see Chapter Fourteen).

Measurements

Footcandles are measured by a footcandle meter (also called a standard light meter). The better light meters are very expensive and may be complicated to use. However, there are pocket meters that are inexpensive, simple to use, and suitable for most architectural applications. These meters provide only approximate values, but if the same instrument is used to take a number of readings, the relative results are very constant.

A simple light meter may include a selenium photoelectric cell, color- and cosine-corrected filters, a multiplier switch and resistor, and a microammeter (see Figure 11.4). The selenium cell converts light into a small amount of electric power that varies with the light's intensity. Since the cell does not "see" the way the human eye does, its reception is modified by a cosine-correction filter (which corrects for response to wide angles of light) and a color filter. The microammeter registers small electrical impulses on a numbered scale. It is valuable to measure levels between 10 and 5000 footcandles, but such a wide range cannot be squeezed onto a small scale. Therefore, a multiplier switch and resistors are used to shunt the meter

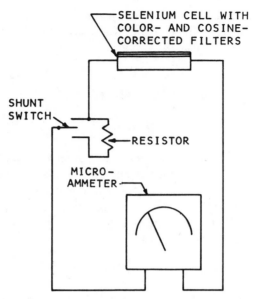

Figure 11.4.   Circuit for a simple light meter.

between several scales. When the switch is in one position, the resistor is not engaged and the meter reads the lower values directly on the scale. When the switch is placed in other positions, resistors are engaged, and the user can read higher illumination values by multiplying the meter indication by an appropriate multiplier or by reading one of several scales.

A typical pocket meter is shown in Figure 11.5. To obtain a footcandle reading on any surface, place the bottom of this meter against that surface so

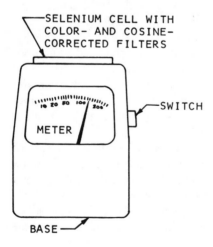

Figure 11.5.   Pocket footcandle meter.

that light strikes the filters covering the cell. There are three rules to remember when using the meter. (1) Always make sure that the microammeter dial is either vertical or face up. The meter needle will not move accurately if it is face down or on its side. (2) Be sure that the multiplier switch is in the correct position for either high- or low-level readings. (3) Do not allow shadows to fall across the face of the meter.

Graphic Presentations

Isofootcandle charts (also called diagrams) are drawn with a single line showing selected footcandle values projected on any plane located at some angle to the source (see Figure 11.6). The distance at which the light source was measured is always indicated, and the footcandle values for other mounting dimensions can usually be found by using an appropriate multiplier. Isofootcandle charts are often used to show the results of using an accented spotlight on a vertical or horizontal plane.

Wall charts (see Figure 11.7) are often provided when a luminaire is being used to wash a vertical surface with light. They indicate the evenness of illumination when the luminaires are placed close together and far apart or at varying distances from the wall.

Quick computation charts are helpful when the designer needs only a rough estimate of the performance of a luminaire. They should not be substituted for accurate measurements or computations of performance.

FOOTLAMBERTS (fL)

Definition

The I.E.S. defines a footlambert as a unit of brightness equal to "the uniform luminance of a perfectly diffusing surface emitting or reflecting light at the rate of one lumen per square foot." Therefore, the average footlamberts on any surface are the product of the footcandles reaching that surface multiplied by the percent reflectance of the surface or its percent transmittance. For example, if 100 footcandles reach a surface painted with a 60% reflective color, 60 footlamberts will be reflected from the surface (0.60 × 100 fc = 60 fL). If 100 footcandles reach a material that offers a 20% transmittance, then the light passing through the material can be measured as 20 footlamberts on the surface opposite the source (0.20 × 100 fc = 20 fL).

To find the percent reflectance of a surface, divide footlamberts by footcandles. Therefore, if 65 footcandles reach a surface and 40 footlamberts

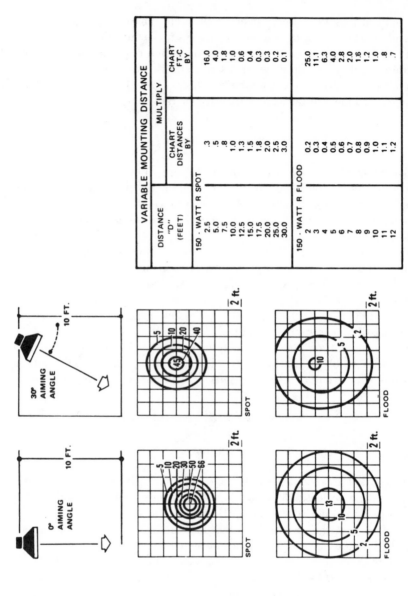

Figure 11.6. Typical isofootcandle chart for 150-watt R40 lamp. (Reprinted, by permission, from *Architectural Lighting Graphics*, by Flynn and Mills, Reinhold, 1962.)

FIXTURE MOUNTED 2 FEET OUT FROM WALL

FOOTCANDLE DISTRIBUTION ON WALL SINGLE UNITS

DISTANCE FROM CEILING IN FEET		1'	2'	3'
0	9.0	8.0	5.0	3.5
1	27.0	20.0	10.0	6.0
2	26.0	21.0	12.0	7.0
3	17.0	13.0	9.5	9.0
4	12.0	10.0	7.0	6.0
5	8.5	7.5	5.5	4.0
6	6.5	6.0	5.0	3.0
7	4.5	4.5	4.0	2.0
8	3.5	3.0	3.0	2.0
9	3.0	2.5	2.0	1.5
10	2.0	1.5	1.0	1.0

FOOTCANDLE DISTRIBUTION ON WALL FOR MULTIPLE INSTALLATIONS

Spacing: 1'—2'—1'—1'—2'—1'—1'

12.0	13.0	12.0	13.0	12.0
47.0	49.0	47.0	49.0	47.0
50.0	53.0	50.0	53.0	50.0
36.0	44.0	36.0	44.0	36.0
26.0	32.0	26.0	32.0	26.0
19.5	23.0	19.5	23.0	19.5
16.5	18.0	16.5	18.0	16.5
12.5	13.0	12.5	13.0	12.5
9.5	10.0	9.5	10.0	9.5
7.0	8.0	7.0	8.0	7.0
4.0	5.0	4.0	5.0	4.0

Spacing: 1.5'—3'—1.5'—1.5'—3'—1.5'—3'—1.5'

11.0	10.0	11.0	10.0	11.0	11.0
39.0	34.0	39.0	34.0	39.0	39.0
40.0	36.0	40.0	36.0	40.0	40.0
35.0	31.0	35.0	31.0	35.0	35.0
24.0	17.0	24.0	17.0	24.0	24.0
16.5	13.0	16.5	13.0	16.5	16.5
12.5	11.0	12.5	11.0	12.5	12.5
8.5	8.5	8.5	8.5	8.5	8.5
7.5	6.0	7.5	6.0	7.5	7.5
6.0	5.5	6.0	5.5	6.0	6.0
4.0	4.0	4.0	4.0	4.0	4.0

Figure 11.7. Wall chart with footcandle performance for a typical smoothing wall washer luminaire.

are reflected from it, the reflectance will be about 62% (40 fL ÷ 64 fc = 0.615, or 62%). If 75 footcandles reach the incident surface of a transmitting material and 15 footlamberts are measured on the side opposite the source, then the material offers a 20% transmittance (15 fL ÷ 75 fc = 0.20, or 20%).

Measurements

Electronic brightness meters are used to measure footlamberts directly. These relatively expensive and delicate meters consist of a phototube that produces a small amount of current. The current is electronically amplified and then measured on a microammeter. To read the footlamberts on a surface, the brightness meter phototube is aimed at the surface, and footlamberts are read directly from the meter scale.

A pocket light meter designed to directly measure footcandles can also be used to read footlamberts issuing from a diffuse surface. To measure the brightness of a diffusely transmitting surface, place the filters covering the cell in direct contact with the surface. When the brightness of a diffusely reflecting surface is to be measured, place the filters in direct contact with the surface, and then draw the meter back until the reading remains constant (about 2 to 5 in.). Footlamberts rather than footcandles are being read because the meter is "seeing" the number of lumens per square foot diffusely leaving the surface. Be sure to take the same precautions as when reading footcandles.

If you wish to find the percent reflectance of a surface using a pocket meter, two systems may be used. The *known-sample comparison method* requires the use of a sample card with a known reflectance (at least 8 by 10 inches). To find the reflectance of an unknown surface, take a footlambert reading in the usual way. Then place the card over the area and take a second reading of the card. The value of the first surface is then divided by the value of the card. The result is multiplied by the known reflectance value of the card and the product is the approximate reflectance of the first surface. Therefore, if the reading of the first surface (without the card) is 20 footlamberts and the reading with an 80% reflectance card is 60 footlamberts, then the reflectance of the first surface is about 27% (20 fL ÷ 60 fL = 0.333; 0.33 times 0.80 = 0.266, or 27%).

Although the known-sample comparison method is relatively accurate, it requires the use of a standardized card that must be carried whenever the test is performed and must also be kept clean and checked frequently for accuracy. The *reflected-incident light method* is not quite as dependable, but it does not require a test card. Simply take a reading of the footcandles and footlamberts of a diffuse surface. Divide the resulting footlamberts by the measured footcandles and the approximate percent reflectance will be found. If a nonglossy wall has 100 footcandles falling on it and reflects 70 footlamberts, the surface is approximately 70% reflective (70 fL ÷ 100 fc = 0.70, or 70%). To find the percent transmittance of a material measure the footlamberts passing through the material and divide by the footcandles falling directly on the side nearest the source. When 80 footcandles fall directly and 33 footlamberts are transmitted, then the material has approximately 41% transmittance (33 fL ÷ 80 fc = 0.4125, or 41%).

Footlamberts represent the light that we see (we do not see objects by footcandles). Unfortunately, there are few tables of recommended minimum footlambert values. We do use footlamberts to establish brightness ratios. (Brightness ratios are discussed in a later chapter.)

BIBLIOGRAPHY

General Electric, *Light Measurement and Control*, TP-118 (Nela Park, Cleveland, 1965).

Illuminating Engineering Society, "Definitions," *I.E.S. Lighting Handbook*, 5th ed. (New York, 1972), Chapter 1.

Chapter Twelve

The Control of Light

The control of light is a very broad subject, and for purposes of discussion may be broken down into eight divisions. Those most important to the lighting designer include (1) reflection [which includes subtopic (2) diffusion], (3) transmission, (4) refraction, (5) absorption, and (6) polarization. Because the other divisions, (7) interference and (8) diffraction, are less important to the designer, they are not discussed here.

REFLECTION

Degrees of Reflection

Specular reflection, shown in Figure 12.1, is the reflection that we get from a mirror or other highly polished surface. The following rule applies to specular reflectors: The angle between the reflected light ray and a line perpendicular to the reflecting surface is equal to the angle between the same perpendicular line and the incident light ray. In other words, the angle of incidence equals the angle of reflection.

Reflectors made of specular materials redirect light in precise beam patterns if the source of light is comparatively small. Therefore, very accurate reflected light patterns require that the light source be as small and as compact as possible.

Three reflector shapes are commonly used in lighting equipment. Each can be formed by passing a plane through a conic section. (1) The parabolic

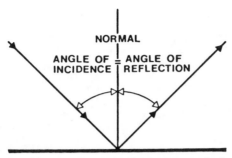

Figure 12.1.   Specular reflection—the angle of reflection equals the angle of incidence.

shapes, shown in Figure 12.2, are among the most useful. When a point light source is placed at the focus of a parabolic reflector section, all the light rays reflected from the surface are parallel. (2) The elliptical reflector (sometimes called an ellipsoidal reflector) has two focal points, as shown in Figure 12.3. When the point light source is placed at one focus, the rays leaving the reflector converge at the second focus. This second focal point is called the "conjugate focal point." Note that the image of the light source is reversed after it has passed through the conjugate focal point. This characteristic crossing of the rays at a second point in front of the reflector makes it possible to direct a relatively large spread of light through a very small opening. (3) The circular reflector section, the simplest of all the reflector shapes commonly used in lighting, is shown in Figure 12.4. When a point source of light is placed at the center of the circle, the reflected rays pass back directly through the source, increasing the apparent intensity of the source.

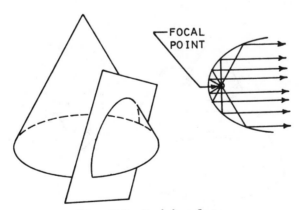

Figure 12.2.   Parabolic reflector.

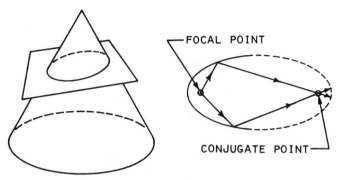

Figure 12.3.   Elliptical reflector.

Spread reflection is a second degree of reflecxtion. The spread reflector has numerous small surfaces that lie only on an average plane (see Figure 12.5). For this reason, the majority of light rays striking the spread surface from a point light source follow the direction indicated by the reflector even though in each case the direction is slightly out of line. The result is to maintain the general direction but to "spread" the light a little.

You may note that the surfaces of so-called specular reflectors are frequently roughened to provide a slight degree of diffusion. This process serves to hide beam irregularities caused by filament striations or other light source imperfections.

Diffuse reflection occurs where the reflecting surface redirects incident light in all directions (see Figure 12.6). This obviously eliminates any directionality of the reflected light and tends to offset the effect of a reflector shape. Flat white paint and unfinished white plaster are good examples of diffuse surfaces. Highly diffusing materials appear nearly equal in brightness from all angles of view.

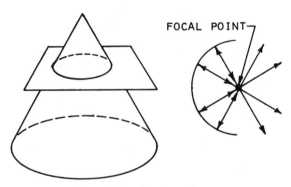

Figure 12.4.   Circular reflector.

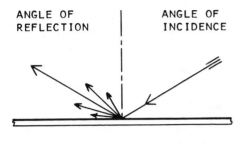

ANGLE OF
REFLECTION

ANGLE OF
INCIDENCE

Figure 12.5.   Spread reflection.

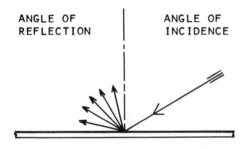

ANGLE OF
REFLECTION

ANGLE OF
INCIDENCE

Figure 12.6.   Diffuse reflection.

Most materials exhibit characteristics of all three degrees of reflection: specular, spread, and diffuse.

Total Reflection

Total reflection occurs when light travels inside a transmitting medium. Fiber optics is one example of this phenomenon. Light entering one end of a glass or plastic fiber of optical quality is transmitted to the other end by the process of total internal reflection. As shown in Figure 12.7, light rays that strike the core at the acceptance angle are reflected back and forth inside the core and travel to the other end of the fiber in a zig zag path of successive reflections. The transparent core is coated with a transparent sheath to provide optical insulation; it permits the fiber to be embedded into other materials without loss of light from the sides of the core.

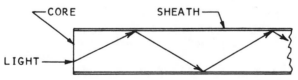

CORE   SHEATH

LIGHT

Figure 12.7.   Enlarged section of an optical fiber—light entering one end is transmitted to the other end through total internal reflection.

In addition to its application in optical fibers, the phenomenon of total reflection is used in edge-illuminated signs and luminous art. When an edge-illuminated transparent material is etched, gouged, or terminated, the indentation appears as a luminous form.

TRANSMISSION

In this discussion, we consider transmission to be the passage of light through any medium without reference to changes in direction in the light beam.

Reflections at the Surface

A certain portion of light entering a transmitting material is returned; this is called first surface reflection. Second suface reflection occurs when the light beam attempts to pass out through the second surface (see Figure 12.8). When light strikes perpendicular to a glass pane with parallel sides, about 4% is reflected from the first surface and between 3 and 4% from the second surface. As the angle of incidence increases, reflection also increases. At an 85% angle of incidence, there is nearly a total first-surface reflection. When major first-surface reflection occurs, we say that we have *grazing illumination*.

Degrees of Absorption Within the Transmitting Material

Direct transmission is a nearly perfect transmission, one essentially free of absorption (see Figure 12.9). In fact, however, all materials absorb some

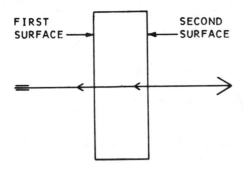

FIRST SURFACE   **SECOND SURFACE**

Figure 12.8.   Reflections at the surface—some light is returned at the first and second surfaces.

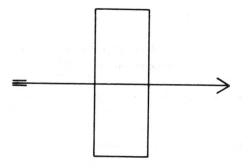

Figure 12.9. Direct transmission.

light, but materials with direct transmission absorb the least. These materials are called "transparent."

Spread transmission occurs when blockages within the material or surface configurations on at least one side of a transmitting material cause light passing through it to be emitted at angles wider than its angle of incidence (see Figure 12.10). However, the general direction of the entering light beam remains the same. This type of material is termed "translucent.'"

Diffuse transmission occurs when the light rays leaving a transmitting medium are scattered in all directions (see Figure 12.11). This phenomenon obscures the directional characteristics of the incident light beam and hides the shape of the light source.

Blocked transmission exists when all light is prohibited from passing through an object. When all light is blocked, we say that the material is "opaque."

Mixed transmission refers to a spectrally selective transmission of light when certain wavelengths are passed directly and others are diffused. An example of mixed transmission occurs in fine opal glass.

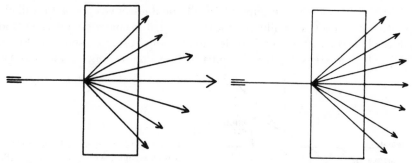

Figure 12.10. Spread transmission.   Figure 12.11. Diffuse transmission.

REFRACTION

Refraction occurs when a light ray leaves one material and enters another of greater or lesser optical density, thus changing the velocity of light. Refraction can be illustrated by placing a pencil in a clear glass of water. If the pencil enters at an angle to the water's surface, it appears to be bent.

Transparent Media with Parallel Sides

Unless the light ray enters at right angles to a flat surface of a transparent medium with parallel sides, the change in velocity is always accompanied by a bending of the light (see Figure 12.12). Note that when the light ray enters a denser medium (e.g., glass or water), it is bent toward a line perpendicular to the surface. If the material is less dense, the ray is bent away from a line perpendicular to the surface. The light rays entering a parallel-sided transparent medium at a specific angle will exit at the same angle (parallel to the entering rays), but with a slight displacement.

Transparent Media with Nonparallel Sides

Not all *prisms* are shaped in the common triangular form. They may have many more sides; as the number of sides increase, a lens of continuous curvature is formed (see Figure 12.13). If a lens is thicker at the center and thinner at the edges, parallel light rays passing through it converge. Conversely, if a lens is thinner at its center than at its edges, parallel light rays passing through it will diverge.

Several *lens shapes* are possible. (1) The double-concave lens (also called a negative lens) causes parallel light rays striking it to diverge (see Figure 12.14). (2) As shown in Figure 12.15, the double-convex lens (also called a positive lens) causes parallel light rays striking it to converge. (3) The plano-convex lens consists of one flat side and one convex side, as shown in Figure 12.16. It converges light rays similarly to a double-convex lens. (4) The

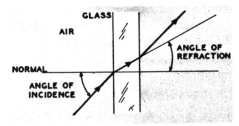

Figure 12.12.   Refraction through a transparent medium with parallel sides. (Reprinted, by permission, from General Electric, TP-118.)

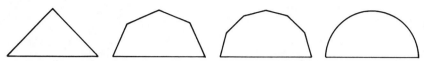

Figure 12.13. As the number of sides of a prism increases, a lens of continuous curvature is formed.

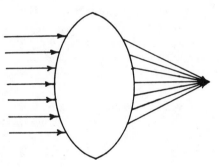

Figure 12.14. Double-concave lens (a negative or diverging lens).

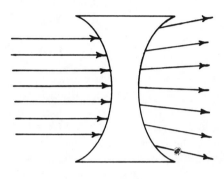

Figure 12.15. Double-convex lens (a positive or converging lens).

Figure 12.16. Plano-convex lens.

Figure 12.17.   Plano-concave lens.

plano-concave lens consists of one flat side and one concave surface (see Figure 12.17). It diverges light rays like a double-concave lens. Other lenses fall into one of the following categories: (5) Concave-convex, or meniscus lens, and (6) convexo-concave (see Figures 12.18 and 12.19). Complex optical systems may consist of several of these lenses used together.

The Fresnel lens (shown in Figure 12.20) is really a plano-convex lens with part of the glass removed. Note that the curved ridges of the Fresnel surface are parallel to those displaced (the curve of each compresed section is the same as the curve of a full convex section). Remember that it is the curved portion of the lens that bends light rays. The plano side of the lens and the surfaces parallel to the light source do not appreciably affect the direction of the light beams passing through them. The Fresnel lens offers several advantages over the plano-convex shape: It is smaller in depth and lighter in weight.

Variations of the basic prism, double-convex lens, plano-convex lens, and Fresnel lens are the refractors most often used in architectural lighting practice.

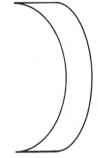

Figure 12.18.   Concave-convex lens (meniscus).

Figure 12.19.   Convexo-concave lens.

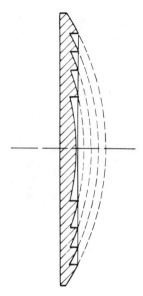

Figure 12.20.   Fresnel lens.

ABSORPTION

Some light absorption is always present when one tries to achieve complete reflection or perfect transmission. In such cases, absorption is undesirable. However absorption is beneficial in the creation of baffles, louvers, and other light-blocking devices. Remember, however, that no surface offers complete absorption; if enough light is directed on a black surface, for example, it will appear light gray.

Some materials (e.g., black paint) offer nearly complete absorption and others perform selective absorption. Selective absorption occurs when certain wavelengths are absorbed in preference to others, which are reflected. Nearly every colored object owes its characteristic hue to selective absorption.

POLARIZATION

Polarization is the process of affecting light radiations so that the vibrations of the waveform assume a definite pattern. Unpolarized light vibrates in an infinite number of planes. Although polarization can be created by reflecting or transmitting materials, lighting applications are mostly of a transmitting nature in the form of closures (lenses) for luminaires and translucent covers for glare-prone surfaces.

Although theoretically complex, it is known that for any one ray of light, polarization in a plane perpendicular to the seeing task tends to reduce veiling reflections (glare). This reduction is less important at small viewing angles and greatest at larger angles. Polarizers of greatest use in lighting have been called "radial polarizers," becuase they produce an equal reduction in glare at all angles.

Polarizing luminaire closures are occasionally used to reduce veiling glare. In recent years, polarizers have also been applied to the glass screens of cathode-ray tube (CRT) computer terminals and other visual display terminals (VDT) with television-like screens. In the CRT/VDT application, they are called contrast enhancement filters because not only do they greatly reduce glare from the first surface of the screen, but they also tend to sharpen the transilluminated image.

EXAMPLES

The condenser lens projector consists of a reflector, a lamp, a condenser (two plano-convex lenses), a beam-shaping device, and an objective (double-convex lens) enclosed in a light-absorbing body. In Figure 12.21, the circular reflector redirects light back through the point source of the incandescent lamp filament. The reflected and incident light is picked up by one plano-convex lens of the condenser and converged on the second plano-convex lens. The second plano-convex lens of the condenser converges the light through the beam-shaping device, which absorbs unwanted rays. The double-convex objective lens collects the resulting light and converges it toward a target. This optical system is common in framing projectors used in architectural practice.

The projector without a condenser lens system controls the first shaping of the light rays with only a reflector (see Figure 12.22). This type of

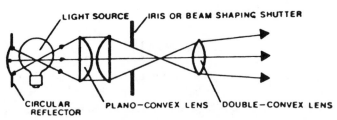

Figure 12.21.   Example of a projector with a condenser lens system and objective lens. (Reprinted, by permission, from General Electric, TP-118.)

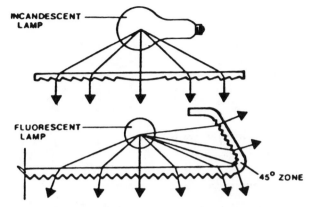

Figure 12.22. Example of a projector without a condenser lens system. (Reprinted, by permission, from General Electric, TP-118.)

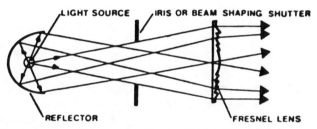

Figure 12.23. Examples of light control without reflectors. (Reprinted, by permission, from General Electric, TP-118.)

projector is common in theatrical work. It is also possible to control light with only a lens and no reflector, or with only a reflector and no lens (see Figure 12.23). In both cases, light control lacks accuracy.

BIBLIOGRAPHY

General Electric, *Light Measurement and Control*, TP-118 (Nela Park, Cleveland, 1965).

Illuminating Engineering Society, "Light Control and Luminaire Design," *I.E.S. Lighting Handbook*, 5th ed. (New York, 1972), Chapter 6.

Kook, Edward F., *Images in Light for the Living Theatre* (New York, 1963).

Chapter Thirteen

Brightness Relationships

VISUAL RESPONSE TO BRIGHTNESS

The standard used today to determine the acceptability of a lighting installation is a measure of the light falling on an environment (which is expressed in footcandles). However, the eye does not react to incident light; it responds to reflected light (which is expressed in footlamberts). Footcandles are simply calculable quantities indirectly used in developing light levels for seeing. Incident light is modified by the effects of object size, simultaneous contrast, viewing time, and color before we perceive the visual response of light as it is directly involved in the seeing process.

Tolerance variations of the eye to differing levels of reflected or transmitted light are phenomenal. Under controlled circumstances, the eye can perceive minimum variations in brightness of approximately 2 to 1, and variations between the brightest and darkest areas of a seeing task can range from a maximum of 100 down to 1, respectively. However, extreme contrasts between high and low areas of brightness can strain the eyes and slow the seeing process, particularly if the viewer is subjected to these conditions for long periods of time or engaged in detailed tasks. On the other hand, some contrast is essential (both physiologically and psychologically) if seeing is to be comfortable and effective. The problem is to control reflected light for optimum effects.

Brightness can be divided into two categories. *Subjective brightness* is the conscious light sensation resulting in the feeling of intensity. Here we have a vast range of words to describe the effect including dark and light, dim and bright, and so on. *Photometric brightness* refers to a measured amount of brightness. Photometric brightness is also called luminance.

UNWANTED BRIGHTNESS VARIATIONS

Glare

Unwanted brightness variations are described as glare. The Illuminating Engineering Society defines glare as "the sensation produced by luminance within the visual field that is sufficiently greater than the luminance to which the eyes are adapted to cause annoyance, discomfort, or loss in visual performance and visibility." They go on to say, "The magnitude of the sensation of glare depends upon such factors as the size, position and luminance of a (light) source, the number of sources and the luminance to which the eyes are adapted."

Types of Glare

Blinding glare is defined by the I.E.S. as "glare that is so intense that for an appreciable length of time no object can be seen." The I.E.S. describes *direct glare* as "glare resulting from high luminances or insufficiently shielded light sources in the field of view or from reflecting areas of high luminance." Most direct glare comes from poorly shielded luminaires, bright windows, or intensely illuminated ceilings. *Disability glare* is simply glare that results in reduced visual performance. *Veiling glare* is a disabling glare that results when *extreme* contrast within a task prevents the viewer from properly discerning the task (e.g., the reflections from shiny magazine paper that prevent the magazine page from being easily read). *Discomfort glare* does not necessarily prevent accurate seeing, but it does produce discomfort. *Reflected glare* results from specular reflections from highly polished areas next to the seeing task. Reflected glare does not always prevent the viewer from observing his or her task.

Glare Control

There are two methods for controlling direct glare. (1) The amount of light emitted in the direction of the eye can be limited. Many types of shielding devices are employed for this purpose, including baffles, louvers, and recessed lighting elements. (2) The overall area of brightness can be increased. In effect, the area of brightness is *spread* so that the average brightness is within the limits of visible comfort. Luminous ceilings employ this principle; diffuse transmitting materials spread the light over a large area.

There are also two principal methods for controlling reflected glare. (1) Remove or reduce the materials causing the glare. (2) Alter the reflective characteristics of the glare-producing object. As an example, nonglare glass is often used to diminish the glare of protected paintings (the paintings are unavoidably dulled in the process). Dulling sprays and films are sometimes applied to offensive specular surfaces.

DECORATIVE BRIGHTNESS VARIATIONS FOR INTEREST AREAS

Use

In controlled environments, designers make excellent use of high luminance levels to create interest zones and thus prevent boredom, attract attention, and stimulate movement.

Terms

Several terms are used to describe these effects. *Sheen* refers to a subdued sparkle approaching, but just short of, specular reflection. *Shine* (luster) is spread transmission or reflection. *Sparkle* (glitter) is controlled spread reflection giving the impression of scintillation.

CONTRAST RELATIONSHIPS FOR OPTIMAL SEEING AREAS

Current research indicates that there are optimum contrast releationships between the several zones encompassing most seeing tasks.

Zones

Three zones are usually considered as a minimum. The *first zone* refers to the task itself. A task is anything that is within the primary focus of the eye. The *second zone* is the surface(s) immediately surrounding the task. The *third zone* is the general surrounding area. For example, if you are in a room and reading a book at a table, the book is zone 1, the desk top is zone 2, and the room's walls and floor comprise zone 3. We always consider the contrast ratios between the zones 1 and 2 and between the zones 1 and 3; it is not usual practice to directly compare the relationships between zones two and three.

Zonal Contrast

Our first consideration is within the task itself (zone 1). In order to be visible, each critical detail within the task must differ from its background in brightness, texture, or color. For the purpose of this discussion, we consider only brightness contrasts. When reading, for example, we generally think that we are looking at black ink on white paper. In fact, we are viewing a dark gray subject on a light gray surface. When the ink is darker and the paper is lighter, the contrast is higher and it becomes easier to read.

After looking within the task, the task can next be compared to the zones that surround it. The I.E.S. suggests that optimum comfort is achieved when the task is only slightly lighter than the surfaces that immediately surround it (zone 2). Research has indicated that substantial areas of the general surround (zone 3) should be not less than one-fifth of the task brightness nor more than five times the task brightness, under normal conditions.

Tables 13.1 and 13.2 indicate the average contrast ratios and average reflectances in typical installations.

Table 13.1. Recommended Contrast Ratios[a]

| | | Ratio of the Zone Footlamberts to the Task (Task = 1) | | | |
| | | Desirable | | Minimum Acceptable | |
Area	Zone	Low	High	Low	High
General	2	1/3	equal	1/5	equal
	3	1/5	5×	1/10	10×
Offices	2	1/3	equal		
	3	1/5	5×		
Residences	2	1/3	equal	1/5	5×
	3	1/5	5×	1/10	10×
Schools	2	1/3	equal		
	3	1/3	5×		
Industry	2	1/3	3×	1/5	5×
	3	1/10	10×	1/20	20×

[a]Values derived from *I.E.S. Handbook*, 5th ed. (New York, 1972), pp. 11-3, 11-12, and 15-2.

Table 13.2. Recommended Surface Reflectances[a]

| Area | Reflectances (Percent Reflectivity) | | | | | |
	Ceilings	Walls	Floors	Partitions	Furniture	Drapes
Standard[b]	80	50	20			
General	60–90	30–70	15–50			
Education	70–90	40–60[c]	30–50		35–50	40–60
Health	80–90	40–60	20–40		25–45	
Offices	80+	50–70	20–40	40–70	25–45	
Residences	60–90	30–60[d]	15–35[e]			45–85

[a]Values derived from the *I.E.S. Lighting Handbook*, 1981 Application Volume.
[b]Often used for photometric approximations.
[c]Including cabinets, cupboards, and tackboards.
[d]40% minimum for walls where specific visual tasks (as contrasted with general seeing) are performed.
[e]25% minimum for floors where specific visual tasks are performed.

In current open-plan ("landscaped") furniture layouts, there may be no permanent walls. Instead, relatively low, flexible partitions are used to divide the space into work stations. The typical station area may be 5 feet square with partition heights of 61 inches. In the resulting tightly enclosed space, all visible surfaces are typically in zone 2—furniture, partitions, office equipment, and the like. A subjective study by Nuckolls (unpublished) suggests that the most comfortable reflectances on all surfaces should be relatively high; ambient illumination in zone 2 might be maintained at 30 footcandles where task lighting is typically between 70 and 100 footcandles.

Interest Versus Optimal Seeing Areas

From the previous discussion, it can be determined that interior spaces might be divided into *interest areas* and *optimal seeing areas* in terms of their luminous treatments. While optimal seeing areas should be relatively close in their brightness relationships to allow optimal physical operation of the seeing process, interest areas might employ more extreme contrasts for psychological relief. We stress that *both* areas are important and should be provided in any interior scheme—commercial, institutional, or residential. In open-plan offices, for example, the ideal secretarial work station should be designed as an optimal seeing area; however, interest area treatments might apply to atria, lobbies, corridors, lavatories, in-house dining facilities, and so on.

Examples

Using the general division of Table 13.1, the following questions can be answered. If the principal task (zone 1) involves white printed paper with a 60% (0.60) reflectance, what will be the most desirable percent reflectance of the second zone if it is to carry the lowest reflectance? (Answer: $0.60 \div 3 = 0.20$, or 20%) Using the same task, what will be the minimum acceptable percent reflectance of the second zone if it is to carry the lowest possible reflectance? (Answer: $0.60 \div 5 = 0.12$ or 12%)

Calculations of contrast relationships are often considered from a different standpoint. If 100 footcandles are striking a task surface that is 60% reflective, how much brightness will you receive from the task? (Answer: 0.60×100 fc = 60 fL) How much brighter might the second zone be if the highest desirable contrast were required under general conditions (see Table 13.1)? (Answer: 60 fL) How much brighter might the third zone be if it has the highest desirable contrast? (Answer: 60 fL $\times$ 5 = 300 fL)

In recent years, engineers and scientists have attempted to formulate a system that will concisely define the interaction of intensity and brightness relationships. The following systems have been proposed and are accepted by some professionals.

EQUIVALENT SPHERE ILLUMINATION (ESI)

The Illuminating Engineering Society defines equivalent sphere illumination (ESI) as "the level of sphere illumination which would produce the task visibility equivalent to that produced by a specific lighting environment." In other words, ESI is the amount of light from a reference uniform system that gives the same visual performance as the actual lighting system. The reflectance is a sphere of uniform luminosity.

ESI accounts for luminaire photometry, space dimensions, room reflectances, and viewer position. For any change in these details, for example, if different viewing directions were substituted, a new ESI value must be considered.

The method of calculating predicted numerical values of ESI is very complex and calculations are best performed on a computer. There are several computer programs available for computing ESI values.

Although ESI is a valuable computational technique, its use is not without limitations. It is often impossible to predetermine viewer position while planning spaces, even if the designer can pin down the other details. Computer programs are expensive to run on small projects. The reference sphere may not represent an appropriate design base.

VISUAL COMFORT PROBABILITY (VCP)

The evaluation of glare that is presently accepted by the Illuminating Engineering Society is known as the visual comfort probability method. With VCP, one number expresses (1) the location of light sources, (2) the sources' luminance, (3) the size of the sources, and (4) the effects of the overall luminance of the environment. As defined by the I.E.S., the number represents the "percent of people who, if seated in the most undesirable location, will be expected to find (an installation) acceptable."

The longhand production of VCP tables is time-consuming and complex; most of the work is done with the aid of computers. However, standard VCP tables are now provided by some manufacturers. They are developed for a specified number of task footcandles (usually 100 fc) and surface reflectances (standard surface reflectances are: walls, 50%; ceilings, 80%; and floors, 20%).

A designer's use of this material must be guided by his or her evaluation of its suitability and accuracy for each illuminated space. (See Chapter Fourteen.)

BIBLIOGRAPHY

Helms, Ronald N., "Fundamentals of Lighting Design," *Electrical Consultant* (November 1972): 26–30.

Jones, William F., "Light Design for Visual Effectiveness," *Electrical Consultant* (July 1973): 6–18.

National Electrical Manufacturers Association, "Veiling Reflections," *Electrical Consultant* (December 1972): 20–22.

Illuminating Engineering Society, *I.E.S. Lighting Handbook*, 5th ed. (New York, 1972), "Dictionary of Lighting Terms," pp. 1-1–1-27; "Light and Vision," pp. 3-24, 3-26.

———, *I.E.S. Lighting Handbook*, Reference Volume, (New York, 1981), "Dictionary of Lighting Terms," p. 1-13.

———, *Visual Comfort Ratings for Interior Lighting*, I.E.S. Transaction LM-25 (New York 1966).

Part Two

A Review of
Lighting Techniques

Chapter Fourteen

Calculations

Most aestheticians are more than a little frightened by quantitative calculations. However, with the application of simple logic and basic mathematics, this need not be true. Vast numbers of calculations are possible for solving the many problems encountered in all phases of lighting design. Those most commonly used by designers concern light loss, intensity, visual comfort, and energy usage.

For a detailed review of most of the accepted calculations available to the designer, a recent edition of the Illuminating Engineering Society *Handbook* should be consulted. Only the most frequently applied computations, using data available to the designer, will be outlined below. Examples of each computation and associated work sheets may be found at the end of this chapter.

QUANTITY OF LIGHT

Footlamberts are the most direct way of estimating the amount of light that will be satisfactory for a given visual task (see Chapters Eleven and Thirteen). Table 14.1 indicates the minimum general footlambert levels often recommended for typical tasks.

Footcandles, although not as directly related to seeing and the human consumption of light, are the most frequently used unit of light measurement. In any ultimate evaluation, they should be converted to footlamberts by taking into account the reflectivity or transmission percentage of the surfaces that return footcandles to the human eye. Table 14.2

Table 14.1. Summation of General Footlambert Requirements (Minimums) for Typical Seeing Tasks

Interior Visual Task	Footlamberts
I. Near Vision Tasks	
A. Good contrast, large, leisurely time schedule	16–40
B. Poor contrast, small, rushed time schedule	80–160
II. Circulation Spaces	
A. Route perception	3–5
B. Intersection, destination or hazard identification	8–10
C. Emergency lighting at night	0.05–1.0

indicates the minimum general footcandle levels often recommended for typical tasks.

With publication of the Reference Volume of its *Lighting Handbook* in 1981, the IES outlined a comparatively precise method of determining illuminance (illumination) in either footcandles (English measure) or lux (metric measure). The conversion of lux to footcandles is easy; for an approximate value, multiply footcandles by 10 (10 footcandles are roughly equal to 100 lux).

To fully investigate the I.E.S. footcandle recommendation procedure, refer to Appendix Section A, Illuminance Selection, Reference Volume, *I.E.S. Lighting Handbook,* Illuminating Engineering Society of North America (New York, 1981), pp. A-1 to A-22. We will review this procedure in its simplest form.

First of all, identify the visual task; typical visual tasks are listed in Table 14.15. Record the illuminance category letter (e.g., A–I) in the illuminance selection work sheet.

Table 14.2. Summation of General Footcandle Requirements (Minimums) for Typical Seeing Tasks. Standard Room Reflectances Are Assumed (80% Ceilings, 50% Walls, 20% Floors). Illumination Levels in Maintained Footcandles.

Interior Visual Task	Footcandles
I. Near Vision Tasks (80% Assumed Average Reflectance)	
A. Good contrast, large, leisurely time schedule	20–50
B. Poor contrast, small, rushed time schedule	100–200
II. Circulation Spaces (50% Assumed Average Reflectance)	
A. Route perception	6–10
B. Intersection, destination or hazard identification	15–20
C. Emergency lighting at night	1.0–2.0

PROJECT: _____   WORK SHEET

DESIGNER: _____

DATE: ___-___-___.

SUBJECT: ILLUMINANCE SELECTION—IES, NA.

I.   SUBJECT AREA: _____   TEST NUMBER: _____

II. ILLUMINANCE FACTORS:

   A. VISUAL TASK IDENTIFICATION: _____

      _____

   B. ILLUMINANCE CAT. (LETTER): _____.

   C. ILLUMINANCE—[ ] LUX, [ ] FC: _____-_____-_____.

III ILLUMINANCE TARGET VALUES:

   A. FOR LOW AND HIGH ILLUMINANCE CATEGORIES—OCCUPANT'S AGE:
      [ ] −40; [ ] 40–55; [ ] 55 +.

   B. FOR LOW ILLUMINANCE CATS.—AVERAGE WEIGHTED REFLECTION OF SURFACES
      ENCOMPASSING VISUAL TASK/SURROUND: [ ] −0.30; [ ] 0.30–0.70;
      [ ] 0.70 +

   C. FOR HIGH ILLUMINANCE CATEGORIES:

      1. SPEED/ACCURACY: [ ] NOT IMPORTANT; [ ] IMPORTANT;
                     [ ] CRITICAL.

      2. REFLECTANCE/BACKGROUND: [ ] −0.30; [ ] 0.30–70; [ ] 0.70 +.

V.   ILLUMINANCE SELECTION—[ ] LUX; [ ] FC: _____.

Next, to determine the *general lighting* throughout a space (illuminance categories A–C), find the occupants age (criteria is established for ages below 40, between 40 and 55, or above 55) and the average surface reflectances (below 30% reflective, between 30 and 70%, or over 70%). If you are concerned with the *illuminance on a task* (illuminance categories D–I), rather than on the general lighting, then you should also establish the demand for speed and/or accuracy (defined as "not important," "important," or "critical"). Using Table 14.3, the recommended lux will be found for these user, room, and task characteristics. For illuminance in footcandles, divide the resulting lux by 10.

Table 14.3. *Illuminance Values, Maintained, in Lux, for a Combination of Illuminance Categories and User, Room, and Task Characteristics*[a]

a. General Lighting Throughout Room

Weighting Factors		Illuminance Categories		
Average of Occupants Ages	Average Room Surface Reflectance (%)	A	B	C
Under 40	Over 70	20	50	100
	30–70	20	50	100
	Under 30	20	50	100
40–55	Over 70	20	50	100
	30–70	30	75	150
	Under 30	50	100	200
Over 55	Over 70	30	75	150
	30–70	50	100	200
	Under 30	50	100	200

b. Illuminance on Task

Weighting Factors			Illuminance Categories					
Average of Workers Ages	Demand for Speed and/or Accuracy[b]	Task Background Reflectance (%)	D	E	F	G[c]	H[c]	I[c]
Under 40	NI	Over 70	200	500	1000	2000	5000	10,000
		30–70	200	500	1000	2000	5000	10,000
		Under 30	300	750	1500	3000	7500	15,000
	I	Over 70	200	500	1000	2000	5000	10,000
		30–70	300	750	1500	3000	7500	15,000
		Under 30	300	750	1500	3000	7500	15,000
	C	Over 70	300	750	1500	3000	7500	15,000
		30–70	300	750	1500	3000	7500	15,000
		Under 30	300	750	1500	3000	7500	15,000
40–55	NI	Over 70	200	500	1000	2000	5000	10,000
		30–70	300	750	1500	3000	7500	15,000
		Under 30	300	750	1500	3000	7500	15,000

Table 14.3. (*Continued*)

b. Illuminance on Task

Weighting Factors			Illuminance Categories					
Average of Workers Ages	Demand for Speed and/or Accuracy[b]	Task Background Reflectance (%)	D	E	F	G[c]	H[c]	I[c]
40–55 (*continued*)	I	Over 70	300	750	1500	3000	7500	15,000
		30–70	300	750	1500	3000	7500	15,000
		Under 30	300	750	1500	3000	7500	15,000
	C	Over 70	300	750	1500	3000	7500	15,000
		30–70	300	750	1500	3000	7500	15,000
		Under 30	500	1000	2000	5000	10,000	20,000
Over 55	NI	Over 70	300	750	1500	3000	7500	15,000
		30–70	300	750	1500	3000	7500	15,000
		Under 30	300	750	1500	3000	7500	15,000
	I	Over 70	300	750	1500	3000	7500	15,000
		30–70	300	750	1500	3000	7500	15,000
		Under 30	500	1000	2000	5000	10,000	20,000
	C	Over 70	300	750	1500	3000	7500	15,000
		30–70	500	1000	2000	5000	10,000	20,000
		Under 30	500	1000	2000	5000	10,000	20,000

[a]For illuminance in footcandles, divide by 10. Reprinted, by permission, from the *I.E.S. Handbook* (New York, 1981).

[b]NI = not important; I = important; and C = critical

[c]Obtained by a combination of general and supplementary lighting.

Example

If we are determining the maintained task footcandles recommended for a school laboratory in an educational facility that also doubles as a lecture room demonstration area, an illuminance category F might be selected. Category F carries a range of illuminances between 1000 and 2000 lux (100 and 200 fc).

If we modify this category by assuming over 70% reflectance for the tabletops (task background reflectance), where the demand for speed and accuracy is important, and an average student under 40 years of age, we can determine a recommended illuminance value of 1000 lux or 100 maintained footcandles.

LIGHT LOSS

Luminaires and lamps lose efficiency with age. In all calculations dealing with the quantity of light, it is the preferred practice to include a factor for this light loss. (A factor is a number multiplied into a formula to adjust the formula.) Therefore, if we calculate 100 *initial* footcandles on a subject, and we determine that there will be a light loss factor of 0.80, then the maintained illumination will be 80 footcandles $(100 \times 0.80 = 80)$.

Light Loss Factors Not to Be Recovered

The *luminaire ambient temperature* can have a strong effect on light loss. Incandescent and HID lamps are less sensitive than fluorescent lamps. Variations in *voltage to the luminaire* are particularly important for incandescent sources; a 1% voltage change can cause about a 3% change in lumen output. Fluorescent and HID (regulated ballast) luminaires are affected less. If the ballast actually supplied with a luminaire differs from that used in computing the luminaires light output, an appropriate *ballast factor* may have to be considered. (In general, these factors are not applicable to new construction. It is assumed that a correct ambient temperature will be encountered, voltage will be properly controlled, and ballasts will be optimal.)

Luminaire surface depreciation results from natural changes in materials. Although anodized aluminum, porcelain, and glass offer negligible depreciation, other materials gradually fail; for example, plastics lose transmittance, baked or painted surfaces permanently discolor, and polished metals scratch. Unfortunately, because of the combination of materials found in most luminaires, it is difficult to predict the total surface depreciation of a luminaire.

The factors that cannot be recovered are assumed not to be present in new construction, not fully understood, or not predictable. For this reason, although their occurrence *should* be studied, they are not usually considered in the planning of installations. For calculation purposes, therefore, a factor of 1.0 is used, which does not affect the computation.

Light Loss Factors to Be Recovered

Area atmosphere, room surface dirt depreciation, lamp burnouts, lamp lumen depreciation, and luminaire dirt depreciation are recoverable factors always considered in determining a total light loss factor.

Area atmosphere includes the dirt, water vapor, corrosive vapors, and explosive gases that may be present in the illuminated space. Areas may fall into one of the following five categories: (1) very clean, (2) clean, (3) medium, (4) dirty, and (5) very dirty. Table 14.4 describes these classifications.

Room surface dirt depreciation accounts for the reduction in the amount of light reflected and interreflected on the work surface caused by dirt

Table 14.4.   Area Atmosphere[a]

	Very Clean	Clean
Generated dirt	None	Very little
Ambient dirt	None (or none enters area)	Some (almost none enters)
Removal of filtration	Excellent	Better than average
Adhesiveness of dirt	None	Slight
Examples	High grade offices, not near production; laboratories; clean rooms	Offices in older buildings or near production; light assembly; inspection

	Medium	Dirty	Very Dirty
Generated dirt	Noticeable but not heavy	Accumulates rapidly	Constant accumulation
Ambient dirt	Some enters area	Large amount enters area	Almost none excluded
Removal or filtration	Poorer than average	Only fans or blowers if any	None
Adhesiveness of dirt	Enough to be visible after some months	High—probably due to oil, humidity, or static	High
Examples	Mail offices; paper processing; light machining	Heat treating: high speed printing; rubber processing	Similar to dirty but luminaires within immediate area of contamination

[a]Source: Westinghouse Electric Corporation, *Lighting Handbook*, Revised October 1969. Lamp Divisions, Bloomfield, New Jersey. pp. 6–5 and 6–6.

accumulation. This form of depreciation is predicted by using the following steps: (1) Find the appropriate area atmosphere in Table 14.4. (2) Determine the time between cleaning (in months). (3) Find the percent expected dirt depreciation from the small graph in Table 14.5. (4) Locate the room cavity ratio by selecting the width, length, and depth in Table 14.6. (5) Determine the room surface dirt depreciation factor (RSDD) from Table 14.5 according to the luminaire distribution type (see pages 229 and 240).

The *lamp burnout* factor predicts the number of lamps that will burn out before the time of planned replacement. It relies on the quality of the building's maintenance program. This factor is a ratio of the lamps remaining on to the total lamps used. In a formula, if LBO = the lamp burnout factor:

$$LBO = \frac{\text{lamps remaining on}}{\text{total lamps used}}$$

Lamp lumen depreciation must be determined from manufacturer's data, taking into account the amount of time that the lamp is run after it is turned on (hours per start). Lamp lumen depreciation (LLD) can be determined from the following formula:

$$LLD = \frac{\text{maintained lumens}}{\text{initial lumens}}$$

Table 14.7 lists approximate lamp lumen depreciation factors, which may also be used. However, manufacturing improvements constantly increase these approximated and averaged factors. The only accurate source of information is the lamp manufacturers' most current catalogs.

Luminaire dirt depreciation predicts the extent to which accumulation of dirt on the luminaire reduces its performance. To find this figure, use the following steps: (1) Determine the area atmosphere (Table 14.4). (2) Using Table 14.8, select the appropriate luminaire maintenance category. (3) Determine the time between cleaning (in months). (4) From Table 14.9, find the luminaire dirt depreciation factor (LDD).

The total *light loss factor* is found by multiplying all of the preceding factors; thus

$$LLF = (RSDD)\ (LBO)\ (LLD)\ LDD)$$

The total light loss factor represents the percentage of lumens remaining within a space after the area, luminaire, and lamp have depreciated. The work sheet provided for light loss factors may be used to properly organize the required information (see page 217).

Table 14.5. *Percent Expected Dirt Depreciation, Room Surface Dirt Depreciation*[a]

Per cent expected Direct Depreciation	Luminaire Distribution Type																			
	Direct				Semi-Direct				Direct-Indirect				Semi-Indirect				Indirect			
Room Cavity Ratio	10	20	30	40	10	20	30	40	10	20	30	40	10	20	30	40	10	20	30	40
1	98	96	94	92	97	92	89	84	94	87	80	76	94	87	80	73	90	80	70	60
2	98	96	94	92	96	92	88	83	94	87	80	75	94	87	79	72	90	80	69	59
3	98	95	93	90	96	91	87	82	94	86	79	74	94	86	78	71	90	79	68	58
4	97	95	92	90	95	90	85	80	94	86	79	73	94	86	78	70	89	78	67	56
5	97	94	91	89	94	90	84	79	93	86	78	72	93	86	77	69	89	78	66	55
6	97	94	91	88	94	89	83	78	93	85	78	71	93	85	76	68	89	77	66	54
7	97	94	90	87	93	88	82	77	93	84	77	70	93	84	76	68	89	76	65	53
8	96	93	89	86	93	87	81	75	93	84	76	69	93	84	76	68	88	76	64	52
9	96	92	88	85	93	87	80	74	93	84	76	68	93	84	75	67	88	75	63	51
10	96	92	87	83	93	86	79	72	93	84	75	67	92	83	75	67	88	75	62	50

[a]Illuminating Engineering Society, "General Procedure for Calculating Maintained Illumination, LM–34," *Illuminating Engineering*, Vol. 65, No. 10.

Table 14.6. Cavity Ratios

Room Dimensions		Cavity Depth																			
Width	Length	1.0	1.5	2.0	2.5	3.0	3.5	4.0	5.0	6.0	7.0	8	9	10	11	12	14	16	20	25	30
8	8	1.2	1.9	2.5	3.1	3.7	4.4	5.0	6.2	7.5	8.7	10.0	11.2	12.5	—	—	—	—	—	—	—
	10	1.1	1.7	2.2	2.8	3.4	3.9	4.5	5.6	6.7	7.9	9.0	10.1	11.2	12.4	—	—	—	—	—	—
	14	1.0	1.5	2.0	2.5	2.9	3.4	3.9	4.9	5.9	6.9	7.9	8.8	9.8	10.8	11.8	—	—	—	—	—
	20	0.9	1.3	1.7	2.2	2.6	3.1	3.5	4.4	5.2	6.1	7.0	7.9	8.7	9.6	10.5	12.2	—	—	—	—
	30	0.8	1.2	1.6	2.0	2.4	2.8	3.2	4.0	4.7	5.5	6.3	7.1	7.9	8.7	9.5	11.1	12.7	—	—	—
	40	0.7	1.1	1.5	1.9	2.2	2.6	3.0	3.7	4.5	5.2	6.0	6.7	7.5	8.2	9.0	10.5	12.0	—	—	—
10	10	1.0	1.5	2.0	2.5	3.0	3.5	4.0	5.0	6.0	7.0	8.0	9.0	10.0	11.0	12.0	—	—	—	—	—
	14	0.9	1.3	1.7	2.1	2.6	3.0	3.4	4.3	5.1	6.0	6.9	7.7	8.6	9.4	10.3	12.0	—	—	—	—
	20	0.7	1.1	1.5	1.9	2.2	2.6	3.0	3.7	4.5	5.2	6.0	6.7	7.5	8.2	9.0	10.5	12.0	—	—	—
	30	0.7	1.0	1.3	1.7	2.0	2.3	2.7	3.3	4.0	4.7	5.3	6.0	6.7	7.3	8.0	9.3	10.7	—	—	—
	40	0.6	0.9	1.2	1.6	1.9	2.2	2.5	3.1	3.7	4.4	5.0	5.6	6.2	6.9	7.5	8.7	10.0	12.5	—	—
	60	0.6	0.9	1.2	1.5	1.7	2.0	2.3	2.9	3.5	4.1	4.7	5.2	5.8	6.4	7.0	8.2	9.3	11.7	—	—
12	12	0.8	1.2	1.7	2.1	2.5	2.9	3.3	4.2	5.0	5.8	6.7	7.5	8.3	9.2	10.0	11.7	—	—	—	—
	16	0.7	1.1	1.5	1.8	2.2	2.6	2.9	3.6	4.4	5.1	5.8	6.6	7.3	8.0	8.7	10.2	11.7	—	—	—
	24	0.6	0.9	1.2	1.6	1.9	2.2	2.5	3.1	3.7	4.4	5.0	5.6	6.2	6.9	7.5	8.7	10.0	12.5	—	—
	36	0.6	0.8	1.1	1.4	1.7	1.9	2.2	2.8	3.3	3.9	4.4	5.0	5.6	6.1	6.7	7.8	8.9	11.1	—	—
	50	0.5	0.8	1.0	1.3	1.5	1.8	2.1	2.6	3.1	3.6	4.1	4.6	5.2	5.7	6.2	7.2	8.3	10.3	12.9	—
	70	0.5	0.7	1.0	1.2	1.5	1.7	2.0	2.4	2.9	3.4	3.9	4.4	4.9	5.4	5.9	6.8	7.8	9.8	12.2	—
14	14	0.7	1.1	1.4	1.8	2.1	2.5	2.9	3.6	4.3	5.0	5.7	6.4	7.1	7.9	8.6	10.0	11.4	—	—	—
	20	0.6	0.9	1.2	1.5	1.8	2.1	2.4	3.0	3.6	4.2	4.9	5.5	6.1	6.7	7.3	8.5	9.7	12.1	—	—
	28	0.5	0.8	1.1	1.3	1.6	1.9	2.1	2.7	3.2	3.7	4.3	4.8	5.4	5.9	6.4	7.5	8.6	10.7	—	—
	42	0.5	0.7	1.0	1.2	1.4	1.7	1.9	2.4	2.9	3.3	3.8	4.3	4.8	5.2	5.7	6.7	7.6	9.5	11.9	—
	60	0.4	0.7	0.9	1.1	1.3	1.5	1.8	2.2	2.6	3.1	3.5	4.0	4.4	4.8	5.3	6.2	7.0	8.8	11.0	—
	90	0.4	0.6	0.8	1.0	1.2	1.4	1.7	2.1	2.5	2.9	3.3	3.7	4.1	4.5	5.0	5.8	6.6	8.3	10.3	12.4
17	17	0.6	0.9	1.2	1.5	1.8	2.1	2.4	2.9	3.5	4.1	4.7	5.3	5.9	6.5	7.1	8.2	9.4	11.8	—	—
	25	0.5	0.7	1.0	1.2	1.5	1.7	2.0	2.5	3.0	3.5	4.0	4.4	4.9	5.4	5.9	6.9	7.9	9.9	12.4	—
	35	0.4	0.7	0.9	1.1	1.3	1.5	1.7	2.2	2.6	3.1	3.5	3.9	4.4	4.8	5.2	6.1	7.0	8.7	10.9	—
	50	0.4	0.6	0.8	1.0	1.2	1.4	1.6	2.0	2.4	2.8	3.2	3.5	3.9	4.3	4.7	5.5	6.3	7.9	9.9	11.8
	80	0.4	0.5	0.7	0.9	1.1	1.2	1.4	1.8	2.1	2.5	2.9	3.2	3.6	3.9	4.3	5.0	5.7	7.1	8.9	10.7
	120	0.3	0.5	0.7	0.8	1.0	1.2	1.3	1.7	2.0	2.3	2.7	3.0	3.4	3.7	4.0	4.7	5.4	6.7	8.4	10.1
20	20	0.5	0.7	1.0	1.2	1.5	1.7	2.0	2.5	3.0	3.5	4.0	4.5	5.0	5.5	6.0	7.0	8.0	10.0	12.5	—
	30	0.4	0.6	0.8	1.0	1.2	1.5	1.7	2.1	2.5	2.9	3.3	3.7	4.2	4.6	5.0	5.8	6.7	8.3	10.4	12.5
	45	0.4	0.5	0.7	0.9	1.1	1.3	1.4	1.8	2.2	2.5	2.9	3.2	3.6	4.0	4.3	5.1	5.8	7.2	9.0	10.8
	60	0.3	0.5	0.7	0.8	1.0	1.2	1.3	1.7	2.0	2.3	2.7	3.0	3.3	3.7	4.0	4.7	5.3	6.7	8.3	10.0
	90	0.3	0.5	0.6	0.8	0.9	1.1	1.2	1.5	1.8	2.1	2.4	2.7	3.1	3.4	3.7	4.3	4.9	6.1	7.6	9.2
	150	0.3	0.4	0.6	0.7	0.8	1.0	1.1	1.4	1.7	2.0	2.3	2.5	2.8	3.1	3.4	4.0	4.5	5.7	7.1	8.5
24	24	0.4	0.6	0.8	1.0	1.2	1.5	1.7	2.1	2.5	2.9	3.3	3.7	4.2	4.6	5.0	5.8	6.7	8.3	10.4	12.5
	32	0.4	0.5	0.7	0.9	1.1	1.3	1.5	1.8	2.2	2.6	2.9	3.3	3.6	4.0	4.4	5.1	5.8	7.3	9.1	10.9
	50	0.3	0.5	0.6	0.8	0.9	1.1	1.2	1.5	1.8	2.2	2.5	2.8	3.1	3.4	3.7	4.3	4.9	6.2	7.7	9.2
	70	0.3	0.4	0.6	0.7	0.8	1.0	1.1	1.4	1.7	2.0	2.2	2.5	2.8	3.1	3.4	3.9	4.5	5.6	7.0	8.4
	100	0.3	0.4	0.5	0.6	0.8	0.9	1.0	1.3	1.5	1.8	2.1	2.3	2.6	2.8	3.1	3.6	4.1	5.2	6.5	7.7
	160	0.2	0.4	0.5	0.6	0.7	0.8	1.0	1.2	1.4	1.7	1.9	2.2	2.4	2.6	2.9	3.4	3.8	4.8	6.0	7.2

Room Dimensions		Cavity Depth																			
Width	Length	1.0	1.5	2.0	2.5	3.0	3.5	4.0	5.0	6.0	7.0	8	9	10	11	12	14	16	20	25	30
30	30	0.3	0.5	0.7	0.8	1.0	1.2	1.3	1.7	2.0	2.3	2.7	3.0	3.3	3.7	4.0	4.7	5.4	6.7	8.4	10.0
	45	0.3	0.4	0.5	0.7	0.8	1.0	1.1	1.4	1.6	1.9	2.2	2.5	2.7	3.0	3.3	3.8	4.4	5.5	6.9	8.2
	60	0.3	0.4	0.5	0.6	0.7	0.9	1.0	1.2	1.4	1.7	2.0	2.2	2.5	2.7	3.0	3.5	4.0	5.0	6.2	7.4
	90	0.2	0.3	0.4	0.6	0.7	0.8	0.9	1.1	1.3	1.5	1.8	2.0	2.2	2.5	2.7	3.1	3.6	4.5	5.6	6.7
	150	0.2	0.3	0.4	0.5	0.6	0.7	0.8	1.0	1.1	1.4	1.6	1.8	2.0	2.2	2.4	2.8	3.2	4.0	5.0	5.9
	200	0.2	0.3	0.4	0.5	0.6	0.7	0.8	1.0	1.0	1.3	1.5	1.7	1.8	2.0	2.2	2.6	3.0	3.7	4.7	5.6
36	36	0.3	0.4	0.6	0.7	0.8	1.0	1.1	1.4	1.7	1.9	2.2	2.5	2.8	3.0	3.3	3.9	4.4	5.5	6.9	8.3
	50	0.2	0.4	0.5	0.6	0.7	0.8	1.0	1.2	1.4	1.7	1.9	2.0	2.5	2.6	2.9	3.3	3.8	4.8	5.9	7.2
	75	0.2	0.3	0.4	0.5	0.6	0.7	0.8	1.0	1.2	1.4	1.6	1.8	2.0	2.3	2.5	2.9	3.3	4.1	5.1	6.1
	100	0.2	0.3	0.4	0.5	0.6	0.7	0.7	0.9	1.1	1.3	1.5	1.7	1.9	2.1	2.3	2.6	3.0	3.8	4.7	5.7
	150	0.2	0.2	0.3	0.4	0.5	0.6	0.7	0.9	1.0	1.2	1.4	1.6	1.7	1.9	2.2	2.4	2.8	3.5	4.3	5.2
	200	0.2	0.2	0.3	0.4	0.5	0.6	0.7	0.8	1.0	1.1	1.3	1.5	1.6	1.8	2.0	2.3	2.6	3.3	4.1	4.9
42	42	0.2	0.4	0.5	0.6	0.7	0.8	1.0	1.2	1.4	1.6	1.9	2.1	2.4	2.6	2.8	3.3	3.8	4.7	5.9	7.1
	60	0.2	0.3	0.4	0.5	0.6	0.7	0.8	1.0	1.2	1.4	1.6	1.8	2.0	2.2	2.4	2.8	3.2	4.0	5.0	6.0
	90	0.2	0.3	0.3	0.4	0.5	0.6	0.7	0.9	1.0	1.2	1.4	1.6	1.7	1.9	2.1	2.4	2.8	3.5	4.4	5.2
	140	0.1	0.2	0.3	0.4	0.4	0.5	0.6	0.7	0.9	1.0	1.2	1.4	1.5	1.7	1.9	2.2	2.5	3.1	3.9	4.6
	200	0.1	0.2	0.3	0.4	0.4	0.5	0.5	0.7	0.8	1.0	1.1	1.3	1.4	1.6	1.7	2.0	2.3	2.9	3.6	4.3
	300	0.1	0.2	0.2	0.3	0.4	0.4	0.5	0.7	0.8	0.9	1.1	1.3	1.4	1.5	1.7	1.9	2.2	2.8	3.5	4.2
50	50	0.2	0.3	0.4	0.5	0.6	0.7	0.8	1.0	1.2	1.4	1.6	1.8	2.0	2.2	2.4	2.8	3.2	4.0	5.0	6.0
	70	0.1	0.2	0.3	0.4	0.5	0.6	0.7	0.9	1.0	1.2	1.4	1.5	1.7	1.9	2.0	2.4	2.7	3.4	4.3	5.1
	100	0.1	0.2	0.3	0.4	0.4	0.5	0.6	0.7	0.9	1.0	1.2	1.3	1.5	1.6	1.8	2.1	2.4	3.0	3.7	4.5
	150	0.1	0.2	0.3	0.3	0.4	0.5	0.5	0.7	0.8	0.9	1.1	1.2	1.3	1.5	1.6	1.9	2.1	2.7	3.3	4.0
	300	0.1	0.2	0.2	0.3	0.3	0.4	0.5	0.6	0.7	0.8	0.9	1.0	1.1	1.3	1.4	1.6	1.9	2.3	2.9	3.5
60	60	0.1	0.2	0.3	0.4	0.5	0.6	0.7	0.8	1.0	1.1	1.3	1.5	1.7	1.8	2.0	2.3	2.7	3.3	4.2	5.0
	100	0.1	0.2	0.2	0.3	0.4	0.5	0.5	0.7	0.8	0.9	1.0	1.2	1.3	1.5	1.6	1.9	2.1	2.7	3.3	4.0
	150	0.1	0.1	0.2	0.3	0.3	0.4	0.4	0.6	0.7	0.8	0.9	1.0	1.2	1.3	1.4	1.6	1.9	2.3	2.9	3.5
	300	0.1	0.1	0.2	0.2	0.3	0.3	0.3	0.5	0.6	0.7	0.8	0.9	1.0	1.1	1.2	1.4	1.6	2.0	2.5	3.0
75	75	0.1	0.2	0.3	0.3	0.4	0.5	0.5	0.7	0.8	0.9	1.1	1.2	1.3	1.5	1.6	1.9	2.1	2.7	3.3	4.0
	120	0.1	0.1	0.2	0.3	0.3	0.4	0.4	0.5	0.6	0.8	0.9	1.0	1.0	1.2	1.3	1.5	1.7	2.2	2.7	3.3
	200	0.1	0.1	0.2	0.2	0.3	0.3	0.4	0.5	0.5	0.6	0.7	0.8	0.9	1.0	1.1	1.3	1.5	1.8	2.3	2.7
	300	0.1	0.1	0.2	0.2	0.2	0.3	0.3	0.4	0.5	0.6	0.7	0.7	0.8	0.9	1.0	1.2	1.3	1.7	2.1	2.5
100	100	0.1	0.1	0.2	0.2	0.3	0.3	0.4	0.5	0.6	0.7	0.8	0.9	1.0	1.1	1.2	1.4	1.6	2.0	2.5	3.0
	200	0.1	0.1	0.1	0.2	0.2	0.2	0.3	0.4	0.4	0.5	0.6	0.7	0.7	0.8	0.9	1.0	1.2	1.5	1.9	2.2
	300	0.1	0.1	0.1	0.2	0.2	0.2	0.3	0.3	0.4	0.5	0.5	0.6	0.7	0.7	0.8	0.9	1.1	1.3	1.7	2.0
150	150	0.1	0.1	0.1	0.2	0.2	0.2	0.3	0.3	0.4	0.5	0.5	0.6	0.7	0.7	0.8	0.9	1.1	1.3	1.7	2.0
	300	—	0.1	0.1	0.1	0.1	0.2	0.2	0.2	0.3	0.3	0.4	0.4	0.5	0.5	0.6	0.7	0.8	1.0	1.2	1.5
200	200	—	0.1	0.1	0.1	0.1	0.2	0.2	0.2	0.3	0.3	0.4	0.5	0.5	0.6	0.6	0.7	0.8	1.0	1.2	1.5
	300	—	0.1	0.1	0.1	0.1	0.1	0.1	0.2	0.2	0.3	0.3	0.4	0.4	0.5	0.5	0.6	0.7	0.8	1.0	1.2
300	300	—	—	0.1	0.1	0.1	0.1	0.1	0.2	0.2	0.2	0.3	0.3	0.3	0.4	0.4	0.5	0.5	0.6	0.7	0.8
500	500	—	—	—	—	0.1	0.1	0.1	0.1	0.1	0.1	0.2	0.2	0.2	0.2	0.2	0.3	0.3	0.4	0.5	0.6

ᵃIlluminating Engineering Society, I.E.S. Lighting Handbook, Fifth Edition, 1972. New York, p. 9-9.

Table 14.7. Lamp Lumen Depreciation Factors[a,b]

Category	Name	Shape	Color	Nominal Wattage	LLD Factor
Incandescent	Extended Service	A,PS	c	15 – 750	0.85
	General Service	A,PS,S		to 40	0.85
				50 –1500	0.89
	Projector	PAR 38–64		75 –1000	0.84
	Reflector	R 40		150– 500	0.86
		R 52–57		500–1000	0.81
	Rough Service	A,PS		50 – 200	0.79
	Showcase	T–10		25 – 40	0.78
	Silver Bowl	A,PS		200– 500	0.75
	Three Light	A,T		30 – 150	0.85
		PS		100– 300	0.72
	Tungsten–Halogen	T		200–1500	0.96
	Vibration	A–19		50	0.72
Fluorescent	Rapid Start	U–12	CW	40	0.84[c]
	430 ma.	T–12	CW	30	0.81[c]
				40	0.88[c]
HID	Mercury Vapor	E17	DX	50	0.76
		E17	DX	75	0.80
		E23	Clear	100	0.81
		E23	DX	100	0.84
		R40 FL	Frosted	100	0.78
		R40 WFL	DX	100	0.80
		E28	Clear	175	0.92
		E28	DX	175	0.86
		E28	WDX	175	0.89
		R40 FL	Frosted	175	0.88
		R40 WFL	DX	175	0.88
		E28	Clear	250	0.92
		E28	DX	250	0.86
		E28	WDX	250	0.80
		E37	Clear	400	0.91
		E37	DX	400	0.85
		E37	WDX	400	0.82
		R60 FL	Frosted	400	0.83
		R60 WFL	DX	400	0.76
		R60 SP	Frosted	400	0.80
		BT46	Clear	700	0.89
		BT46	DX	700	0.80
		BT56	Clear	1000	0.85
		BT56	DX	1000	0.75
		BT56	WDX	1000	0.68

[a]Percentage of initial lumens produced at 70% of life.

[b]All lamps run at 120 volts (measured at the ballast for all discharge sources). All lamps measured for vertical burning.

[c]3 hour per start for cool white, warm white and daylight colors. For color improved types (deluxe cool white and deluxe warm white), multiply by 0.93. Fluorescent and Incandescent factors from I.E.S. Handbook, 5th ed. HID factors from GE Large Lamp Catalog 9200, effective 27 March 1974.

Table 14.8. Luminaire Maintenance Category[a]

To assist in determining Luminaire Dirt Depreciation (LDD) factors, luminaires are separated into six maintenance categories (I through VI). To arrive at categories, luminaires are arbitrarily divided into sections, a *Top Enclosure* and a *Bottom Enclosure*, by drawing a horizontal line through the light center of the lamp or lamps. The characteristics listed for the enclosures are then selected as best describing the luminaire. Only one characteristic for the bottom enclosure should be used in determining the category of a luminaire. Percentage of uplight is based on 100% for the luminaire.

The maintenance category is determined when there are characteristics in both enclosure columns. If a luminaire falls into more than one category, the lower numbered category is used.

Maintenance Category	Top Enclosure	Bottom Enclosure
I	1. None.	1. None
II	1. None 2. Transparent with 15% or more uplight through apertures. 3. Translucent with 15% or more uplight through apertures. 4. Opaque with 15% or more uplight through apertures.	1. None 2. Louvers or baffles
III	1. Transparent with less than 15% upward light through apertures. 2. Translucent with less than 15% upward light through apertures. 3. Opaque with less than 15% uplight through apertures.	1. None 2. Louvers or baffles
IV	1. Transparent unapertured. 2. Translucent unapertured. 3. Opaque unapertured.	1. None 2. Louvers
V	1. Transparent unapertured. 2. Translucent unapertured. 3. Opaque unapertured.	1. Transparent unapertured 2. Translucent unapertured
VI	1. None. 2. Transparent unapertured. 3. Translucent unapertured. 4. Opaque unapertured.	1. Transparent unapertured 2. Translucent unapertured 3. Opaque unapertured

[a]Illuminating Engineering Society, "General Procedure for Calculating Maintained Illumination, LM-34," *Illuminating Engineering*, Vol. 65, No. 10.

Table 14.9. Luminaire Dirt Depreciation Factors

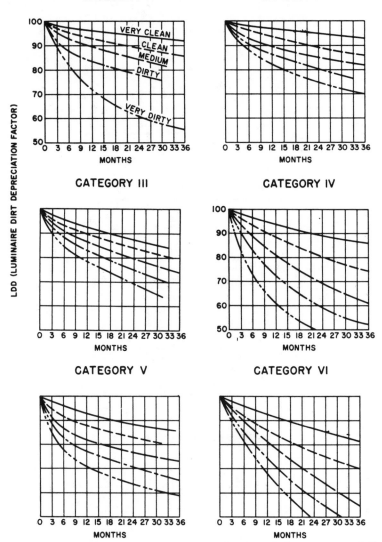

CATEGORY I

CATEGORY II

CATEGORY III

CATEGORY IV

CATEGORY V

CATEGORY VI

[a]Illuminating Engineering Society, "General Procedure for Calculating Maintained Illumination, LM-34," *Illuminating Engineering*, Vol. 65, No. 10.

INTENSITY

There are two methods by which the number of footcandles falling on a surface can be computed. The point-by-point method assumes that one point source of light is directed at a specific object in a space relatively free of interreflections. The zonal cavity method, by contrast, considers both the interreflections of light from room surfaces and the contributions of several light sources. Several formulas are used to calculate incident light under these conditions, and most may be found in publications issued by the Illuminating Engineering Society.

Point-by-Point Method

To use the point-by-point method correctly, the right conditions must exist: (1) The dimension of the light source should be no larger than one-fifth the distance from the source to the task; (2) a candlepower distribution curve must be available; (3) only one source should be considered at a time; (4) the target (task surface) should be relatively small; and (5) the space in which the source and target are located should be free of interreflecting surfaces that would influence the calculations. We illustrate this method in the following problems.

PROBLEM 1

Problem.   The light source is pointing straight down and is located directly over the horizontal task surface (the target) (see Figure 14.1).

Known.   (a) Candlepower at 0° (straight down—called the "normal angle"); (b) the distance between the source and the target.

Source Materials Required.   Candlepower distribution chart (supplied by the lamp and/or luminaire manufacturer).

Solution.   Candlepower (read in candelas from a chart) divided by the distance squared equals the footcandles on the surface.

Formula. $\text{fc} = \dfrac{I}{D^2}$

where I is the candlepower in candelas and D is the distance between the source and the surface.

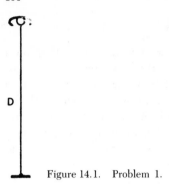

Figure 14.1.   Problem 1.

PROBLEM 2

Problem.   The source is pointing straight down but is located to one side and above the horizontal task surface (see Figure 14.2).

Known.   (a) The candlepower of the source at all angles; (b) the angle θ between normal (straight down) and the target (to one side); (c) the distance D between the source and the target.

Source Materials Required.   (a) Candlepower distribution chart; (b) trigonometric function table (Table 14.10).

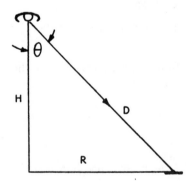

Figure 14.2.   Problems 2 and 3.

Solution. Candlepower at the appropriate angle multiplied by the cosine of that angle and then divided by the distance squared equals the footcandles on the surface.

Formula. $\quad \text{fc} = \dfrac{(I) \ (\cos \ \theta)}{D^2}$

where I is the candlepower in candelas, θ is the angle (called "theta") between the normal and the target, and D is the distance between the source and the target.

PROBLEM 3

Problem. The source is pointing straight down but is located above and to one side of the horizontal task surface.

Unknown. The angle θ between normal (straight down) and the target (to one side).

Known. (a) The candlepower of the source at all angles; (b) the horizontal space (R) between the source and the target; (c) the vertical height (H) of the source above the target.

Source Materials Required. (a) Candlepower distribution chart; (b) point-by-point calculation table (Table 14.11).

Solution. (1) Find values for H and R in feet rounded off to the nearest decimal (5 ft 6 in. becomes 5.5 ft). (2) From the point-by-point calculation table, locate the appropriate horizontal space (R) and the height (H) columns and determine the point at which these columns intersect. (3) Find θ by looking for the top figure at the intersection. (4) From the candlepower distribution chart, find the appropriate number of candelas for theta (no need to use the cosine). (5) Multiply the candlepower (in candelas) by the multiplier located earlier in the point-by-point table (bottom number). (6) To obtain footcandles, move the decimal point two places to the left (since the multiplier is for footcandles for each 100 cp).

Formula. No formula is required.

Table 14.10. *Trigonometric Function Table*

Sines and Cosines of Angles

θ°	sin θ	cos θ	θ°	sin θ	cos θ	θ°	sin θ	cos θ	θ°	sin θ	cos θ
0	0.0000	1.000	26	0.438	0.899	52	0.788	0.616	72	0.951	0.309
1	.0175	1.000	27	.454	.891	53	.799	.602	73	.956	.292
2	.0349	0.999	28	.470	.883	54	.809	.588	74	.961	.276
3	.0523	.999	29	.485	.875	55	.819	.574	75	.966	.259
4	.0698	.998	30	.500	.866	56	.829	.559	76	.970	.242
5	.0872	.996	31	.515	.857						
6	.105	.995	32	.530	.848	57	.839	.545	77	.974	.225
7	.122	.993	33	.545	.839	58	.848	.530	78	.978	.208
8	.139	.990	34	.559	.829	59	.857	.515	79	.982	.191
9	.156	.988	35	.574	.819	60	.866	.500	80	.985	.174
10	.174	.985	36	.588	.809	61	.875	.485	81	.988	.156
11	.191	.982	37	.602	.799						
12	.208	.978	38	.616	.788	62	.883	.470	82	.990	.139
13	.225	.974	39	.629	.777	63	.891	.454	83	.993	.122
14	.242	.970	40	.643	.766	64	.899	.438	84	.995	.105
15	.259	.966	41	.656	.755	65	.906	.423	85	.996	.0872
16	.276	.961	42	.669	.743	66	.914	.407	86	.9976	.0698
17	.292	.956	43	.682	.731						
18	.309	.951	44	.695	.719	67	.921	.391	87	.9986	.0523
19	.326	.946	45	.707	.707	68	.927	.375	88	.9994	.0349
20	.342	.940	46	.719	.695	69	.934	.358	89	.9998	.0175
21	.358	.934	47	.731	.682	70	.940	.342	90	1.0000	0.0000
22	.375	.927	48	.743	.669	71	.946	.326			
23	.391	.921	49	.755	.656						
24	.407	.914	50	.766	.643						
25	.423	.906	51	.777	.629						

Table 14.11. Point-by-Point Calculation Table[a]

HORIZONTAL DISTANCE FROM AXIS OF LIGHT SOURCE—FEET																											
Height of Light Source Above Surface—Feet	0	1	2	3	4	5	6	7	8	9	10	11	12	13	14	15	16	18	20	22	24	26	28	30	35	40	50
									FOOTCANDLES FOR EACH 100 CANDLEPOWER																	
2	0°0' / 25.00	27° / 17.85	45° / 8.850	56° / 4.275	63° / 2.245	68° / 1.298	71° / .802	74° / .528	76° / .355	78° / .255	79° / .190	80° / .142	81° / .113	81° / .090	82° / .070	82° / .058	83° / .048	84° / .038	84° / .025	85° / .020	85° / .015	86° / .013	86° / .008	86° / .007	87° / .004	87° / .000	87° / .000
3	0°0' / 11.11	18° / 9.500	34° / 6.400	45° / 3.933	53° / 2.400	59° / 1.522	63° / 1.000	67° / .680	69° / .477	72° / .356	73° / .264	75° / .205	76° / .161	77° / .126	78° / .100	79° / .084	80° / .070	81° / .050	81° / .036	82° / .027	83° / .021	83° / .016	84° / .012	84° / .011	85° / .007	86° / .004	87° / .002
4	0°0' / 6.250	14° / 5.707	27° / 4.472	37° / 3.200	45° / 2.210	51° / 1.524	56° / 1.066	60° / .764	63° / .559	66° / .419	68° / .320	70° / .249	72° / .198	73° / .159	74° / .130	75° / .107	76° / .090	78° / .064	79° / .047	80° / .037	81° / .028	81° / .021	82° / .018	82° / .015	84° / .009	84° / .006	86° / .003
5	0°0' / 4.000	11° / 3.771	22° / 3.202	31° / 2.522	39° / 1.904	45° / 1.414	50° / 1.050	54° / .785	58° / .595	61° / .458	63° / .358	66° / .283	67° / .228	69° / .185	70° / .152	72° / .126	73° / .106	74° / .077	76° / .057	77° / .044	78° / .034	79° / .027	80° / .022	81° / .017	82° / .010	83° / .006	84° / .004
6	0°0' / 2.778	9° / 2.673	18° / 2.372	27° / 1.987	34° / 1.600	40° / 1.260	45° / .982	49° / .766	53° / .600	56° / .474	59° / .378	61° / .305	63° / .249	66° / .205	67° / .170	68° / .142	69° / .120	71° / .088	73° / .066	75° / .051	76° / .040	77° / .032	78° / .026	79° / .021	80° / .013	81° / .009	83° / .005
7	0°0' / 2.041	8° / 1.980	16° / 1.814	23° / 1.585	30° / 1.336	36° / 1.100	41° / .893	45° / .722	49° / .583	52° / .473	55° / .385	58° / .316	60° / .261	62° / .218	63° / .183	65° / .154	66° / .131	69° / .097	71° / .074	72° / .057	74° / .045	75° / .036	76° / .029	77° / .024	79° / .016	80° / .010	82° / .006
8	0°0' / 1.563	7° / 1.527	14° / 1.427	21° / 1.283	27° / 1.118	32° / .953	37° / .800	41° / .672	45° / .552	48° / .458	51° / .381	54° / .318	56° / .267	58° / .225	60° / .191	62° / .163	63° / .140	66° / .105	68° / .080	70° / .063	71° / .050	73° / .040	74° / .032	75° / .026	76° / .018	77° / .012	80° / .007
9	0°0' / 1.235	6° / 1.212	13° / 1.148	18° / 1.054	24° / .943	29° / .825	34° / .711	38° / .607	42° / .515	45° / .437	48° / .370	51° / .314	53° / .267	55° / .228	57° / .196	59° / .168	61° / .146	63° / .110	66° / .085	68° / .067	69° / .053	71° / .043	72° / .035	73° / .029	76° / .013	76° / .024	80° / .008
10	0°0' / 1.000	5°43' / .985	11° / .943	17° / .879	22° / .801	27° / .716	31° / .631	35° / .550	39° / .476	42° / .411	45° / .354	48° / .305	50° / .263	52° / .227	54° / .196	56° / .171	58° / .149	61° / .115	63° / .089	65° / .071	67° / .057	67° / .046	69° / .038	70° / .032	72° / .021	75° / .014	79° / .008
11	0°0' / .826	5°12' / .816	10° / .787	15° / .742	20° / .686	24° / .623	27° / .559	32° / .496	35° / .437	39° / .383	42° / .335	45° / .292	47° / .255	50° / .223	52° / .195	54° / .171	56° / .150	59° / .117	61° / .092	63° / .074	63° / .060	67° / .049	67° / .040	70° / .034	73° / .023	75° / .015	78° / .009
12	0°0' / .694	4°46' / .687	9° / .668	14° / .634	18° / .593	23° / .546	27° / .497	30° / .448	34° / .400	37° / .356	40° / .315	43° / .278	45° / .246	47° / .217	49° / .191	51° / .169	53° / .150	56° / .119	59° / .094	61° / .076	63° / .063	65° / .051	67° / .043	68° / .036	71° / .024	73° / .017	77° / .009
13	0°0' / .592	4°24' / .587	9° / .571	13° / .547	17° / .517	21° / .481	25° / .447	30° / .404	32° / .366	35° / .329	38° / .295	40° / .263	43° / .235	45° / .209	47° / .187	49° / .166	51° / .148	54° / .119	57° / .096	59° / .078	62° / .064	63° / .053	65° / .044	67° / .037	70° / .025	72° / .017	76° / .010
14	0°0' / .510	4°5' / .506	8° / .495	11° / .477	16° / .454	20° / .426	23° / .396	25° / .365	30° / .329	32° / .304	36° / .275	38° / .248	41° / .223	43° / .201	45° / .181	47° / .162	49° / .146	52° / .118	55° / .096	58° / .079	60° / .065	62° / .054	63° / .046	65° / .039	68° / .026	71° / .018	75° / .011
15	0°0' / .444	3°49' / .442	8° / .433	11° / .419	15° / .401	18° / .380	22° / .356	25° / .331	28° / .305	31° / .280	34° / .256	36° / .233	39° / .212	41° / .192	43° / .174	45° / .157	47° / .142	51° / .117	53° / .096	56° / .079	58° / .066	60° / .055	62° / .047	63° / .040	67° / .027	69° / .019	73° / .011
16	0°0' / .391	3°35' / .388	7° / .382	10° / .371	14° / .357	17° / .339	21° / .321	24° / .300	27° / .280	29° / .259	32° / .238	35° / .219	37° / .200	39° / .183	41° / .167	43° / .152	45° / .138	48° / .115	51° / .095	54° / .080	56° / .067	58° / .056	60° / .048	62° / .041	66° / .028	68° / .020	72° / .012
17	0°0' / .346	3°22' / .344	7° / .339	10° / .331	13° / .319	16° / .306	20° / .290	22° / .274	25° / .256	28° / .239	30° / .222	33° / .205	35° / .189	37° / .174	39° / .159	41° / .146	43° / .134	47° / .112	50° / .094	52° / .079	55° / .069	57° / .057	59° / .048	60° / .042	64° / .029	67° / .021	71° / .012
18	0°0' / .309	3°11' / .307	6° / .303	9° / .297	13° / .287	16° / .276	18° / .264	21° / .250	24° / .236	27° / .221	29° / .206	31° / .192	34° / .178	36° / .165	38° / .152	40° / .140	42° / .129	45° / .109	48° / .092	51° / .079	53° / .067	55° / .057	57° / .049	59° / .042	63° / .030	66° / .021	70° / .012
19	0°0' / .277	3°' / .276	6° / .273	9° / .267	12° / .260	15° / .251	18° / .240	19° / .229	22° / .217	24° / .205	27° / .192	29° / .180	32° / .167	34° / .156	36° / .145	38° / .134	40° / .124	43° / .106	46° / .090	48° / .077	50° / .066	52° / .057	54° / .049	56° / .042	60° / .030	63° / .022	68° / .013
20	0°0' / .250	2°51' / .249	5°43' / .246	9° / .242	14° / .236	14° / .228	17° / .219	19° / .210	22° / .200	24° / .190	26° / .179	29° / .168	29° / .158	33° / .147	37° / .137	37° / .128	39° / .119	42° / .103	45° / .088	48° / .076	50° / .066	52° / .057	54° / .049	56° / .043	60° / .030	63° / .022	68° / .013

(continued)

167

Table 14.11. Point-by-Point Calculation Table[a] (Continued)

Each cell lists the angle (degrees) over the footcandle multiplier. Upper section (heights 21–70 ft): **FOOTCANDLES FOR EACH 100 CANDLEPOWER**. Lower section (heights 80–200 ft): **FOOTCANDLES FOR EACH 100,000 CANDLEPOWER**.

Height of Light Source Above Surface—Feet \ Horizontal Distance from Axis of Light Source—Feet	0	1	2	3	4	5	6	7	8	9	10	11	12	13	14	15	16	18	20	22	24	26	28	30	35	40	50
21	0°0' .227	2°44' .226	5°26' .224	8° .220	11° .215	13° .210	16° .201	18° .194	21° .185	23° .176	25° .167	28° .158	30° .144	32° .139	34° .131	36° .122	37° .114	41° .099	44° .086	46° .075	49° .065	51° .056	53° .049	55° .043	59° .031	62° .023	67° .014
22	0°0' .207	2°36' .206	5°10' .205	8° .201	10° .196	13° .192	15° .185	17° .179	20° .171	21° .164	25° .155	27° .148	31° .140	33° .132	34° .124	36° .114	39° .109	42° .096	45° .084	47° .073	50° .064	54° .056	58° .049	61° .043	66° .031	61° .023	66° .014
23	0°0' .189	2°29' .189	4°58' .187	7° .184	10° .181	13° .176	15° .171	17° .165	19° .159	21° .153	24° .146	26° .139	28° .132	29° .125	31° .118	33° .111	35° .105	38° .092	41° .081	44° .071	46° .063	49° .055	51° .049	53° .043	57° .031	60° .023	65° .014
24	0°0' .174	2°23' .173	4°45' .172	7° .170	10° .166	13° .158	15° .154	17° .148	18° .143	20° .137	23° .130	25° .124	27° .118	28° .112	30° .106	32° .100	34° .089	36° .079	39° .070	42° .061	44° .054	46° .048	48° .042	51° .031	56° .024	59° .014	64° .014
25	0°0' .160	2°17' .160	4°34' .158	7° .154	9° .147	12° .143	14° .138	16° .133	18° .128	20° .123	22° .118	24° .112	26° .106	27° .101	29° .096	31° .086	33° .060	36° .053	39° .047	42° .042	44° .041	46° .041	48° .040	52° .031	55° .024	58° .015	63° .015
27	0°0' .137	2°7' .137	4°14' .136	6° .135	8° .133	10° .130	12° .128	13° .124	15° .121	17° .117	20° .113	22° .109	23° .105	25° .100	27° .096	29° .079	31° .064	34° .057	37° .045	39° .046	41° .041	43° .039	45° .039	49° .031	52° .024	56° .015	62° .015
30	0°0' .111	1°54' .111	3°50' .111	5°43' .109	8° .108	10° .107	11° .105	13° .103	15° .100	17° .098	18° .095	20° .092	22° .089	23° .086	25° .083	27° .080	28° .070	31° .058	34° .053	36° .048	38° .043	40° .039	42° .039	45° .039	49° .024	53° .024	59° .015
33	0°0' .092	1°44' .092	3°28' .091	5°12' .090	7° .089	9° .087	10° .086	12° .084	14° .082	15° .080	17° .078	18° .076	20° .074	22° .072	23° .069	24° .067	26° .062	29° .049	31° .049	34° .045	36° .041	38° .037	40° .037	42° .030	47° .030	50° .024	57° .015
36	0°0' .077	1°36' .077	3°11' .077	4°46' .076	6° .075	7° .074	9° .073	10° .072	12° .070	13° .067	14° .066	16° .064	18° .062	21° .059	22° .055	23° .061	24° .059	27° .055	29° .044	31° .041	34° .038	36° .040	38° .040	40° .029	44° .029	48° .024	54° .015
40	0°0' .063	1°26' .062	2°52' .062	4°17' .062	5°43' .061	7° .060	8° .060	9° .058	11° .057	13° .056	14° .055	15° .054	16° .051	17° .050	18° .059	19° .055	21° .050	24° .047	27° .039	28° .037	30° .034	32° .032	34° .035	37° .027	41° .022	45° .013	51° .015
45	0°0' .049	1°16' .049	2°33' .049	3°49' .049	5°5' .049	6° .048	7° .048	8° .047	9° .047	10° .046	11° .045	12° .044	13° .043	14° .042	15° .042	16° .041	18° .040	20° .038	22° .036	24° .034	26° .032	28° .030	30° .028	32° .025	35° .022	39° .021	45° .013
50	0°0' .040	1°9' .040	2°17' .040	3°26' .040	4°34' .040	5°43' .039	7° .039	8° .039	9° .039	10° .038	11° .037	12° .037	13° .036	14° .036	15° .035	16° .035	18° .033	20° .033	22° .032	24° .030	26° .028	28° .027	31° .025	33° .022	36° .019	39° .018	45° .013
55	0°0' .033	1°2' .033	2°5' .033	3°7' .033	4°10' .034	5°9' .033	6° .032	7° .032	8° .032	9° .032	10° .031	11° .031	12° .031	13° .031	14° .030	15° .030	16° .029	18° .028	20° .027	22° .026	24° .024	25° .023	27° .022	29° .022	33° .020	36° .018	42° .013
60	0°0' .028	0°57' .028	1°55' .028	2°52' .028	3°50' .028	4°46' .028	5°43' .027	7° .027	8° .027	9° .026	10° .026	11° .026	12° .026	13° .025	14° .025	15° .025	15° .024	18° .024	20° .023	22° .022	23° .022	25° .021	27° .021	30° .018	34° .020	34° .018	40° .013
70	0°0' .020	0°49' .020	1°38' .020	2°34' .020	3°16' .020	4°5' .020	4°54' .020	5°43' .020	7° .020	8° .020	9° .020	10° .020	11° .019	11° .019	12° .019	13° .019	14° .019	14° .018	16° .018	17° .018	19° .017	20° .017	22° .016	23° .016	27° .015	30° .013	36° .011
80	0°0' 15.63	0°43' 15.62	1°26' 15.61	2°9' 15.59	2°52' 15.57	3°35' 15.53	4°17' 15.49	5°0' 15.45	5°43' 15.39	6° 15.35	7° 15.27	8° 15.19	9° 15.09	9° 15.04	10° 14.93	11° 14.82	11° 14.75	13° 14.49	14° 14.27	15° 14.03	17° 13.71	18° 13.44	19° 13.16	21° 12.79	24° 12.02	27° 11.14	32° 9.53
100	0°0' 10.00	0°34' 9.999	1°9' 9.994	1°43' 9.987	2°17' 9.976	2°52' 9.963	3°26' 9.946	4° 9.927	4°34' 9.905	5° 9.880	5°43' 9.852	6° 9.826	7° 9.785	8° 9.761	9° 9.712	10° 9.660	11° 9.630	11° 9.539	13° 9.439	14° 9.330	15° 9.175	16° 9.048	17° 8.914	19° 8.819	21° 8.440	22° 7.993	27° 7.160
125	0°0' 6.400	0°28' 6.399	0°55' 6.398	1°22' 6.395	1°50' 6.390	2°17' 6.385	2°45' 6.378	3°12' 6.370	3°40' 6.361	4° 6.351	4°34' 6.339	5° 6.313	6° 6.297	6° 6.262	7° 6.250	8° 6.209	9° 6.168	10° 6.113	11° 6.059	12° 6.001	13° 5.938	14° 5.872	16° 5.708	18° 5.521	19° 5.120	18° 5.120	32° 5.120
150	0°0' 4.444	0°23' 4.444	0°46' 4.443	1°9' 4.440	1°32' 4.437	1°55' 4.434	2°17' 4.430	2°40' 4.424	3° 4.416	3°26' 4.415	3°49' 4.402	4° 4.395	4°34' 4.387	5° 4.370	6° 4.357	6° 4.343	7° 4.324	9° 4.290	10° 4.249	11° 4.216	12° 4.195	13° 4.102	15° 4.009	19° 3.813			
175	0°0' 3.265	0°20' 3.265	0°39' 3.264	0°59' 3.263	1°19' 3.261	1°38' 3.260	1°58' 3.258	2°17' 3.255	2°37' 3.252	2°57' 3.249	3°16' 3.246	3°36' 3.242	3°55' 3.238	4° 3.234	4°34' 3.230	5° 3.225	5°43' 3.213	6° 3.191	7° 3.174	8° 3.145	8° 3.124	9° 3.076	10° 3.024	13° 2.899	16° 2.899		
200	0°0' 2.500	0°17' 2.500	0°34' 2.499	0°52' 2.498	1°9' 2.497	1°26' 2.495	1°43' 2.494	2° 2.492	2°17' 2.490	2°35' 2.489	2°52' 2.487	3°9' 2.484	3°26' 2.482	3°43' 2.479	4° 2.476	4°34' 2.470	5°43' 2.463	6° 2.446	6° 2.428	7° 2.415	8° 2.440	9° 2.428	10° 2.415	11° 2.390	14° 2.360		2.282

[a]For illumination of vertical surfaces, reverse the table headings when determining the multiplier. From Westinghouse Electric Corporation, Lighting Handbook (Bloomfield, New Jersey 1969). Revised January 1974. pp. 6-32, 6-33.

PROBLEM 4

Problem.   The source is pointing straight down but is located above and to one side of the vertical task surface (see Figure 14.3).

Known.   (a) The candlepower of the source at all angles; (b) the angle between normal and the target; (c) the distance D between the source and the target.

Source Materials Required.   (a) Candlepower distribution chart, (b) trigonometric function table (Table 14.10).

Solution.   Candlepower at the appropriate angle (read in candelas on the chart) multiplied by the sine of that angle and then divided by the distance squared equals the footcandles on the surface.

Formula. $\text{fc} = \dfrac{(I)\ (\sin\ \theta)}{D^2}$

where I is candlepower in candelas, θ is the angle between normal and the target, and D is distance between the source and the target.

PROBLEM 5

Problem.   The source is pointing straight down but is located above and to one side of the vertical task surface.

Unknown.   Theta.

Known.   (a) The candlepower of the source at all angles; (b) the horizontal space (R) between the source and the target; (c) the vertical height (H) of the source above the target.

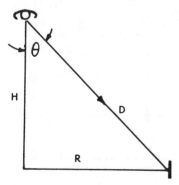

Figure 14.3.   Problems 4 and 5.

Source Materials Required. (a) Candlepower distribution table; (b) point-by-point calculation table (Table 14.11).

Solution. (1) Find the values for H and R in decimal feet. (2) From the point-by-point calculation table, locate the horizontal space (R) and the height columns (H) and determine the point at which the column intersect. (3) Find theta (θ) by looking for the top figure at the point of intersection. (4) From the candlepower distribution chart, find the appropriate number of candelas at theta (no need to use the sine). (5) *Reverse the headings on the table* (so that Height becomes Horizontal Distance) and multiply the candlepower by the multiplier given in the point-by-point table (bottom figure). (6) Move the decimal point two places to the left.

Formula. No formula required.

ZONAL CAVITY METHOD OF CALCULATING AVERAGE ILLUMINATION LEVELS AT THE WORK SURFACE

The zonal cavity method is based on the assumption that typical rooms can be divided into three spatial areas or "cavities" (see Figure 14.4). The ceiling cavity (CC) is defined as the area between the bottom line of suspended luminaires and the finished ceiling. The room cavity (RC) is the area between the bottom of the suspended luminaires and the top of the principal work surface. The floor cavity (FC) is the area between the top of the

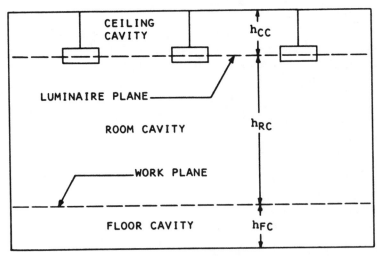

Figure 14.4.   Zonal cavities.

principal work surface and the floor. Each cavity has a specific effective reflectance with respect to the work plane and the other cavities.

When the cavity sizes and finishes have been established, numerical relationships for each are calculated; these are called "cavity ratios." The cavity ratios are first used to determine the effective reflectances of the ceiling and the floor.

A *coefficient of utilization* is next determined by using the cavity ratios. The coefficient of utilization is a ratio of the lumens from a luminaire received on the work plane to the total lumens emitted by the lamps used in the luminaire.

Calculation Procedure

1. Determine the cavity ratios. Many of these can be found in the cavity ratios table for each of the three cavities required (Table 14.6). However, the most accurate way to determine specific cavity ratios is by using the following formulas:

Ceiling cavity ratio (CCR) $= (5\ h_{CC})(L\ +\ W)\ /\ (L)(W)$
Room cavity ratio (RCR) $= (5\ h_{RC})(L\ +\ W)\ /\ (L)(W)$
Floor cavity ratio (FCR) $= (5\ h_{FC})(L\ +\ W)\ /\ (L)(W)$

where h_{CC} is the distance in feet from the luminaire to the ceiling, h_{RC} is the distance in feet from the luminaire to the work plane, h_{FC} is the distance in feet from the work plane to the floor, L is the length in feet of the room, and W the width in feet of the room.

2. Determine the cavity reflectances. These data are available in Table 14.12. Effective cavity reflectances must be determined for the ceiling cavity ρCC and the floor cavity ρFC.

To use the table, find the column with the appropriate percent ceiling reflectance and wall reflectance (found by analyzing the finishes on these areas (see Chapter Thirteen). Then find the horizontal column with the applicable ceiling cavity ratio (see Table 14.6). The number at the intersection of these two columns is the effective ceiling cavity reflectance. To obtain the effective floor cavity reflectance, repeat this procedure using the percent floor reflectance and the floor cavity ratio.

Remember that if there is no ceiling cavity (e.g., the luminaires are recessed) or there is no floor cavity (the floor surface may be the work surface), the CCR and FCR are the same as the actual reflectances on the planes of these single surfaces.

Table 14.12. *Effective Cavity Reflectance*[a]

% Base Reflectance[b]	90										80									
% Wall Reflectance	90	80	70	60	50	40	30	20	10	0	90	80	70	60	50	40	30	20	10	0
Cavity Ratio																				
0.2	89	88	88	87	86	85	85	84	84	82	79	78	78	77	77	76	76	75	74	72
0.4	88	87	86	85	84	83	81	80	79	76	79	77	76	75	74	73	72	71	70	68
0.6	87	86	84	82	80	79	77	76	74	73	78	76	75	73	71	70	68	66	65	63
0.8	87	85	82	80	77	75	73	71	69	67	78	75	73	71	69	67	65	63	61	57
1.0	86	83	80	77	75	72	69	66	64	62	77	74	72	69	67	65	62	60	57	55
1.2	85	82	78	75	72	69	66	63	60	57	76	73	70	67	64	61	58	55	53	51
1.4	85	80	77	73	69	65	62	59	57	52	76	72	68	65	62	59	55	53	50	48
1.6	84	79	75	71	67	63	59	56	53	50	75	71	67	63	60	57	53	50	47	44
1.8	83	78	73	69	64	60	56	53	50	48	75	70	66	62	58	54	50	47	44	41
2.0	83	77	72	67	62	56	53	50	47	43	74	69	64	60	56	52	48	45	41	38
2.2	82	76	70	65	59	54	50	47	44	40	74	68	63	58	54	49	45	42	38	35
2.4	82	75	69	64	58	53	48	45	41	37	73	67	61	56	52	47	43	40	36	33
2.6	81	74	67	62	56	51	46	42	38	35	73	66	60	55	50	45	41	38	34	31
2.8	81	73	66	60	54	49	44	40	36	34	73	65	59	53	48	43	39	36	32	29
3.0	80	72	64	58	52	47	42	38	34	30	72	65	58	52	47	42	37	34	30	27
3.2	79	71	63	56	50	45	40	36	32	28	72	65	57	51	45	40	35	33	28	25
3.4	79	70	62	54	48	43	38	34	30	27	71	64	56	49	44	39	34	32	27	24
3.6	78	69	61	53	47	42	36	32	28	25	71	63	54	48	43	38	32	30	25	23
3.8	78	69	60	51	45	40	35	31	27	23	70	62	53	47	41	36	31	28	24	22
4.0	77	69	58	51	44	39	33	29	25	22	70	61	53	46	40	35	30	26	22	20
4.2	77	62	57	50	43	37	32	28	24	21	69	60	52	45	39	34	29	25	21	18
4.4	76	61	56	49	42	36	31	27	23	20	69	60	51	44	38	33	28	24	20	17
4.6	76	60	55	47	40	35	30	26	22	19	69	59	50	43	37	32	27	23	19	15
4.8	75	59	54	46	39	34	28	25	21	18	68	58	49	42	36	31	26	22	18	14
5.0	75	59	53	45	38	33	28	24	20	16	68	58	48	41	35	30	25	21	18	14
6.0	73	61	49	41	34	29	24	20	16	11	66	55	44	38	31	27	22	19	15	10
7.0	70	58	45	38	30	27	21	18	14	08	65	53	41	35	28	24	19	16	12	07
8.0	68	55	42	35	27	23	18	15	12	06	62	50	38	32	25	21	17	14	11	05
9.0	66	52	38	31	25	21	16	14	11	05	61	49	36	30	23	19	15	13	10	04
10.0	65	51	36	29	22	19	15	11	09	04	59	46	33	27	21	18	14	11	08	03

[a]Reprinted, by permission, Illuminating Engineering Society, *I.E.S. Lighting Handbook* (New York, 1981).

[b]Ceiling, floor or floor of cavity.

Table 14.12. **Effective Cavity Reflectance** *(Continued)*

% Base Reflectance[b]	70										60									
% Wall Reflectance	90	80	70	60	50	40	30	20	10	0	90	80	70	60	50	40	30	20	10	0
Cavity Ratio																				
0.2	70	69	68	68	67	67	66	66	65	64	60	59	59	59	58	57	56	56	55	53
0.4	69	68	67	66	65	64	63	62	61	58	60	59	59	58	57	55	54	53	52	50
0.6	69	67	65	64	63	61	59	58	57	54	60	58	57	56	55	53	51	51	50	46
0.8	68	66	64	62	60	58	56	55	53	50	59	57	56	55	54	51	48	47	46	43
1.0	68	65	62	60	58	55	53	52	50	47	59	57	55	53	51	48	45	44	43	41
1.2	67	64	61	59	57	54	50	48	46	44	59	56	54	51	49	46	44	42	40	38
1.4	67	63	60	58	55	51	47	45	44	41	59	56	53	49	47	44	41	39	38	36
1.6	67	62	59	56	53	47	45	43	41	38	59	55	52	48	45	42	39	37	35	33
1.8	66	61	58	54	51	46	42	40	38	35	58	55	51	47	44	40	37	35	33	31
2.0	66	60	56	52	49	45	40	38	36	33	58	54	50	46	43	39	35	33	31	29
2.2	66	60	55	51	48	43	38	36	34	32	58	53	49	45	42	37	34	31	29	28
2.4	65	60	54	50	46	41	37	35	32	30	58	53	48	44	41	36	32	30	27	26
2.6	65	59	54	49	45	40	35	33	30	28	58	53	48	43	39	35	31	28	26	24
2.8	65	59	53	48	43	38	33	30	28	26	58	53	47	43	38	34	29	27	24	22
3.0	64	58	52	47	42	37	32	39	27	24	57	52	46	42	37	32	28	25	23	20
3.2	64	58	51	46	40	36	31	28	25	23	57	51	45	41	36	31	27	23	22	18
3.4	64	57	50	45	39	35	29	27	24	22	57	51	45	40	35	30	26	23	20	17
3.6	63	56	49	44	38	33	28	25	22	20	57	50	44	39	34	29	25	22	19	16
3.8	63	56	49	43	37	32	27	24	21	19	57	50	43	38	33	29	24	21	19	15
4.0	63	55	48	42	36	31	26	22	20	17	57	49	42	37	32	28	23	20	18	14
4.2	62	55	47	41	35	30	25	22	19	16	56	49	42	37	32	27	22	19	17	14
4.4	62	54	46	40	34	29	24	21	18	15	56	49	42	36	31	27	22	19	16	13
4.6	62	53	45	39	33	28	24	21	17	14	56	49	41	35	30	26	21	18	16	13
4.8	62	53	45	38	32	27	23	20	16	13	56	48	41	34	29	25	21	18	15	12
5.0	61	52	44	36	31	26	22	19	16	12	56	48	40	34	28	24	20	17	14	11
6.0	60	51	41	35	28	24	19	16	13	09	55	45	37	31	25	21	17	14	11	07
7.0	58	48	38	32	26	22	17	14	11	06	54	43	35	30	24	20	15	12	09	05
8.0	57	46	35	29	23	19	15	13	10	05	53	42	33	28	22	18	14	11	08	04
9.0	56	45	33	27	21	18	14	12	09	04	52	40	31	26	20	16	12	10	07	03
10.0	55	43	31	25	19	16	12	10	08	03	51	39	29	24	18	15	11	09	07	02

173

Table 14.12. **Effective Cavity Reflectance** *(Continued)*

% Base Reflectance[b]	50									40								
% Wall Reflectance	90	80	70	60	50	40	30	20	10	0	90	80	70	60	50	40	30	20	10	0

Cavity Ratio	90	80	70	60	50	40	30	20	10	0	90	80	70	60	50	40	30	20	10	0
0.2	50	50	49	49	48	48	47	46	46	44	40	40	39	39	39	38	38	37	36	36
0.4	50	49	48	48	47	46	45	45	44	42	41	40	39	39	38	37	36	35	34	34
0.6	50	48	47	46	45	44	43	42	41	38	41	40	39	38	37	36	34	33	32	31
0.8	50	48	47	45	44	42	40	39	38	36	41	40	38	37	36	35	33	32	31	29
1.0	50	48	46	44	43	41	38	37	36	34	42	40	38	37	35	33	32	31	29	27
1.2	50	47	45	43	41	39	36	35	34	29	42	40	38	36	34	32	30	29	27	25
1.4	50	47	45	42	40	38	35	34	32	27	42	39	37	35	33	31	29	27	25	23
1.6	50	47	44	41	39	36	33	32	30	26	42	39	37	35	32	30	27	25	23	22
1.8	50	46	43	40	38	35	31	30	28	25	42	39	36	34	31	29	26	24	22	21
2.0	50	46	43	40	37	34	30	28	26	24	42	39	36	34	31	28	25	23	21	19
2.2	50	46	42	38	36	33	29	27	24	22	42	39	36	33	30	27	24	22	19	18
2.4	50	46	42	37	35	31	27	25	23	21	43	39	35	33	29	27	24	21	18	17
2.6	50	46	41	37	34	30	26	23	21	20	43	39	35	32	29	26	23	20	17	15
2.8	50	46	41	36	33	29	25	22	20	19	43	39	35	32	28	25	22	19	16	14
3.0	50	45	40	36	32	28	24	21	19	17	43	39	35	31	27	24	21	18	16	13
3.2	50	44	39	35	31	27	23	20	18	16	43	39	35	31	27	23	20	17	15	13
3.4	50	44	39	35	30	26	22	19	17	15	43	39	34	30	26	23	20	17	14	12
3.6	50	44	39	34	29	25	21	18	16	14	44	39	34	30	26	22	19	16	14	11
3.8	50	44	38	34	29	25	21	17	15	13	44	38	33	29	25	22	18	16	13	10
4.0	50	44	38	33	28	24	20	17	15	12	44	38	33	29	25	21	18	15	12	10
4.2	50	43	37	32	28	24	20	17	14	12	44	38	33	29	24	21	17	15	12	10
4.4	50	43	37	32	27	23	19	16	13	11	44	38	33	28	24	20	17	14	11	09
4.6	50	43	36	31	26	22	18	15	13	10	44	38	32	28	23	19	16	14	11	08
4.8	50	43	36	31	26	22	18	15	12	09	44	38	32	27	22	19	16	13	10	08
5.0	50	42	35	30	25	21	17	14	12	09	45	38	31	27	22	19	15	13	10	07
6.0	50	42	34	29	23	19	15	13	10	06	44	37	30	25	20	17	13	11	08	05
7.0	49	41	32	27	21	18	14	11	08	05	44	36	29	24	19	16	12	10	07	04
8.0	49	40	30	25	19	16	12	10	07	03	44	35	28	23	18	15	11	09	06	03
9.0	48	39	29	24	18	15	11	09	07	03	44	35	26	21	16	13	10	08	05	02
10.0	47	37	27	22	17	14	10	08	06	02	43	34	25	20	15	12	08	07	05	02

Table 14.12. **Effective Cavity Reflectance** (*Continued*)

% Base Reflectance[b]	30										20									
% Wall Reflectance	90	80	70	60	50	40	30	20	10	0	90	80	70	60	50	40	30	20	10	0
Cavity Ratio																				
0.2	31	31	30	30	29	29	29	28	28	27	21	20	20	20	20	20	19	19	19	17
0.4	31	31	30	30	29	28	28	27	26	25	22	21	20	20	20	19	19	18	18	16
0.6	32	31	30	29	28	27	26	26	25	23	23	21	21	20	19	19	18	18	17	15
0.8	32	31	30	29	28	26	25	25	23	22	24	22	21	20	19	19	18	17	16	14
1.0	33	32	30	29	27	25	24	23	22	20	25	23	22	20	19	18	17	16	15	13
1.2	33	32	30	28	27	25	23	22	21	19	25	23	22	20	19	17	17	16	14	12
1.4	34	32	30	28	26	24	22	21	19	18	26	24	22	20	18	17	16	15	13	12
1.6	34	33	29	27	25	23	22	20	18	17	26	24	22	20	18	17	16	15	13	11
1.8	35	33	29	27	25	23	21	19	17	16	27	25	23	20	18	17	15	14	12	10
2.0	35	33	29	26	24	22	20	18	16	14	28	25	23	20	18	16	15	13	11	09
2.2	36	32	29	26	24	22	19	17	15	13	28	25	23	20	18	16	14	12	10	09
2.4	36	32	29	26	24	22	19	16	14	12	29	26	23	20	18	16	14	12	10	08
2.6	36	32	29	25	23	21	18	16	14	12	29	26	23	20	18	16	14	11	09	08
2.8	37	33	29	25	23	21	17	15	13	11	30	27	23	20	18	15	13	11	09	07
3.0	37	33	29	25	22	20	17	15	12	10	30	27	23	20	17	15	13	11	09	07
3.2	37	33	29	25	22	19	16	14	12	10	31	27	23	20	17	15	12	11	09	06
3.4	37	33	29	25	22	19	16	14	11	09	31	27	23	20	17	15	12	10	08	06
3.6	38	33	29	24	21	18	15	13	10	09	32	27	23	20	17	15	12	10	08	05
3.8	38	33	28	24	21	18	15	13	10	08	32	28	23	20	17	15	12	10	07	05
4.0	38	33	28	24	21	18	14	12	09	07	33	28	23	20	17	14	11	09	07	05
4.2	38	33	28	24	20	17	14	12	09	07	33	28	23	20	17	14	11	09	07	04
4.4	39	33	28	24	20	17	14	11	09	06	34	28	24	20	17	14	11	09	07	04
4.6	39	33	28	24	20	17	13	10	08	06	34	29	24	20	17	14	11	09	07	04
4.8	39	33	28	24	20	17	13	10	08	05	35	29	24	20	17	13	10	08	06	04
5.0	39	33	28	24	19	16	13	10	08	05	35	29	24	20	16	13	10	08	06	04
6.0	39	33	27	23	18	15	11	09	06	04	36	30	24	20	16	13	10	08	05	02
7.0	40	33	26	22	17	14	10	08	05	03	36	30	24	20	15	12	09	07	04	02
8.0	40	33	26	21	16	13	09	07	04	02	37	30	23	19	15	12	08	06	03	01
9.0	40	33	25	20	15	12	09	07	04	02	37	29	23	19	14	11	08	06	03	01
10.0	40	32	24	19	14	11	08	06	03	01	37	29	22	18	13	10	07	05	03	01

Table 14.12. Effective Cavity Reflectance (Continued)

% Base Reflectance[b]	10										0									
% Wall Reflectance	90	80	70	60	50	40	30	20	10	0	90	80	70	60	50	40	30	20	10	0
Cavity Ratio																				
0.2	11	11	11	10	10	10	10	09	09	09	02	02	02	01	01	01	01	00	00	0
0.4	12	11	11	11	11	10	10	09	09	08	04	03	03	02	02	02	01	01	00	0
0.6	13	13	12	11	11	10	10	09	08	08	05	05	04	03	03	02	02	01	01	0
0.8	15	14	13	12	11	10	10	09	08	07	07	06	05	04	04	03	02	02	01	0
1.0	16	14	13	12	12	11	10	09	08	07	08	07	06	05	04	03	02	02	01	0
1.2	17	15	14	13	12	11	10	09	07	06	10	08	07	06	05	04	03	02	01	0
1.4	18	16	14	13	12	11	10	09	07	06	11	09	08	07	06	04	03	02	01	0
1.6	19	17	15	14	12	11	09	08	07	06	12	10	09	07	06	05	03	02	01	0
1.8	19	17	15	14	13	11	09	08	06	05	13	11	09	08	07	05	04	03	01	0
2.0	20	18	16	14	13	11	09	08	06	05	14	12	10	09	07	05	04	03	01	0
2.2	21	19	16	14	13	11	09	07	06	05	15	13	11	09	07	06	04	03	01	0
2.4	22	19	17	15	13	11	09	07	06	05	16	13	11	09	08	06	04	03	01	0
2.6	23	20	17	15	13	11	09	07	06	04	17	14	12	10	08	06	05	03	02	0
2.8	23	20	18	16	13	11	09	07	05	03	17	15	13	10	08	07	05	03	02	0
3.0	24	21	18	16	13	11	09	07	05	03	18	16	13	11	09	07	05	03	02	0
3.2	25	21	18	16	13	11	09	07	05	03	19	16	14	11	09	07	05	03	02	0
3.4	26	22	18	16	13	11	09	07	05	03	20	17	14	12	09	07	05	03	02	0
3.6	26	22	19	16	13	11	09	06	04	03	20	17	15	12	10	08	05	04	02	0
3.8	27	23	19	17	14	11	09	06	04	02	21	18	15	12	10	08	05	04	02	0
4.0	27	23	20	17	14	11	09	06	04	02	22	18	15	13	10	08	05	04	02	0
4.2	28	24	20	17	14	11	09	06	04	02	22	19	16	13	10	08	06	04	02	0
4.4	28	24	20	17	14	11	08	06	04	02	23	19	16	13	10	08	06	04	02	0
4.6	29	25	20	17	14	11	08	06	04	02	23	20	17	13	11	08	06	04	02	0
4.8	29	25	20	17	14	11	08	06	04	02	24	20	17	14	11	08	06	04	02	0
5.0	30	25	20	17	14	11	08	06	04	02	25	21	17	14	11	08	06	04	02	0
6.0	31	26	21	18	14	11	08	06	03	01	27	23	18	15	12	09	06	04	02	0
7.0	32	27	21	17	13	11	08	06	03	01	28	24	19	15	12	09	06	04	02	0
8.0	33	27	21	17	13	10	07	05	03	01	30	25	20	15	12	09	06	04	02	0
9.0	34	28	21	17	13	10	07	05	02	01	31	25	20	15	12	09	06	04	02	0
10.0	34	28	21	17	12	10	07	05	02	01	31	25	20	15	12	09	06	04	02	0

3. Select the coefficient of utilization. Use the table printed by the luminaire manufacturer for this purpose. Base your selection on the data found in procedures 1 and 2: room cavity ratio, effective ceiling cavity reflectance, effective floor cavity reflectance, and the largest area of wall reflectance (ρW). Note that all tables are printed for 20% effective floor cavity reflectance (ρFC). If the ρFC reflectance varies widely from 20%, then correct the coefficient by multiplying it by the appropriate factor given in Table 14.13.

4. Determine the light loss factor. This is the expected light loss due to depreciation of the luminaire surfaces and room surfaces and lamp degeneration. See page 154.

5. Compute the *average footcandle level*. This is accomplished by using the formula for maintained footcandles.

$$\text{fc} = \frac{\text{(number of luminaires) (lamps per luminaire)}}{\text{(initial lumens per lamp) (CU) (LLF)}}}{\text{total room area in square feet}}$$

If the desired footcandle level is known, this formula can be rewritten to calculate the number of luminaires needed to obtain it.

$$\text{number of luminaires} = \frac{\text{(fc) (total room area in square feet)}}{\text{(lamps per luminaire) (initial lumens per lamp) (CU) (LLF)}}$$

The resulting values can be checked against the recommendations of the Illuminating Engineering Society (see Table 14.15)

VISUAL COMFORT PROBABILITY

A VCP rating is defined as the percent of people who, if seated in the most undesirable location, will be expected to find a lighting installation acceptable. It has already been discussed in Chapter Thirteen.

The computation of VCP is complex and rarely attempted by designers in the field. However, some manufacturers are providing VCP tables for their equipment. These tables assume the following: (1) 80% effective ceiling cavity reflectance, 50% wall reflectance, and 20% effective floor cavity reflectance; (2) a work surface illumination of 100 footcandles; (3) luminaire mounting heights of 8.5, 10.0, 13.0, or 16.0 feet above the floor; (4) rooms of stated lengths and widths; (5) a layout of luminaires uniformly distributed throughout the space; (6) an observer whose eyes are 4 feet above the floor

Table 14.13. *Factor for Effective Floor Cavity Reflectances Other than 20%*[a]

Multiplying Factors for 10 Per Cent Effective Floor Cavity Reflectance (20 Per Cent = 1.00)

% Effective Ceiling Cavity Reflectance, ρ_{cc}	80				70				50			30			10		
% Wall Reflectance, ρ_w	70	50	30	10	70	50	30	10	50	30	10	50	30	10	50	30	10
ROOM CAVITY RATIO																	
1	.923	.929	.935	.940	.933	.939	.943	.948	.956	.960	.963	.973	.976	.979	.989	.991	.993
2	.931	.942	.950	.958	.940	.949	.957	.963	.962	.968	.974	.976	.980	.985	.988	.991	.995
3	.939	.951	.961	.969	.945	.957	.966	.973	.967	.975	.981	.978	.983	.988	.988	.992	.996
4	.944	.958	.969	.978	.950	.963	.973	.980	.972	.980	.986	.980	.986	.991	.987	.992	.996
5	.949	.964	.976	.983	.954	.968	.978	.985	.975	.983	.989	.981	.988	.993	.987	.992	.997
6	.953	.969	.980	.986	.958	.972	.982	.989	.977	.985	.992	.982	.989	.995	.987	.993	.997
7	.957	.973	.983	.991	.961	.975	.985	.991	.979	.987	.994	.983	.990	.996	.987	.993	.997
8	.960	.976	.986	.993	.963	.977	.987	.993	.981	.988	.995	.984	.991	.997	.987	.993	.998
9	.963	.978	.987	.994	.965	.979	.989	.994	.983	.990	.996	.985	.992	.998	.988	.994	.999
10	.965	.980	.989	.995	.967	.981	.990	.995	.984	.991	.997	.986	.993	.998	.988	.994	.999

Multiplying Factors for 30 Per Cent Effective Floor Cavity Reflectance (20 Per Cent = 1.00)

% Effective Ceiling Cavity Reflectance, ρ_{cc}	80				70				50			30			10		
% Wall Reflectance, ρ_w	70	50	30	10	70	50	30	10	50	30	10	50	30	10	50	30	10
Room Cavity Ratio																	
1	1.092	1.082	1.075	1.068	1.077	1.070	1.064	1.059	1.049	1.044	1.040	1.028	1.026	1.023	1.012	1.010	1.008
2	1.079	1.066	1.055	1.047	1.068	1.057	1.048	1.039	1.041	1.033	1.027	1.026	1.021	1.017	1.013	1.010	1.006
3	1.070	1.054	1.042	1.033	1.061	1.048	1.037	1.028	1.034	1.027	1.020	1.024	1.017	1.012	1.014	1.009	1.005
4	1.062	1.045	1.033	1.024	1.055	1.040	1.029	1.021	1.030	1.022	1.015	1.022	1.015	1.010	1.014	1.009	1.004
5	1.056	1.038	1.026	1.018	1.050	1.034	1.024	1.015	1.027	1.018	1.012	1.020	1.013	1.008	1.014	1.009	1.004
6	1.052	1.033	1.021	1.014	1.047	1.030	1.020	1.012	1.024	1.015	1.009	1.019	1.012	1.006	1.014	1.008	1.003
7	1.047	1.029	1.018	1.011	1.043	1.026	1.017	1.009	1.022	1.013	1.007	1.018	1.010	1.005	1.014	1.008	1.003
8	1.044	1.026	1.015	1.009	1.040	1.024	1.015	1.007	1.020	1.012	1.006	1.017	1.009	1.004	1.013	1.007	1.003
9	1.040	1.024	1.014	1.007	1.037	1.022	1.014	1.006	1.019	1.011	1.005	1.016	1.009	1.004	1.013	1.007	1.002
10	1.037	1.022	1.012	1.006	1.034	1.020	1.012	1.005	1.017	1.010	1.004	1.015	1.009	1.003	1.013	1.007	1.002

[a]Illuminating Engineering Society, "Zonal-Cavity Method of Calculating Coefficients of Utilization," *Illuminating Engineering* New York, May 1964. LM–23.

and 4 feet in front of the center of the rear wall; (7) a line of sight looking directly forward; (8) a field of view limited to an angle of 53 degrees above and directly forward.

When all of the above conditions are met, the planned installation may be compared with a VCP table prepared by the equipment manufacturer. The Illuminating Engineering Society states that direct glare will not be a problem (the installation will be comfortable to most people) if the following conditions are met: "(1) the VCP is 70 or more; (2) the ratio of maximum-to-average luminaire luminance (footlamberts seen while looking at the luminaire) does not exceed five to one (preferably three to one) at 45, 55, 67, 75 and 85 degrees from nadir (straight down) crosswise and lengthwise; and (3) maximum luminaire luminances crosswise and lengthwise do not exceed the following values:"*

Degrees from Nadir	Maximum Luminance
45	2250
55	1605
65	1125
75	750
85	495

In other words, the I.E.S. is suggesting that the surface brightness of a large and evenly luminous ceiling area may be more comfortable than that of a single, relatively small-apertured luminaire when both are producing the same amount of light in the same space. The same might be said for the benefits of using many recessed ceiling-mounted luminaires of lower aperture brightness compared to the disadvantages of using a few luminaires with higher aperture brightness to produce equal light levels. There is a similar inference that low aperture brightness in recessed luminaires (or at least aperture brightness equaling that of surrounding ceiling surfaces) is helpful in optimal seeing areas.

EQUIVALENT SPHERE ILLUMINATION

ESI calculations require the use of a computer. Several companies have developed computer programs for these calculations under limited conditions, and they should be contacted when an ESI check is appropriate for an installation design.

*Illuminating Engineering Society, *I.E.S. Lighting Handbook*, 5th ed. (New York, 1972), p. 3–26.

ENERGY USAGE

In the initial design of most projects, the consulting electrical engineer and air-conditioning or heating engineers need to know the amount of electrical power that will be required for lighting equipment

By using Table 14.14, a preliminary estimate of energy usage can be made if the following factors are known: (1) the basic type of light source (incandescent, fluorescent, or HID), (2) the approximate type of luminaire (direct, indirect, general-diffuse, direct/semidirect), and (3) the maintained level of footcandles preferred throughout the space (for even illumination). Table 14.14 readings are only approximate values. They are based on a room cavity ratio of 2.5 and on reflectances of 80% for the ceiling cavity, 50% for walls, and 20% for the floor cavity.

EXAMPLES

Point-by-Point Calculations

PROBLEM 1

Stated. You have a 150PAR38/SP lamp casting light directly on a horizontal surface 5 feet away (see Figure 14.5). How many footcandles are produced on the surface directly under the lamp?

Given. $D = 5.0$ feet (convert all inches to decimals since it makes the math easier; i.e., 5 ft. 6 in. equals 5.5 ft. in decimals).

Find. From the candlepower distribution chart, find that a 150PAR/SP lamp produces 12,000 candelas at 0°.

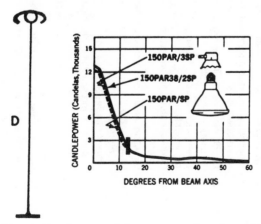

Figure 14.5.   Problem 1. (Graph reprinted, by permission, from General Electric, 212-399.)

Table 14.14. Preliminary Watts per Square Foot[a]

Approximate wiring capacity to provide a given maintained illuminance level in a room of 2.5 Room Cavity Ratio by means of the following:

A – Indirect, incandescent filament (silvered bowl)

B – Direct, incandescent filament (with diffuser)

C – Direct, incandescent filament (downlight)

D – General diffuse, incandescent filament

E – Direct, incandescent filament (lens)

F – Direct, incandescent filament (industrial)
Indirect, fluorescent (cove)

G – Indirect, fluorescent (extra high output)

H – Direct, fluorescent (extra high output) (louvered)

I – Direct, fluorescent (louvered)

J – Luminous ceiling, fluorescent
Direct, HID (mercury)

K – Direct, fluorescent (lens)

L – Direct/Semi-direct, fluorescent (industrial)

M – Direct, metal halide

N – Direct, high pressure sodium

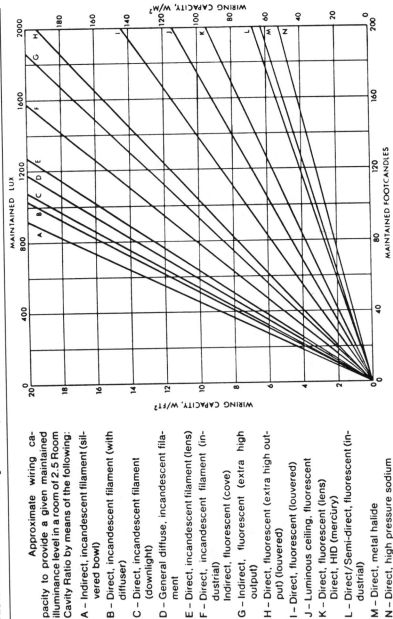

[a]Illuminating Engineering Society, *I.E.S. Lighting Handbook*, (New York, 1981).

Formula.   fc $= \dfrac{I}{D^2}$

Substitute.   fc $= \dfrac{12,000}{(5)\ (5)} = \dfrac{12,000}{25} = 480$

PROBLEM 2

Stated.   You are working with one light source that gives off 3000 candelas (candlepower) at an angle of 10° from the vertical (see Figure 14.6). The light is traveling to a horizontal surface 10.0 feet away. How many footcandles will be found at that point?

Given. $D = 10.0$ feet, $\theta = 10°$, $I = 3000$ at 10°.

Find.   Cosine of $10° = 0.985$ (from Table 14.10).

Formula.   fc $= \dfrac{(I)\ (\cos\ \theta)}{D^2}$

Substitute.   fc $= \dfrac{(3000)\ (0.985)}{(10)\ (10)} = 29.55$

PROBLEM 3

Stated.   You are using one 150PAR38/FL lamp in a shallow, recessed luminaire to light a desk sitting in the center of a darkly painted hotel lobby (see Figure 14.7). The desk is placed 2 feet to one side of the light source.

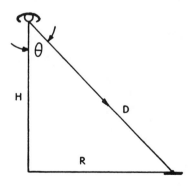

Figure 14.6.   Problem 2.

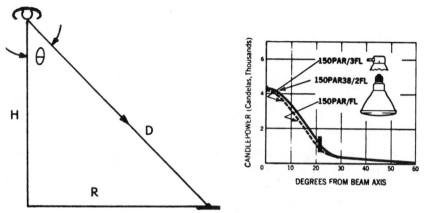

Figure 14.7.   Problem 3. (Graph reprinted, by permission, from General Electric, 212-399.)

The ceiling is 10 feet 6 inches from the floor. How many footcandles will there be on the desk top?

Given. $R = 2.0$ feet, $H = 8.0$ feet (the distance from the ceiling to a point below the lamp in line with the desk top). Desk tops are normally 2.5 feet from the floor. Therefore, the height of the luminaire above the level of the target will be $10.5 - 2.5$, or 8.0 feet.

Find.   From Table 14.11, find that θ is 14° when $R = 2.0$ feet and $H = 8.0$ feet. from the candlepower distribution chart, find that the lamp produces 2000 candelas at 14°. From Table 14.11 find that the multiplier is 1.43 (rounded from 1.427) when $R = 2.0$ feet and $H = 8.0$ feet.

Calculate. $(1.43)\ (2000) = 2860.$

Adjust.   Move the decimal point two places to the left (because values are for 100 candlepower amounts). Therefore, 2860 becomes 28.6, which is the number of footcandles on the desk top.

PROBLEM 4

Stated.   You are working with one light source that produces 3000 candelas at an angle of 10° from nadir (straight down) (see Figure 14.8). This light is striking a vertical surface at an angle of 10° from the source. How many footcandles will be found on that surface if it is 10 feet from the light?

Given. $D = 10.0$ feet, $\theta = 10°$, $I = 3000$

Find.   Sine of $10° = 0.174$ (from Table 14.10)

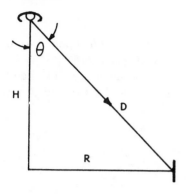

Figure 14.8.   Problem 4.

Formula.   fc $= \dfrac{(I)\ (\text{sine } \theta)}{D^2}$

Substitute.   fc $= \dfrac{(3000)\ (0.174)}{(10)\ (10)} = 5.19$ or 5.2

PROBLEM 5

Stated.   You have used one 500PAR64/WFL lamp 2 feet away from a black wall (see Figure 14.9). On the wall, you have placed a small painting the center of which is 6 feet down from the ceiling. How many footcandles will reach the painting?

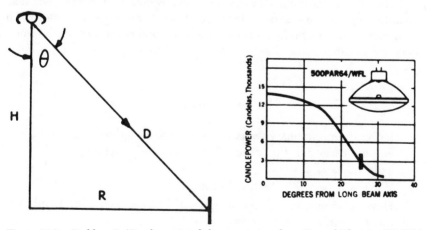

Figure 14.9.   Problem 5. (Graph reprinted, by permission, from General Electric, 212-399.)

Given. $R = 2.0$ feet, $H = 6.0$ feet.

Find.   From Table 14.11 find that θ is 18° when $R = 2.0$ feet and $H = 6.0$ feet. From the candlepower distribution chart, find that a 500PAR64/WFL lamp produces 9000 candelas at 18°. *Reverse the headings* of Table 14.11 and find that the multiplier is 0.802, since H has become 2.0 feet and R has become 6.0 feet.

Calculate. $(9000)\,(0.802) = 7218.0$

Adjust.   72.18, or 72 footcandles

ZONAL CAVITY, VISUAL COMFORT PROBABILITY, AND ENERGY USAGE CALCULATION EXAMPLES

Stated

You have designed the lighting for a school laboratory in an educational facility. The reflectances are as follows: ceiling, 80% (0.80); walls between the luminaire and the work plane, 50%; walls below the work plane, 10%; and the floor, 30%. The dimensions of the space are 30.0 feet long by 20.0 feet wide by 10.0 feet high. The working surface (task) of the lab benches is 3.0 feet above the floor.

You have decided to use 30 of the example luminaires in five continuous rows (see Figure 14.10a–g). Since detailed tasks may be performed at any point in the space, a uniform level of illumination is required.

Laboratory experiments are easily spoiled by dust, and so an excellent air-conditioning system has been installed to keep the space very clean. The total space, including fully recessed luminaires and room surfaces, is cleaned once every 18 months. Lamps are replaced as soon as they burn out.

Questions

1. Using the preliminary watts per square foot method, what will be the energy usage in the room if a maintained lighting level of 100 footcandles is desired?
2. What will be the light loss factor?
3. How many maintained footcandles can be predicted to uniformly light the top surfaces of the tasks?

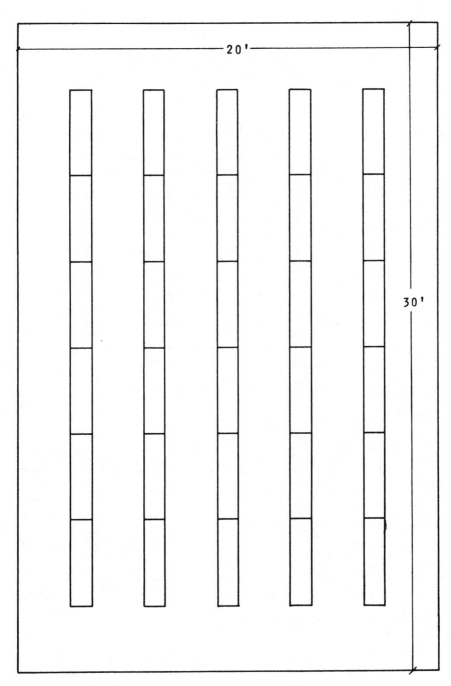

(a) Reflected ceiling plan of a school laboratory.

Figure 14.10.

187

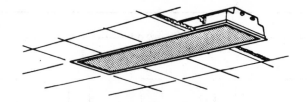

(b) Perspective luminaire illustration.

FLOORS	20%						
CEILING	80%				50%		
WALLS	70%	50%	30%	10%	50%	30%	10%
1	.61	.59	.57	.55	.55	.54	.53
2	.56	.53	.50	.48	.50	.48	.46
3	.53	.48	.45	.42	.46	.43	.41
R C R 4	.49	.44	.40	.37	.42	.39	.36
5	.45	.40	.35	.32	.38	.34	.32
6	.42	.36	.32	.29	.35	.31	.29
7	.39	.33	.29	.26	.32	.28	.26
8	.36	.30	.26	.23	.29	.25	.23
9	.34	.27	.23	.20	.26	.22	.20
10	.31	.25	.21	.18	.24	.20	.18

(c) Luminaire zonal cavity coefficients of utilization.

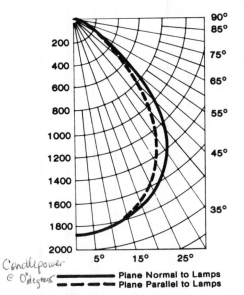

Candlepower
© 0°degrees ───── Plane Normal to Lamps
━ ━ ━ Plane Parallel to Lamps

(d) Luminaire candlepower distribution.

CROSSWISE

Angle	Maximum	Average
45°	1200	1040
55°	850	780
65°	570	560
75°	450	440
85°	430	430

LENGTHWISE

Angle	Maximum	Average
45°	1080	1020
55°	880	820
65°	580	550
75°	390	390
85°	420	420

(e) Luminaire brightness in footlamberts.

Figure 14.10. (Continued)

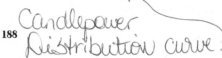
Candlepower Distribution curve.

188

100 FC. ROOM		REFLECTANCES 80/50/20							
		LUMINAIRES LENGTHWISE				LUMINAIRES CROSSWISE			
W	L	8.5	10.0	13.0	16.0	8.5	10.0	13.0	16.0
20	20	73	77	82	83	73	79	84	85
20	30	67	70	76	78	66	71	78	80
20	40	64	67	71	73	63	67	72	76
20	60	62	64	67	69	60	63	67	70
30	20	73	77	81	83	74	78	83	85
30	30	66	70	74	77	66	70	76	79
30	40	63	66	69	71	62	65	70	73
30	60	61	62	64	66	59	61	64	67
30	80	59	61	62	64	57	60	62	64
40	20	74	78	82	84	75	79	83	85
40	30	67	70	74	77	67	71	76	79
40	40	63	66	68	71	63	65	69	73
40	60	61	62	64	66	59	61	63	66
40	80	59	61	61	63	57	59	60	63
40	100	58	60	60	61	57	58	59	61
60	30	68	71	74	77	68	71	75	78
60	40	64	66	68	71	63	66	69	72
60	60	61	62	63	65	60	61	63	66
60	80	59	60	60	62	57	59	60	62
60	100	58	59	59	60	56	58	58	60
100	40	67	68	70	72	66	68	70	73
100	60	63	64	64	66	62	63	64	67
100	80	61	62	61	63	59	61	60	63
100	100	60	60	59	61	58	59	58	60

(f) Luminaire visual comfort probability data.

Figure 14.10. (Continued)

189

MATERIALS: PLASTIC LENS, SHEET STEEL HOUSING.

DISTRIBUTION: DIRECT DOWN.

LUMINAIRE EFFICIENCY: 54%

SPACING: FOR MAXIMUM UNIFORMITY, SPACING NOT TO EXCEED
(1.1)(MOUNTING HEIGHT ABOVE THE WORK PLANE).

TEST LAMPS: TWO, F40T12/CW.   3150 INITIAL LUMENS EACH.

DIMENSIONS: 1'-0" (NOMINAL) WIDE
4'-0" (NOMINAL) LONG

(g) Additional luminaire data.

Figure 14.10. (*Continued*)

4. Does this footcandle level meet the standards of the Illuminating Engineerng Society?

5. Will the layout diagram of luminaires satisfy maximum spacing criteria? (See Chapter Fifteen.)

6. Using visual comfort probability criteria, will the installation be satisfactory?

7. Does the installation contain recommended surface reflectances?

Answers

1. The preliminary watts per square foot are found by referring to Table 14.14. The question has stated that the maintained footcandle level is to be 100. By looking at the data given in Figure 14.10g, you find that the luminaire distribution is directly down, that the source is fluorescent, and that it uses a lens for light control; these clues lead you to select a type K luminaire in Figure 14.11. By joining the appropriate lines in the graph, you will estimate approximately 4.8 watts per square foot as the preliminary power requirement.

2. The light loss factor can be determined by filling in the blanks on the appropriate work sheet (see Figure 14.12). The first blank is for "light loss factors not to be recovered." Since we have no knowledge of these factors, the blank is assigned unity (1.0). A factor of 1.0 does not affect the computation in any way.

   The problem states that the area atmosphere is very clean and that the installation is cleaned every 18 months. By intersecting the graph

Approximate wiring capacity to provide a given maintained illuminance level in a room of 2.5 Room Cavity Ratio by means of the following:

A – Indirect, incandescent filament (silvered bowl)

B – Direct, incandescent filament (with diffuser)

C – Direct, incandescent filament (downlight)

D – General diffuse, incandescent filament

E – Direct, incandescent filament (lens)

F – Direct, incandescent filament (industrial)
Indirect, fluorescent (cove)

G – Indirect, fluorescent (extra high output)

H – Direct, fluorescent (extra high output) (louvered)

I – Direct, fluorescent (louvered)

J – Luminous ceiling, fluorescent

K – Direct, fluorescent (lens)
Direct, HID (mercury)

L – Direct/Semi-direct, fluorescent (industrial)

M – Direct, metal halide

N – Direct, high pressure sodium

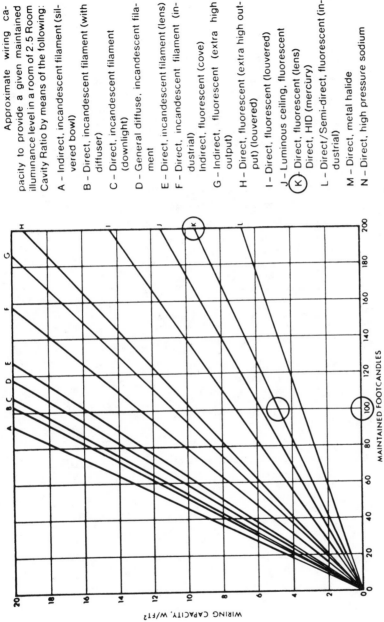

Figure 14.11. Approximately 4.8 watts per square foot.

191

```
PROJECT:    Example problem                          WORK SHEET
DESIGNER:   Author
DATE:          -       -

SUBJECT:    LIGHT LOSS FACTOR FOR LUMINAIRE TYPE:  Example

LAMP DESCRIPTION:   MANUFACTURER:  Example
                     ANSI NUMBER:  F40T12/CW
                    INITIAL LUMENS:  3150
                 MAINTAINED LUMENS:  2770

                                                    ESTIMATED
FACTOR DESCRIPTION:                                 FACTOR

1. LIGHT LOSS FACTORS NOT TO BE RECOVERED...........:  1.0

2. LIGHT LOSS FACTORS TO BE RECOVERED:

   A. AREA ATMOSPHERE:  Very clean

   B. ROOM SURFACE DIRT DEPRECIATION:
      1. AREA ATMOSPHERE..............:  Very clean
      2. TIME BETWEEN CLEANINGS.....:  18 months
      3. EXPECTED DIRT DEPRECIATION.:  .10
      4. ROOM CAVITY RATIO..........:  2.9
                                         RSDD:    .98
   C. LAMP BURN-OUTS:  LAMPS REMAINING ON
                       TOTAL LAMPS USED
                                         LBO:  1.0
   D. LAMP LUMEN DEPRECIATION:  MAINTAINED LUMENS
                                INITIAL LUMENS
                                         LLD:    .88
   E. LUMINAIRE DIRT DEPRECIATION:
      1. AREA ATMOSPHERE............:  Very clean
      2. LUMINAIRE MAINTENANCE
            CATEGORY................:  V
      3. TIME BETWEEN CLEANINGS.....:  18 months
                                         LDD:    .90


LIGHT LOSS FACTOR = (RSDD)(LBO)(LLD)(LDD)........LLF:    .78
```

Figure 14.12. Work sheet: light loss factor.

lines in Figure 14.13 for Very Clean and 18 months, a 10% expected dirt depreciation is predicted.

Table 14.6 shows possible cavity ratios. The problem states that the width of the room is 20.0 feet, the length 30.0 feet, and the room cavity (the space between the top of the work surface and the bottom of the luminaire) 7.0 feet. By connecting the columns of Figure 14.14, a room cavity ratio of 2.9 is found.

Returning to Figure 14.13, the 10% expected direct depreciation column for Direct luminaire distribution is located. Since the actual room cavity ratio figure (2.9) is very close to 3, this figure is selected from the RCR column. The columns are intersected and predict a 98% (0.98) expected dirt depreciation (called room surface dirt depreciation).

We are told that the lamps will be replaced as soon as they burn out, and so unity (1.0) is assigned to the lamp burnouts blank on the work sheet.

Lamp lumen depreciation is predicted in one of two ways: (1) Maintained lumens are divided by initial lumens, or (2) Table 14.7 is consulted (as shown in Figure 14.15). The resulting 0.88 figure is placed in the LLD blank.

After repeating the description of area atmosphere (Very Clean), Table 14.8 is consulted to determine the luminaire maintenance category and a translucent, unapertured bottom enclosure. For these reasons, it falls in luminaire maintenance category V, as shown in Figure 14.16. By selecting graph V in Table 14.9, a Luminaire Dirt Depreciation factor of 0.90 is determined for a Very Clean atmosphere and 18-month period between cleanings as shown in Figure 14.17.

By multiplying all the estimated factors together $(1.0 \times 0.98 \times 1.0 \times 0.88 \times 0.90)$, a Light Loss Factor of 0.78 is predicted (0.776 rounded to two places).

3. *Maintained footcandles* are predicted by filling in the blanks on the work sheets shown in Figure 14.18 and 14.19.

Most of the information requested on the test area work sheet is either given to you in the stated problem or derived from earlier questions. The area of the space is its length times its width. The spacing ratio required for the maximum spacing blank, as well as the lamp catalog number, the quantity of lamps per luminaire, and the initial lumens produced by each lamp can be found in Figure 14.10g.

On the coefficient of utilization work sheet (Figure 14.19) the room cavity ratio has been previously determined from Table 14.6. There is no ceiling cavity since the luminaires are fully recessed. The Floor cavity ratio is also found with the aid of Table 14.6. Since the depth of

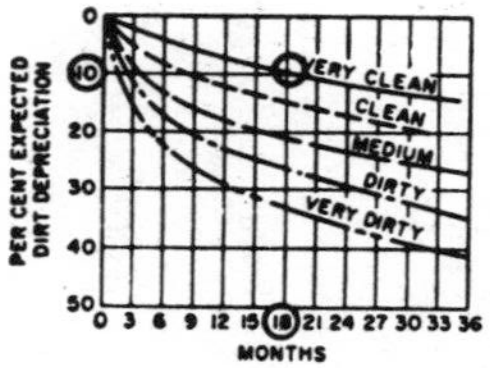

Luminaire Distribution Type

Room Cavity Ratio	Direct				Semi-Direct				Direct-Indirect				Semi-Indirect				Indirect			
Per cent expected Direct Depreciation	10	20	30	40	10	20	30	40	10	20	30	40	10	20	30	40	10	20	30	40
1	98	96	94	92	97	92	89	84	94	87	80	76	94	87	80	73	90	80	70	60
2	98	96	94	92	96	92	88	83	94	87	80	75	94	87	79	72	90	80	69	59
3	98	95	93	90	96	91	87	82	94	86	79	74	94	86	78	71	90	79	68	58
4	97	95	92	90	95	90	85	80	94	86	79	73	94	86	78	70	89	78	67	56
5	97	94	91	89	94	90	84	79	93	86	78	72	93	86	77	69	89	78	66	55
6	97	94	91	88	94	89	83	78	93	85	78	71	93	85	76	68	89	77	66	54
7	97	94	90	87	93	88	82	77	93	84	77	70	93	84	76	68	89	76	65	53
8	96	93	89	86	93	87	81	75	93	84	76	69	93	84	76	68	88	76	64	52
9	96	92	88	85	93	87	80	74	93	84	76	68	93	84	75	67	88	75	63	51
10	96	92	87	83	93	86	79	72	93	84	75	67	92	83	75	67	88	75	62	50

Figure 14.13. Expected dirt depreciation, 10%; surface dirt depreciation factor, 0.98.

Room Dimensions		Cavity Depth																			
Width	Length	1.0	1.5	2.0	2.5	3.0	3.5	4.0	5.0	6.0	7.0	8	9	10	11	12	14	16	20	25	30
8	8	1.2	1.9	2.5	3.1	3.7	4.4	5.0	6.2	7.5	8.8	10.0	11.3	12.5	12.4	—	—	—	—	—	—
	10	1.1	1.7	2.2	2.8	3.4	3.9	4.5	5.6	6.7	7.9	9.0	10.1	11.3	10.7	11.7	—	—	—	—	—
	14	1.0	1.5	2.0	2.5	3.0	3.4	4.0	4.8	5.9	6.9	8.0	8.8	9.8	9.6	10.5	13.2	11.8	—	—	—
	20	0.9	1.3	1.7	2.2	2.6	3.1	3.5	4.4	5.2	6.1	7.0	7.9	8.8	8.7	9.6	11.1	—	—	—	—
	30	0.8	1.1	1.6	2.0	2.4	2.8	3.2	4.0	4.7	5.5	6.3	7.1	8.0	8.1	8.8	10.3	—	—	—	—
	40	0.7	1.1	1.5	1.9	2.3	2.6	3.0	3.7	4.5	5.3	6.0	6.8	7.4	—	—	—	—	—	—	—
10	10	1.0	1.5	2.0	2.5	3.0	3.5	4.0	4.9	6.0	7.0	8.0	9.0	10.0	11.0	12.0	12.8	12.0	—	—	—
	14	0.7	1.1	1.5	1.9	2.3	2.8	3.4	4.2	5.1	6.0	6.9	7.8	8.6	8.3	10.4	10.5	10.6	12.5	—	—
	20	0.7	1.0	1.4	1.7	2.0	2.8	3.7	4.0	4.7	6.0	5.3	6.8	7.5	7.3	9.0	9.4	10.0	11.0	—	—
	30	0.6	0.9	1.2	1.6	1.9	2.2	2.5	3.3	4.0	4.7	5.3	6.0	6.8	6.9	7.5	8.7	9.8	10.2	—	—
	40	0.6	0.9	1.2	1.5	1.7	2.0	2.3	2.9	3.5	4.1	4.7	5.3	5.9	6.0	7.1	8.2	9.4	9.7	12.2	—
12	12	0.8	1.2	1.7	2.1	2.5	2.9	2.9	4.2	5.0	5.8	6.7	7.5	8.4	9.2	10.4	11.7	11.6	12.5	—	—
	16	0.7	1.1	1.5	1.8	2.2	2.5	2.4	3.1	4.4	5.1	5.8	6.5	7.2	8.3	9.0	10.7	9.8	11.0	11.9	—
	24	0.6	1.0	1.2	1.6	1.9	2.2	2.8	3.7	3.7	4.4	5.3	6.0	6.5	7.3	8.0	9.4	8.4	10.5	11.0	—
	36	0.5	0.8	1.1	1.3	1.7	1.9	2.5	3.3	3.3	3.9	4.4	5.5	5.8	6.2	7.5	7.3	8.8	9.8	10.3	—
	50	0.5	0.7	1.0	1.2	1.5	1.8	2.1	3.1	3.1	3.4	3.9	4.4	4.9	6.4	7.1	6.8	7.8	9.7	—	12.4
14	14	0.7	1.1	1.4	1.8	2.1	2.5	2.9	3.6	4.3	5.0	5.7	6.4	7.1	7.8	9.0	10.0	9.4	—	—	—
	20	0.6	0.9	1.2	1.5	1.8	2.1	2.4	3.0	3.6	4.2	4.9	5.5	6.1	6.7	8.2	8.6	9.0	—	11.9	11.6
	30	0.5	0.8	1.0	1.3	1.6	1.8	1.9	2.6	3.3	3.7	4.2	5.0	5.5	6.0	6.3	7.3	7.0	9.5	10.3	10.9
	42	0.4	0.7	0.9	1.1	1.4	1.7	1.8	2.4	2.8	3.0	3.8	4.3	4.7	5.2	5.7	6.1	7.6	8.8	9.0	10.1
	60	0.4	0.6	0.8	1.0	1.2	1.4	1.6	2.0	2.5	3.4	3.3	3.7	4.1	4.5	5.0	5.8	6.6	6.3	10.3	10.1
17	17	0.6	0.7	1.0	1.3	1.5	1.7	2.0	2.5	3.5	4.1	4.7	5.3	6.4	6.5	7.0	7.8	9.4	11.7	12.5	12.4
	25	0.5	0.6	1.0	1.1	1.3	1.5	1.9	2.3	3.0	3.1	3.5	4.3	4.6	4.9	5.2	7.0	8.0	10.5	10.9	11.8
	35	0.4	0.5	0.8	0.9	1.2	1.4	1.3	1.7	2.2	3.1	3.3	3.3	4.4	4.3	4.7	6.1	7.0	8.7	10.7	11.6
	50	0.4	0.5	0.7	0.8	1.1	1.2	1.2	1.7	1.8	2.5	2.9	3.3	3.6	4.0	4.3	5.1	5.8	7.3	9.0	10.1
	80	0.4	0.5	0.7	0.7	0.8	1.0	1.1	1.4	1.7	2.3	2.4	2.6	3.0	3.7	4.0	4.5	5.1	6.7	8.4	10.1
	120	0.3	0.4	0.6	0.7	0.7	0.8	1.0	1.3	1.4	1.9	1.9	2.1	2.4	2.6	3.2	3.3	4.6	6.7	—	—
20	20	0.5	0.6	0.8	0.9	1.2	1.4	1.7	2.0	3.0	3.0	4.0	4.5	5.0	5.5	6.0	7.0	8.0	10.0	12.5	12.4
	35	0.4	0.5	0.7	0.8	1.1	1.3	1.7	2.0	2.2	2.5	3.3	3.7	4.1	4.4	4.9	5.8	6.6	8.3	10.3	12.4
	60	0.4	0.4	0.6	0.7	0.8	1.1	1.3	1.7	2.0	2.3	2.7	3.0	3.3	4.3	4.3	5.1	7.0	7.7	9.1	9.4
	90	0.4	0.4	0.5	0.7	0.8	1.0	1.1	1.4	1.8	2.1	2.4	2.7	3.0	4.0	4.0	4.2	4.8	6.7	8.2	9.0
	150	0.3	0.4	0.5	0.6	0.7	0.8	1.0	1.3	1.7	2.0	2.3	2.6	3.4	3.7	3.4	4.0	4.6	6.7	7.2	8.6
24	24	0.4	0.6	0.8	0.9	1.2	1.5	1.7	2.1	2.5	2.9	3.3	3.7	4.1	4.5	5.0	5.8	6.7	8.2	10.3	12.4
	33	0.4	0.5	0.7	0.8	1.1	1.3	1.5	1.8	2.2	2.6	2.9	3.3	3.6	4.4	4.3	5.1	5.8	7.2	8.8	11.0
	50	0.3	0.4	0.6	0.7	0.8	1.0	1.2	1.4	1.7	2.1	2.4	3.0	3.1	3.7	3.3	3.8	4.4	5.5	6.9	9.4
	70	0.3	0.4	0.5	0.6	0.8	0.9	1.0	1.3	1.7	1.8	2.1	2.6	2.8	3.0	3.3	3.7	4.2	5.2	6.9	8.2
	100	0.2	0.4	0.5	0.6	0.7	0.8	1.0	1.3	1.4	1.7	2.1	2.4	2.4	2.8	2.9	3.3	3.8	4.7	6.9	7.1

Figure 14.14. Cavity ratio 2.9.

195

CATEGORY	NAME	SHAPE	COLOR	NOMINAL WATTAGE	LLD FACTOR
INCANDESCENT	EXTENDED SVCE.	A,PS		15-750	.85
	GENERAL SERVICE	A,PS,S		TO 40	.85
				50-1500	.89
	PROJECTOR	PAR 38-64		75-1000	.84
	REFLECTOR	R40		150-500	.86
		R 52-57		500-1000	.81
	ROUGH SERVICE	A,PS		50-200	.79
	SHOWCASE	T-10		25-40	.78
	SILVER BOWL	A,PS		200-500	.75
	THREE LIGHT	A,T		30-150	.85
		PS		100-300	.72
	TUNGSTEN-HALOGEN	T		200-1500	.96
	VIBRATION	A-19		50	.72
FLUORESCENT	RAPID START	U-12	CW	40	.84*
	430 MA.	T-12	CW	30	.81*
				40	(.88*)
H.I.D.	MERCURY VAPOR	E17	DX	50	.76
		E17	DX	75	.80
		E23	CLEAR	100	.81
		E23	DX	100	.84
		R40 FL	FROSTED	100	.78
		R40 WFL	DX	100	.80
		E28	CLEAR	175	.92
		E28	DX	175	.86
		E28	WDX	175	.89
		R40 FL	FROSTED	175	.88
		R40 WFL	DX	175	.88
		E28	CLEAR	250	.92
		E28	DX	250	.86
		E28	WDX	250	.80
		E37	CLEAR	400	.91
		E37	DX	400	.85
		E37	WDX	400	.82
		R60 FL	FROSTED	400	.83
		R60 WFL	DX	400	.76
		R60 SP	FROSTED	400	.80
		BT46	CLEAR	700	.89
		BT46	DX	700	.80
		BT56	CLEAR	1000	.85
		BT56	DX	1000	.75
		BT56	WDX	1000	.68

NOTES: ALL LAMPS RUN AT 120 VOLTS (MEASURED AT THE BALLAST FOR ALL DISCHARGE SOURCES).
ALL LAMPS MEASURED FOR VERTICAL BURNING.
*3 HOUR PER START FOR COOL WHITE, WARM WHITE AND DAYLIGHT COLORS. FOR COLOR IMPROVED TYPES (DELUXE COOL WHITE AND DELUXE WARM WHITE) MULTIPLY BY .93.

Figure 14.15.   Lamp lumen depreciation factor 0.88.

To assist in determining Luminaire Dirt Depreciation (LDD) factors, luminaires are separated into six maintenance categories (I through VI). To arrive at categories, luminaires are arbitrarily divided into sections, a *Top Enclosure* and a *Bottom Enclosure*, by drawing a horizontal line through the light center of the lamp or lamps. The characteristics listed for the enclosures are then selected as best describing the luminaire. Only one characteristic for the bottom enclosure should be used in determining the category of a luminaire. Percentage of uplight is based on 100 per cent for the luminaire.

The maintenance category is determined when there are characteristics in both enclosure columns. If a luminaire falls into more than one category, the lower numbered category is used.

Maintenance Category	Top Enclosure	Bottom Enclosure
I	1. None.	1. None
II	1. None 2. Transparent with 15% or more uplight through apertures. 3. Translucent with 15% or more uplight through apertures. 4. Opaque with 15% or more uplight through apertures.	1. None 2. Louvers or baffles
III	1. Transparent with less than 15% upward light through apertures. 2. Translucent with less than 15% upward light through apertures. 3. Opaque with less than 15% uplight through apertures.	1. None 2. Louvers or baffles
IV	1. Transparent unapertured. 2. Translucent unapertured. 3. Opaque unapertured.	1. None 2. Louvers
(V)	1. Transparent unapertured. 2. Translucent unapertured. (3.) Opaque unapertured.	1. Transparent unapertured (2.) Translucent unapertured
VI	1. None. 2. Transparent unapertured. 3. Translucent unapertured. 4. Opaque unapertured.	1. Transparent unapertured 2. Translucent unapertured 3. Opaque unapertured

Figure 14.16.   Luminaire maintenance factor V.

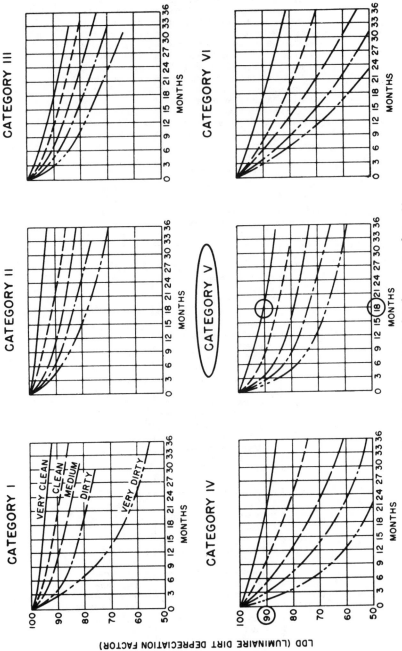

Figure 14.17. Luminaire dirt depreciation factor 90.

198

PROJECT: **Example problem** _____ WORK SHEET

DESIGNER: **Author** _____

DATE: _____-_____-_____

SUBJECT: DESCRIPTION OF THE TEST AREA, LUMINAIRE AND LAMP
FOR USE WITH THE IES ZONAL CAVITY METHOD

SUBJECT AREA: **school laboratory** _____ TEST NUMBER: **1**

DESCRIPTION OF THE AREA:

DIMENSIONS:

LENGTH = **30**.**0** ' WIDTH = **20**.**0** ' AREA = **600**.**0** SQ. FT.

TOTAL HEIGHT OF THE SPACE = **10**.**0** '

HEIGHT BETWEEN LUMINAIRE AND WORK PLANE = HRC = **7**.**0** '

DISTANCE FROM LUMINAIRE PLANE TO CEILING = HCC = **0**.**0** '

HEIGHT OF WORK PLANE ABOVE FLOOR = HFC = **3**.**0** '

ROOM SURFACE REFLECTANCES:

CEILING = PC = **.80**

WALLS ABOVE LUMINAIRE MOUNTING PLANE = PW = **.00**

WALLS BETWEEN LUMINAIRE AND WORK PLANE = PW = **.50**

WALLS BELOW WORK PLANE = PW = **.10**

FLOOR = PF = **.30**

LUMINAIRE:

MANUFACTURER: **Example** _____ QUANTITY USED IN DESIGN: **30**

LUMINAIRE CATALOG NUMBER: **Example luminaire** _____

MAXIMUM SPACING =

(SPACING RATIO)(MOUNTING HEIGHT ABOVE WORK PLANE)

= (**1.1**)(**7.0**) = **7.7**

LIGHT LOSS FACTOR = LLF = **.78**

LAMP:

MANUFACTURER: **Example** _____ LAMPS PER LUMINAIRE: **2**

CATALOG OR ORDERING NUMBER (ANSI NUMBER): **F40T12/CW** _____

INITIAL LUMENS PRODUCED BY EACH LAMP: **3150** _____

Figure 14.18.   Work sheet: description of the test area, luminaire, and lamp for use with the I.E.S. zonal cavity method.

PROJECT: **Example problem**   WORK SHEET

DESIGNER: **Author**

DATE: -   -

SUBJECT: COEFFICIENT OF UTILIZATION AND FOOTCANDLE LEVELS
          DERIVED FROM THE IES ZONAL CAVITY METHOD

TEST NUMBER: **1**

COEFFICIENT OF UTILIZATION:

CAVITY RATIOS: ROOM = **2.9**   CEILING = **0.0**   FLOOR = **1.2**

EFFECTIVE CEILING CAVITY REFLECTANCE = PCC = **.80**

EFFECTIVE FLOOR CAVITY REFLECTANCE = PFC = **.20**

CU (USING MANUFACTURER'S DATA FOR 20% PFC) = **.48**

IF THE EFFECTIVE FLOOR CAVITY REFLECTANCE DIFFERS SIGNIFICANT-
   LY FROM 20%, THIS CU IS CORRECTED BY THE APPROPRIATE FACTOR:
          (CU AT .20 PFC)(CORRECTION FACTOR) = CORRECTED CU
          (.____)(__.__) = .**not applicable**

CALCULATION FOR FOOTCANDLES:

   (NO. OF LUMINAIRES)(LAMPS/LUMINAIRE)(INITIAL LUMENS/LAMP)(CU)(LLF)
                (TOTAL AREA OF THE SPACE IN SQ. FT.)

        FOOTCANDLES = (**30**)(**2**)(**3150**)(**.48**)(**.78**)
                                    (**600**)

        FOOTCANDLES = **118.0**

CALCULATION FOR THE QUANTITY OF LUMINAIRES:

        (FOOTCANDLES)(AREA IN SQ. FT.)
   (LAMPS/LUMINAIRE)(INITIAL LUMENS/LAMP)(CU)(LLF)
          LUMINAIRE QUANTITY = ____(____)(____)____
                                ( )( )(.)(.)
          LUMINAIRE QUANTITY = **not applicable**

Figure 14.19.   Work sheet: coefficient of utilization and footcandle levels derived from the I.E.S. zonal cavity method.

the floor cavity is 3.0 feet, the floor cavity ratio is 1.2, as shown in Figure 14.20. Remember that cavity ratios can also be found by using the simple formulas given previously.

The effective ceiling cavity reflectance (ρCC) is the same as the reflectance of the ceiling surface (0.80) since there is no cavity involved.

The effective floor cavity reflectance is determined by intersecting the appropriate columns in Table 14.12, as shown in Figure 14.21. The floor reflectance is 0.30, the walls below the work plane are 0.10 and the Floor Cavity Ratio is 1.2. The resulting ρFC is .20.

By consulting the chart for zonal cavity coefficients of utilization shown in Figure 14.22, the coefficient of utilization for this specific luminaire may be determined. In this instance, the floors are 20% (ρFC), the ceilings 80% (ρCC), the largest wall mass is 50% (ρW) reflective, and the 2.9 RCR is closest to the "3" figure on the chart. The resulting coefficient of utilization is 0.48. The zonal cavity coefficients of utilization chart is calculated for a floor cavity reflectance (ρFC) on 20% only. If the floor cavity reflectance was 10%, then we would have to multiply the coefficient of utilization by a factor found in Table 14.13 (0.951). However, since the effective floor cavity reflectance in this problem is 20%, this step can be omitted.

The calculation for maintained footcandles is merely a matter of placing previously collected data into the proper equation. The resulting predicted footcandles are 117.94, rounded to 118.

4. The *sufficiency of the predicted footcandle level* can be checked by consulting Table 14.15, under the heading Educational Facilities and the subheading Lecture Rooms. Since 100 footcandles are recommended, the predicted lighting is sufficient by I.E.S. standards.

5. The layout diagram shows that the luminaires are placed on 3.5-foot centers. Since the *maximum* tolerable spacing is 7.7 feet, the layout satisfies *maximum spacing criteria.*

6. Referring to Figure 14.23, it is possible to determine that *visual comfort probability* has been satisfied: (1) For a room with ρCC = 80, ρW = 50, and ρFC = 20 measuring 20.0 feet by 30.0 feet by 10.0 feet and receiving 100 footcandles, the lengthwise VCP is 70 and the crosswise VCP is 71; (2) the ratio of maximum-to-average luminaire luminance does not exceed five to one at the requisite degrees from nadir; and (3) the maximum luminaire luminances, both lengthwise and crosswise, do not exceed allowable values.

7. Referring to Table 13.2 under education, it can be seen that range of reflectance percentages is satisfactory for most of the space. The wall area below the work surface is largely out of view in this installation so that its 10% surface reflectance need not be considered.

| Room Dimensions | | Cavity Depth | | | | | | | | | | | | | | | | | | | |
Width	Length	1.0	1.5	2.0	2.5	3.0	3.5	4.0	5.0	6.0	7.0	8	9	10	11	12	14	16	20	25	30
8	8	1.2	1.9	2.5	3.1	3.7	4.4	5.0	6.2	7.5	8.8	10.0	11.2	12.5	—	—	—	—	—	—	—
	10	1.1	1.7	2.2	2.8	3.4	4.1	4.5	5.6	6.7	7.9	9.0	10.1	11.3	12.4	—	—	—	—	—	—
	14	1.0	1.5	2.0	2.5	3.0	3.4	3.9	4.9	5.9	6.9	7.8	8.8	9.7	10.7	11.7	12.2	—	—	—	—
	20	0.9	1.3	1.7	2.2	2.6	3.1	3.5	4.4	5.2	6.1	7.0	7.9	8.8	9.7	10.5	11.0	11.8	12.5	—	—
	30	0.8	1.2	1.6	2.0	2.4	2.8	3.2	4.0	4.7	5.5	6.3	7.1	7.9	8.7	9.5	10.3	—	11.7	—	—
	40	0.7	1.1	1.5	1.9	2.3	2.6	3.0	3.7	4.5	5.3	5.9	6.5	7.4	8.1	8.8	—	11.8	—	—	—
10	10	1.0	1.5	2.0	2.5	3.0	3.5	4.0	4.8	6.1	7.0	8.0	9.0	10.0	11.0	12.0	—	—	—	—	—
	14	0.9	1.3	1.7	2.1	2.6	3.0	3.4	4.3	5.1	6.0	6.9	7.8	8.6	9.5	10.4	12.0	12.0	12.5	—	—
	20	0.7	1.1	1.5	1.9	2.3	2.6	2.7	3.7	4.0	4.7	6.0	6.8	7.5	8.3	9.0	9.4	10.6	13.0	—	—
	30	0.7	1.0	1.3	1.6	2.0	2.3	2.5	3.1	3.7	4.4	5.3	6.6	6.2	7.3	8.0	8.7	9.4	11.0	—	—
	40	0.6	0.9	1.2	1.5	1.7	2.0	2.3	2.9	3.5	4.1	4.7	5.3	5.9	6.5	7.1	8.2	9.4	9.7	12.2	—
12	12	0.8	1.2	1.7	2.1	2.5	2.9	3.3	4.2	5.0	5.8	6.7	7.5	8.4	9.2	10.0	11.7	11.6	12.3	12.5	—
	16	0.7	1.1	1.5	1.9	2.2	2.5	2.9	3.6	4.4	5.1	5.8	6.5	7.2	8.0	8.7	10.2	10.0	10.5	10.9	—
	24	0.6	0.9	1.2	1.4	1.9	2.2	2.7	3.1	3.3	4.2	5.0	6.0	6.2	6.9	7.5	7.8	8.8	9.5	9.7	11.6
	36	0.6	0.8	1.1	1.3	1.7	1.9	2.1	2.8	3.1	3.6	4.4	5.6	5.5	6.0	6.6	7.2	7.8	8.8	9.0	10.9
	50	0.5	0.7	1.0	1.2	1.5	1.8	2.0	2.4	2.9	3.4	3.9	4.4	4.9	5.4	5.8	6.8	7.8	8.3	8.4	10.1
14	14	0.7	1.1	1.4	1.8	2.1	2.5	2.9	3.6	4.3	5.0	5.7	6.4	7.1	7.8	8.5	10.0	11.4	11.7	—	—
	20	0.6	0.9	1.2	1.5	1.8	2.1	2.4	3.0	3.6	4.3	4.9	5.5	6.1	6.7	7.3	8.6	9.8	10.0	12.3	—
	30	0.5	0.8	1.0	1.3	1.6	1.8	1.9	2.6	3.1	3.6	4.2	4.7	5.2	5.8	6.3	7.3	8.4	9.5	10.2	11.9
	42	0.5	0.7	0.9	1.1	1.4	1.6	1.8	2.2	2.6	3.1	3.6	4.3	4.7	5.2	5.7	6.7	7.6	7.7	9.0	10.9
	60	0.5	0.6	0.9	1.0	1.2	1.5	1.6	2.0	2.5	2.9	3.5	3.9	4.4	4.8	5.3	6.1	7.0	7.5	7.6	8.6
	90	0.4	0.6	0.8	1.0	1.1	1.4	1.6	2.0	2.5	2.9	3.3	3.7	4.1	4.5	5.0	5.7	6.6	6.7	8.4	10.1
17	17	0.6	0.9	1.2	1.5	1.8	2.1	2.3	2.9	3.5	4.1	4.7	5.3	5.9	6.5	7.0	8.2	9.4	11.7	12.5	—
	25	0.5	0.7	0.9	1.2	1.4	1.7	1.9	2.4	3.0	3.4	4.0	4.5	5.0	5.5	6.1	7.0	8.0	10.0	10.9	11.6
	35	0.5	0.7	0.8	1.0	1.3	1.5	1.7	2.2	2.6	3.1	3.5	3.9	4.4	4.8	5.2	6.1	7.2	9.5	9.7	10.9
	50	0.4	0.5	0.7	0.9	1.2	1.4	1.6	2.0	2.4	2.8	3.1	3.5	3.9	4.3	4.6	5.4	7.0	7.7	9.0	10.9
	80	0.4	0.5	0.7	0.8	1.1	1.2	1.3	1.8	2.0	2.3	2.9	3.3	3.4	3.7	4.0	4.7	5.4	7.2	7.5	9.0
	120	0.3	0.5	0.6	0.7	1.0	1.2	1.3	1.7	2.0	2.3	2.7	3.0	3.4	3.7	4.0	4.6	5.4	6.7	8.4	10.1
20	20	0.5	0.7	1.0	1.2	1.2	1.7	2.0	2.5	3.0	3.5	3.9	4.5	5.0	4.5	5.0	5.8	6.7	8.2	10.3	12.4
	30	0.4	0.6	0.8	1.0	1.0	1.5	1.7	2.1	2.5	2.9	3.5	3.7	4.1	4.4	4.7	5.1	5.8	7.2	9.1	10.4
	45	0.4	0.5	0.7	0.8	1.0	1.3	1.4	1.8	2.1	2.6	3.1	3.3	3.6	4.0	4.3	5.1	5.4	6.6	8.4	10.9
	60	0.3	0.5	0.6	0.7	0.9	1.2	1.3	1.5	2.0	2.3	2.8	3.0	3.4	3.7	4.0	4.2	5.4	6.7	9.0	10.1
	90	0.3	0.5	0.6	0.7	0.8	1.1	1.2	1.4	1.6	2.0	2.4	2.7	3.0	3.3	3.6	4.0	4.6	6.0	7.5	9.6
	150	0.3	0.4	0.5	0.6	0.7	0.8	1.1	1.3	1.4	1.7	2.3	2.4	2.9	3.2	3.4	3.8	4.6	5.7	7.2	8.6
21	24	0.4	0.6	0.8	1.0	1.2	1.5	1.7	2.1	2.5	2.9	3.3	3.7	4.1	4.5	5.0	5.8	6.7	8.2	10.3	12.4
	32	0.4	0.5	0.7	0.9	0.9	1.3	1.5	1.8	2.2	2.6	2.9	3.3	3.6	4.0	4.3	5.1	5.8	7.2	7.8	11.0
	50	0.3	0.5	0.6	0.7	0.9	1.1	1.3	1.5	1.8	2.1	2.5	2.8	3.0	3.4	3.7	4.4	5.4	6.6	7.5	8.2
	70	0.3	0.4	0.6	0.6	0.8	1.0	1.1	1.4	1.6	1.8	2.2	2.5	2.8	3.0	3.3	3.8	4.2	6.0	6.5	7.7
	100	0.3	0.4	0.5	0.6	0.8	0.9	1.0	1.3	1.4	1.7	2.1	2.4	2.6	2.9	3.1	3.7	4.2	5.2	6.5	6.9
	160	0.2	0.4	0.5	0.6	0.7	0.8	1.0	1.2	1.4	1.7	1.9	2.1	2.4	2.6	2.8	3.3	3.8	4.7	5.9	7.1

Figure 14.20. Floor cavity ratio 1.2.

Cavity Ratio	90				80				70			50			(30)				10		
PER CENT WALL REFLECTANCE	90	70	50	30	80	70	50	30	70	50	30	70	50	30	65	50	30	(10)	50	30	10
0.1	90	90	90	90	80	80	80	80	70	70	70	50	50	50	30	30	30	30	10	10	10
0.2	90	89	88	87	80	79	78	80	69	69	68	50	49	48	30	30	29	29	10	10	10
0.3	89	88	86	85	79	78	77	78	68	67	66	49	48	47	30	29	29	28	10	10	9
0.4	89	87	85	83	78	77	75	76	68	66	64	49	47	46	30	29	28	27	11	10	9
0.5	88	86	83	81	78	76	74	74	67	65	61	48	46	45	30	28	27	26	11	10	9
0.6	88	85	80	78	77	75	73	72	65	64	59	47	46	43	29	28	26	25	11	10	9
0.7	88	84	78	76	76	74	71	70	65	62	58	47	45	42	29	28	26	24	11	10	8
0.8	87	83	77	76	75	73	70	68	64	61	56	47	44	41	29	27	25	23	11	10	8
0.9	87	82	76	73	75	73	69	66	63	60	55	46	43	40	29	27	25	22	11	9	8
1.0	86	80	74	71	74	71	68	65	63	59	53	46	42	39	29	27	24	22	11	9	8
1.1	86	79	73	69	74	71	66	63	62	58	52	46	41	38	29	26	24	21	11	9	8
(1.2)	86	78	72	67	73	70	65	61	61	57	50	45	41	37	29	26	23	(20)	12	9	7
1.3	85	78	70	65	72	69	64	60	60	56	48	45	40	36	29	26	23	20	12	9	7
1.4	85	77	69	64	72	68	63	58	60	55	48	45	40	35	28	26	22	19	12	9	7
1.5	85	76	68	62	71	68	62	57	59	54	47	44	39	34	28	25	22	18	12	9	7
1.6	85	75	66	61	71	67	61	55	59	53	45	44	39	33	28	25	21	18	12	9	7
1.7	84	74	65	59	71	66	60	53	58	52	44	44	38	32	28	25	21	17	12	9	7
1.8	84	73	64	58	70	65	59	52	57	51	43	43	37	32	28	25	21	17	12	9	6
1.9	84	73	63	56	70	65	58	51	57	50	42	43	37	31	28	25	20	16	12	9	6
2.0	83	72	62	55	69	64	57	49	56	49	41	43	37	30	28	24	20	16	12	9	6
2.1	83	71	61	53	69	63	56	48	56	48	40	43	36	29	28	24	20	16	13	9	6
2.2	83	70	60	52	68	63	55	47	55	47	39	42	36	29	28	24	19	15	13	9	6
2.3	83	69	59	51	68	62	54	45	54	46	38	42	35	28	28	24	19	15	13	9	6
2.4	82	68	58	50	67	61	53	44	54	45	37	42	35	27	28	24	19	15	13	9	6
2.5	82	68	57	47	67	61	51	42	53	44	36	41	34	27	27	23	18	14	13	9	6

Figure 14.21. Effective floor cavity reflectance 20.

203

FLOORS	20%						
CEILING	80%				50%		
WALLS	70%	50%	30%	10%	50%	30%	10%
1	.61	.59	.57	.55	.55	.54	.53
2	.56	.53	.50	.48	.50	.48	.46
3	.53	.48	.45	.42	.46	.43	.41
4	.49	.44	.40	.37	.42	.39	.36
5	.45	.40	.35	.32	.38	.34	.32
6	.42	.36	.32	.29	.35	.31	.29
7	.39	.33	.29	.26	.32	.28	.26
8	.36	.30	.26	.23	.29	.25	.23
9	.34	.27	.23	.20	.26	.22	.20
10	.31	.25	.21	.18	.24	.20	.18

(left margin label: R C R)

Figure 14.22.   Coefficient of utilization 0.48.

Table 14.15. Recommended Illuminance Categories[a]

I. Illuminance Categories and Illuminance Values for Generic Types of Activities in Interiors

Category	Ranges of Illuminances	Type of Activity and Category Reference Work Plane
A	20–30–50 lux[b]	Public spaces with dark surroundings.
B	50–75–100 lux	Simple orientation for short temporary visits. Reference: general lighting throughout spaces.
C	100–150–200 lux	Working spaces where visual tasks are only occasionally performed.
D	200–300–500 lux	Performance of visual tasks of high contrast or large size.
E	500–750–1,000 lux	Performance of visual tasks of medium contrast of small size. Reference: illuminance on the task.
F	1,000–1,500–2,000 lux	Performance of visual tasks of low contrast or very small size.
G	2,000–3,000–5,000 lux	Performance of visual tasks of low contrast and very small size over a prolonged period. Reference: illuminance on task, obtained by a combination of general and local (supplementary) lighting.
H	5,000–7,500–10,000 lux	Performance of very prolonged and exacting visual tasks. Reference: illuminance on task, obtained by a combination of general and local (supplementary) lighting.
I	10,000–15,000–20,000 lux	Performance of very special visual tasks of extremely low contrast and small size. Reference: illuminance on task, obtained by a combination of general and local (supplementary) lighting.

Table 14.15. **Recommended Illuminance Categories**[a] (*Continued*)

II (*continued*). Extract of Illuminances Recommended by the I.E.S. NA for Commercial, Institutional, Residential, and Public Assembly Interiors. (For full listings, see the 1981 Reference Volume, I.E.S. Lighting Handbook.)

Category	Area/Activity
C[c]	Armories
	Auditoriums:
C[c]	Assembly
B	Social activity
	Banks (also see Reading):
C	Lobby: General
D	Lobby: Writing area
E	Teller's stations
E	Barbershops and Beauty Parlors
D	Club and Lodge Rooms: Lounge and reading
D	Conference Rooms: Conferring
	Courtrooms:
C	Seating area
E	Court activity area
B	Dance Halls and Discotheques
	Drafting:
	Mylar:
E	High contrast media
F	Low contrast media
	Vellum:
E	High contrast media
F	Low contrast media
	Tracing paper:
E	High contrast media
F	Low contrast media
	Prints:
E	Blue line
E	Blueprints
F	Sepia prints
	Educational Facilities:
	Classrooms:
	General (see Reading)
	Home economics (see Residences)
E	Science laboratories
	Lecture rooms; Audience (see Reading)
F	Lecture rooms: Demonstration
	Music rooms (see Reading)
F	Sight-saving rooms
	Study halls (see Reading)

Table 14.15. (Continued)

II (*continued*). Extract of Illuminances Recommended by the I.E.S. NA for Commercial, Institutional, Residential, and Public Assembly Interiors. (For full listings, see the 1981 Reference Volume, I.E.S. Lighting Handbook.)

Category	Area/Activity
	Educational Facilities (Continued)
	Typing (see Reading)
	Cafeterias (see Food Service Facilities)
	Dormitories (see Residences)
C	Elevators: freight and passenger
C[c]	Exhibition halls
	Food Service Facilities:
	Dining areas:
D	Cashier
C	Cleaning
B[d]	Dining
	Food displays (see Merchandising Areas)
E	Kitchen
	Graphic Design and Material:
F[e]	Color selection
F	Charting and mapping
E	Graphs
F	Keylining
F	Layout and artwork
E[g]	Photographs, moderate detail
	Hotels:
D	Bathrooms, for grooming
D	Bedrooms, for reading
C	Corridors, elevators, and stairs
E	Front desk
	Linen room:
F	Sewing
C	General
	Lobby:
C	General lighting
D	Reading and working areas
	Libraries:
	Reading areas (see Reading)
	Book stacks (at a point 30 in. above floor):
D	Active stacks
B	Inactive stacks
D	Book repair and binding
D	Cataloging
E	Card files

Table 14.15. Recommended Illuminance Categories[a] (Continued)

II (continued). Extract of Illuminances Recommended by the I.E.S. NA for Commercial, Institutional, Residential, and Public Assembly Interiors. (For full listings, see the 1981 Reference Volume, I.E.S. Lighting Handbook.)

Category	Area/Activity
	Libraries (Continued)
	Carrels, individual study areas (see Reading)
D	Circulation desks
	Map, picture and print rooms (see Graphic Design and Material)
D	Audiovisual areas
D	Audio listening areas
	Microfilm areas (see Reading)
C	Locker rooms
	Merchandising Areas:
F	Alteration Room
	Fitting rooms:
D	Dressing areas
F	Fitting areas
D	Stockrooms
D	Wrapping and packaging
E	Sales transaction area
	Municipal Buildings—Fire and Police:
	Police:
F	Identification records
D	Jail cells and interrogation rooms
D	Fire hall
	Museums:
D	Displays of nonsensitive materials
	Displays of sensitive materials (see Chapter Twenty-six.)
C	Lobbies, general gallery areas, corridors
E	Restoration or conservation shops and laboratories
	Offices:
	Accounting (see Reading)
	Conference areas (see Conference Rooms)
	Drafting (see Drafting)
	General and private offices (see Reading)
	Libraries (see Libraries)
C	Lobbies, lounges and reception areas
E	Mail sorting
D	Offset printing and duplicating area
	Post Offices (see Offices)

Table 14.15. (Continued)

II (*continued*). Extract of Illuminances Recommended by the I.E.S. NA for Commercial, Institutional, Residential, and Public Assembly Interiors. (For full listings, see the 1981 Reference Volume, I.E.S. Lighting Handbook.)

Category	Area/Activity
	Reading:
	Copied tasks:
E	Ditto copy
$B^{f,g}$	Microfiche reader
D	Mimeograph
E^g	Photographs, moderate detail
F	Thermal copy, poor copy
D	Xerograph
E	Xerograph, third generation and greater
	Electronic data processing tasks:
$B^{f,g}$	CRT screens
D	Impact printer, good ribbon
E	Impact printer, poor ribbon
E	Impact printer, second carbon and greater
D	Ink jet printer
D	Keyboard reading
	Machine rooms:
D	Active operations
D	Tape storage
C	Machine area
E^h	Equipment service
E	Thermal print
	Handwritten tasks:
E	#3 pencil and softer leads
F	#4 pencil and harder leads
D	Ball-point pen
D	Felt-tip pen
E	Handwritten carbon copies
F	Non photographically reproducible colors
E	Chalkboards
	Printed tasks:
E	6 point type
D	8 and 10 point type
D^g	Glossy magazines
E	Maps
D	Newsprint
D	Typed originals
E	Typed second carbon and later
E	Telephone books

Table 14.15. Recommended Illuminance Categories[a] (Continued)

II (continued). Extract of Illuminances Recommended by the I.E.S. NA for Commercial, Institutional, Residential, and Public Assembly Interiors. (For full listings, see the 1981 Reference Volume, I.E.S. Lighting Handbook.)

Category	Area/Activity
	Residences:
	General lighting:
B	Conversation, relaxation, and entertainment
B	Passage areas
	Specific visual tasks:[i]
C	Dining
D	Grooming: Makeup and shaving
D	Grooming: Full-length mirror
	Handcrafts and hobbies:
D	Workbench hobbies: Ordinary tasks
E	Workbench hobbies: Difficult tasks
F	Workbench hobbies: Critical tasks
E	Easel hobbies
D	Ironing
	Kitchen duties:
E	Kitchen counter: Critical seeing
D	Kitchen counter: Noncritical
E	Kitchen range: Difficult seeing
D	Kitchen range: Noncritical
E	Kitchen sink: Difficult seeing
D	Kitchen sink: Noncritical
	Laundry:
D	Preparation and tubs
D	Washer and dryer
	Music study (piano or organ):
D	Simple scores
E	Advanced scores
F	Substandard-size scores
	Reading:
D	In a chair: Books, magazines, and newspapers
E	In a chair: Reproductions and poor copies
D	In bed: Normal
E	In bed: Prolonged, serious, or critical
D	Desk: Primary task plane, casual
E	Desk: Primary task plane, study
	Sewing:
F	Hand sewing: Dark fabrics, low contrast
E	Hand sewing: Light to medium fabrics
D	Hand sewing: Occasional, high contrast

Table 14.15. *(Continued)*

II *(continued)*. Extract of Illuminances Recommended by the I.E.S. NA for Commercial, Institutional, Residential, and Public Assembly Interiors. (For full listings, see the 1981 Reference Volume, I.E.S. Lighting Handbook.)

Category	Area/Activity
	Sewing (Continued)
F	Machine sewing: Dark fabrics, low contrast
E	Machine sewing: Light to medium fabrics
D	Machine sewing: Occasional, high contrast.
D	Table games
	Service Spaces:
C	Stairways, corridors.
C	Elevators: freight, and passenger.
C	Toilets and washrooms.
	Transportation Terminals:
C	Waiting room and lounge
E	Ticket counters
D	Baggage checking
B	Concourse
C	Boarding area

[a]Extract of illuminance categories and illuminance values for lighting design (target maintained levels) currently recommended by the I.E.S. Reference Volume, *I.E.S. Lighting Handbook*, Illuminating Engineering Society of North America (New York, 1981). Reprinted by permission. According to the I.E.S., "This listing is intended to guide the lighting designer in selecting an appropriate illuminance for design and evaluation of lighting systems. Guidance provided ...[represents] a range of illuminances ...given in *lux* and as such are intended as *target* (nominal) values with deviations expected. These target values also represent *maintained* values. ...In all cases the recommendations in this table are based on the assumption that lighting will be properly designed to take into account the visual characteristics of the task. For full information, refer to the 1981 Reference Volume, *I.E.S. Lighting Handbook*.

[b]Conversions: To change lux into footcandles, multiply the lux figures by 0.0929. Multiply footcandles by 10.76 to obtain lux. These multipliers can be rounded to 1.0 and 10.0, respectively, for approximate conversions that are satisfactory under most conditions.

[c]Include provisions for higher levels for exhibitions.

[d]Provide higher level over food service or selection areas.

[e]For color matching, the spectral quality of the color of the light source is important.

[f]Veiling reflections may be produced on glass surfaces. It may be necessary to treat plus weighting factors as minus in order to obtain proper illuminance.

[g]Especially subject to veiling reflections. It may be necessary to shield the task or to reorient it.

[h]Only when actual equipment service is in process. May be achieved by a general lighting system or by localized or portable equipment.

[i]General lighting should not be less than one-third of visual task illuminance nor less than 200 lux (20 fc).

100 FC. ROOM		REFLECTANCES 80/50/20								
		LUMINAIRES LENGTHWISE				LUMINAIRES CROSSWISE				
W	L	8.5	10.0	13.0	16.0	8.5	10.0	13.0	16.0
20	20	73	77	82	83	73	79	84	85
20	30	67	70	76	78	66	71	78	80
20	40	64	67	71	73	63	67	72	76
20	60	62	64	67	69	60	63	67	70
30	20	73	77	81	83	74	78	83	85
30	30	66	70	74	77	66	70	76	79
30	40	63	66	69	71	62	65	70	73
30	60	61	62	64	66	59	61	64	67
30	80	59	61	62	64	57	60	62	64
40	20	74	78	82	84	75	79	83	85
40	30	67	70	74	77	67	71	76	79
40	40	63	66	68	71	63	65	69	73
40	60	61	62	64	66	59	61	63	66
40	80	59	61	61	63	57	59	60	63
40	100	58	60	60	61	57	58	59	61
60	30	68	71	74	77	68	71	75	78
60	40	64	66	68	71	63	66	69	72
60	60	61	62	63	65	60	61	63	66
60	80	59	60	60	62	57	59	60	62
60	100	58	59	59	60	56	58	58	60
100	40	67	68	70	72	66	68	70	73
100	60	63	64	64	66	62	63	64	67
100	80	61	62	61	63	59	61	60	63
100	100	60	60	59	61	58	59	58	60

Figure 14.23. Visual comfort probability 70 and 71.

212

SHORTCUT CALCULATION AIDS

Manufacturers often provide quick-calculation charts to help environmentalists approximate luminaire performance. These guidelines are only as good as their assumptions and accuracy. See Figure 14.24a and b for two formats that are typically used for down lighting. See Figures 14.25 for a typical accent light chart, and Figure 14.26 for a representation of wall washer performance.

For down-lighting luminaires, most manufacturers make the following assumptions. Seeing tasks are taken to be horizontal, flat, and diffusely finished. All rooms are rectilinear and have diffuse surfaces with flat ceilings that are 80% reflective, walls 50% reflective, and floors 20% reflective. Footcandles are measured at a point 2.5 feet (30 in.) above the finished floor.

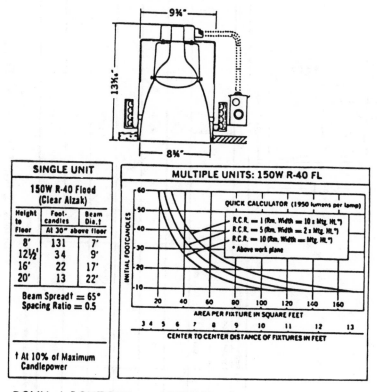

DOWN LIGHTING - METHOD A

(a)

Figure 14.24. Typical down-lighting illumination chart—Methods A and B.

Initial Footcandles—Single Unit*
150 W R-40 Flood

At Edge	Center	Diameter
3.6	34	9'
2.3	21	12'
1.6	15	15'
1.2	11	18'
.9	8	20'
.7	7	22'

Ceiling to Floor

	12'6"
	15'0"
	17'6"
	20'0"
	22'6"
	25'0"

Initial Footcandles—Multiple Units*

	Ceiling 80%	Walls 50%	Floor 20%
Max. Spacing Over Work Plane	RCR 1	RCR 3	RCR 8
8'6"	57	40	30
7'0"	36	31	24
8'3"	25	22	17
9'8"	18	16	12
11'0"	14	12	10
12'4"	11	10	8

9¾"   13¾"   8¾"

*At work plane 30" above floor. Apply maintenance factor.

DOWN LIGHTING – METHOD B

(b)

Figure 14.24. (Continued)

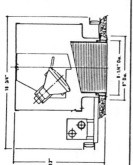

		ILLUMINATION ON VERTICAL PLANE											
		AIMING ANGLE (A) 30° FROM VERTICAL											
Mtg. Dist. (D) in Ft.		2'			4'			6'			8'		
LAMP TYPE		CENTER TO CENTER (S)	F.C.	BEAM HEIGHT (H)	CENTER TO CENTER (S)	F.C.	BEAM HEIGHT (H)	CENTER TO CENTER (S)	F.C.	BEAM HEIGHT (H)	CENTER TO CENTER (S)	F.C.	BEAM HEIGHT (H)
150W PAR-38 FL		2.6'	116	4.0'	5.2'	29	8.0'	7.8'	13	12.0'	10.4'	7	16.0'
150W PAR-38 SP		1.4'	344	3.2'	2.8'	86	6.4'	4.2'	39	9.6'	5.6'	22	12.8'
150W R-40 FL		5.0'	38	5.0'	10.0'	9	10.0'	15.0'	4	15.0'	20.0'	2	20.0'
150W R-40 SP		1.2'	219	3.5'	2.4'	55	7.0'	3.6'	25	10.5'	4.8'	14	14.0'
250W PAR-38 FL (T.H.)		2.6'	203	4.0'	5.2'	51	8.0'	7.8'	23	12.0'	10.0'	13	16.0'
250W PAR-38 SP (T.H.)		1.2'	783	3.0'	1.9'	195	6.0'	2.9'	88	9.0'	3.8'	50	12.0'
300W R-40 FL		4.6'	78	5.0'	9.2'	20	10.0'	13.8'	9	15.0'	18.5'	5	20.0'
300W R-40 SP		1.6'	423	3.5'	3.2'	105	7.0'	4.8'	47	10.5'	6.4'	27	14.0'

EXAMPLE: At a mounting distance (D) of 2' from a vertical surface, a single 150 Watt PAR-38 Flood lamp will provide 116 footcandles and the beam height (H) will be 4.0'. The fixtures, should be installed 2.6' on center (S) for even illumination.

NOTES: (1) FC is average initial footcandles in center of beam.

(2) Beam Height (H) and Beam Length (L) is to the point where illumination drops to approximately 10% of maximum or where illumination becomes insignificant.

(3) Center to Center (S) is the maximum spacing of fixtures for even illumination.

ACCENT LIGHTING

Figure 14.25. Typical accent light illumination chart.

215

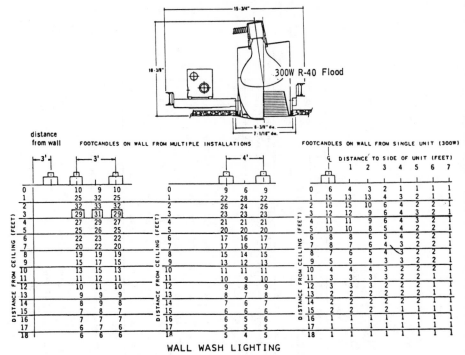

WALL WASH LIGHTING

Figure 14.26. Typical wall washer illumination chart.

When a beam diameter is mentioned, it is assumed that the footcandles at its edge are 10% of those found at its center. All footcandles are given in initial values (not maintained). If your installation varies from these assumptions, then the footcandle values will also vary.

The initial values found in shortcut calculation aids can be converted to maintained values using estimated light loss factors: 0.75 for very clean spaces with excellent maintenance; 0.65 for clean spaces; and 0.55 for dirty spaces.

Although these shortcuts can be useful for preliminary estimations, complete calculations are advised for final planning.

PROJECT: _____   WORK SHEET
DESIGNER: _____
DATE: _____-_____-_____

SUBJECT: LIGHT LOSS FACTOR FOR LUMINAIRE TYPE: _____

LAMP DESCRIPTION: MANUFACTURER: _____
                      ANSI NUMBER: _____
                      INITIAL LUMENS: _____
                      MAINTAINED LUMENS: _____

FACTOR DESCRIPTION: ESTIMATED
                                             FACTOR

1. LIGHT LOSS FACTORS NOT TO BE RECOVERED........:___.____

2. LIGHT LOSS FACTORS TO BE RECOVERED:

   A. AREA ATMOSPHERE: _____

   B. ROOM SURFACE DIRT DEPRECIATION:
      1. AREA ATMOSPHERE............: _____
      2. TIME BETWEEN CLEANINGS.....: ___months____
      3. EXPECTED DIRT DEPRECIATION.: ._____
      4. ROOM CAVITY RATIO..........: _____
                                          RSDD:___.____

   C. LAMP BURN-OUTS: LAMPS REMAINING ON
                      TOTAL LAMPS USED
                                          LBO:___.____

   D. LAMP LUMEN DEPRECIATION: MAINTAINED LUMENS
                               INITIAL LUMENS   LLD:___.____

   E. LUMINAIRE DIRT DEPRECIATION:
      1. AREA ATMOSPHERE............: _____
      2. LUMINAIRE MAINTENANCE
         CATEGORY................: _____
      3. TIME BETWEEN CLEANINGS.....: ___months____
                                          LDD:___.____

LIGHT LOSS FACTOR = (RSDD)(LBO)(LLD)(LDD)........LLF:___.____

217

```
PROJECT: _____                    WORK SHEET
DESIGNER: _____
DATE:       _____-_____-_____


SUBJECT:  DESCRIPTION OF THE TEST AREA, LUMINAIRE AND LAMP
          FOR USE WITH THE IES ZONAL CAVITY METHOD
_____


SUBJECT AREA: _____TEST NUMBER:____


DESCRIPTION OF THE AREA:
    DIMENSIONS:
    LENGTH = ___.___'  WIDTH = ___.___'  AREA = ____.___SQ. FT.
    TOTAL HEIGHT OF THE SPACE = ___.___'
    HEIGHT BETWEEN LUMINAIRE AND WORK PLANE = HRC = ___.___'
    DISTANCE FROM LUMINAIRE PLANE TO CEILING = HCC = ___.___'
    HEIGHT OF WORK PLANE ABOVE FLOOR = HFC = ___.___'
    ROOM SURFACE REFLECTANCES:
    CEILING = PC = .___
    WALLS ABOVE LUMINAIRE MOUNTING PLANE = PW = .___
    WALLS BETWEEN LUMINAIRE AND WORK PLANE = PW = .___
    WALLS BELOW WORK PLANE = PW = .___
    FLOOR = PF = .___ ,


LUMINAIRE:
MANUFACTURER:_____QUANTITY USED IN DESIGN:_____
LUMINAIRE CATALOG NUMBER:_____
MAXIMUM SPACING =
            (SPACING RATIO)(MOUNTING HEIGHT ABOVE WORK PLANE)
          = (___.___)(___.___) = ___.___
LIGHT LOSS FACTOR = LLF = .___


LAMP:
MANUFACTURER:_____LAMPS PER LUMINAIRE:_____
CATALOG OR ORDERING NUMBER (ANSI NUMBER):_____
INITIAL LUMENS PRODUCED BY EACH LAMP:_____
```

218

PROJECT: _____   WORK SHEET
DESIGNER: _____
DATE: _____-_____-_____

SUBJECT: COEFFICIENT OF UTILIZATION AND FOOTCANDLE LEVELS
           DERIVED FROM THE IES ZONAL CAVITY METHOD

TEST NUMBER:_____

COEFFICIENT OF UTILIZATION:
CAVITY RATIOS: ROOM =___.___   CEILING =___.___   FLOOR =___.___
EFFECTIVE CEILING CAVITY REFLECTANCE = PCC = .___
EFFECTIVE FLOOR CAVITY REFLECTANCE = PFC = .___
CU (USING MANUFACTURER'S DATA FOR 20% PFC) = .___
IF THE EFFECTIVE FLOOR CAVITY REFLECTANCE DIFFERS SIGNIFICANT-
   LY FROM 20%, THIS CU IS CORRECTED BY THE APPROPRIATE FACTOR:
        (CU AT .20 PFC)(CORRECTION FACTOR) = CORRECTED CU
        (.____)(___.___) = .___

CALCULATION FOR FOOTCANDLES:

   (NO. OF LUMINAIRES)(LAMPS/LUMINAIRE)(LUMENS/LAMP)(CU)(LLF)
              (TOTAL AREA OF THE SPACE IN SQ. FT.)
        FOOTCANDLES = (____)(____)(_____)(.____)(.____)
                               (_____)
        FOOTCANDLES = _____.___

CALCULATION FOR THE QUANTITY OF LUMINAIRES:

   ____(FOOTCANDLES)(AREA IN SQ. FT.)____
   (LAMPS/LUMINAIRE)(LUMENS/LAMP)(CU)(LLF)
        LUMINAIRE QUANTITY = ___(____)(_____)___
                             (__)(____)(.__)(.__)
        LUMINAIRE QUANTITY = _____

Chapter Fifteen

Recommendations for Standard Interior Luminaires Based on Data Sheet Information

The basic source of equipment information for selecting standard catalog luminaires is the manufacturer's data sheet. A well-designed data sheet contains all the necessary details for choosing the right luminaires.

Although it is impossible to list every pertinent item that might appear on such a data sheet, the following descriptions illustrate the general information that should appear in every luminaire recommendation.

ILLUSTRATIONS

Illustrations help acquaint the designer with unfamiliar equipment. A clear line drawing or unretouched photograph of the installed luminaire is very helpful. Also helpful is a cross section of the luminaire, containing all pertinent dimensional information and illustrating its internal structure.

DIMENSIONS

All data sheets should contain detailed luminaire dimensions. The following dimensions are critical:

1. The depth required for recessing the luminaire (its recessing "height"). This dimension is particularly important when the luminaire is to be

used in a renovation, since only 3 to 9 inches may be available for recessing. The space available for recessing must be slightly greater than the luminaire body dimensions, because the luminaire must stand free from all flammable building materials or be suitably insulated.

2. The diameter or greatest horizontal dimension of the luminaire, including the junction box, mounting brackets, and so on. This is essential if the luminaire is to be placed between the beams of an existing structure.

3. The vertical and horizontal dimensions of all visible parts flush with or below the ceiling line.

4. The aperture dimension (size of the hole through which the light emanates).

5. The width of the overlapping ceiling flange in recessed luminaires. This flange goes around the luminaire's aperture and provides a finishing detail between the aperture and the ceiling; here, one must weigh the visual desirability of a thinner flange with the desirability of a wider flange to cover errors in cutting the aperture hole through crumbly ceiling materials (see Chapter Eighteen, *Trims—Flanges*).

HOUSINGS

The housing, or the enclosure for the luminaire's working parts, will also be specified in the data sheet. Housings for recessed luminaires are usually metal. The data sheet will specify the type and gauge, or thickness, of metal used (note that the smaller the gauge number, the thicker the metal). The following are typical: (1) 16-, 18-, 20-, or 22-gauge sheet steel (see Table 15.1) (2) 16- or 20-gauge sheet aluminum, and (3) cast or die-formed aluminum. The housing may contain holes allowing convective drafts to naturally vent the luminaire housing.

The housings of surface-mounted or portable equipment may be constructed of any material. Luminaires that will be handled during operation should be insulated against heat generated by the lamp.

MOUNTING

Recessed

If the luminaire is to be recessed into a ceiling, the designer must know whether the ceiling construction is either wet (plaster) or dry (metal pan, dry wall, or acoustic tile) to choose an appropriate mounting frame. When used

Table 15.1.   Conversion of Typical Sheet Metal Gauges to Thickness in Inches and Centimeters. Note That When a Metal is Spun or Otherwise Processed, Resulting Thickness May Be Less.

Gauge	Steel	Galvanized Steel	Stainless Steel	Brass	Copper	Aluminum
16	0.0598 in.	0.0637 in.	0.0625 in.	0.0508 in.	0.0650 in.	0.0500 in.
	0.152 cm	0.162 cm	0.159 cm	0.129 cm	0.165 cm	0.127 cm
18	0.0478 in.	0.0516 in.	0.0500 in.	0.0403 in.	0.0490 in.	0.0400 in.
	0.121 cm	0.131 cm	0.127 cm	0.102 cm	0.124 cm	0.102 cm
20	0.0359 in.	0.0396 in.	0.0375 in.	0.0320 in.	0.0350 in.	0.0320 in.
	0.091 cm	0.1001 cm	0.095 cm	0.081 cm	0.089 cm	0.008 cm
22	0.0299 in.	0.0336 in.	0.0312 in.	0.0254 in.	0.0280 in.	0.0250 in.
	0.076 cm	0.085 cm	0.079 cm	0.065 cm	0.071 cm	0.064 cm
24	0.0239 in.	0.0276 in.	0.0250 in.	0.0201 in.	0.0220 in.	0.0200 in.
	0.061 cm	0.070 cm	0.064 cm	0.051 cm	0.056 cm	0.051 cm

in plaster, frames must be prepared with a solid bond between the plaster and the frame's metal sides.

Some incandescent frames are reversible; the side suitable for dry construction has a covering flange that hides the rough edge of the cut tile, and the other side is designed with a minimum trim for plaster.

Most frames are constructed with one of the following materials: (1) steel, usually 20 gauge, (2) aluminum, generally 18 gauge (aluminum does not rust and will not stain a wet ceiling), and (3) 24-gauge stainless steel. Stainless steel frames are not affected by certain corrosive substances, such as those found in acoustic plasters, and should be used if the wet ceiling material is unknown.

The selection of mounting frames for fluorescent luminaires can be very complex. We discuss fluorescent luminaires in Chapter Nineteen (see page 266).

Several devices are used to attach the luminaire to the building structure. In incandescent luminaires, the device usually consists of two flanges extending from the luminaire's mounting frame. These flanges fit into mounting bars (usually 18 in.-long shafts of steel) or steel channels or wire, which are directly attached to building structure. The mounting flanges are adjustable, so the luminaire may be raised or lowered to ensure a flush fit with the ceiling line. Additional leveling adjustments that precisely orient the luminaire's baffle to the ceiling surface may be available.

The mounting equipment for fluorescent luminaires is an integral part of the particular hanging system for the ceiling type that is specified.

Semirecessed

Partially recessed luminaires may be selected for aesthetic reasons or if recessing space is limited. The baffle is frequently extended below the ceiling while the reflector and lamp are hidden above. These luminaires are attached to the building structure by methods similar to those used with fully recessed luminaires.

Surface

The housings of surface-mounted luminaires attach directly to any finished surface (ceiling or floor). Wall-mounted (see page 224) luminaires fall in a separate category.

When luminaires are attached directly to a flammable surface, or a surface that may warp or discolor from luminaire heat, an insulating pad must be placed between the surface and the luminaire.

Pendant

If the luminaire is to hang freely below the surface of the ceiling, a pendant (cord or stem) is required. A swivel should be used with a rigid stem, since rigid pendants can break when hit or may loosen with normal building vibration. Chains are occasionally used to hang fluorescent luminaires or chandeliers.

Portable

Equipment that can be easily moved is usually self-contained in a decorative housing and is supplied with a cord and plug. This description applies to architectural equipment, such as floor-mounted up lights, as well as table and floor lamps.

Track

A track system consists of a linear or curved electrified wireway to which lamp holders can be attached. The tracks may be recessed in, or surface-mounted to, many architectural surfaces. A track system has a vast number of individual parts, and the manufacturer's ordering directions should be followed carefully.

Bracket

When a luminaire is attached to a vertical plane, a bracket mounting is used. The mounting is usually an arm joining the luminaire body and an electrical junction box attached to a wall. When a similar luminaire is attached to the slender vertical pier separating the glass of a window or screen, an adaptation of the bracket, called a "mullion mounting," is used.

Panel

The panel mounting method is used with a transilluminated surface, such as a luminous ceiling (called a "louver-all" ceiling) or luminous wall.

Of the various types of lighting equipment, recessed luminaires are the most difficult to specify and the least understood (even by professionals). Semirecessed luminaires are much like the fully recessed models. For this reason, the remainder of this chapter will stress fully recessed and semirecessed lighting equipment. Pendant, portable, bracket, or track conditions will be specially noted where appropriate.

Seismic

Where earthquakes are prevalent or other forms of vibration are critical, special mounting techniques are recommended. For example, luminaires may be attached directly to the building structure rather than being allowed to rest on hung ceiling framing. Pendant movement is often constrained so that hung luminaires can shift, but not swing.

APERTURE PLATES

Normal luminaire maintenance (cleaning or relamping) often requires the removal of the plate surrounding the aperture, the lens holder, or the baffle holder. These items are cumbersome to hold or, worse yet, may fall and cause injury during luminaire servicing if they are not secured to the luminaire housing. For this reason, there is usually a way to hold these items after they have been removed from the luminaire.

A *jack chain* is a beaded, flexible, metal chain that fastens any removable part to the luminaire's housing.

A *torsion spring* is a V-shaped metal spring resembling an oversized hairpin. By pulling the spring through a slot that contains the spread arms of the V, or by pinching the legs together, the removable item attached to the spring can be lowered but remain attached to the luminaire.

After luminaire servicing, the aperture plate, or lens or baffle holder, must be returned to its operating position and secured. If a torsion spring is used, it returns to its open V shape and maintains its holding function. If the luminaire is not designed to use a torsion spring, then some other form of holding device is necessary. *Latches,* similar to those used for closet or cupboard doors, provide a good mechanical connection. Light items can be held by *magnetic fasteners;* heavier items are frequently attached with *bayonet connectors* or *bolts.*

FINISHES

The metal housings and exterior parts of recessed luminaires are usually finished with paint over metal or in various colors of anodized aluminum.

Paint

Paint finishes must withstand continuous heat conditions (without discoloring or flaking) and handling abuse during installation and maintenance. Enamels baked to the surface are particularly strong and therefore are superior to air-dried finishes. A primer bond is often applied to the naked metal to obtain better paint adhesion. There are several methods for cleaning and preparing the metal surfaces, such as phosphate coatings, the patented Bonderizing, and other proprietary processes.

Anodizing

Anodizing is a process used on aluminum in which electrical and chemical treatments cause the surface of the metal to develop a permanent color and specularity. High-purity anodized aluminum reflectors are the most widely used precision reflectors. "Alzak" is a common patented anodizing process.

Protection

Visible surfaces, both painted and anodized, must be protcted during installation. Baffles with highly specular finishes are often enclosed in translucent plastic during installation (bagged fluorescent louvers will still provide a limited amount of light during construction) or they may not be delivered until after all surfaces have been cleaned by the installing contractor. Under certain conditions, installers may be required to wear soft white cotton gloves when they place particularly delicate baffles—an instruction that is rarely followed.

REFLECTORS

Luminaire reflectors are usually fabricated from one of the following: (1) sheet steel, painted white for diffuse reflectance; (2) 16-, 18-, 20-, or 22-gauge sheet anodized aluminum that has a polished specular, etched spread, diffuse, or embossed reflective surface (depending on the intended performance of the luminaire). Glass was once very popular in specular reflectors, but is seldom seen today except in industrial luminaires. Chrome reflectors are rarely used now because of their high cost and low reflectivity.

In addition to the pattern of reflectance (specular, spread, diffuse, or a combination thereof), specifiers should always note the minimum percentage of reflectance required (painted surfaces should be at least 85% reflective), since the quality of the reflector is partly judged on this basis.

ELECTRICAL REQUIREMENTS

Most data sheets devote one section to electrical requirements, including socket type, and size of wire supplied. Note that incandescent or HID lamp holders with porcelain shells are most desirable, since they can withstand the high temperatures that prevail in the base of the lamp. Plastic lamp-holder shells are used only in low-temperature conditions.

Wire Sizes and Types

Generally, incandescent luminaires using less than 300 watts are internally wired with 18- or 16-gauge AF wire (asbestos covered). (Remember that the smaller the gauge number, the more power the wire will carry.) If the incandescent luminaire draws from 300 to 1000 watts, 16- or 14-gauge silicone-covered wire is typical. HID luminaires usually employ the same wiring as their incandescent counterparts. In fluorescent luminaires, 18- or 16-gauge 150°C SPT wire (thermoplastic covered) is generally supplied. Thermoplastic coverings are satisfactory for low temperatures; silicone insulators are preferred for high-heat conditions.

Manufacturers usually supply 5-foot leads for connecting recessed luminaires to the power distribution system. They also supply either a ⅜- or ½-inch flexible conduit connector. The installing contractor supplies the flexible conduit (popularly called "greenfield;" the connector is therefore a "greenfield connector").

Ballasts

Ballasts should carry the following ratings and/or approvals. (1) *Type* should always be indicated (for fluorescent: rapid start, dimming/flashing, etc.; for HID: autotransformer, constant wattage, etc. (2) The *sound classification* is important (A is the quietest; B, C, and D are progressively louder). (3) *Power factor* should usually be rated as "high" (even though a "low" is generally cheaper). (4) *Class* is a UL indication denoting safety devices such as the generally accepted Class P with automatic resetting (indicating internal thermal protection). (5) Particularly for external applications, the *minimum starting temperature* is important. (6) *Label requirements* must be noted. These include: ETL—certified by the Electrical Testing Laboratories; CBM compliance—satisfies Certified Ballast Manufacturers specifications for performance; UL listed—meets Underwriters Laboratories requirements for safety; and CSA—meets Canadian Standards Association requirements for use in Canadian installations. Most important, the ballast must be designed for the exact type of lamp used in the luminaire. (See Chapters Seven and Eight for additional details and explanations). Thermal cutouts may be required.

STANDARD AND PREWIRED LUMINAIRES

The terms "standard," and "prewired," refer to the method by which wires leading to a recessed luminaire are terminated.

The standard luminaire usually has a greenfield connector attached to the greenfield flexible conduit which joins the luminaire to an electrical junction box provided by an electrical contractor. The junction box, or "JB," is connected to a rigid metal conduit that distributes the building's electric power from centralized circuit-breaker panels. In addition to the greenfield connector, the luminaire manufacturer may also include a 4- to 6-foot length of appropriately sized wire. The installing contractor then supplies the actual greenfield flexible conduit and threads the wire through it to connect the luminaire and the junction box.

The luminaire, however, can also be prewired. Prewired luminaires are supplied with a junction box already attached to the luminaire's mounting frame; both the wiring and greenfield between the junction box and the luminaire are also supplied by the manufacturer. Although this system saves considerable installation time, it is not permitted in some localities. Therefore, if rulings are unknown, order "standard wired" luminaires.

In certain states (Connecticut is one), the junction boxes supplied with prewired luminaires must be suitable for "through wiring," which means that the installer can electrically link several luminaires, rather than returning each luminaire's wiring to a power distribution point. Local regulations regarding the size of the junction box and its attachment to the luminaire must be followed where prewired conditions are required or desired.

ACCESS

In the initial building design phase, it must be decided whether the lighting installation will be serviced from below the ceiling or from an attic area above the luminaire. Thus luminaires may be chosen according to the ease of accessibility of the lamp and reflector from either the top or bottom.

In certain localities, building codes require that luminaires be installed or removed through the finished ceiling aperture. This access plan is also advantageous if equipment orders are rushed. The manufacturer can often supply the mounting frame from stock and deliver the luminaire body at a later date, thereby expediting completion of the building's ceiling installation. Remember that if the luminaire is totally removable through the ceiling aperture or if the luminaire body is to be installed later, the luminaires must have housings no larger than their apertures or aperture plates. However, if the luminaire body is larger than its ceiling aperture, it must be placed in the ceiling cavity before the ceiling is closed. In this case, the contractor should be aware that he or she must install the total luminaire before closing the ceiling.

PHOTOMETRICS

The photometric test data developed for any luminaire should be calculated by an agency independent of the manufacturer. In this way, the user can be fairly certain that the data is objective and not distorted by the enthusiasm of a manufacturer for its product. Two companies are well known for independent testing. They are the Independent Testing Laboratories (ITL) and the Electrical Testing Laboratories (ETL).

The following data should be available for any luminaire.

C.I.E. Classification

The Commission International de l'Eclairage has established five basic luminaire classifications, to which the U.S. Illuminating Engineering Society has added a sixth and this author has added a seventh. These classifications describe the luminous performance of the luminaire.

Asymmetric. (Author's category) Very simply, the light distribution is not symmetrical about the vertical axis of the luminaire; it is directed permanently or flexibly to one or more sides of the vertical axis. Two major categories of luminaires cast asymmetric light patterns: accent lights and wall washers. Accent lights allow the designer to highlight objects or surfaces by directing the light beam at an angle away from the vertical axis. Wall washers cast light patterns over vertical surfaces, thereby evenly "washing" them with light. Wall washers include luminaires designed to make surfaces appear smooth and those designed to accentuate surface textures.

Direct. To be classified as a direct lighting system, luminaires must emit 90–100% of their light output downward. The spread of the light beam may be either wide or narrow.

Semidirect. Although an upward amount of light is present, 60–90% of the total light output is directed downward in semidirect lighting.

General-diffuse. The upward and downward light emissions are equal (producing about 40–60% of the total light output).

Semi-indirect. Between 60 and 90% of the total output is directed upward.

Indirect. From 90 to 100% of the total light output is directed upward.

Direct-indirect (I.E.S. category). The distribution is similar to general-diffuse, but very little light is emitted at angles near horizontal.

Lamp Information

Two variables affect a photometric evaluation: the luminaire's optical features and the lamp used. Because any change in the lamp type may heavily influence a luminaire's photometric performance, lamps should be accurately described by standard codes, not by abbreviated descriptions. The initial lumens of the lamp should also be given, as this quantity may vary from manufacturer to manufacturer or increase if a particular lamp type has been improved.

Spacing Ratio

The maximum distance between luminaires that results in even lighting is determined by the maximum spacing ratio. It is usually stated in relation to the luminaire's mounting height above the work surface (spacing ratio multiplied by the luminaire's height above the work surface). For example, a luminaire with a ratio of 0.5 can be used on 5-foot centers if mounted 10 feet above the work surface.

Candlepower Distribution Curve

Candlepower distribution data should be presented graphically (see Chapter Eleven).

Photometric Summaries in Table Form

Candlepower may be stated numerically at angles of 0° (straight down), 15°, 25°, and so on (which facilitates reading small charts). For rectangular fluorescent luminaires, readings are stated parallel to the lamps, at 45° to them, and at normal (right) angles. Other luminaires with asymmetric light distributions (e.g., oval-beam PAR lamp holders) have their data presented for more than one significant angle. A *lumen summary* may state total lumens as increments of 0–30°, 0–40°, and so on. *Average footlamberts*, *maximum footlamberts*, and *footlambert ratios* may also be presented at 0°, 45°, 55°, and other significant angles to aid in direct glare evaluation (see Chapter Fourteen, *Visual Comfort Probability*).

Coefficient of Utilization Chart

The coefficient of utilization should be developed to facilitate use of the zonal cavity method of calculation (see Chapter Fourteen).

Isofootcandle Diagrams

Isofootcandle diagrams illustrate a luminaire's light pattern as it will look when it hits any surface (see Chapter Eleven). These diagrams are usually developed for accent lights and exterior luminaires.

Quick Computation Charts

Quick computation charts allow the designer to arrive at a rough estimate of luminaire performance without making extensive calculations.

LABELS

In addition to the labeling requirements outlined in this chapter, luminaires may carry other information. In all cases, the labels should be placed on the luminaire itself, hidden from normal viewing angles, but in full view to a maintenance person making adjustments or changing lamps.

Manufacturer

The name, address, and telephone number of the manufacturer of the luminaire should be listed.

Wattage and Lamp Type

The maximum wattage the luminaire can accommodate must be listed. In addition, the catalog abbreviation or code (ANSI) of the lamp designated for each luminaire is helpful when changing lamps.

Underwriters Laboratories (UL)

The luminaire itself, as well as the ballast, may carry a UL label. This label assures the user that Underwriters Laboratories has found sample luminaires to be electrically safe; the UL label says nothing about other performance features. In some localities, a UL label is required on all luminaires used in public construction. The Canadian Standards Association (CSA) label is the Canadian counterpart of UL, although its requirements may differ from those of UL.

Union Labels

If an appropriate union label is not attached to a luminaire, union electricians may refuse to install it. In certain parts of the country, a local union must wire the luminaire; a special local union number is then required. In New York City, for example, all luminaires must carry the IBEW (International Brotherhood of Electrical Workers) Local #3 label. If a designer intends to use a large number of luminaires wired by another union in the IBEW, Local #3 will ask to dismantle and rewire them.

SPECIAL REQUIREMENTS

Manufacturers frequently include "special requirements" paragraphs on their data sheets. The special requirements are limitations to luminaire use. For example, the luminaire may be approved only "for fireproof construction." This indicates that, unless the building is constructed of fireproof materials, the luminaire must be specially insulated.

ACCESSORIES

Luminaire data sheets often include lists of accessories that can be used with the luminaire. The most common items are described below.

Sloping ceiling adapters are used when a luminaire is mounted in a slanted ceiling. They keep the luminaire housing vertical and the light directed straight down.

Concrete pour boxes provide a strong housing for luminaires installed in wet concrete construction.

Scallop shields can be used in luminaires with reflectors to block out part of the light beam. The shield will prevent a luminaire placed close to a vertical surface from casting scallops of light on the surface.

When used with certain luminaires, *air handling systems* make them an integral part of the air-conditioning system.

Louvers may be supplied to control objectionable light spill or to prevent direct viewing of the light source.

Color filters can be added to some luminaires. Unfortunately, all color filters fade with usage, so provisions must be made for replacement. Light pink and light blue are most commonly used although they are also the most fragile of all colors. Coated filters are more fragile than filters in which the color permeates the glass. If a luminaire operates with intense heat, precautions must be made against filter cracking. Heat-resistant filters can be made of borosilicate glass, or ordinary glass may be divided into strips to allow for expansion; the split marks do not affect light output and do *not* indicate that the filter is broken.

Auxiliary *lenses* may be added to modify light beam patterns of some luminaires. The 50° spread lens is especially common. This lens increases the luminaire's light distribution in one axis of its beam.

GUARANTEE

All manufacturers should guarantee that their products will be free of defects in material and workmanship for a period of more than 1 year *after delivery*. Guarantees are usually limited to the replacement of the defective part or total luminaire and do not cover the labor costs of removing and reinstalling equipment on the job site.

ORDERING DATA

Data sheets contain lists of numbers and letters that comprise luminaire ordering codes. Since each manufacturer codes equipment differently, it would be impossible to list all of the elements of the various codes.

If the designer recommends a luminaire that is in any way different from a manufacturer's standard, the code "SP" should be placed after the standard ordering code. If a part of the ordering information cannot be determined when the luminaire is recommended, a question mark should be substituted for that part of the ordering code.

If a sales representative who has provided aid in the selection of a luminaire gets a commission on sales, it would be generous to place his or her code letter/number or initials at the beginning or end of the ordering code.

THERMAL PROTECTION

Luminaires using fluorescent and HID light sources are thermally protected through their ballasts. For example, the Class P requirement (see Chapter Seven, *Auxiliary Equipment—Ballasts*) provides an automatic thermal protector built into the ballast case that deactivates the ballast when it exceeds a permissible temperature.

After October 1982, UL also requires thermal insulation protectors on all recessed incandescent luminaires, with the exception of those installed in poured concrete or installed in cavities where the building's thermal insulation would be in direct contact with the luminaire.

These incandescent luminaire thermal protectors consist of a heating coil and thermostat located in a housing that protrudes from the luminaire. The heater maintains a constant temperature for the thermostat. If insulation is laid too close to the luminaire, the heat generated from the heating coil will not be dissipated. The resulting heat buildup will cause the thermostat to disconnect the luminaire. These switches are called insulation detectors because they sense the presence of insulation.

Chapter Sixteen

Glossary of Construction Materials for Lighting Equipment

Construction methods, products and specific applications are discussed in chapters dealing with luminaires. Only the distinguishing aspects of common materials are described in this topic.

Acetate.   *See* Cellulose Acetate.

Acrylic.   *See* Polymethyl Methacrylate.

Asbestos.   A fibrous mineral. Properties: electrically and thermally nonconducting, incombustible, chemically resistant. Applications: electrical and thermal insulators. This is a dangerous material, and many of its applications have been outlawed.

Acrylonitrile-butadiene-styrene (ABS).   A thermoplastic. Properties: nontransparent, resilient to impact, slow burning, exceptional dimensional stability in the presence of heat, resistant to flex-fatigue, scuffs, and stains, can be chrome plated. Processing: heat formed, machined, laminated, nailed, screwed, stapled. Applications: luminaire housings when resistance to corrosion and harsh handling is important.

Aluminum.   A nonferrous metal. Properties: soft, easily formed, good electrical conductor, good heat conductor; can be anodized. Processing: formed, die-cast, extruded. Applications: reflectors, housings, lightweight electrical conductors. Cost comparison: moderate to expensive.

Brass.   An alloy of copper and zinc. Properties: medium hard, resistant to corrosion. Processing: formed, die-cast, extruded. Applications: fittings requiring corrosion resistance and structural stability. Cost comparison: expensive.

Bronze.   An alloy of copper and tin. Properties: medium hard, resistant to corrosion. Processing: formed, die-cast, extruded. Applications: fittings requiring corrosion resistance and structural stability. Cost comparison: expensive.

Butyrate.   See Cellulose Acetate Butyrate.

Cellulose Acetate (Acetate).   A thermoplastic. Properties: self-extinguishing in the presence of fire. Processing: bent, heat-formed, cut. Applications: photographic and drafting film, protective laminate.

Cellulose Acetate Butyrate (Butyrate).   A thermoplastic. Properties: more bluish than acetate, unpleasant odor, high impact resistance, yellows and loses strength in the presence of ultraviolet, possesses good light transmission with slight diffusion, becomes brittle with age. Processing: molded and heat formed. Applications: formed shapes used for exterior luminaire closures where vandalism is prevalent.

Copper.   A nonferrous metal. Properties: superior conductor of heat and electricity, soft, subject to verdigris (a poisonous surface pigment that develops in the presence of moisture). Applications: decorative surfaces, electrical conductors. Cost comparison: expensive.

Glass.   Most commonly a silica, soda, and lime combination. Types: crystal glass for decorative luminaires, opal glass for diffusion, borosilicate glass for thermal shock resistant uses, soft lead-crystal glass for optical-quality lens systems and chandelier pendants. Properties: hard, dimensionally stable, does not change shape or color with age, excellent light transmission and refraction, fireproof, readily available, economic to maintain, will not support a static charge and attract dust. Processing: hot formed or cold cut. Applications: lenses, reflectors.

Impact Polymethyl Methacrylate (Impact Acrylic).   A thermoplastic similar to regular polymethyl methacrylate, but with improved impact resistance. Properties: impact strength five to eight times that of standard acrylic, transparency good but slightly diffuse, thermal resistance less satisfactory than standard acrylic, good scratch resistance. Processing: same as acrylic. Applications: impact resistant closures. Cost comparison: moderately expensive.

Melamine-Formaldehyde.   A thermoset plastic. Properties: resistant to heavy wear, impervious to most chemicals and stains, brittle unless laminated to a suitable substructure, not transparent. Applications: laminated to decorative exterior finishes. Trade names: Formica, Micarta, Texolite.

Nylon. A thermoplastic polyamide resin. Properties: slick surface, resistant to corrosive chemicals and impact. Applications: gears, electrical connector bodies, gaskets, insulators.

Phenolic. One of the oldest thermoplastics. Properties: fireproof, heat resistant, dark colored, excellent insulation. Applications: luminaire baffles, electrical plugs, face plates.

Polycarbonate. A thermoplastic. Properties: toughest transparent plastic available for lenses, good electrical insulator, self-extinguishing in the presence of fire, 87% light transmission (clear sheet), not as stable as standard impact acrylic with regard to ultraviolet radiation. Processing: cold formed, extruded/embossed, injection molded. Applications: bulletproof canopies and shields, vandal-resistant luminaires.

Polyester. A thermoset plastic that is called fiber glass when reinforced with glass fibers, burlap, jute, sisal, or decorative fabrics. Processing: hand formed. Applications: simulated stained glass, architectural forms (such as ceiling coffers produced in small quantities). Cost comparison: moderate to inexpensive.

Polyethylene. A thermoplastic. Properties: flexible as a thin film, clear to milky-white, yellows in the presence of ultraviolet radiation, low heat sensitivity (can be heat sealed at low temperatures), stains easily. Applications: protective sheets and temporary films. Cost comparison: inexpensive.

Polymethyl Methacrylate (Acrylic). The most popular thermoplastic used in lighting. Properties: superior optical properties, superior light stability, freedom from inherent colorations, superior impact strength (but not as good as polycarbonate or impact acrylic), good thermal resistance (but not equal to polycarbonate), will not smoke when heated, odorless. Processing: drilled, sanded, sawed, heat bent, extruded/embossed, injection molded. Applications: for closures in structures governed by strict lighting codes. Cost comparison: moderate. Trade names: Plexiglas, Lucite, Acrilyte, Perspex.

Polypropylene. A thermoplastic. Properties: can be bent repeatedly without breaking, lightest plastic in terms of weight. Applications: lightweight structures, "living hinges" (extruded, one-piece, noiseless piano-type hinges).

Polystyrene (Styrene). A popular thermoplastic. Properties: good initial optical properties, poor stability in the presence of ultraviolet radiation or heat (material yellows and becomes brittle), low thermal resistance, produces black smoke when heated. Processing: extruded/embossed, injection molded. Applications: low-cost transparent or translucent closures and structures where a short life is anticipated, yellowing is acceptable, and fire regulations do not apply. Cost comparison: inexpensive.

Polyvinyl Chloride (PVC). A thermoplastic. Properties: poor ultraviolet stability (yellows), self-extinguishing in the presence of fire, odorless, transparent or opaque, rigid or flexible. Applications: flexible rear-screen projection surfaces, treated films resembling leather or fabrics.

Silicone. A thermoset plastic. Properties: Nothing will adhere to the surface once it has "set"; it remains flexible. Applications: gaskets, caulking, adhesives, insulators.

Stabilized Plastics. Plastics that are treated to prevent rapid deterioration from ultraviolet or infrared light. Examples: stabilized polystyrene, stabilized butyrate, stabilized polycarbonate. Properties: similar to their unstabilized counterparts. Applications: long-life installations. Processing: similar to their unstabilized counterparts. Cost comparison: slightly more expensive than their unstabilized counterparts.

Steel. A ferrous material. Properties: dimensionally stable, great tensile strength, wear resistance, susceptible to oxidation. Processing: bent, molded by several processes. Applications: luminaire housings and hardware. Cost comparison: inexpensive.

Steel, Stainless. A ferrous metal. Like steel, but resistant to rust and chemical corrosion. Cost comparison: more expensive than steel.

Styrene. *See* Polystyrene.

Thermoset Plastics. One of the two major families of plastic materials. Thermoset plastics are infusible and insoluble once they have been heat softened, molded, and chemically set.

Thermoplastics. One of the two major families of plastic materials. Thermoplastics may be continuously softened by heat and then hardened by cooling.

BIBLIOGRAPHY

Clarkson, Clarence W., "Through a Glass Lightly," *Lighting Design and Application* (December 1973): 48–51.

Weil, Luis G., "Picking a Plastic," *Lighting Design and Application* (December 1973): 37–39.

Winfield, Armand G., "Plastics are Everywhere," *Display World* (May 1970): 20–21, 45–50.

Zarosi, Robert W., "Diffusers: Which One, Where and Why?" *Illuminating Engineering* (July 1970): 412–19.

Chapter Seventeen

Luminaire Categories

An abundant variety of luminaire designs are available today; to describe them all or predict those that may soon be on the market would be impossible. Initially, luminaire design was limited to decorative items, such as chandeliers, sconces, and table or floor lamps. To those basic items were added "practical fixtures"—mostly functional luminaires. In the recent era of comparatively sophisticated application, the demand for both decorative and functional luminaires has increased substantially, and there has been a corresponding increase in types of equipment and number of manufacturers.

The variety of detail in luminaire design has grown to be overwhelming. In this limited space, only the major categories of luminaire design and function can be discussed.

Most architectural luminaires currently on the market can be divided into the following categories. The categories are cumulative as the list progresses. Several subcategories may apply within any one heading. Most categories have been previously described in detail. For a discussion of baffles and trims, see Chapters Eighteen, Nineteen, and Twenty.

Use:
  Decorative
  Emergency
  Utilitarian
Source of Light:
  Cold-cathode
  Fluorescent*

*Most frequently used.

High Intensity Discharge (HID)*
Incandescent (standard high- and low-voltage, tungsten–halogen)*
Mounting:
  Bracket (including cove, mullion, sconce)
  Panel (luminous ceiling/wall, soffit, canopy)
  Pendant
  Portable
  Recessed (in dry wall, wet plaster, or suspended surfaces)
  Semirecessed (in dry wall, wet plaster, or suspended surfaces)
  Surface (permanently attached)
  Track
Distribution of Light:
  Asymmetric:
    Accent (variable light beam axis)
    Wall/ceiling washers:
      Shadowless effect on surfaces
      Grazing of surface irregularities
  Direct (C.I.E. classifaction: 90–100% light output downward)
  Direct-indirect (I.E.S. up and down, little from sides)
  General-diffuse (C.I.E.: output equal about the source)
  Indirect (C.I.E.: 90–100% output upward)
  Semi-direct (C.I.E.: 60–90% downward, 10–40% upward)
  Semi-indirect (C.I.E.: 10–40% downward, 60–90% upward)
Control (final light controlling element or light-emitting closure):
  Diffuser:
    Shape (dropped, drum, flat, regressed, spherical, etc.)
    Type (opal/albalite/lucent, ceramic paint, decorative, etc.)
  Lamp (when the lamp also serves as the luminaire optics):
    Aperture (a special fluorescent or incandescent lamp)
    Decorative (globe-shaped, chimney, flame, etc.)
    Parabolic aluminized reflector (PAR shape)
    Reflector (R shape)
  Lens
  Louver (parabolic wedge, etc.)
  Open reflector (without lens)
  Reflector and transparent closure
  Refractor:
    Shape (dropped, flat, recessed, tubular, etc.)
    Type:
      Conical prismatic
      Fresnel

*Most frequently used.

Linear ribbed prismatic
Planoconvex
Spread (in degrees)
Stepped
Baffle:
  Annular ring
  Collar
  Decorative
  Housing (housing serves as its own baffle)
  Louver (concentric ring, egg crate, parallel blade, decorative)
  Miniature groove
  None (e.g., when a lens is used in a fluorescent luminaire)
  Reflector (Cone)
Trim (for recessed luminaires):
  Type:
    Air handling
    Connector cover (bracket/mullion, plate, junction box cover, etc.)
    Decorative (Ornamental Shaped Bezel, etc.)
    Eyelid (for wall washers)
    Flange (minimum trim)
    Hidden (for semirecessed luminaires, etc.)
    Plate (an aperture cover which may be surface or flush) ·
    Regressed return
    Splay (straight or curved) return
    Trimless
  Shape (rectangular, round, square)
  Ceiling construction:
    Dry (for wall board, ceiling tile, etc.)
    Wet (for plaster)
Housing (for surface-mounted or semirecessed luminaires):
  Cylindrical
  Decorative
  Rectilinear
  Spherical
Accessories:
  Air handling attachments
  Concrete pour box
  Emergency auxiliary source
  Filter/lens holder
  Scallop shield
  Sloping ceiling adapter

Chapter Eighteen

Recessed Utilitarian
Incandescent Luminaires

In this chapter, we restrict our discussion of luminaires of the following types: (1) Recessed equipment, or luminaires whose housings are hidden above the ceiling line. (Semirecessed and surface-mounted luminaires are similar, but part or all of their mechanism is enclosed in a simple exposed housing). (2) Utilitarian equipment, which is used when lighting output is more important than the mechanical appearance. (3) Equipment for incandescent light sources (which are frequently adapted for HID sources). (4) Equipment with direct or asymmetric distribution, which include downlights, accent lights, and wall washers.

LUMINAIRES DESCRIBED BY FUNCTION

Downlights

Incandescent downlights usually have a direct light distribution (most of the useful light is directed downward). Their inherent control of highlights develops the quality and character of shadow. General downlighting is frequently used as the total illumination for an area, although it can be effectively supplemented with other types of lighting.

From the designer's point of view, the best possible downlight should: (1) have exposed surfaces with a pleasing and appropriate design; (2) use virtually all the light produced by the lamp effectively and efficiently; (3) be easy to maintain and last a lifetime; (4) be adaptable to changes in intensity, color, and character of the light; and (5) have a controlled apparent brightness.

Application Tips

Reflected glare and inappropriate harsh shadows on tasks must be minimized. These problems can be controlled if the units are placed on tight centers (close together), or if the light output is spread over a large area. If narrow distribution outputs are used, additional wall lighting and/or highly reflective vertical surfaces are advisable. In fact, in all cases a high reflectance on all surfaces improves brightness relationships.

Downlight luminaires placed too close to a wall create scallops of light on wall surfaces. If scallops are not desired as a decorative effect, luminaires should be placed at least half of the maximum spacing distance from the wall.

Open Reflector Downlights

One of the most common, and often the most efficient, downlight luminaires uses an inexpensive general service lamp in a polished reflector to produce controlled light without a lens (see Figure 18.1). The reflector serves two purposes. It redirects (by reflection) the otherwise wasted upward component of the light source down through the aperture and distributes it in a useful pattern. The reflector may also be used to minimize the bright glare that may be visible at normal viewing angles. To be effective for this second purpose, the reflector must be located in the luminaire's housing so that the reflection or direct image of the lamp is cut off at 45° above nadir (straight down).

Relamping for open reflector downlights is easy. One simply replaces the lamp through the open aperture. Since no other part of the luminaire is handled, maintenance personnel do not have to remove plates (which are eventually covered with dirty fingerprints), baffles (which may become twisted or scratched), or lenses (which may break).

One major disadvantage of the open reflector design is that the reflector is not protected from dust and general grime. This is particularly serious in atmospheres dense with grease (kitchens), dust (any modern city), corrosive vapors (industrial plants and locations near salt water), or water vapor (bathrooms, etc.)

Open reflector downlights are frequently used in protected areas with low ceilings (8–10 ft) if it is desirable to have the illumination produce a medium shadow value on objects. They are also installed where luminaires with inexpensive relamping costs are desired.

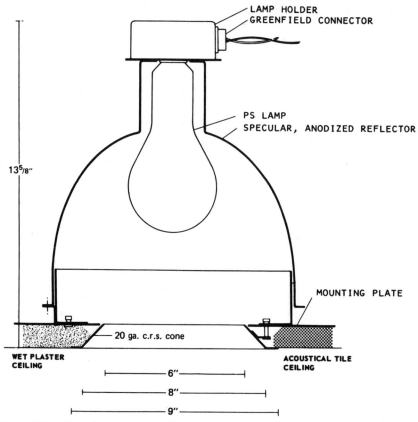

Figure 18.1.   Typical open reflector down light. (Reproduced, by permission, from Lighting and Electronics Co.)

There are many sophisticated designs for open reflector downlights. One example uses a silver-bowl lamp in a luminaire that resembles (and is often called) a mushroom (see Figure 18.2). The lamp's light is directed up into the reflector and then reflected down through the aperture. The result is a carefully controlled illumination pattern that is very low in aperture brightness at normal viewing angles. Unfortunately, this reflector system is costly and requires a deep recessing area. Another example features a multiple-part reflector: Most of the reflector is dedicated to down lighting, but certain segments direct light to wall surfaces. These luminaires, while simultaneously providing down lighting, also light one wall, two walls, three walls, or four walls. Although their wall washing is not as dramatic as with luminaires dedicated only to this purpose, they do allow the wall washing of

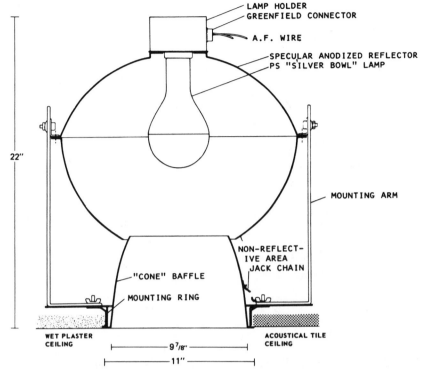

Figure 18.2.   Typical open reflector down light with a "mushroom" reflector. (Reproduced, by permission, from Lighting and Electronics Co.)

two or more right-angle or opposing surfaces from a single aperture (a technique that is outside the abilities of their dedicated counterparts).

Reflector with Lens or Diffuser

One downlight type usually combines a general service lamp with a reflector and a refractor, as shown in Figure 18.3. (The Fresnel lens is the most popular refractor, although stepped and prismatic lenses are also used.) The lens provides additional directional control of the light as it leaves the luminaire and may also soften the shadow of value of the illumination. The lens covers the ceiling aperture, thus keeping dust from the reflector and providing a heat shield. Luminaires using a diffuser rather than a refractor merely inefficiently scatter the light beam in all directions.

There are two disadvantages to this luminaire type. The surface of the lens collects light (particularly if it is partially diffuse), so the viewer may be

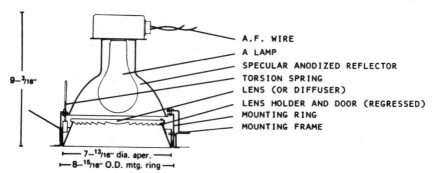

Figure 18.3. Typical down light with a reflector and lens or diffuser. (Reproduced, by permission, from Lighting and Electronics Co.)

conscious of a bright spot at the aperture. To some extent, this brightness may be controlled by regressing the lens above the ceiling line or by painting the bright but optically inert edges of the lens (a process called "colouvering"). A second disadvantage is that maintenance is more difficult, since the lens must be removed when a lamp change or cleaning is required.

Fresnel lens luminaires are often used where ceilings are low, heat is a problem, and the atmosphere is wet, corrosive, or dirty.

No Reflectors or Lenses

Downlights without reflectors or lenses are commonly called "cans." They have cylindrical housings and usually rely on a PAR or R lamp for optical control (see Figure 18.4).

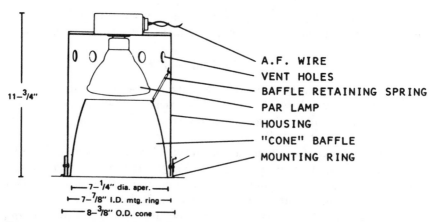

Figure 18.4. Typical downlight without reflectors and lenses. (Reproduced, by permission, from Lighting and Electronics Co.)

The housing design may be very simple or include complicated baffling. The simple "can" is comparatively low in initial cost, but the reflectorized lamps needed in it are relatively expensive. Therefore, the original installations can be a bargain, but the client may pay heavily in relamping costs for the rest of the installation's life.

However, reflectorized lamp installations have several advantages over other types of downlights: (1) The lamps are long-lived and efficient. (2) When the lamp is changed, the reflector and lens (integral parts of the lamp) are also replaced. In effect, the optical system is renewed every 2000–4000 hours. (3) Downlights placed in high ceilings that use high-wattage PAR and (to a lesser extent) R lamps provide efficient point-source illumination.

Luminaires with Asymmetric Light Distributions

Any luminaire whose light pattern may be permanently or temporarily focused away from nadir (straight down) has an asymmetric light distribution. The accent light and wall washer are the two types most commonly used in architectural installations.

Accent Lights

The accent light has a flexibile lamp (and therefore light beam) position. It is used to emphasize objects or areas at some lighting angle other than perpendicular to the floor. This discussion concerns luminaires used to accent statues, paintings, moldings, graphics, and so on.

Since it is easy to misapply accent lights, the designer should keep the following points in mind: (1) Accent lights are designed to "spotlight" rather than evenly cover walls; they cannot evenly illuminate vertical surfaces. (2) Most accent lights are only adjustable to 35° from nadir (see Figure 18.5). Although completely recessed models that tilt up to 50° would be ideal, there are baffle, glare, and other problems with this extent of flexibility. (3) Accent lights usually have a limited rotation, which prevents their internal electric wiring from twisting inside the housing. Usually 358° of rotation is sufficient for accenting (the swivel-stopping mechanism takes the remaining 2°), provided the accented object is not placed within the forbidden 2° zone.

Application Tips. (1) Accurately compute the aiming angle so the subject will be totally illuminated. Isolux diagrams and manufacturer's guides are helpful. (2) To ensure that the accented object will not fall within the unusable 2° when the luminaire is installed, place an arrow on each accent light symbol shown on the reflected ceiling plan. The arrow will indicate the principal direction of focus. (3) If installation and maintenance problems are

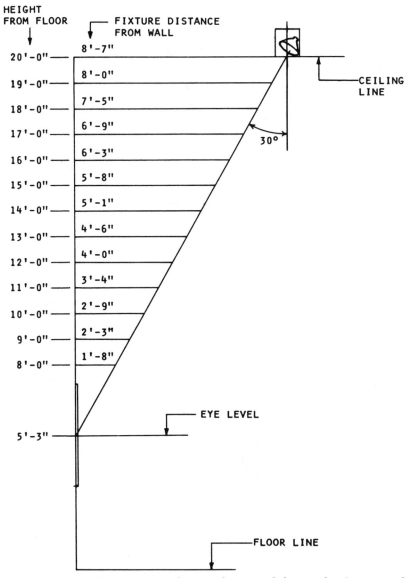

Figure 18.5. Typical fixture mounting locations for picture lighting with 30° aiming angle. (Reproduced, by permission, from Lighting Services Co.)

to be avoided, recommend a recessed unit without a lens or framing device. (4) Accent lights can effectively be used as downlights in sloped ceilings if the housing is installed at the angle of the ceiling line and the lamp is aimed straight down.

One subcategory of accent light uses an adjustable reflectorized lamp without a separate lens or reflector (see Figures 18.6 and 18.7). These lamps spotlight an area but do not provide precise definition. To achieve the optimal performance of these luminaires, the following conditions should prevail: (1) The luminaire should be capable of 358° of rotation. (2) It should have a minimum tilt of 35°. (3) An accent light should accommodate color filters and spread lenses and be able to hold both the filter and the lens at the same time. (4) It should have adequate baffling to prevent direct sight of the lamp from normal viewing angles when the lamp is tilted. (5) The luminaire's working components should be easily accessible from either below or above the ceiling line in order to adjust direction, change lamps, change color filters and lenses, and/or change the orientation of the light pattern produced by the lamp (some of the larger incandescent PAR lamps produce oval beam patterns). (6) It should be possible to lock all adjustable features in place once they have been focused by the lighting designer so that maintenance personnel do not inadvertently alter the light scheme. (7) An accent light should accommodate a variety of lamp wattages and beam distributions without the need for external adapters. (8) Any accent light should be efficient; some direct most of their light inside the lamp housing when "tilted" more than 10°.

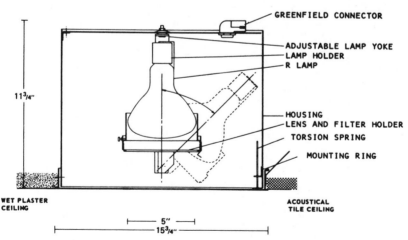

Figure 18.6. Typical accent light using an adjustable reflector lamp without lenses or reflectors. (Reproduced, by permission, from Lighting and Electronics Co.)

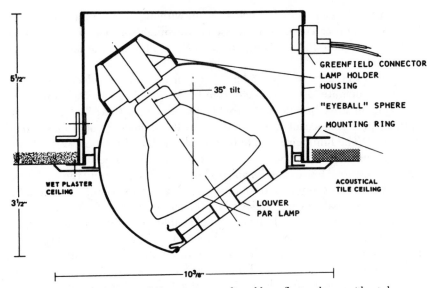

Figure 18.7. Typical accent light using an adjustable reflector lamp without lenses or reflectors—variation called "eyeball." (Reproduced, by permission, from Lighting and Electronics Co.)

A second subcategory of accent light, which uses a lens and reflector system with framing devices, produces a sharply defined beam pattern (see Figure 18.8). These devices are often used to accent paintings; the light pattern terminates in a straight, hard line at the edge of the canvas or frame. Although the lighting produced by these units can be both effective and dramatic, there are many application and maintenance problems. These ongoing troubles include: relatively short lamp life in some models, maintenance headaches, difficulty in precise framing, impermanence of framing once completed, inappropriate light color for the subject, and difficulties in electrical control.

Optimum conditions for this kind of accent light are similar to those for lensless accent lights. Installations must be carefully planned or one may fall into numerous design traps: It is easy to cut off the tops of an object if the projector is placed too far from that object; one may inadvertently select an optical system that does not fully cover the subject after the framing shutters or template are pushed in place; unpleasantly sharp shutter images and harsh shadows can appear on wall surfaces adjacent to paintings, behind sculpture, and so on. If one framing projector does not fully cover a painting, do not try to use additional units on the same painting; no matter how carefully one tries to join each light field, bright streaks or shadow lines will appear where two or more light projections overlap.

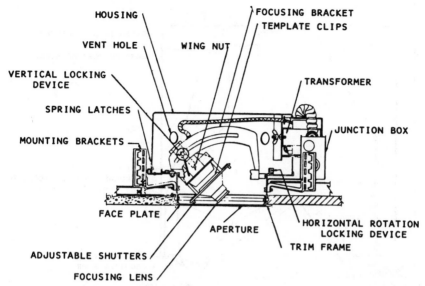

Figure 18.8.   Typical accent light using reflectors and lenses. (Reproduced, by permission, from Lightolier.)

Wall Washers

There is an increasing trend toward the use of luminaires to illuminate the vertical surfaces independently of the horizontal working planes. Walls then act as a "lighting surround" that partially establishes a space's mood and balances its lighting contrasts. In wall washers, the asymmetrical distribution of the luminaire is usually predetermined by the manufacturer.

The first subcategory of wall washers provides shadlowless coverage. These luminaires coat the vertical surface with an even "wash" of light, which obscures undesirable unevenness of the surface. These units are usually placed 3–4 feet form any surface they illuminate.

There are two types of shadlowless wall washers: luminaires that use a lens at the ceiling opening (see Figure 18.9) and those that use lensless apertures (see Figure 18.10). Generally, the latter offers a better cutoff of unwanted light spill at the bottom and sides, but the former provides slightly more even illumination.

Application Tips.   (1) A "one-to-one" installation spacing ratio usually applies. In other words, for each unit of distance from the vertical surface (starting at 3 ft), luminaires must be located an equal unit of distance from

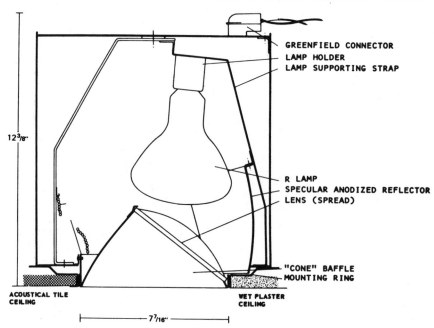

Figure 18.9.   Typical shadowless wall washer with a lens at the ceiling opening. (Reproduced, by permission, from Lighting and Electronics Co.)

center to center. Therefore, if wall washers are placed in a line 3 feet from (and parallel to) a wall, they should be placed no more than 3 feet apart in a row. Placement at greater distances will cause uneven illumination (2) Most wall washers cannot be placed closer than 2.5 feet to a wall (3 ft is optimal for 8-ft walls) or "hot spots" will be created on the wall directly opposite the luminaire. (3) Wall washing intensities decrease toward the bottom third of the wall. This decrease should not be a source of concern, however, since the room's general lighting will begin to contribute to the wall illumination at this point. (4) It is not usually necessary to place down lighting near a wall washed with shadowless light. Wall washing also provides light for the horizontal surfaces located near the subject wall. (5) Specular surfaces *cannot* be wall washed by luminaires intended for shadowless illumination. Glossy surfaces (such as polished marble, oiled wood, or smooth terrazzo) will produce a mirror image of the light source, causing a condition called veiling glare. (6) Caution is necessary when directing wall washers at walls with doors or windows. Glare from wall washers aimed at a door may stun anyone entering the room. If the area contains windows, those outside may be offended by the lamp image (and those inside may experience veiling glare).

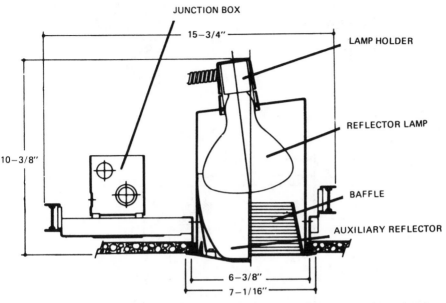

JUNCTION BOX

15−3/4″

LAMP HOLDER

REFLECTOR LAMP

10−3/8″

BAFFLE

AUXILIARY REFLECTOR

6−3/8″

7−1/16″

Figure 18.10. Typical shadowless wall washer with aperture not having a lens. (Reproduced, by permission, from Prescolite, 93065.)

Wall washers in a line down the center of a hall (or worse yet, in a line past the hall's center) will create a row of glare sources. As a general rule, place the wall washer nearest a wall opening no closer than the full recommended spacing dimension between units.

Grazing coverage is the second subcategory of wall washers (see Figure 18.11). Grazing wall washers highlight desirable textures in a plane surface (such as decorative stucco, rough brick, or "unfinished" wood). This method consists of using closely spaced reflectorized lamp units (often with spread lenses) placed near, and parallel with, the subject wall.

Application Tips.   (1) Grazing wall washing is very dramatic but inefficient. While the luminaires in a shadowless system may consist of 150-watt lamps placed on 3-foot centers, the grazing system may use 200-watt lamps on 1-foot centers. (2) With the grazing system, the total vertical surface is not the illumination task. The principal task is to highlight the top surfaces of the wall's irregularities (requiring the units to be placed as close as 1 ft from the wall). Therefore, the frontal surface of a painting projecting from the surface of a grazed wall will not be effectively illuminated.

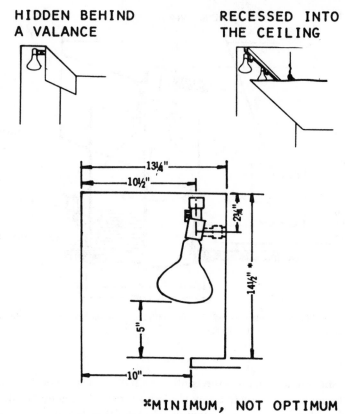

HIDDEN BEHIND
A VALANCE

RECESSED INTO
THE CEILING

✗MINIMUM, NOT OPTIMUM

Figure 18.11. Typical grazing wall washer system. (Reproduced, by permission, from Lightolier.)

LUMINAIRES DESCRIBED BY APPEARANCE

In the preceding section, we briefly reviewed the common types of luminaires according to their function; in this section we discuss luminaire appearance.

Six considerations should be weighed before determining luminaire appearance: (1) Will the visible aspects of the luminaire coordinate with the total design? (2) Should the aperture be open or closed (should there be an open or closed hole in the ceiling)? (3) Should the aperture be darker or lighter than the surrounding ceiling? (4) What is the optimal dimension for the aperture? (5) Is the luminaire to be unimportant to the visual design (i.e., blend in so that it is inconspicuous) or is it to be an active decorative element? (6) Should the ceiling trim be emphasized or as subtle as possible?

Baffles

Baffles are devices that shield an observer from a luminaire's brightness in the normal field of view. They also serve as the major decorative feature of recessed units. Three factors should be kept in mind when selecting baffles: (1) The baffle should be consistent with the design concept—not necessarily the manufacturer's idea of what is fashionable. (2) The baffle should effectively prevent direct viewing of a luminaire's bright interior. (3) The baffle should be free of extraneous nuts, notches, screws, bolts, clasps, fasteners, springs, clips, ripples, welds, overlaps, jagged edges, badly formed corners, scratches, paint spray, finger marks, discoloring, bumps, slots, advertising, labels, or any other imperfections that can be found on inferior equipment.

Round baffles are the most popular, although other shapes are available. Several manufacturers have introduced square baffles, and design possibilities should include ovals, polygons, and rectangles.

Reflectors (Cones)

One of the most commonly used baffles is the cone (see Figure 18.12). The cone serves two purposes. It can act as an aperture shield to reduce luminaire brightness in normal viewing angles and/or as a multiplier of light output.

In section, the cone looks like part of an ellipse or parabola. Its inner surface, the surface one sees, is often highly polished (specular) and serves to remove all visible stray light above 45° from nadir. It is not uncommon for an observer to be unaware that a luminaire is on when the cone baffle is used.

Cones are constructed of several materials and come with a variety of finishes. (1) Polished aluminum spinnings, with a highly specular finish of anodized aluminum or paint, are most often desirable for very low brightness. Anodized aluminum surfaces do not chip and can support the highest specularity; however, they do tend to scratch and discolor. Specular paint (used for all but the natural aluminum surfaces) may chip, but it does not discolor. (2) Compression-molded phenolic (a plastic) is also common. Phenolic cones cannot be as highly polished and therefore may show some surface brightness, but their surfaces do not chip, scratch, or discolor as easily as those of the aluminum cone. Phenolic cones may also age relatively poorly.

When a cone is designed as a light "multiplier," it is shaped so as to baffle the light output and also redirect some of the lamp's otherwise wasted light into a useful field.

Cones are often supplied with "black mirror" surfaces. A specular natural aluminum or pale gold color is also common. Other colors are available, but usually on "special order." When placing a special order, it may be necessary

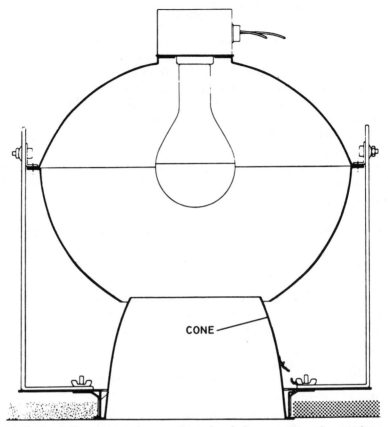

Figure 18.12.   Baffles—a typical cone. (Reproduced, by permission, from Lighting and Electronics Co.)

to order large quantities and pay an elevated price. Bronze, brass, gray, pink, and deep gold are typical special colors.

Collars

The simplest form of baffle is a collar (cylinder) of black-painted metal that shields the observer's eye from the reflector or lamp (see Figure 18.13). The best vertical-sided baffles are perfect cylinders that have no visible imperfections.

Rings

Rings are designed to create shadow patterns that keep the aperture dark and limit the field of view. Remember that black is only black when no light

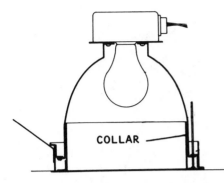

Figure 18.13. Baffles—a typical collar. (Reproduced, by permission, from Lighting and Electronics Co.)

falls on its painted surface. The hidden top sides of the rings block light and therefore present a dark bottom surface to the viewer.

Annular ring baffles consist of large flat rings of sheet metal tacked to the luminaire's interior (see Figure 18.14). *Miniature groove baffles* are formed surfaces of multiple rings that are also designed to produce a dark shadow pattern (see Figure 18.15). Good miniature grooved baffles are precisely

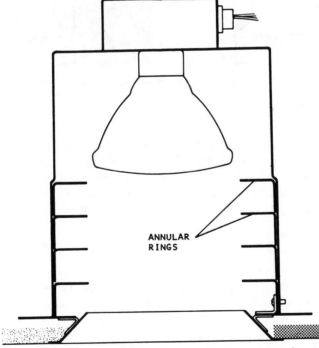

Figure 18.14. Baffles—typical annular rings. (Reproduced, by permission, from Lighting and Electronics Co.)

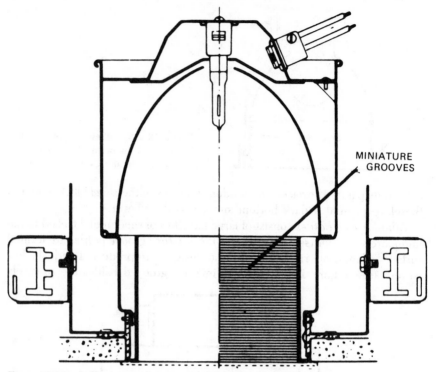

Figure 18.15.   Baffles—typical miniature grooves. (Reproduced, by permission, from Strand Century, Inc.)

formed with no less than eight rings per vertical inch and have sharp visible edges (a dull edge catches light). Many manufacturers have trade names for their miniature grooved baffles, but the word "groove" is usually a part of the name—for example, Minigroove, Microgroove, or Polygroove. Both aluminum and phenolic are possible construction materials.

Louvers

Louvers consist of a series of fins covering the aperture with the fin orientation parallel to the light direction (see Figure 18.16). Louvers are not currently popular because they give installations a barred and prisonlike look. They are most effective when baffling the internal parts of accent lights. They are at their worst when they appear to be prominent wire guards for the luminaire. Several types of louvers are available: concentric ring, spiral ring, parallel blade, egg crate, or honeycomb.

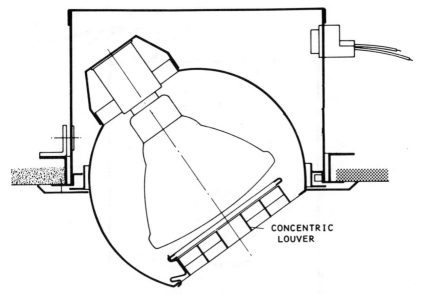

CONCENTRIC
LOUVER

Figure 18.16.   Baffles—typical louver. (Reproduced, by permission, from Lighting and Electronics Co.)

Housings as Baffles

The luminaire housing may serve as its own baffle (see Figure 18.17). If the housing is made of a decorative material, such as wood or bronze anodized aluminum, the effect can be aesthetically pleasing, although brightness is relatively high.

Trims

A trim is that part of a luminaire used to finish off the space between the aperture and the ceiling line. In the past, trim types were limited, but manufacturers are now skillfully expanding the designer's options. (Naturally, all trims should be free of extraneous nuts, notches, screws, bolts, etc.)

Plates

Although a plate (shown in Figure 18.18) is the least imaginative trim design, it may resolve such problems as sloppy luminaire design, awkward building codes (certain communities require that the complete luminaire be removable from below the ceiling without breaking open the ceiling), rough ceiling plaster, and several mechanical, maintenance, and installation difficulties.

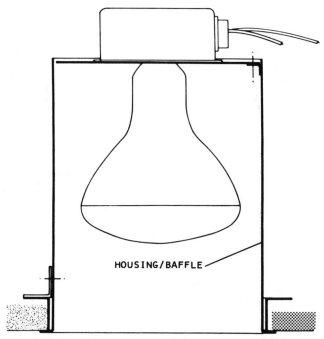

HOUSING/BAFFLE

Figure 18.17. Baffles—typical luminaire with the housing used as a baffle.(Reproduced, by permission, from Lighting and Electronics Co.)

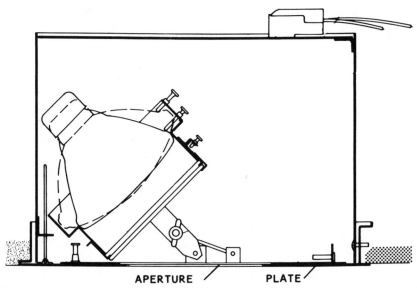

APERTURE PLATE

Figure 18.18. Trims—a typical plate. (Reproduced, by permission, from Lighting and Electronics Co.)

Unless used as a decorative accent, the plate should blend with the decor. Plates may be installed flush with the ceiling line or slightly below the ceiling surface.

Flanges

A flange trim is actually a plate of minimum size used to cover only the rough edge caused by cutting a hole in the ceiling material (see Figure 18.19). Flanges are always recommended when dry ceiling materials are used. Acoustic tile, for example, is difficult to cut neatly. Flanges are also called "minimum trims."

Eyelid

Another variation of the plate, called the "eyelid," usually masks half of the aperture (see Figure 18.20). It is often used for lensless wall washers.

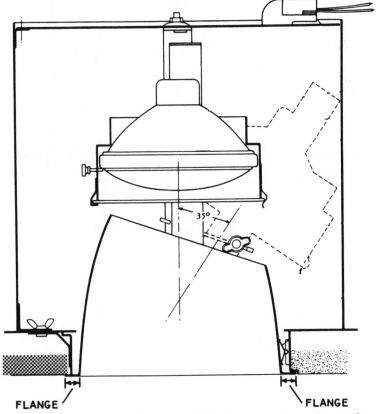

FLANGE   FLANGE

Figure 18.19. Trims—a typical flange. (Reproduced, by permission, from Lighting and Electronics Co.)

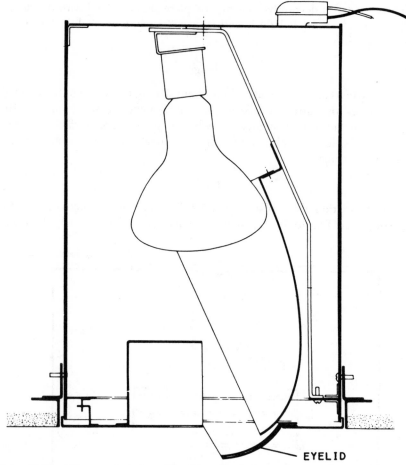

EYELID

Figure 18.20.   Trims—a typical eyelid. (Reproduced, by permission, from Lighting and Electronics Co.)

Regressed Return

The regressed return is an angled ring that slants upward from the ceiling line into the aperture (see Figure 18.21). Regressions are used to hold a Fresnel lens or diffuser slightly above the ceiling line in order to minimize annoying surface brightness.

Splays

The straight or curved splay is simply a narrow regression (see Figure 18.22). These trims are used to conceal the structural thickness of the ceiling

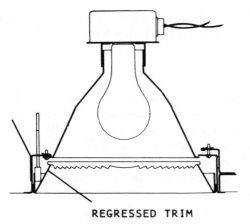

REGRESSED TRIM

Figure 18.21.   Trims—regressed. (Reproduced, by permission, from Lighting and Electronics Co.)

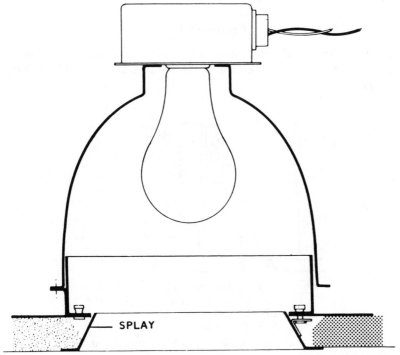

SPLAY

Figure 18.22.   Trims—a typical splay. (Reproduced, by permission, from Lighting and Electronics Co.)

construction. When they are formed, the angle or curve of the splay may be calculated to keep light off the return surface.

Trimless

Trimless luminaires have no visible hardware between the edge of the ceiling line and the edge of the aperture (see Figure 18.23). The detail is very clean and subtly integrates the baffle with the ceiling. This system is usually limited to wet plaster construction and is only successful when the plastering entails fine craftsmanship. If the designer questions the quality of the plastering, a minimum trim luminaire should be recommended.

Air Handling

Some trim details integrate a structure's air-handling system and the luminaire aperture. They always appear as a black slot around the aperture. Some manufacturers supply total air-handling luminaires; others use enclosures supplied by air-conditioning manufacturers.

Connector Covers

Bracket, mullion, and other junction box mounted luminaires are supplied with connector covers, which shield the luminaire's physical and electrical connections.

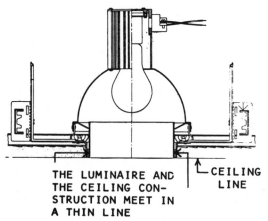

THE LUMINAIRE AND | ⌐CEILING
THE CEILING CON- | LINE
STRUCTION MEET IN
A THIN LINE

Figure 18.23.   Trims—a typical trimless luminaire. (Reproduced, by permission, from Gotham Lighting.)

Decorative

Ornamental trims abound, and they are only limited by the designer's or manufacturer's imagination.

Hidden

When a luminaire is semirecessed, the trim detail may be hidden by the exposed portion of the luminaire's housing.

Chapter Nineteen

Utilitarian Fluorescent
Luminaires

This chapter is devoted to a description of utilitarian, fluorescent luminaires that are recessed or permanently surface mounted. Semirecessed fluorescents are usually a modification of recessed or surface types. Panel, pendant, and bracket equipment will also be considered. Only the more typical systems will be considered. New products are regularly introduced.

MATERIALS AND FINISHES

Housings

Materials

Generally, the opaque housings that contain the electrical, mechanical and optical components of fluorescent luminaires are made of 20-gauge (0.0359-in.-thick) cold rolled prime steel (C.R.S.) that is electrically welded. The socket holders may be supplied in 18- (0.478 in.) to 20-gauge C.R.S. Reflectors, usually flat or angled sheets that may also cover some of the electrical components, are often made of 20- to 24-(0.0239 in.) gauge C.R.S. Sheet-metal parts are usually mass produced by automated formers, but they can also be shaped by hand. A section of a typical housing is shown in Figure 19.1.

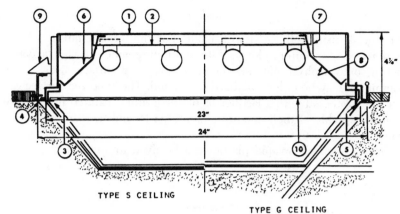

TYPE S CEILING

TYPE G CEILING

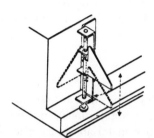

LEGEND: 1 HOUSING
         2 SOCKET HOLDER AND REFLECTOR
         3 CLOSURE FRAME ("DOOR")
         4 CONCEALED HINGE TO HOLD DOOR
            IN THE OPEN POSITION
         5 LATCH FOR HOLDING DOOR IN
            CLOSED POSITION
         6 BALLAST COVER AND WIREWAY
            (ALSO PART OF THE REFLECTOR)
         7 BALLAST
         8 REFLECTOR (ALSO BALLAST COVER)
         9 MOUNTING SUPPORT BRACKET
            (SEE DETAIL)
        10 LENS

DETAIL OF MOUNTING SUPPORT BRACKET:

LUMINAIRE IS PLACED INTO THE CEILING
THROUGH THE CEILING OPENING WITH THE
BRACKET FLAT AGAINST THE HOUSING.
THE SCREW OPENS THE BRACKET AND PULLS
THE LUMINAIRE FLUSH TO THE CEILING
LINE.

Figure 19.1.   Section of a typical recessed fluorescent luminaire. (Adapted, by permission, from Mark Lighting Fixture Co., Inc.)

Some housings are formed of cast, extruded, or sheet aluminum when structural weight is undesirable or corrosive factors are expected. Plastics, such as ABS, phenolic, or polypropylene, may be used when an electrically nonconductive, vandal-proof, or corrosion-retardant luminaire is required.

The transparent or translucent lenses used in fluorescent luminaires may be held in a frame, called a "door," that opens for maintenance. These frames are constructed of extruded plastic and aluminum, or formed sheet steel. Some refractors and diffusers are frameless—the opening and closing devices are incorporated in the closure material.

Finishes

Sheet steel is usually finished with paint. For the interior finish, a high-reflectivity (85% or better), glossy white, synthetic enamel is baked (at 350°F or better) onto a physically and chemicaly prepared surface.

Aluminum may be either anodized or painted. The anodized surface can be further protected with a lacquer or plastic coating. Painted finishes are often as acceptable as their anodized counterparts, and they are much less expensive.

Housings made of opaque plastics can be dyed to any color.

Closures

A closure (also termed a "light shield") is any device that covers the luminaire's working parts while allowing the passage of illumination. Closures include louvers, refractors, and diffusers.

Materials

Translucent, transparent, or opaque plastics used in closures include cellulose acetate butyrate (for vandal-resistant applications), polymethyl methacrylite (acrylic, by far the most popular material), impact acrylic, polycarbonate (if the closure will receive rough handling), and polystyrene (used where low cost is the guiding factor). Glass is also used if shape retention and fire or smoke problems are important. Louvers are constructed of sheet steel, aluminum, or plastic.

Finishes

Opaque plastics for louvers are usually dyed white or black; they may also be supplied with special metallic finishes. Lenses are usually made in colorless materials, although slightly tinted materials are available. Opal (not really opalescent, but rather "milk white") diffusers are common.

Closure Types

There are innumerable methods for covering the light-emitting side of a fluorescent luminaire, but most can be divided into the following five basic types.

Egg-Crate Louver

The "egg crate" consists of vertical fins set at right angles to form a series of repetitive cells. These louvers offer from 45–60° shielding for the fluorescent lamp and are typically supplied in 2- by 4-foot panels of plastic or metal. A variety of cell dimensions are available. Some egg crates have elaborate configurations on their visible edges. These often are proprietary items supplied by fluorescent luminaire or luminous ceiling manufacturers. See Figure 19.2.

Parallel-Blade Louvers

The parallel-blade louver resembles the egg-crate louver, but has one disadvantage. If these louvers are viewed from the nonshielded direction, the observer will be able to see into the luminaire. A parabolic shape (described in the following section) may be given to the louver blade.

Parabolic-Section Louver

As Figure 19.3 shows, the parabolic-section louver has cells shaped with a parabolic curve. Each cell has a specular or spread surface that redirects wasted light toward the work surface, resulting in an effect similar to that created by the incandescent cone—the louver will appear to be dark even when the lamp is operating. The cells can be constructed of aluminum or plastic. Two types are currently available.

The small-cell parabolic louver looks very much like a special egg crate.

PERSPECTIVE VIEW

SECTION

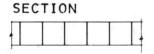

Figure 19.2. Egg-crate louver. (Reproduced, by permission, from Contemporary Ceilings, Inc.)

PERSPECTIVE VIEW

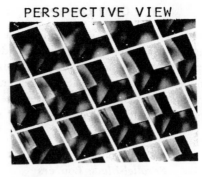

SECTION

Figure 19.3. Parabolic-section louver. (Reproduced, by permission, from Contemporary Ceilings, Inc.)

Each cell is about ½ inch square and approximately ½ inch deep. Its plastic cell surfaces are finished with a clear or colored specular metallic film. Unfortunately, once the comparatively unprotected mirrorlike cell surfaces become soiled, the louver begins to show the light passing through it. For this reason, the louver surface may receive a slightly spread finish (resulting in a brighter aperture). Specular finishes should only be used where installation, airborne dust, and maintenance can be carefully controlled. These cells are not easily cleaned. Metal types are available, but they are not as typical as types constructed of plastic.

The large-cell parabolic louver has cells that may be greater than 8 inches square and 6 inches deep. When manufactured with sufficient depth and in an accurate parabolic shape, they are one of the most successful closures found today for the following reasons: Aperture brightness is low; because they are typically constructed of aluminum, they avoid the electrostatic accumulations of dirt that are typical of plastic closures; they are high in efficiency (exceeding 80% in some cases).

Although louvers are supplied in flat panels, refractors and diffusers may be supplied as sheets, domes, "wrap-arounds," or "dropped dishes." The wrap-around covers several sides of a luminaire; the dropped dish curves downward from its supporting edges.

Diffusers

Diffusers simply scatter the illumination into a space. They may be fully diffuse or "opalescent." Opal diffusers may have combined diffuse and translucent qualities; they may also appear iridescent.

Refractors

Dr. McPhail patented a system of clear, prismatic optical control in 1949. He demonstrated that a flat sheet of small, 30–35° prisms will bend light striking it above 45°, returning the light to the luminaire's housing and redirecting it toward the working plane. Refractor sheets composed of numerous small, pyramidal prisms are the most popular lenses based on this principal. Parallel, ribbed refractors, as well as other special refractor designs, are also available. Refractors composed of many small hemispherical lenses are a new development offering very low brightness.

PHOTOMETRICS

The user must refer to a manufacturer's data sheet for detailed information about any luminaire's photometric performance. However, certain general comments are possible.

Closure Contribution

Closures Producing Directed Light Distributions

Conical and Pyramid Prismatic Refractors. These transparent sheets are flat on one side and have conical or pyramidal prisms on the other (see Figure 19.4). Both raised (male) and recessed (female) prisms (four- or six-sided) are available in various sizes. These prisms direct useful light to the work surface and reflect the luminaire light rays that strike them at angles over 45°. Their accuracy depends on the precision of the prism's angles,

PERSPECTIVE VIEW

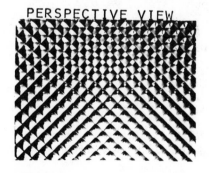

SECTION

Figure 19.4.   Refractor. (Reproduced, by permission, from Contemporary Ceilings, Inc.)

Figure 19.5.   Hemispherical refractor. (Reproduced, by permission, from Holophane Company Inc., A Johns-Manville Company.)

flatness of the reflecting surface, cleanliness, transparency, and prismatic error. In general, larger prisms are more accurate, but give the refractor a visible texture. A larger number of smaller prisms give the appearance of a soft surface, but suffer from inaccuracies caused by the rounding of the prism structure during manufacture.

Parallel-Ribbed Prismatic Refractors.   A ribbed design is often used to spread light in one or two directions. These refractors may also be combined with other prismatic structures.

Hemispherical Refractors.   A new refractor design consists of a transparent sheet containing a hexagonal array of hemspherical refractive elements (see Figure 19.5). One surface consists of many constant-radius convex surfaces, and the other has matching concave shapes. When illuminated, the refractor has a very low brightness. For this reason, and because the surfaces of this solid sheet are easily maintained, it can often be substituted for parabolic-wedge louvers. Although lamps used with this refractor are obscured at normal viewing angles, they are plainly visible from directly below the closure. An "interface" diffuser may be installed directly above (and bonded to) the refractor's top surface. In addition to obscuring the lamps, the interface lowers the surface brightness of this refractor with a sacrifice of between 10 and 20% of its light output.

Polarizers.   These transparent lenses are specially coated to transmit light rays in controlled directions. They are used to minimize glare.

Diffuser Closures

Diffusers scatter light in all directions.

Etched, Frosted, Ground, and Sandblasted Diffusers.   These closures usually offer poor diffusion and lamp shielding, with low absorption and high transmission of light.

Opalescent Diffusers.   Fair diffusion, some iridescence, and lower transmission than the previous materials are achieved with these diffusers. True opal diffusers are glass. *Flashed (cased) opal diffusers* have a thin opal coating over a clear glass layer and offer excellent transmission with low absorption. *Solid opal glass diffusers* are most effective when an excellently diffuse white is desired.

White Plastic Diffusers. These diffusers are often used in place of solid opal glass. Their generally high absorption, excellent diffusion, and great flexibility make them a superior lighting closure.

Louver Closures for Direct Light Distribution

An enormous selection of louvers is available, so general comment is particularly difficult. Exotic designs are usually the proprietary products of luminous ceiling manufacturers.

Egg Crates. These louvers eliminate a minimum of 50% of the light incident to them. They should be constructed to provide 45° shielding (or better). They are correctly blamed for contributing to reflected glare, since the lamps are openly exposed to work surfaces directly below them.

Parabolic-Section Louvers with Specular or Spread Surfaces. A special variation of the egg crate, these panels of precise, parabolic-surfaced cells largely eliminate high-angle direct glare with 45° shielding. Direct and asymmetric distributions are available for small-cell louver types. Small-cell (with cell dimensions that are usually ½ in. square by ½ in. deep) parabolic louvers are not particularly efficient in their ability to allow the passage of light. Large-cell (typically larger than 8 in. square and 6 in. deep) parabolic louvers made of aluminum are very efficient.

Combined Closures for Varied Light Distributions

Asymmetric Refractors. These refractors generally use a combination of refractive elements to direct light in a nonuniform pattern. They are frequently used in fluorescent wall washers.

Wrap-Around Refractors. When used on surface and pendant-hung luminaires, these refractors direct light downward and upward while also removing illumination from the offending zone. The upward light component adds illumination to the ceiling, thereby reducing the brightness contrast between the luminaire and the ceiling surface. The bottom portion of these refractors may be composed of pyramidal prism, while the sides are parallel ribbed.

Bat-Wing Refractors. A combination of refractor designs produces a candlepower distribution that is lobed in two directions on a single vertical plane (as shown in Figure 19.6). The result is light distriubtion to either side with only a small amount emanating directly down from the bottom of the luminaire. When overlapping bat-wing luminaires are correctly placed, the task surface is illuminated primarily from the side so that glare reflections on the task are directed away from the viewer.

Refractor-Diffuser-Louver Combinations. These designs may be used for particular purposes. Some lenses are a combination of pyramidal and ribbed prisms while others use a diffusing element to soften light distributions. Lenses are sometimes used above open louvers to prevent direct viewing of the luminaire interior or to the alter the louver's photometrics. Similarly, the hemispherical refractor may be ordered with an optical interface, a diffuser attached to the top of the refractor, which obscures the lamps if

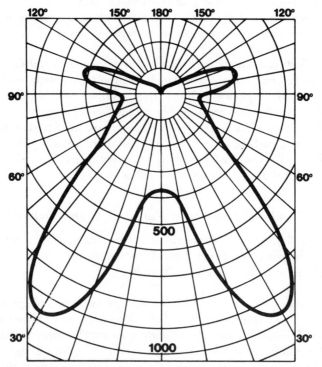

Figure 19.6. Bat-wing candlepower distribution. (Reproduced, by permission, from Holophane Company Inc., A Johns-Manville Company.)

viewed from directly below. Of course, it must be remembered that efficiency is reduced with each additional light controlling element.

Housing Contribution

The opaque structure enclosing the optical, mechanical, and electrical components also affects the photometric distribution of a luminaire.

Direct Light Distribution

Fully recessed fluorescent luminaires only emit light directly downward. Semirecessed and pendant-mounted luminaires have a similar effect when all sides except the bottom panel are opaque. Bright luminous panels may create excessive contrasts between the luminaire and the ceiling surface surrounding it. For this reason, the optimal recessed luminaire installation uses closures with low surface brightness in spaces with highly reflective floors, walls, and ceilings.

Indirect Light Distribution

Indirect illumination can be very diffuse in distribution, but it is also inefficient. Examples include indirect coves, up-lighting brackets, pendant-mounted luminaires, furniture-mounted/integrated ambient units and free-standing torchiere.

Semidirect Light Distribution

Housings function as a wrap-around refractor if luminous apertures appear on their side surfaces. The effect is to illuminate some of the ceiling surface near the luminaire and thus reduce the brightness contrast between the ceiling and the principal luminous closure. These luminaires are usually semirecessed or pendant-mounted.

Direct-Indirect Light Distribution

Bracket-mounted housings with opaque vertical surfaces, as well as pendants, can issue equal amounts of illumination both upwards and downwards. With careful planning, it is possible to use these sources to totally illuminate a space.

TYPICAL DIMENSIONS AND LAMP CONFIGURATIONS

Special fluorescent luminaires can be manufactured with various unusual dimensions and lamp configurations. However, only typical architectural lighting equipment will be itemized in Tables 19.1 and 19.2.

Table 19.1. Typical Square and Rectangular Fluorescent Luminaires (Recessed, Semirecessed, and Pendant)

Luminaire Width (in ft)	Luminaire Length (in ft)[a]	Number of Lamps
0.50	2	1
0.50	4	1
0.50	8	1, 2 (in tandem)
1	2	2, 3
1	4	2, 3
1	8	2, 3, 4 (in tandem if 4-ft lamps used)
2	2	2^b, 3^b, 4
2	4	2, 3, 4
2	8	4, 6 (in tandem if 4-ft lamps used)
3	3	2^b, 3^b, 4, 6
4	4	4, 6, 8
4	8	4, 6 (in tandem if 4-ft lamps used)

Table 19.2. Typical Round Fluorescent Luminaires (Recessed)

Luminaire Diameter	Lamp Length	Number of Lamps
2	24	2^b, 4, 6
3	36	2^b, 4, 6
4	48	6, 8
5	48	8, 10

Notes to Tables 19.1 and 19.1:

[a]Luminaire length = nominal lamp length.

[b]May use U-shaped lamps.

Luminaire and lamp dimensions are nominal. Luminous closures and lamps may be smaller. Luminaire housings may be larger.

Although 3- and 8-foot (nominal) lamps are available, 3-foot lamps are rarely used in standard cataloged luminaires, and 8-foot lamps are difficult to transport and install. Therefore, two 4-foot lamps, in tandem, are usually used in 8-foot luminaires.

LUMINAIRE TYPES AND MOUNTING SYSTEMS

Fluorescent luminaires are often categorized by their installation method. Therefore, luminaire types and mounting systems will be considered simultaneously.

Recessed and Semirecessed Luminaires

Ceiling Types

The type of ceiling and the luminaire's installation method must be considered when selecting a recessed or semirecessed luminaire. Obviously, the luminaires and the ceilings must be compatible, but choosing the right luminaire is a complex process, and conflicts do occur here—they can be merely awkward problems or expensive errors. For example, there may be gaps between the luminaire surface and the ceiling surface, or the luminaire's closure may be impossible to open once installation is completed.

There are two major considerations in matching a luminaire to a ceiling. (1) What is the ceiling support system: Does the luminaire support the ceiling, are the ceiling and the luminaire independently supported, does the ceiling support the luminaire, is the major support at the ends or at either side of the luminaire? (2) Will there be proper clearances in the ceiling: What is the relationship between the aperture size and the luminaire body size, what is the shape of the luminaire in relation to the aperture and framing, will the luminaire's trim match the ceiling elements, what are the necessary vertical clearances above the ceiling (particularly in the case of air-handling luminaires with their accessory fittings)?

There are two basic types of ceilings: wet (plaster) or dry construction. Dry construction includes ceilings made of dry plaster, hardboard, sheet-rock, or similar materials, and those that are mechanically hung or suspended. The mechanically hung ceiling is, perhaps, the most complex, since there are many specific products on the market. In an attempt to classify hung ceilings, NEMA (National Electrical Manufacturers Association) has established the following five categories.

Type F (Flange). This is used for both wet and dry ceiling construction (see Figure 19.7). In either case, the luminaire trim must conceal the spaces between the visible luminaire surface and the ceiling.

Type G (Grid). In exposed grid ceilings, luminaires used with these ceilings "lay in" between the grid supports. (Type G is often incorrectly called a "T-bar" system; the more correct term is "exposed, inverted T.")

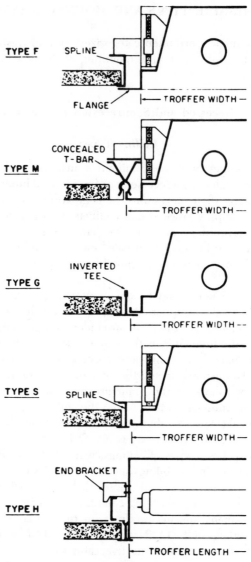

Figure 19.7. Hung ceiling types. (Reproduced, by permission, from NEMA Publication No. LE 1-1963, "Standards Publication, Recessed Fluorescent Luminaires.")

Type H (Hook).   In this case, the luminaire hooks itself to the structure that also supports the ceiling. This method is often used for luminaires supported at the ends (rather than the sides) of their housings.

Type M (Metal Pan).   This is a true T-bar system when used with a metal pan type of ceiling construction.

Type S (Spline). Many variations are included within this ceiling type such as "Z-spline," or "concealed Z" (no spline shows from below).

Many proprietary systems are too exotic to fit within the preceding categories. Often, luminaires must be specially constructed to be used with these ceilings.

Luminaire Components

Although specific luminaires may differ in details, most have similar components.

Housing. The housing serves as an opaque protective body that encloses all other components. Since the ballast is usually mounted within the housing, it must provide an effective thermal dissipator (heat sink) as well as a noise suppressor. In particular, loose components in the housing may amplify the buzz that is inherent in ballast operation.

Fluorescent luminaires can be very large (4 ft by 4 ft is not atypical), heavy, and awkward to install. Housings must, therefore, be strong enough to resist distortion during installation and rigid enough to maintain their shape after installation.

If fluorescent luminaires are to be used in tandem (end to end, forming continuous rows), some provision should be made in the luminaire for continuous wiring. A wiring trough is often provided as part of the ballast enclosure so that electrical connections can be made between luminaires. Appropriate "knockouts" should also be provided (knockouts, or "K.O.'s" are circular indentations in sheet metal that may be pried out as needed for wiring connections).

Hanging System. (See *Ceiling Types.*) Some method of adjusting the luminaire's recessing height from inside the housing should be provided. This enables the installer to precisely align the luminaire with the finished ceiling surface, and it also permits installation of the luminaire (when the housing is smaller than the ceiling aperture) after the ceiling is closed.

Ballast and Ballast Housing. (See *Chapter Seven, Auxiliary Equipment— Ballasts*) Since ballasts can burst under abnormal conditions, such as overheating, they are usually placed inside a ballast enclosure mounted to a convenient surface of the housing. This enclosure may be parallel to and directly behind the lamps along the length of the housing. When mounted in this way, the ballast housing also serves as a reflector, starting aid, socket holder, and wiring channel. In all luminaires, the ballast and wiring must be accessible for maintenance from below and/or above the luminaire.

Reflector. The fluorescent reflector is often a simply bent sheet of metal finished with a highly reflective coating of white synthetic enamel paint;

here, reflectors act as diffusers. When parabolic-section louvers are supplied with specular or spread surfaces of anodized aluminum, these may act to alter the light pattern (direct or bat-wing asymmetric distributions are typical). However, the control of fluorescent light through the use of reflectors cannot be as precise as it is with compact-filament incandescent or metal halide light sources. This is due to the diffuse nature of the fluorescent source.

Lamp Sockets. Appropriate sockets for the specific lamp type must be firmly attached to the housing. This is particulary important when compression lampholders are used (typical with high output lamps). If the sockets wobble or spread apart during relamping, electrical contact will be poor and the lamps can fall from their mounting positions.

Closure Door. The light-emitting closure may be strengthened and attached to the housing by a "door" (also called a "frame"). The door will also hold the necessary hardware to lock the closure in its proper position. In better luminaires, all hardware (and even the door itself) is hidden. Frameless luminaires are also available. Here, the strengthening, fastening, and supporting features are molded into the closure itself.

Some closure doors offer universal access—they may be opened from either side for lamp replacement and luminaire maintenance.

The closure door may have a variety of functional and/or decorative trims.

Trim. Air-handling trims are used when air enters or leaves a space through slots located on the luminaire's sides. Flanges (minimum trims) are very popular for covering rough edges surrounding the aperture. Regressed trims are used to raise the luminaire's closure above the ceiling line. Splays (minimal regressions) are also typical.

Trims are not always necessary, however. Trimless luminaires can be used in either wet or dry ceilings. If the luminaire will fit within a straight-line ceiling module, for example, difficult aperture cuts are not necessary in dry ceiling materials so that ragged edges are not present.

Surface-Mounted Luminaires

Surface-mounted units are similar to recessed luminaires, except that the housing may also serve a decorative function. Although fully exposed, standard surface-mounted luminaires may function like recessed luminaires in terms of direct light distribution, but they can also be modified to create semidirect lighting. They are often easier and less expensive to install, and it is possible to add decorative elements to their exposed vertical surfaces.

One basic surface-mounted unit is not enclosed. It consists of a lamp, lamp sockets, and a ballast housing. The housing also serves as a wiring channel, starting aid, and reflector. Because of its minimal construction, this basic unit is called a "skeleton strip" or "channel." Skeleton strips are used as is, with architectural baffling (such as in a cove or niche), or as components of other systems (special luminaires, luminous panels, etc.).

Pendant-Mounted Luminaires

Pendant-mounted fluorescent luminaires are often simply surface-mounted units suspended from the ceiling on a pipe (called a "stem") or chain. They are particularly useful in providing semidirect, direct-indirect, and indirect illumination. General-diffuse luminaires are also available.

With all pipe pendants, a "hang-straight," or swivel, should be attached where the pendant connects to the ceiling (see Figure 19.8). The hang-straight allows the luminaire to adjust to variations in hanging position without breaking.

Bracket-Mounted Luminaires

Any fluorescent luminaire attached to a wall is considered a bracket luminaire. One specific type consists of a skeleton strip placed behind a thin, horizontal baffle that is either opaque or translucent. Brackets may produce

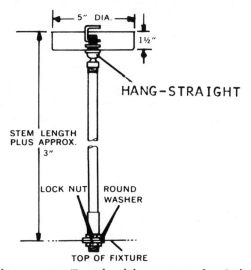

Figure 19.8.   Pendant mounting. (Reproduced, by permission, from Lighting Products, Inc.)

direct, indirect, direct-indirect, semidirect/indirect or general-diffuse light distributions. They can, if properly constructed, provided the total light for a space.

Although bracket-mounted luminaires are usually attached to walls, they can also be found under counters, in self-contained bookshelf lights, and around mirrors, where they serve as self-contained shaving or makeup lights.

Panels

A lighting panel is the combination of an architectural element and a lighting instrument. Lighting panels hung overhead are called luminous or "louverall" ceilings. When mounted vertically, they are termed luminous wall panels. Panels are illuminated from the rear ("transilluminated").

Luminous Wall Panels

Complete panels are not usually supplied by lighting equipment manufacturers. Instead, they are developed from architectural elements and lighting equipment combined by installers in the field (see Figure 19.9).

Because luminous panels are more decorative than practical, many design forms are possible, and the lighting variations they produce cannot be simply described. If the wall panels are constructed with materials typical for luminous ceilings (described below), many of the ceiling comments apply. Designers must ensure that the luminous panel does not cast objects in front of it into inappropriate silhouette or create annoying brightness areas.

Luminous Ceilings

When used as practical lighting units, luminous ceilings spread luminous intensity over a large area in an attempt to diffuse the light source (see Figure 19.10). The result is a very soft and shadowless illumination on the task.

The simplest luminous ceiling has the following components:

1. "Black iron," which is the steel structure that supports the ceiling and the hanging wires (rods).
2. The hanging wires (usually 12 gauge) attach to the black iron and support the runners that form a grid supporting the visible ceiling.
3. The main grid runners are often inverted T-bars that hang in parallel rows along the greatest length of the space.

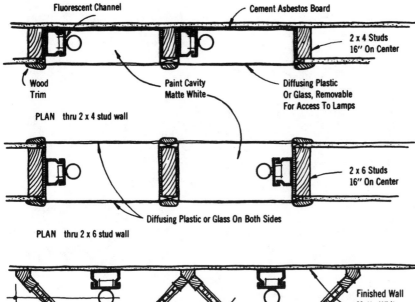

PLAN   thru 2 x 4 stud wall

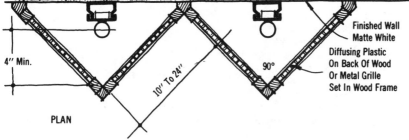

PLAN   thru 2 x 6 stud wall

PLAN

Figure 19.9.   Examples of luminous wall panels. (Reproduced, by permission, from General Electric, TPC-12-R.)

4. Short crossbars are snapped at right angles into the main runners and form a square or rectangular grid (2 by 2 and 2 by 4 ft are common, nominal, dimensions for openings in the grid).

5. Edging strips terminate the grid where it meets with wall surfaces.

6. Closures are fitted into the grid.

7. Skeleton strips are suspended from the black iron above the closure.

There are many variations of this simplified system. When an invisible grid is desirable, for example, special runners may be substituted for the inverted T-bars. Or the complete system may attach to the structure without the use of black iron. In effect, any system is possible if it satisfies lighting safety, and architectural requirements.

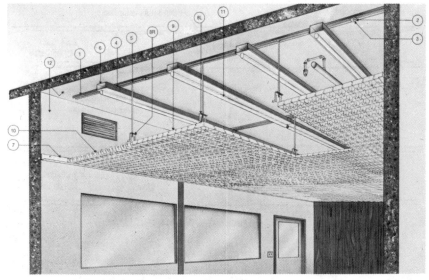

LEGEND: 1 Black Iron (structural channel)
           2 Supporting bolt
           3 Supporting plate
           4 Skeleton strip support hanger
           5 Hanging wires
           6 Skeleton Strips
           7 Edging strip
           8 Louver Hangers
           9 Louver (This special louver does not rest on grid runners. It is self-
             supportng.)
          10 Section of the louver that is specially hinged to give access to the
             skeleton strips for maintenance.
          11 Lamp
          12 Plenum space. Surfaces are painted white.

Figure 19.10.   Luminous ceiling details. (Reproduced, by permission, from Contemporary
Ceilings, Inc.)

The form of the closure can also be varied. Many of the most effective
luminous ceilings are proprietary systems developed by specialized manufacturers. If a proprietary system is used, all of its components (and all of the
responsibility for a fully working system) should be supplied by one
manufacturer.

Luminous ceilings enjoyed a popularity during the 1950s and 1960s,
although in some instances they were poorly applied. This type of ceiling is
only efficient as a practical lighting instrument when placed from 8–10 feet
above the floor. The light it produces is very diffuse, so the resulting

illumination may have the dullness associated with any shadlowless interior. When hung much above 10 feet, luminous ceilings provide a mostly decorative element.

The reflective surfaces behind the panels of both luminous ceilings and walls should be painted flat white. Ideally, all spaces between the closure and the light source should be free of obstructions (air conditioning, sprinkler pipes, sound equipment, etc.) that may cause shadows on the closure. If this is not possible, the light sources must be spaced specifically to avoid casting shadows. To assure even illumination over the closure surface, light sources should be spaced on centers no more than 1½ times the distance between the closure and the light source (an ideal ratio is 1.1).

Chapter Twenty

Other Luminaire Types

HIGH INTENSITY DISCHARGE LUMINAIRES

Application

For many years, designers were cautious in their use of HID light sources in interiors because of their color aberrations, size, and ballast noise. The development of deluxe sources has reduced color distortions to some extent, (or at least given designers acceptable apparent color). The manufacture of lower wattages (50, 75, 100, 175 and 250) has also made these light sources more applicable to interiors. Ballast noise may still be a problem in "quiet" areas.

HID light sources still do not provide a well-balanced spectral distribution. However, they can be useful where color balance is not of major importance. For example, the warmer deluxe colors may be acceptable in design controlled lobbies, reception areas, malls, and other areas principally used as passageways. When used in color-sensitive spaces, such as department stores and supermarkets, they should be expertly handled.

Luminaires

As a result of their slow acceptance for interior applications, HID luminaires have yet to realize fully their own potential. At present, these high output sources are generally used in modified incandescent and fluorescent equipment.

286

ELECTRIFIED TRACKS

Track lighting is more a system of electrical distribution than a lighting technique (see Figure 20.1). It is based on a continuously available linear power source that also acts as an attachment and support system for various lamp holders. Track lighting is principally used for accent lighting (and for specialized forms of wall washing). Its basic advantage is flexibility.

Several manufacturers currently produce totally integrated track–lighting systems. Unfortunately, the components are not interchangeable. Although each proprietary system has different details, all have the same basic parts.

Track

The basis of the system is a linear raceway that can provide electrical power at any point. The housing for the raceway is usually extruded aluminum and may be recessed, surface mounted, or pendant hung. It can also act as the

Figure 20.1. Perspective of track with fixtures attached. (Reproduced, by permission, from Halo Lighting Division, McGraw-Edison Company.)

main grid runners of a suspended ceiling. By adjusting the track connector, some systems can provide an additional two or three separate circuits. Each component of a track system must be ordered separately. The following parts are typical.

Starter Track

The first section of track used in any continuous run contains an electrical connector at one end. Starter tracks are almost universally supplied in 4- or 8-foot lengths. Although it is a difficult task, tracks may be shortened at the job site to meet other dimensional requirements.

Joiner Track

Joiner tracks extend any continuous run, but cannot be used to start a run. It is not practical to join more than 16 feet of track in any one run powered by a 15-amp lighting circuit. Joiner tracks are usually supplied in 8-foot lengths.

Curved Track

Some manufacturers offer curved starter and joiner tracks in standard lengths. As a general rule, track can be curved away from or toward the conductors (the side on which lighting equipment is attached) in a minimum radius of 8 feet. If the conductors are on the bottom, minimum radius of 20 feet must be maintained. Tighter curves will cause the track to buckle and will interfere with the attachment of lighting equipment.

Mounting Systems

Track can be mounted directly to any vertical or horizontal surface, or it can be secured with clips that hold the track slightly away from the surface. The clips speed installation, but they do not hold the track as firmly as direct mountings. Track can also be recessed into surfaces by using an appropriate length of recessed housing (which can be trimless or have minimum trim features). Modified tracks are often supplied for pendant mounting by themselves or in decorative housings (tubes, square beams, and the like). Some manufacturers integrate their tracks into the main grid runners of hung ceiling systems. Other suppliers offer kits that allow the track to be installed along the top of exposed ceiling grids.

Feed Connectors

A variety of methods can be used to connect the building's electrical power to the track: outlet box covers, surface greenfield connectors, pendant kits, grid adapters, and boxes for splicing in recessed track. Surface tracks can be joined continously or at angles; L, T, X, and flexible corner blocks are used to obtain various configurations. Recessed track may be joined at the corners.

Individual points of track are also used with portable lighting equipment (a weighted base with cord and plug is provided) or where equipment is mounted over a single outlet box (a special outlet box cover is provided).

Attachment Fittings

Lighting equipment is both physically and electrically joined to the track with a special fitting. Fittings are designed to support lamp holders, flexible pendants (cords or chains supporting up to 10 lb), or rigid pendants (pipe supporting up to 20 lb).

Track-Mounted Lighting Equipment

A vast selection of utilitarian and decorative fixtures are available. Among them are: bare lamp holders, covered and baffled housings for R and PAR lamps, wall washers (types that both smooth i.e., minimize, and accent wall textures), low-voltage equipment, and framing optical projectors. Many forms of lightweight, surface-mounted equipment not available in a track manufacturer's catalog can be adapted for track mounting.

Limitations

Track lighting is temporary. Electrical codes may specify that each enclosed space be illuminated by a permanent source. Therefore, track lighting should not provide the only illumination in any enclosed space. In addition, codes in certain cities limit lighting track to specific purposes or locations.

Since lighting track accepts various wattages, each track must be supplied with the maximum amount of power for its capacity or estimated needs. In large installations, this requirement can add up to huge electrical service requirements.

The flexibility of track can be its own worst enemy. Anyone can inadvertently change the designer's lighting scheme, including maintenance men or the clients themselves.

Track equipment has a distinct design established by the manufacturer. Although it should not be said that track either "looks commercial" or "looks residential," it is safe to assume that it may intrude inappropriately on certain designs.

SUPPLEMENTARY LIGHTING

The I.E.S. defines supplementary lighting as lighting that provides "an additional quantity and quality of illumination that cannot readily be obtained by a general lighting system and that supplements the general lighting level, ususally for specific work requirements."

The following are general rules for its use: (1) Supplementary lighting should rarely be used by itself. Since, by definition, it covers only a small area with relatively high intensity, it can cause excessive brightness contrasts with surrounding areas. It should always be used with general illumination that is at least 20% of the local level of light. (2) Supplementary lighting should be designed so that it will not cause glare for observers located near the supplemented task. (3) Supplementary lighting sources should be oriented so that they will cause neither direct glare nor reflected glare for the user.

Supplementary lighting equipment can take many forms. Permanent equipment includes downlights, luminous panels (modified as valences and cornices), brackets (often found as luminous soffits and canopies), and accent lights (both recessed and surface-mounted). Portable units may include simple reflectorized spot lamps in appropriate housings, well-shielded fluorescent lamps in concentrating reflector/lens housings, as well as table and floor lamps.

Table and floor lamps (see Figure 20.2) deserve special emphasis. Although they are usually chosen for their decorative value (money is lavished on the shade and base but rarely on the luminous elements), they are expected to provide acceptable supplementary lighting. In some cases, one table or floor lamp is expected to provide the total illumination within a space; however, such a setup is rarely successful.

Table lamps that perform multiple functions within a space (task lighting, general illumination, decoration, etc.) should fulfill the following minimum requirements: (1) The lower edge of the shade should be at eye level if it can be seen by the user when he is concentrating on a task. If the lower edge of the shade must be above eye level for decorative reasons, the light source should be placed slightly behind the user so that its unshielded glare will not be an annoyance. (2) The top edge of the shade should be at eye level when the observer is standing. This will prevent the interior of the luminaire from being observed. If the top edge cannot be in this optimum position, the top of the luminaire should be baffled. (3) Slightly translucent shades are preferred when they are open at the top and bottom. The open top allows light to "bounce" off the ceiling, thereby providing general reflected light if the ceiling has a highly reflective surface. The glowing wall of the shade will also add to the general ambience and will reduce glare. If an opaque shade is

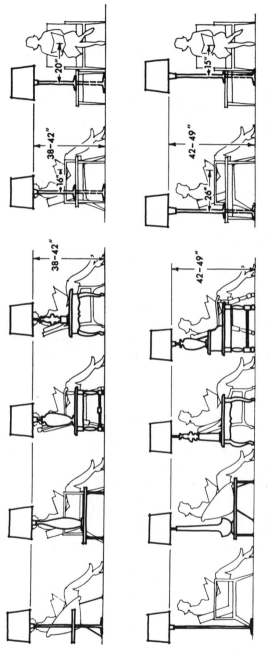

Average seated eye level is 38 to 42 inches above the floor. Lower edge of floor or table lamp shades should be at eye level when lamp is beside user. This is the correct placement for most table lamps, and for floor lamps serving furniture placed against a wall. Floor lamps with built-in tables should have shades no higher than eye level. For user comfort—when floor-lamp height to lower edge of shade or lamp-base-plus-table height is above eye level (42 to 49 inches), placement should be close to right or left rear corner of chair. This placement is possible only when chairs or sofas are at least 10 to 12 inches from wall.

Figure 20.2. Table and floor lamp data. (Reproduced, by permission, from Illuminating Engineering Society, *I.E.S. Lighting Handbook*, 1972.)

used, the light emitted from the top and bottom of the shade may appear excessively bright. The light from the open bottom of the shade can provide direct task illumination. Since these luminaires are usually located closer to the task than they are to the reflective ceiling surface, a diffuser may be used to reduce and soften the downward light component while reinforcing the upward intensities. (4) Highly translucent shades should be used next to highly reflective walls, and low-transmission shades should be placed next to dark walls. (5) The inside of the shade should be highly reflective so that it will redirect light output that would otherwise be wasted. (6) A conical shade is desirable because it tends to laterally spread the light emitted from the bottom of the shade. (7) If possible, lamps should be positioned in the lower portion of the shade so that widespread illumination will reach the task plane. It can be effective to have separate sources for up and down lighting. (8) Dimming should be provided to control the source over a continous range of illumination. If dimmers are not feasible, three-way lamps may be considered. If up and down lighting components are separate, there should be separate control for each light source. (9) Proper placement of the luminaire varies. If the luminaire is in line with the observer's shoulder, center it approximately 20 inches to the left or right of his head. If the luminaire is located slightly behind a seated user, position it approximately 15 inches to the side with the lower edge of the shade from 47 to 49 inches above the floor. (10) Concentrated sources in small reflectors should not be used if a supplementary luminaire is expected to perform both specific and general lighting.

FULLY FURNITURE INTEGRATED LIGHTING*

When you contemplate using fully furniture integrated office lighting you are, in a sense, considering a sophisticated form of the table lamp—a furniture-mounted device, or system of devices, on which you can rely for all lighting needs. This system should direct adequate light on the work at hand (task lighting) while also providing balanced illumination for the rest of the environment (ambient lighting). The system should always be positioned correctly, regardless of the observer's orientation, but it must never be intrusive.

The *direct* task lighting elements may be placed on desk tops, attached to partition walls, or hidden under shelves or cabinets. In furniture integrated lighting practice, the task is often assumed to be a piece of paper resting flat on a horizontal surface 2 feet 6 inches (2.5 ft) above the floor. Where

*Portions reprinted, by permission, from Nuckolls, James L., *Furniture Integrated Lighting*, Copyright © 1979 by the Shaw-Walker Company.

partitioned, open-plan (landscaped) furnishings are contemplated, some task lighting is usually furniture integrated.

In fully furniture integrated systems, most *ambient* lighting equipment is also attached to the furnishings, but it works by bouncing lower light intensities off ceilings. Here, the lighting equipment is attached to partitions, is placed on the tops of cabinets and shelves, or stands free (as with a torchiere or light column). Many ambient light sources are located above eye level (about 5.5 ft above the floor). If they are placed below eye level, then they must be carefully shielded. In certain instances, task and ambient sources of illumination are combined within a single device.

Of course, ambient illumination can also be produced by traditional luminaires recessed within or mounted on the ceiling and walls, but this discussion will be limited to full furniture integration of all luminaires.

Lamps

Fluorescent Applications.   Fluorescent lamps may be used for both task and ambient illumination in furniture integrated lighting systems. For indirect systems, they are most effective when ceiling heights are between 7.5 and 10.0 ft.

HID Applications.   HID lighting is mostly used for the indirect component of furniture integrated lighting systems. It tends to be most effective when ceilings are more than 10.0 ft high. Because of their compact nature, HID lamps may also form the lighting component of freestanding torchiere-type up lights. Clear mercury vapor lamps are never used; color-improved (phosphor-coated) versions offer passable color balance and higher efficiency. Metal halide lamps provide excellent light control possibilities when the clear lamp is needed for optical precision. Phosphor-coated types offer color improvement with a reduction in light control. Metal halide color variances are always a problem; two identical lamps may not look the same when first turned on, and all lamps tend to turn blue-white with age. High-pressure sodium lamps are a very efficient light source and offer excellent optical control. Their poorly balanced, yellow-orange color properties tend to limit acceptance with interior designers and architects. Very high pressure sodium models may be slightly more acceptable.

Illumination Levels

Although footlambert evaluations might be most appropriate, furniture integrated lighting systems are commonly evaluated in footcandles. Generally speaking, average task illumination is between 70 and 100 maintained footcandles. Illumination in zone 2 of optimal seeing areas gains subjective approval in typical installations when a minimum of 30 footcandles are maintained. This assumes that the reflectivity of surfaces is within optimal ranges, tending toward the more reflective of these parameters for furniture and nearby walls (see *Brightness Relationships*). Practical experience suggests that carpeted floors can be provided at only 15% reflectivity (20% and above would be desirable) if tracking and dirt buildup is to be kept under control. Of course, diffuse surfaces are a must, and it is also assumed that lighting reaches visible surfaces from directions that minimize veiling glare.

Light Control—Down (or Task) Lighting

In most applications, incandescent or fluorescent light sources are typical. Light control is accomplished by various methods, depending on whether the system uses fixed or flexibility mounted luminaires.

Flexible Luminaires. Flexible systems are based on adjustable and/or portable luminaires such as architect arm lamps (typical of those made by the Luxo company) or traditional table lamps, swing lamps, and the like. The observer can control veiling glare with these luminaires by simply moving them out of the offending zone.

Fixed Luminaires. These systems include statically mounted luminaires often attached to the underside of cabinets and bins mounted above, and parallel to, the work surface. They are also often located directly in the offending glare zone (Figure 20.3). Because they do not move, light control must be provided by other means.

Continuously linear fluorescent task lighting units may employ a *bat-wing* refractor to reduce veiling glare. When viewed at right angles to the long dimension, these closures split the down-light beam into right and left components, so the task is lighted at an oblique angle, with a minimum of direct down illumination (Figure 20.4). Some fixed systems may consist of two or more separate luminaires, or luminaire elements, that light the task from one or both sides.

In addition to reducing veiling glare, the task illumination must be low in direct glare. This is achieved through the use of precisely positioned refractors or louvers; the latter, however, are often inefficient. The use of simple diffusers may also be unsatisfactory, because they do nothing to minimize either direct or reflected glare. The same can be said of the bare fluorescent tubes often found in under-cabinet lighting.

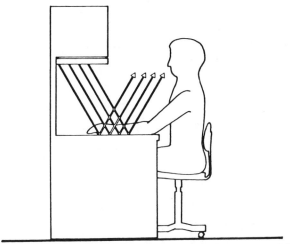

Figure 20.3. Glare-producing light distribution from under-cabinet-mounted fluorescent task luminaire.

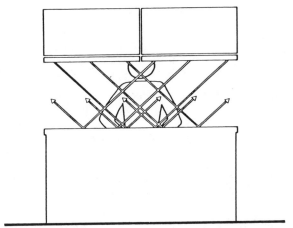

Figure 20.4. Bat-wing light distribution from under-cabinet-mounted fluorescent task luminaire.

Light Control—Up (or Ambient) Lighting

Up-lighting systems frequently use fluorescent or HID sources. Louvers, low-brightness reflectors, or refractors are used to reduce direct glare when observers pass close to indirect lighting mounted below 5.5 feet, as well as to distribute relatively even levels of illumination across the ceiling (most important when ceiling heights are below 9 ft). Solid lenses may also provide physical protection for the lamps and reflectors found within. Airborne dirt can severely reduce light output, for example, where open louvers are used. It is important to remember that any available, flat, uplight surface is inevitably going to hold dripping coffee cups, leaky plant pots, dusty books, and so on.

Mechanical Stability

Because furniture integrated lighting is mounted within the reach of its users, the structures should be able to withstand heavy abuse, particularly where long spans are encountered. A rule of thumb suggests that a 150-pound person should be able to sit on any unit without damaging it. Since this equipment can also be easily jarred or bumped, fasteners between the lighting units and its supporting structures must be designed to withstand these.

Heat

As a general rule, all exposed surfaces of lighting equipment within reach should be comfortable to the touch. "Warm" operation is an acceptable condition. The top surfaces of HID up lights are often very hot. This may also pose a safety problem, even when they are mounted above reachable height or covered with glass shields. The "trash basket" principle suggests that flammable materials will be tossed into any such opening, wherever it is mounted.

Maintenance

One of the great expenses in commercial lighting is the cost of maintenance. Ceiling integrated equipment often requires two electricians for cleaning and relamping. Since the location must be reached with a ladder, there is also a disruption of office activities. This costly inconvenience can be minimized by maintenance programs carried out during off-hours, but the practice may require the payment of overtime wages.

Well-designed furniture integrated lighting can be maintained by one person, standing on the floor, without tools. The relamping and cleaning services can be performed by unskilled workers during regular business hours with little disruption to business routines.

Whenever possible, electric discharge lamps should be used. They last longer than incandescent sources and therefore require less frequent service.

Electric Power Consumption

There is no evidence to suggest that full or partial furniture integration of lighting, per se, will lead to lesser or greater electrical efficiencies. In addition, all reports of very low energy consumption should be considered with care. This is particularly true of predictions made by competing manufacturers before equipment is selected and installed. The best tests of energy efficiency rely on metered readings of working installations taken over long periods of time. Even here, the figures may not be accurate since it is difficult to separate lighting from other equipment that may be connected to an electrical distribution system. Total possible connected electrical load predictions of from 2 to 5 watts per square foot are not unusual; an amount between 1.5 and 2.5 watts per square toot is to be admired.

Electrical Power Distribution

Fully furniture integrated lighting must be wired through the floor and walls or by the use of poles of flexible ducts running to the ceiling.

Floor Systems. The three major types of floor systems may be modified and possibly combined. (1) *Raised floors,* often called "computer floors," offer relatively easy access to all parts of the electrical system. Although they are more expensive than many of their alternatives, they are the most flexible. When the use of communications equipment is extensive (telephones, computer terminals, etc.), access floors are doubly effective. (2) *Wiring channels,* encased in the floor slab, are less expensive, but also less flexible. One must plan to position work stations over the channel grid. (3) *Floor-through* systems allow electrical power to be pulled up from distribution systems concealed in the ceiling of the floor below. With this method, additional plenum height must be provided, and holes will have to be cut in the floor materials whenever work stations are relocated.

Ceiling Poles. Poles that carry electrical wiring and communications from conventional distribution systems in the ceiling to the work station below are inexpensive alternative to floor systems. They are, however, often rejected as a disturbing visual element because they create a "forest" effect in the open plan office. Internally wired floor-to-ceiling partitions eliminate the need for poles.

Voltages.   Because furniture integrated lighting equipment can be touched by the user, current national codes limit the voltage to 120. Standard building electrical distribution systems using 277, 240, or other voltages above 120 are not available in the United States.

Wireways.   Once wires leave the floor, they must be routed through the furnishings. Acceptable furniture systems provide separate raceways and electrical connections for both power and communications. Sufficient outlets are, of course, a necessity for the operation of clocks, typewriters, calculators, terminals, and other desk equipment. Separately enclosed wiring may be required when certain forms of emergency lighting are incorporated within the standard lighting module.

Fast-Track/Phased Construction

In many situations, building materials must be ordered before spaces are fully designed. At the same time, unalterable construction schedules place strain on the design process. This sort of fast-track/phased construction is easily accommodated by furniture integrated lighting. To start with, the designer need only establish the lighting system to be used, density of use, average watts per square foot, and the electrical distribution system. Lighting equipment particulars can then be developed as the use of the space becomes more clearly defined.

Light Patterns

Furniture integrated lighting systems, by intent, will not create unvarying levels of illumination throughout a space. Light levels are *designed* to vary with the use of the space and difficulty of the task. On the other hand, distracting variations in intensity should not occur within a task or between the task and its immediate environment.

In landscaped offices with partitions or other high obstructions, the designer must avoid annoying shadows. When ceiling-mounted lighting systems are used, these obstructions can cause pockets of shadow, particularly under hanging cabinets. Properly designed furniture integrated lighting places lighting equipment under cabinets and within other potentially dark spaces.

Ceiling Heights and Conditions

Extra Floor Space.   With a complete furniture integrated lighting system, it may be possible to add a floor of office space within a 20-story building. The extra floor may be added because furniture integrated lighting does not require as high a ceiling plenum as traditional ceiling recessed lighting. This is possible even when a raised, computer-type access floor is used.

Ceiling Finishes.   Ceiling finishes should be diffuse and highly reflective (80–90%). Although fissured surfaces are acceptable, the ceiling should be generally on a single plane.

Flexibility and Mobility

Furniture integrated lighting systems provide the greatest flexibility when installed in facilities that are owner occupied or where the owner provides the furnishing systems. When the owner does not occupy the space and it is offered for speculative lease or rent, furniture integrated ambient lighting may not be the best for the owner because tenants may object to purchasing these specialized systems. On the other hand, a tenant leaseholder may find that furniture integrated lighting is a flexible and inexpensive way to renovate or improve an existing space. Tenants who buy their own furniture integrated lighting can take their lighting equipment with them should they decide to move.

Plugs Versus *Hard Wiring.*   When plugs are used to connect electric power to the furniture integrated lighting systems, the relocation of work stations is relatively simple. Certain electrical codes may require permanent wiring and prohibit plugging, or they may require special plugging provisions. Permanent wiring, also called "hard wiring," limits flexibility because an electrician must make the connection, which entails extra expense and possible scheduling problems.

Chapter Twenty-one

Electrical Control

The control of electricity is one of the most exciting subjects in the study of lighting, but it is also one of the least understood and poorest applied of the lighting tools. Very few designers realize how much can be accomplished with innovative control.

DIMMING

Full-range dimming is the continuous variation of lighting intensity without steps.

Dimming Curve

The way that light output responds to changes in the control setting is called the dimming curve. If a change in the setting of the dimming control, from full bright to full dim, approximately equals change in the amount of electricity allowed to reach the light source, the dimmer is said to have a linear curve. However, the eye is more sensitive to changes in low light levels than changes at high levels. Lamps also do not respond in a linear way. Even if the electrical output of a dimmer changes in a linear manner, a light source will appear to dim faster at low levels and slower at high light levels. To correct this, dimmers may feature a "square law" dimming curve. Here the dimmer control moves at a constant speed, but causes the light to dim faster at high levels and slower at low levels. To the eye, the effect is a constant dimming speed. Both logarithmic and linear dimming curves are supplied by equipment manufacturers.

Incandescent Dimmers

Dimming methods are first governed by the way in which sources produce light. Separate systems exist for incandescent, fluorescent, and HID light sources. Incandescent dimming has the longest history.

Resistance Dimming

The first dimming system used for incandescent sources was the resistance type. It consisted of a long wire that was attached to the power supply and was formed of metals that resisted the flow of electrons over its entire length. Connected to the incandescent source was a second wire attached to a "shoe" or "wiper" that slid along the resistance wire.

The resistance wire had to be very long so that it could absorb all the energy that was required. For this reason, it was often coiled on itself. Because the shoe actually moved over an exposed section of this coil, the dimming was actually completed in a series of steps (often a minimum of 110 for flickerless control). The shoe was connected to an insulated mechanism, called a "dead front," that prevented the operator from touching any of the electrically "live" parts as he moved the shoe. (All electrical controls should be of the dead-front type.)

In many of the resistance dimmers used for lighting practice, the resistance coils were wound more closely at the bright end of the dimming curve than at the dim end. This feature produced a logarithmic dimming curve.

The chief advantages of the resistance dimmer are its low cost and electrical simplicity. However, the following disadvantages far outweigh this system's usefulness in contemporary architectural lighting: (1) Resistance dimmers are heavy and bulky. (2) They are only effective within a very restricted capacity range. For example, if a dimmer is rated for 50 to 60 watts, a 25-watt lamp will not dim evenly. (3) Resistance dimmers are sensitive to the load they carry. If three lamps are attached to a resistance circuit, they will dim when a fourth is added, even though the control has not been moved. (4) The electrical power that is not used by a lamp in the dimmed position is discarded by the resistance dimmer in the form of heat; the lower the dimmer reading, the hotter the dimmer. This feature wastes electrical energy and creates cooling problems.

Autotransformer Dimming

An advance in incandescent dimming was achieved with the development of variable transformers. A simple transformer consists of two separate coils of wire mounted in such a way that the coils have overlapping magnetic fields. Therefore, the magnetic field created in the "primary" coil by the alternating current passing through it induces another magnetic field to pass through a "secondary" coil. The alternating voltage in the first coil induces voltage in the second coil. By varying the number of turns in the second coil, the amount of voltage it produces can be decreased or increased. If electric power is drawn from different points on the secondary coil, we can (in basic theory) achieve different voltages from the same transformer.

The action of the basic autotransformer is roughly similar to selecting different voltage outputs from a simple transformer, although certain modifications in the circuitry make the continuously variable autotransformer operate effectively.

The autotransformer has the following advantages over the resistance dimmer: (1) It will evenly dim a wide range of wattages, from a few watts to its full electrical rating. (2) It will operate all wattages connected to it through the same dimming range. High-wattage lamps will dim over the same curve as low-wattage lamps. (3) Lamps can be added to or subtracted from an autotransformer controlled circuit without affecting the other lamps already on the circuit. (4) The dimmer is cool in operation since unused power is not dissipated as heat. Most electrical power not used by the lamp is simply not used.

There are, however, three disadvantages: (1) Although frequently smaller than the resistance dimmer, the autotransformer still requires considerable space. As an example, a dimmer used to control only 200 watts requires a wall area measuring 5 inches high by 5 inches wide by 3 inches long. If the wall-mounted autotransformer must control 800 watts, it may require approximately 10 inches by 7½ inches by 3¾ inches. (2) The autotransformer is comparatively expensive. (3) The autotransformer is heavy when compared to newer dimming systems.

Solid-State Dimming

Most solid-state dimming systems are based on the use of a "thyristor." This term encompasses power control devices such as triacs, silicon controlled rectifiers (SCR), and silicon controlled switches (SCS). These solid-state devices allow electric current to flow at full voltage, but only for a portion of the time. This causes the incandescent lamp to dim as if the voltage had been reduced (as with the autotransformer). The timing of the solid-state device is controlled by a low-voltage source that can be remotely varied. A small variable current, therefore, causes a larger one to change.

With one of the most common thyristors, the SCR, two types of circuit can be considered. If there is only one SCR in the dimming circuit, dimming is accomplished by partially or completely eliminating half of an alternating current's cycle. Two SCRs mounted back to back, permit a controlled amount of current to pass during each half cycle of the full AC voltage cycle. With SCRs, control is obtained by what is called "gating action"; a very small and variable DC voltage is applied to the gate (controlling element) of the SCR. This voltage activates the SCR and times the voltage that is allowed to flow.

Solid-state dimming systems have the following advantages: (1) They are very small. A 600-watt dimmer, for example, can fit into a standard wall switch enclosure (about 2½ in. by 3½ in. by 2 in.). (2) Thyristor dimmers are efficient, since there is little power loss caused by the dimmer itself. (3) They are insenstive to changes in incandescent load up to their rated capacity. (4) They are relatively cool in operation. (5) They adapt easily to miniaturization and programmed remote control. (6) The dimmers are inert and require no maintenance. (7) They are comparatively inexpensive, particularly when used to control lower wattages (to 1000 W).

As with all control devices, thyristors have certain disadvantages: (1) They are fragile. Thyristors will take neither the electrical nor physical abuse that can be absorbed by an autotransformer (when they fail, they stay at "full on"). (2) They may cause noise in associated systems. Thyristors can cause lamps to "sing" (a high buzz) and/or create interference with electronic audio or television equipment.

Other Systems

Other types of incandescent dimming systems have been used in the past, but are rarely installed today. These systems, which may be encountered in older installations, are magnetic amplifiers, reactors, and electronic tubes (thyraton tubes).

Fluorescent Dimmers

Fluorescent light sources can be successfully dimmed through the control of electric power. Two systems are commonly used: the autotransformer and the solid-state dimmer. The autotransformer was the first system employed for fluorescent service.

The autotransformer has been largely displaced by the solid-state dimmer. In a simple installation, the solid-state dimming system is comparatively uncomplicated. When large numbers of fluorescent lamps are dimmed, however, the system must be more sophisticated. Advanced systems should be developed by a lighting expert (lighting consultant, engineer, or manufacturer). All components of the system should be supplied by one manufacturer so that they will be coordinated.

Environmental designers should be aware of the following details concerning application of solid-state systems: (1) Only rapid start fluorescent lamps can be used. During the dimming cycle, the electrodes of these lamps must remain heated. Instant start and preheat lamp electrodes are turned off after the lamps are started. (2) A dimming ballast must be used, and this ballast must be compatible with the dimmer or dimming system to be installed. Dimmer and ballast manufacturers will help in the selection of appropriate components. (3) Fluorescent lamps will not dim all the way off. If they are allowed to dim too far, the lamps will flicker or a luminous spiraling form will be seen within the bulb. Most fluorescent dimmers have an adjustment that prevents the user from dimming the lamp beyond a maximum down position. On the smaller and simpler systems, this control is usually found under the face plate and is located near the main adjustment knob. Once the maximum down position has been reached, the lamps must be turned off with a switch. When a fluorescent dimming system is planned, it should be kept in mind that the lamps will still be faintly glowing when dimmed to their maximum. (4) The use of a starting aid is essential. The starting aid should be in the form of a 1-inch wide metal strip placed within approximately 1 inch of the lamp bulb, and it must extend along the entire length of the bulb. A fluorescent housing will often serve as a starting aid. In all cases, the ballast case must be electrically connected to the starting aid. (5) Only 3-and 4-foot lamps can be dimmed by most systems. All lamps controlled by a single system should be of the same length or they will not dim at the same rate. (6) Fluorescent lamps used in dimming systems should be new, and it is a wise practice to install them all at the same time. As some of the lamps grow old and begin to flicker, the complete set of lamps can be moved to a nondimming part of an installation and replaced with a fresh supply.

HID Dimmers

At first, it was not possible to dim HID sources by controlling their electric power. When dimming was absolutely necessary, mechanical methods were used. These mechanial systems consisted of filters, shutters, or louvers that moved in front of the source to selectively block its light output.

Solid-state dimming systems are now a reality. Mercury-vapor light sources are most commonly dimmed, although systems also exist for metal halide and high-pressure sodium.

SWITCHING

Manually Operated Toggle Switches

The most obvious mode of switching control, and the one most frequently used in architectural practice, is the manually operated toggle wall switch.

Circuits

In architectural practice, three circuit types are important. These include circuits controlled from one, two, or three or more positions. Each requires a different switching circuit.

Single-Pole, Single-Throw (SPST).   As described in the topic on electricity, a simple circuit can consist of a single lamp connected to a power source by two wires (see Figure 21.1). If direct current is present, the power flows in one direction, from the negative terminal to the positive terminal of the power supply. With alternating current, electrons also move in one direction, but that direction is reversed at regular intervals. In both instances, the resistance of an incandescent lamp filament, placed in series with the circuit, causes the filament to glow and produce visible energy. Either wire connecting the light source to the power supply can be connected to, and thus controlled by, an SPST toggle switch.

Single-Pole, Double-Throw (SPDT).   When an electrical load must be controlled from two locations, a three-way or SPDT switch is required (see Figure 21.2). This switch allows the cirucit to choose one of two alternative paths to complete (connect) the circuit.

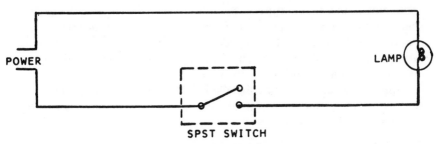

SPST SWITCH

Figure 21.1.   One-way switching circuit.

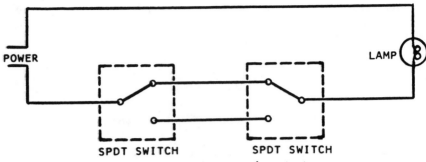

Figure 21.2.   3-way switching circuit.

It is possible to develop standard-voltage wiring circuits to accommodate three or more control positions. However, as the number of control positions increase, so does the wiring complexity. For multiple switching locations, therefore, other switching systems are usually recommended (see *Advanced Concepts for Simple Electrical Control*).

Types

Manually operated toggle switches are available in the following three basic mechanical types.

Toggle Snap.   This type is the most common and least expensive. It makes contact by snapping one metal contact to another.

Mercury Switch.   In this switching instrument, a vial containing liquid mercury is tilted to allow the flow of mercury (an electrically conductive metal) between the switching contacts. Mercury switches are also called "silent action switches" (there is no snap or click).

There are two main advantages in using mercury control devices: (1) The silent action of the switches suggests their use in hospitals, churches, radio or television stations, bedrooms, and similar installations. (2) Since the making and breaking of the electrical circuit is completed within a vial containing a special atmosphere, the spark created by the snapping action of standard switching is minimized. Because this sparking (or arcing) causes corrosion of the metal parts in standard switches, the mercury control has a longer life. The absence of an open spark also recommends mercury controls in explosive or corrosive areas.

Mercury switches must be installed in the specified upright position. If they are not, the mercury will not flow in the correct direction, and the switches may fail to function.

Momentary Contact.   The momentary contact switch, or push button, is used to briefly open or close a circuit. When manual pressure is released, the switch returns to its normal resting position. Push buttons are available with NO (normal open) and NC (normal closed) functions. The NO type maintains a disconnected position when it is not being operated.

Both momentary contact and continuous contact switches can be fitted with light sources that indicate their location and/or operating position. If the lights are used to locate the switches, they are usually placed in the handle of the switch and are normally "on" when the circuit is not energized. Lights that indicate the operating position ("on" or "off") can be located anywhere in the switch or on the face plate covering the switching mechanism.

Certain indicators require separate wiring for the lighting circuit. Others, using neon glow lamps, do not require a separate lamp circuit.

Designs

Simple wall switches are currently available in numerous design configurations. Instead of flipping a control, the user can push, turn, or tilt it. Finishing plates, often called "decorator wall plates," are also numerous. Their design styles change as fast as the fashion of the moment. In spite of this capriciousness, designers should attempt to match thier interior schemes with an appropriate finishing detail and not leave the selection up to the installing electrical contractor.

Advanced Concepts for Simple Electrical Control

Low-Voltage Switching

In effect, the low-voltage control system of multiple light sources is an adaptation of an old-fashioned pull-chain method of switching luminaires on and off. At one time, control of several lights in a room was accomplished by pulling a chain attached to the luminaire. With low-voltage control, the strings are replaced by low-voltage wires that operate a relay to turn the light on or off.

The low-voltage system consists of two main components: (1) A split-coil relay permits "positive control" for on and off functions. In other words, one half of a split electromagnetic coil pulls the higher voltage (120 V or above) switch off, and the other half pulls the switch on. This means that the relay can either be mounted near the higher voltage load or installed in a remote location. Since the low-voltage controls are small and consume little electric power, there can be many of them, and they can be placed wherever desired without running heavily insulated wire. (2) Power regulation is necessary to convert the low-voltage control signal from higher-voltage building service.

The regulator is a transformer that may or may not be attached to the low-voltage system through a rectifier. The rectifier is not essential, but it is added in some systems because the relays react more positively in the presence of direct current.

There are several advantages to low-voltage control: (1) The systems can be inexpensive to install. The branch circuits of higher voltage building current can go directly to the luminaires (where the low-voltage switching element can be located) eliminating costly runs of heavy wire through wall switch locations. Where multiple switching is from three or more locations, savings are excellent. Since the control voltage is relatively harmless, control wiring can be run through an installation without the use, or expense of, conduit. (2) Multiple switching from more than two locations and other control elaborations are feasible. There can be many switches controlling a single lamp, or one switch can operate ("master") many luminaires. (3) Changes in lighting control can be achieved easily by running thin and inexpensive low-voltage wires. Only one power supply is required, no matter how many switches are connected to a system, providing only one switch is energized at a time (the usual circumstance).

There are also certain disadvantages to low-voltage control: (1) It is not a common system of control wiring, so the local electrician may find the installation difficult to understand. (2) Certain building codes limit its use or make it uneconomical. (3) It may be expensive and unnecessarily complex for systems without any need for multiple or centralized control.

Sound-Activated Controls

It is not necessary to manually flip a handle or push a button to turn on lighting equipment; control can be accomplished with sound-activated devices. One of the units first marketed was a hand-clap control. To control illumination, two hand claps, 1 second apart, were all that was needed. The switch responded to the high-frequency component of the sound created by the hand claps; two claps were required to prevent confusion with stray sounds producing the same frequency tones.

Another device uses a high-frequency dog whistle for the same purpose. Other systems rely on electrically produced control tones (similar to those used for the wireless remote control of television sets).

Motion Detection Switching

Motion detection devices are a modified type of high-frequency tone control that was first introduced as a sensor for burglar alarms. These devices send out and receive an invisible ultrasonic beam and operate like a sonar sounding device. Movement of a person or thing within the range of the sensor will activate the switch. Some versions of the device will, when activated, hold the circuit in the on position. Other types can be set to turn on for a few seconds or a full minute and then return to off and automatically reset. Motion detectors are useful in commercial or residential applications that require immediate illumination, whenever occupied, for purposes of safety or crime prevention. They also save electrical power by extinguishing the lighting of unoccupied areas.

Infrared and "radar" detectors offer sophistication to their more common sonic counterparts. Infrared motion detectors can be "tuned" to sense a restricted area within any volume (sonic detectors tend to fill volumes with their signal). Radar sensors pass through certain building materials—not always an advantage.

Carrier-Current Switching

This system consists of two basic components: (1) a transmitter powered by the building voltage that sends a signal through the building wiring, and (2) a receiver that turns a circuit on or off when it senses an appropriate signal. Lighting devices can be attached to one receiver or any number of receivers. Any number of transmitters can control any one receiver. As long as both transmitter and receiver are connected to the same source of a building's standard lighting power, no additional control wiring is required between the transmitter and receiver.

Carrier-current switching is not new; some lighting systems were introduced as "executive toys" during the 1960s. They are now promoted as viable, very low cost, simply installed control systems for both residential and commerical facilities in new installations and retrofits. Both dimming and switching capabilities are typical.

Radio-Frequency Control

Radio waves can also be used to operate lighting. Radio-operated controls are commonly found in automatic garage door openers and model plane and car controls.

Photoelectric Control

These switches rely on a light-sensing element to energize power. They are often used to turn on both residential and commercial light sources when evening approaches. They are also extensively used in commercial counting applications.

In addition to its use as a simple, light-sensitive switching device, two or more sophisticated systems are typical. In one, photoelectric sensors initiate full range dimming to compensate for changes to the natural illumination of interior spaces (e.g., as the sun goes down, the lights dim up).

In another application, the photoelectric sensor adjusts for an artificial lighting system's light loss factor (LLF) (see *Calculations*). We know that lighting levels should always be developed for their maintained intensities; this means that the initial illumination will usually be in excess of the designed level. If the LLF is 50% in a dirty atmosphere with poor predicted maintenance, for example, the initial illumination may be twice what is needed. Here, the photocell tells the dimmer to provide a lower initial light level; that level is increased as the lighting system ages, and the level is reduced again when room surfaces and lighting equipment are cleaned and relamped.

TIMING AND PROGRAMMING

Simplified "on" and "off" timing of electrical circuits is common at present; multiple selection of complex illumination programs is rarely applied in architecture. However, in programmed lighting, switching and dimming of many circuits can be accomplished on command, according to time, or based on other environmental conditions, such as light and sound levels, moisture, and traffic flow.

Chapter Twenty-two

Lighting Layouts and Design Reports

The drawings of the lighting layout and the report that may accompany them indicate the location of equipment and give other information such as: quantities, critical dimensions, direction of luminaire focus, construction details, finishes, mounting systems, manufacturers, recommended lamping, electrical requirements, and any other detail necessary (1) to purchase lighting equipment and to install a working lighting design or (2) for the preparation of specifications.

DRAWINGS

This chapter does not detail the processes of architectural drawing—we assume that the environmental designer is well grounded in this. However, there are techniques and requirements particularly important to a lighting plan, as contrasted with other construction documents. This discussion will cover particular requirements for the lighting aspects of a construction document.

Reflected ceiling plans, elevations and sections, floor plans, and miscellaneous details are the views frequently required to describe a lighting design. They are listed here, roughly in the order of their importance.

Generally, an acceptable drawing must be legible and capable of being reproduced by standard printing equipment. Its style should be pleasing to the client. In particular, the drawing should be concise; unnecessary or repetitive details merely confuse the work.

Focus

When a luminaire is expected to point in a particular direction, the general direction of focus should be noted on the drawing by adding an arrow to the luminaire symbol. Note that certain luminaires only rotate within a 350° arc; the arrow will prevent the installer from locating the axis of major focus in the unusable 10°.

Title Block

A title block, which should appear on each drawing, should contain the following information: designer's name, client's name, project's name or description, project location, date (with additional spaces for date revisions), draftsman's and supervisor's initials, project number, scale, and drawing number.

Wiring and Electrical Control

There are two methods of indicating lighting control wiring on a layout. In one system, each luminaire and its switch or dimmer are connected by an appropriate line (as shown in Figure 22.1e). For the second method, a lowercase letter placed by each luminaire symbol refers to a corresponding control.

When creating a layout with the first method, a single line symbolizes all the wires within a single circuit. The installing contractor or the electrical engineer will determine the number and size of the actual wires, as well as their exact location.

For the second method, the following letters are accepted: a, b, c, d, f, g, h, j, k, m, n, p, q, r, t, u, v, w, y, z. The following letters are not used: e is reserved for emergency circuits (designated by the project engineer), i is confused with 1, l is confused with 1, o is confused with 0, s is reserved for switches, x is reserved for exit light wiring (designated by the project engineer). If one runs out of letters, double letters are used (e.g., aa).

Figure 22.1. Symbols: (a) Incandescent and HID luminaires; (b) fluorescent luminaires.

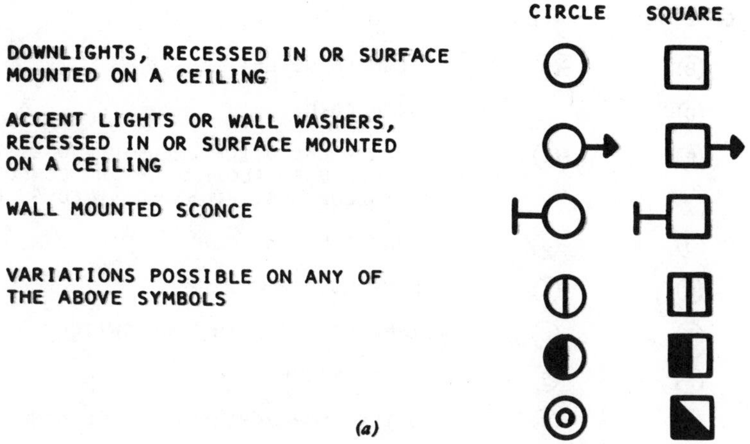

	CIRCLE	SQUARE

DOWNLIGHTS, RECESSED IN OR SURFACE MOUNTED ON A CEILING

ACCENT LIGHTS OR WALL WASHERS, RECESSED IN OR SURFACE MOUNTED ON A CEILING

WALL MOUNTED SCONCE

VARIATIONS POSSIBLE ON ANY OF THE ABOVE SYMBOLS

(a)

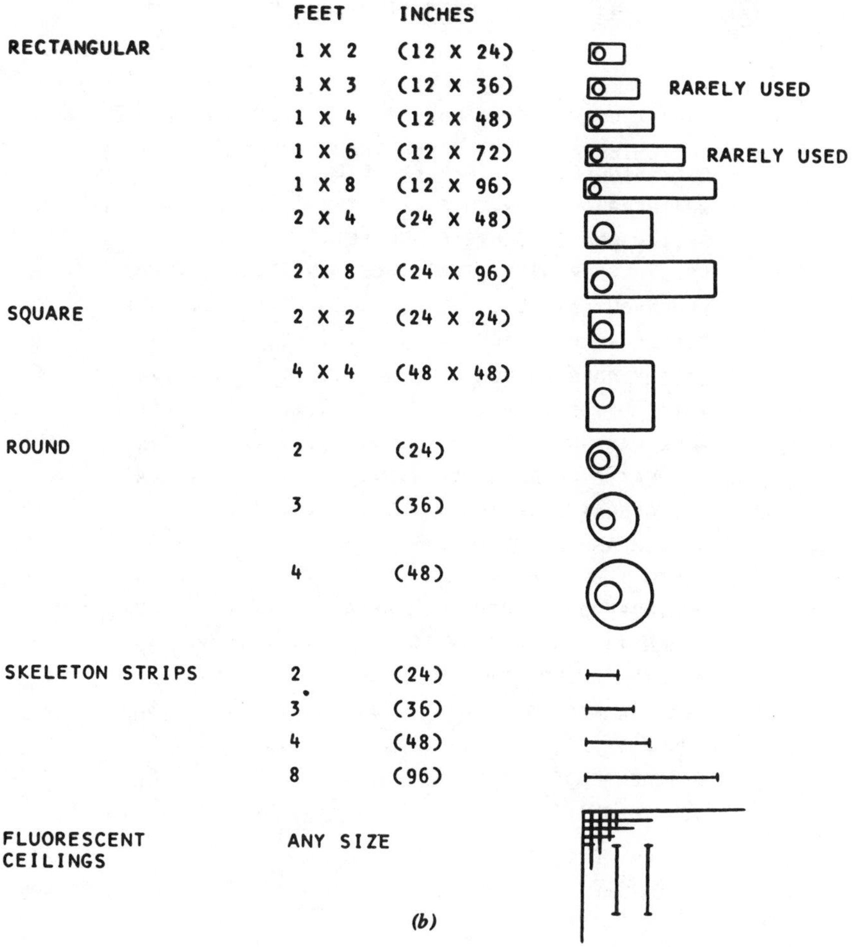

	FEET	INCHES	
RECTANGULAR	1 X 2	(12 X 24)	
	1 X 3	(12 X 36)	RARELY USED
	1 X 4	(12 X 48)	
	1 X 6	(12 X 72)	RARELY USED
	1 X 8	(12 X 96)	
	2 X 4	(24 X 48)	
	2 X 8	(24 X 96)	
SQUARE	2 X 2	(24 X 24)	
	4 X 4	(48 X 48)	
ROUND	2	(24)	
	3	(36)	
	4	(48)	
SKELETON STRIPS	2	(24)	
	3	(36)	
	4	(48)	
	8	(96)	
FLUORESCENT CEILINGS	ANY SIZE		

(b)

313

CEILING   WALL

Ⓑ   ─Ⓑ   BLANKED OUTLET

Ⓓ   DROP CORD

Ⓔ   ─Ⓔ   ELECTRICAL OUTLET; FOR USE ONLY WHEN CIRCLE USED ALONE MIGHT BE CONFUSED WITH COLUMNS, PLUMBING SYMBOLS, ETC.

Ⓙ   ─Ⓙ   JUNCTION BOX

Ⓛ   ─Ⓛ   LAMP HOLDER

Ⓛ$_{PS}$ ─Ⓛ$_{PS}$ LAMP HOLDER WITH PULL SWITCH

Ⓢ   ─Ⓢ   PULL SWITCH

Ⓥ   ─Ⓥ   OUTLET FOR VAPOR DISCHARGE LAMP

Ⓧ   ─Ⓧ   EXIT LIGHT OUTLET

(c)

DUPLEX CONVENIENCE OUTLET.................. ⊖

CONVENIENCE OUTLET OTHER THAN DUPLEX...... ⊖1,3 (1 = SINGLE, 3 = TRIPLEX, ETC.)

WEATHERPROOF CONVENIENCE OUTLET.......... ⊖ WP

SWITCH AND CONVENIENCE OUTLET............. ⊖ S

SPECIAL PURPOSE OUTLET (DES. IN SPEC.).... ◭

FLOOR OUTLET............................. ⊙

SINGLE POLE SWITCH........................S

DOUBLE POLE SWITCH........................S$_2$

THREE WAY SWITCH..........................S$_3$

FOUR WAY SWITCH...........................S$_4$

AUTOMATIC DOOR SWITCH.....................S$_D$

KEY OPERATED SWITCH.......................S$_K$

SWITCH AND PILOT LAMP.....................S$_P$

CIRCUIT BREAKER...........................S$_{CB}$

WEATHERPROOF CIRCUIT BREAKER..............S$_{WCB}$

MOMENTARY CONTACT SWITCH..................S$_{MC}$

REMOTE CONTROL SWITCH.....................S$_{RC}$

WEATHERPROOF SWITCH.......................S$_{WP}$

FUSED SWITCH..............................S$_F$

WEATHERPROOF FUSED SWITCH.................S$_{WF}$

DIMMER SWITCH.............................S$_{DIM}$

(d)

Figure 22.1.   (*c*) Other luminaires or lighting outlets. (*d*) Convenience receptacles and switches.

——— BRANCH CIRCUIT; CONCEALED IN CEILING OR WALL

—·— BRANCH CIRCUIT; CONCEALED IN FLOOR

------ BRANCH CIRCUIT; EXPOSED

→▶▶ HOME RUN TO PANEL BOARD - INDICATE NUMBER OF
CIRCUITS BY NUMBER OF ARROWS
NOTE: ANY CIRCUIT WITHOUT FURTHER DESIGNATION
INDICATES A TWO-WIRE CIRCUIT - FOR A
GREATER NUMBER OF WIRES, INDICATE AS
FOLLOWS: ——————— (3 WIRES),
——————— (4 WIRES), ETC.

$O_{a,b,c,etc.}$
$\Theta_{a,b,c,etc.}$
$S_{a,b,c,etc.}$

ANY STANDARD SYMBOL WITH THE
ADDITION OF A LOWER CASE SUBSCRIPT
LETTER MAY BE USED TO DESIGNATE SOME
SPECIAL VARIATION OF STANDARD EQUIPMENT
OF PARTICULAR INTEREST IN A SPECIFIC
SET OF ARCHITECTURAL PLANS.
WHEN USED THEY MUST BE LISTED IN
THE KEY OF SYMBOLS ON EACH DRAWING
AND IF NECESSARY FURTHER DESCRIBED
IN THE SPECIFICATIONS.

(e)

Figure 22.1. (*e*) Wiring and special variations.

Type Letters

Each luminaire should be identified with a type letter, located next to (not inside) its symbol. Only uppercase letters are used, as lowercase letters are reserved for circuit identification. Single letters (e.g., Type A) refer to luminaires using electric discharge light sources; double letters (Type AA) refer to luminaires with incandescent light sources. If one type of luminaire is very much like another (e.g., a 3-ft long version of a 4-ft skeleton strip), then that subtype is indicated with a number (Type A–1 or AA–1 would be similar to Type A or AA); separate type letters should be assigned whenever one luminaire is substantially different from another. For example, if lighting track were labeled Type TT, track-mounted lamp holders would not be assigned Type TT-1 since they bear no structural resemblance to each other.

Control systems (dimmers, special switches, etc.) can also be assigned type letters. If reserved for incandescent service, four letters are used (Type AAAA might refer to a wall-box-mounted dimmer); three letters are used for electric discharge lighting control. If the electrical control system can operate either kind of light source, three letters are also used.

The following letters are accepted for luminaire and electrical control system identification: A (or AA or AAA or AAAA), B, C, D, F, G, H, J, K, L,

M, N, P, Q, R, T, U, V, W, Y, Z. The following letters are not used: E (or EE) is reserved for emergency equipment (designated by the project engineer), I is confused with 1, O is confused with 0, S is reserved for switches, X is reserved for exit light systems (designated by the project engineer). One does not usually run through all the letters used to designate luminaires with electric discharge lamps or to designate electrical controls. However, one often does exceed the number of available double letters in installations using large amounts of incandescent decorative luminaires (e.g., hotels with sconce, chandeliers, etc.). Here, types such as "AB" or "AC" are used to extend the alphabet.

REPORT

A full written report may or may not accompany a lighting layout. If a report is not used, all detailed information pertaining to the design must be placed on the drawing. In particular, a schedule showing all luminaires by type letter, description, wattage, lamp, and manufacturer should be included.

A report should be prepared if the designer wishes to include exact information about layout. The report should indicate all the information necessary to interpret, evaluate, purchase, install, and maintain the design. A report may include some or all of the following features.

Cover. The cover page identifies the report. It may include the project's name, client's name, designer's name, issue date, revision dates, and project number.

Introduction. The introduction explains how the report is to be used.

References. This page is usually reserved for the names, addresses, and telephone numbers of everyone involved in the project.

Contents. The pages of the report (in its final form) should be numbered and major sections listed in the table of contents. Preliminary report pages are not numbered.

General Comments. The general comments section lists all the considerations and qualifications relative to the project. Where applicable, the following comments are useful:

The Consultant's work is based on dimensions and drawings supplied by the Client and not further verified by the Consultant. It is assumed that:
Construction of the facility is fireproof.
The mounting depth dimensions given to the Consultant represent the total space available for the recessing of a luminaire, after allowances have been made for local

electrical code requirements, and all occasional obstructions such as pipes and air conditioning, ceiling insulation, and wiring.

Unless otherwise noted, the dimension given for luminaire mounting depth includes all socket assembles, maximum adjustments, and wiring connectors.

Prewired luminaires have (or have not) been recommended. All luminaires are standard (or prewired).

Special code and label requirements must be brought to the Consultant's attention. Unless otherwise noted, all standard and catalog luminaires carry the UL label and are constructed according to the standards of the National Electrical Code.

Recommendations containing the latest date supersede all other recommendations. In particular, preliminary recommendations should not be used as construction documents unless they have been approved for that purpose by the Consultant.

Equipment orders should not be placed with suppliers on the basis of information contained in the Budget Estimates page or other condensed schedules (if the full report form is used). The sheet(s) used to fully describe the lighting equipment (identified by a "type" letter in the upper right corner) should be submitted to equipment suppliers together with all lamp information. The purchaser must verify all quantities estimated in the recommendation.

The electrical contractor or electrician who will install the lighting equipment should be asked to supply a cost estimate and comment on installation problems that may be particular to the project *before* equipment is purchased. [This comment is always important when the project involves work with existing structures (not new construction).]

The following lighting layouts and equipment recommendations are the responsibility of others [lighting designers may not be involved in these areas—they are often planned by the project engineer] and are not directly covered in this report.
Emergency lighting systems.
Exit indicators.
Mechanical room illlumination.
[Other specific areas as they apply to each project.]

Budget Estimates. The cost of lighting equipment (usually including luminaires and controls, but excluding lamps) is often stated at the list price if the report is for the client or at the net price (often the discount price to the contractor) if the report is for professional use. Distributor prices are rarely published.

Substitutions. If the designer wishes to list alternative equipment that is approved, he or she should do so on a substitutions page.

Control. Specific comments (if any) concerning control are listed on this page. Comments often include the division of circuits, or dimmer or circuit wattage totals.

Luminaire (Lighting Fixture) Schedule.   This listing offers a summary of the lighting equipment being used on a project. Columns may be established for (1) luminaire symbols (see Figure 22.1*a–e*), (2) type letters, (3) lamp codes, (4) total watts (with ballast loss), and (5) a brief description (see Chapter Seventeen, e.g., "Utilitarian fluorescent luminaire, recessed mounted, with direct light distribution, reflector light control, reflector (cone) baffle, and minimum trim with a scallop-shield accessory"). If a full lighting equipment recommendation is not provided (see the following section), then additional columns are established for (6) the manufacturer's name, and (7) the luminaire or control system catalog number. Whether or not a full lighting equipment recommendation exists, this schedule should be included in either the project's lighting report or drawings (or both).

Lighting Equipment Recommendations.   These pages, indicated with an capital type letter [basic luminaires are listed by letter only ("Type A"), while variations use a number ("Type A–1")], describe the equipment shown in the project's drawings. Each luminaire is described by location, construction, finish, mounting, and suggested manufacturer. These recommendations also list the lamp suggested for the luminaire, as well as its electrical requirements and all other essential details.

Critical Lamp Performance Data, Photometric Reports, Specialized Control Recommendations,   Detail Drawings, and/or an *Appendix* are specialized sections that appear in reports when required.

SPECIFICATIONS

A specification is a detailed and precise statement prepared in the form of a legal document outlining the contract terms of a project. Specifications are used as a base for bidding projects and as an outline for construction. Their wording is based on precedent, and they should only be prepared by experts with extensive experience in the work.

SYMBOLS

Many of the symbols used in lighting layouts are standards listed by independent agencies (see Figure 22.1*a–e*). Variations of standard symbols should be carefully explained on the project drawings.

BASIC CHECKLIST FOR THE SPECIFICATION OF ALL
LUMINAIRES

BRIEF DESCRIPTION OF THE EQUIPMENT:

LOCATION OF THE EQUIPMENT:

IMPORTANT CONSTRUCTION DETAILS:

FINISHES: baffle.........
             exposed surfaces
             housing.........
             other..........

CEILING CONSTRUCTION: ( ) dry, ( ) wet.

MOUNTING: ( ) bracket   MOUNTING DEPTH:
             ( ) panel
             ( ) pendant   MAXIMUM MOUNTING WIDTH:
             ( ) portable
             ( ) recessed
             ( ) semi-recessed
             ( ) surface
             ( ) track

ACCESS: ( ) bottom only, ( ) top only, ( ) bottom & top.

RECOMMENDED MANUFACTURER(S):

CATALOG NUMBER(S):..........

LAMP CODE: QUANTITY OF LAMPS PER LUMINAIRE:

TOTAL WATTS PER LUMINAIRE: ( ) actual, ( ) nominal.

VOLTAGE TO THE LUMINAIRE:

NOTES:

                                        ILLUSTRATION
REFERENCE: REVISION DATE:

319

BASIC CHECKLIST FOR THE SPECIFICATION OF
INCANDESCENT AND H.I.D. LUMINAIRES

---

1. INSTALLATION: ( ) after ceiling is closed.
                  ( ) before ceiling is closed.

2. WIRING: ( ) standard, ( ) prewired.

3. BAFFLE: ( ) annular ring.   ( ) miniature groove.
            ( ) collar.   ( ) none.
            ( ) decorative.   ( ) reflector (cone).
            ( ) housing.   other:
            ( ) louver.

4. TRIM: ( ) air handling.   ( ) none.
          ( ) decorative.   ( ) plate.
          ( ) eyelid.   ( ) "trimless."
          ( ) minimum.   other:

5. ACCESSORIES: ( ) emergency auxiliary light source (HID).
                 ( ) filter/lens holder.
                 ( ) scallop shield.
                 ( ) sloping ceiling adapter.
                 other:

6. BALLAST   certifications: ( ) CBM, ( ) CSA, ( ) ETL,
    DESCRIPTION: ( ) IBEW local   ( ) UL.
    [HID only]   circuit type: ( ) reactor, ( ) autotransformer,
                               ( ) constant watt. autotrans.
                 number of lamps per ballast: ( ) 1, ( ) 2.
                 power factor: ( ) high, ( ) low.
                 sound rating: ( ) A, ( ) B, ( ) C, ( ) D.

7. ADJUSTMENT: maximum vertical tilt from nadir: °.
    [accent   maximum horizontal rotation: °.
    lights only] provision for filters/lenses: ( ) yes, ( ) no.

INCLUDE APPROPRIATE PHOTOMETRICS AND CALCULATIONS.

BASIC CHECKLIST FOR THE SPECIFICATION OF
FLUORESCENT LUMINAIRES

---

1. CEILING TYPE: ( ) "B" (flush)
                ( ) "F" (flange)
                ( ) "G" (exposed grid)
                ( ) "H" (hook)
                ( ) "M" (metal pan)
                Other:

2. CLOSURE TYPE: ( ) diffuser.
                ( ) louver.
                ( ) refractor.
                other:

3. CLOSURE MATERIAL: ( ) acrylic.
                    ( ) aluminum.
                    ( ) steel.
                    ( ) styrene.
                    other:

4. REFLECTANCE OF INTERNAL FINISHES: %.

5. BALLAST   certifications: ( ) CBM, ( ) CSA, ( ) ETL,
   DESCRIPTION: ( ) IBEW local   ( ) UL.
                classification: ( ) instant start
                            ( ) preheat.
                            ( ) rapid start.
                            ( ) trigger start.
             M.A.: ( ) 430 standard
                    ( ) 800 high output.
                  .( ) 1500 very- or super-high output,
                        power groove.
             no. lamps per ballast: ( ) 1, ( ) 2, ( ) 3.
             power factor: ( ) high, ( ) low.
             sound rating: ( ) A, ( ) B, ( ) C, ( ) D.

INCLUDE APPROPRIATE PHOTOMETRICS AND CALCULATIONS.

ABBREVIATIONS

The following abbreviations are used on lighting drawings and in associated literature.

Accent light	accent lt,
Alternating current	ac
Aluminum	alum.
American National Standards Institute	ANSI
American Standards Association	ASA
Ampere	amp or A
Asymmetrical	asym.
Automatic	auto.
Average	avg.
Brightness	(see Footlambert)
Ceiling	clg.
Center line	cl
Centigrade	C
Centimeter	cm
Certified Ballast Manufacturers	CBM
Lighting Division of the Chartered Institution of Building Services	CIBS
Commission Internationale de l'Eclairage	CIE
Conduit	cnd.
Current	(see Ampere)
Degree	deg. or °
Diagram	diag.
Diameter	dia.
Dimension	dimen.
Dimmer switch	dim. or sw-dim.
Direct current	dc
Downlight	dnlt.
Drawing	dwg.
Electric	elec.
Elevation	el or elev.
Equal	eq.
Equipment	equip.
Estimate	est.
Exterior	ext.
Fahrenheit	F
Feet or foot	ft. or '
Fluorescent	fluor.

Footcandle	fc
Footlambert	fl
Gauge	ga.
Hardware	hdw.
High intensity discharge	HID
High pressure sodium	HPS
Horizontal	horiz.
International Brotherhood of Electrical Workers	IBEW
Illuminating Engineering Society, N.A.	IES
Incandescent	incan.
Inch or inches	in. or "
Inside diameter	I.D.
Insulate	ins.
Interior	int.
International Association of Lighting Designers	IALD
International Commission on Illumination	CIE
Junction	jct.
Kilowatt	kW
Knockout	KO
Light	lt.
Lumens per watt	lpw
Manual	man.
Mechanical	mech.
Mercury vapor	MV
Millimeter	mm
Minimum	min.
National Electric Code	NEC
National Electrical Manufacturers Association	NEMA
Natural	nat.
Negative	neg.
Nominal	nom.
Not in Contract	N.I.C.
Not to scale	NTS
On center	O.C.
Outside diameter	O.D.
Panel	pnl.
Perforate	perf.
Permanent	perm.
Perpendicular	perp.
Phase	ph or ∼
Pole	p
Positive	pos.

Receptacle	recpt.
Required	req.
Schedule	sch.
Section	sect.
Similar	sim., e.g.
Special	spl.
Specification	spec.
Square	sq.
Standard	std.
Substitute	sub.
Supersede	supsd.
Switch	s or sw
Switchboard	swbd.
Symmetrical	sym.
System	sys.
Temperature	temp.
That is	i.e.
Transformer	trans.
Typical	typ.
Underwriters Laboratories Inc.	UL
U.S.A. Standards Institute	USASI
Ventilate	vent.
Vertical	vert.
Voltage	volt or V
Wall Washer	ww
Watt	W
With	w/
Without	w/o
Wood	wd.

LIGHTING DESIGN INFORMATION

Manufacturers and Selling Organizations

Perhaps the sources of information in widest use are the fabricators who produce lighting equipment or the organizations representing them. Of course, manufacturers are in business to sell their equipment and not that of their competitors, and so their information may be biased. This bias is enhanced by the particular way in which manufacturers have chosen to view lighting design in addition to their relative isolation from other equipment. For example, if a company is producing modern stylings, they will have little information to offer about antique luminaire application; if they are dedicated to indirect lighting, their evaluation of up- versus down-lighting will probably be prejudiced.

"Sales representatives" are the people who sell for a particular lighting manufacturer, and "sales agents" handle the products of several companies. The quality of their advice varies widely with their interest in the general subject (not just the money involved), their education, quality of their product, and knowledge of the competition. A good agent or representative will tell you when *not* to purchase the represented equipment as well as when to favor her/him with an order. Some agencies and manufacturers offer sales outlets that are well stocked with examples of their lines. These salesrooms offer the invaluable service of actual product contact without the puffery of promotional literature.

Contractors and Electricians

Equipment installers are just that—experts in the technical problems associated with construction. They are not necessarily aestheticians, nor are they often familiar with varying grades of equipment, new devices, or even a wide range of old devices.

Literature

Certain manufacturers (large luminaire suppliers and lamp companies, in particular) offer excellent sources of free information on the general aspects of the areas in which they offer product lines. For the lamp companies, these may include pamphlets on color and light, plant lighting, and the biological implications of different kinds of lighting. Manufacturer's catalogs are, in themselves, an education in equipment types.

Unbiased texts on architectural lighting aesthetics are in short supply, but technical information is better represented. The I.E.S. Library of Recommended Practices, Committee Reports, Measurement and Testing Guidelines, and Energy Management Series, together with the *I.E.S. Lighting Handbooks* and its monthly publication *Lighting Design and Application*, are invaluable. For international practice, turn to publications offered by the C.I.E. and the British Lighting Division of The Chartered Institution of Building Services.

Education

You would think that major colleges offering architecture and interior design degrees would support in-depth courses concerning lighting design, but with a few notable exceptions, they do not. However, their typical one-semester courses may be useful introductions to the subject. Engineering and technical schools are not any better on the average.

The Designers Lighting Forum and the I.E.S. offer a wide range of short-term classes. The biannual Lighting World International convention, sponsored by the International Association of Lighting Designers and the I.E.S., is directed at the design professional. In addition, the annual I.E.S. conference is an important source of technical information.

Other Professionals

Architects, interior designers, store planners, business designers, and electrical engineers all offer advice on lighting. Depending on the particular skills involved, this may be the only advice necessary for the user. When these professionals find complex problems, they may seek specialized consulting.

Architectural Lighting Design Consultants

These professionals, often members of the International Association of Lighting Designers (IALD), concentrate on providing advanced information, just as do acoustic consultants, color consultants, and the like.

They may begin a project by attending preliminary conferences, preparing necessary analysis, and by being available for general orientations. They then prepare design development documents in conformance with their client's project design. They first create outline recommendations reflecting basic materials and types of lighting equiment—both luminaires and electrical control. They also suggest the obtaining of surveys, investigations, or tests necessary for the proper completion of the work, and they may be involved in the development and/or evaluation of mock-ups. After preparing drawings and recommendations, which often become the project's legal construction documents (specifications), they assist in analyzing bids for construction or installation. Lighting design consultants may inspect the project site during installation to assure conformance with the plans. Very often, they will make on-site observations or approvals as the work progresses and finally target adjustable equipment. These full services are tailored to the project requirements through the consultant's contract.

The full services of an architectural lighting design consultant can be enormously expensive—particularly for small projects. On the other hand, finding out the information on your own or from any other source may also consume irritating and expensive amounts of time. As a result, a great many projects never see the light of well-planned illumination.

Some architectural lighting design consultants will make available a less costly but more limited form of lighting design. Be sure to call your chosen consultant in advance, however, because the service is not offered by all.

This type of consulting is usually restricted to architects, interior designers, business planners or other environmentalists who have a nodding acquaintance with lighting layouts (possibly achieved through experience or by taking an introductory lighting course). These professionals are often seeking innovation in *their* lighting designs or solutions to problems that they perceive as either unusual or difficult. In this situation, the consultant may offer verbal recommendations, copy pertinent data from manufacturer's catalogs, direct you to other sources of both information or equipment, and occasionally suggest additional consulting services or special investigations. On simple projects, the total consultation can take place during a single meeting that may occupy from 1 to 3 hours.

The following services may *not* be included—they are usually provided under full-service contracts for larger projects: client meetings, written reports, formal written or drawn specifications, specially designed equipment, extensive follow-up or involved techniques. Because the consultant will not be checking on the application of this information, you may be asked to sign a statement limiting the consultant's liability. It is unwise to apply this consulting technique to complicated or larger projects.

A face-to-face conference in the consultant's office is the most useful and least expensive form of meeting, since it results in a free flow of ideas and materials for future reference. Under certain circumstances, however, the entire process may be concluded on a job site, by mail, or with the help of a telephone-coupled facsimile machine.

Request the consultant's hourly charge rate. This rate varies widely depending on the consultant's location, experience level, and reputation. In addition to the time you are actually in conference, the consultant may charge for the hours involved in preparation, billing, and so on. There will be a charge for all expenses (long-distance telephone, copying, printing, etc.), and there may be minimum billings imposed. You should request a statement of these policies. Also, ask if the consultant requires payment at the completion of the meeting or if billing is provided for these limited services.

PREPARATION IS THE SECRET

Regardless of the form of consulting, the location of your meeting, or the person providing lighting design advice, careful preparation and planning saves significant time and money in addition to improving the accuracy of the results.

Consultants often book their time 2 or more weeks in advance. Although every effort is made to accommodate urgent schedules, travel and conference commitments may make the consultant unavailable. Rushed projects inevitably cost more than those on an orderly timetable. It is best to confirm your appointment the day before it is scheduled since you may be difficult to reach when emergencies require a last-minute change in the consultant's plans.

Over the telephone, tell the consultant about the lighting problems you wish to discuss. This allows the preparation of both ideas and materials prior to your arrival. There may be no charge for short telephone conferences.

Before you seek advice, complete the following checklist.

Drawings

( )   Floor Plans: Show furniture placement.
( )   Reflected Ceiling Plans: Show surface beams and other obstructions, if any.
( )   Section or Elevations: These are particularly valuable when sculpture or wall-hung art is to be illuminated.
( )   Drawing Scale: ¼ inch = 1 foot is ideal; ⅛ inch = 1 foot and 1/16 inch = 1 foot may lead to measurement inaccuracies: ½ inch = 1 foot is unusual but appreciated; "details" can be at any appropriate size. *Always indicate scale on each drawing!* All drawings should be detailed and accurate (i.e., "hard line").
( )   Paper Size: 8½ inches × 11 inches, 8½ inches × 14 inches for xerographic reproduction—but be careful, the scale may change when originals are copied. 18 inch × 24 inch and 24 × 36 inch sizes should be in the form of sepia reproducibles so the consultant can keep a reference copy. Other sizes are acceptable.

Pictorials

( )   Photographs: If the space to be designed already exists (if it is ready for renovation or restoration), provide a photograph and include a person for scale. Instant photographs (Polaroid, Kodak, etc.) are welcome.
( )   Perspectives or Isometrics: Simple views give the consultant an idea of your design intent, even if they are not entirely accurate.

Finishes

( ) Reflectivity: It is important to know the amount of light returned by the surfaces you plan to use, such as wall coverings, carpets, tiles and furnishings. If the project is commercial, the supplier of the surface may give you this information. If reflectances are not known, bring a sample to the consultant. For accurate testing, the sample should be at least 2 feet square; however, any size is useful.

( ) Sample Boards: If these have been prepared for your client's review, be sure to include them.

( ) Surfaces: If walls are not flat, bring this to the consultant's attention.

Information

( ) Ceiling Heights: Most important.

( ) Hidden Building Beams: Indicated on the reflected ceiling plan.

( ) Total Recessing Space Available for Lighting Equipment. Take into account sprinkler pipes and heads, air-conditioning ducts and registers, sound system locations, and all other obstructions.

( ) Building Materials: Is the ceiling made of concrete, suspended tiles (what size and suspension system), plasterboard?

( ) Project Scheduling: This will guide the consultant in determining project complexity, selecting equipment (to lessen delivery problems), and planning additional work if indicated. Include lighting design completion date, bidding or purchasing time, installation period and move-in deadline.

Part Three

A Survey of
Lighting Design

Chapter Twenty-three

Theatrical and Photographic Lighting Design

The design effects of controlled electrical illumination were first studied and applied in the theater. In fact, instrumentation used in architectural lighting was first developed for the stage. Some of the earliest examples of controlled electric lighting were originally demonstrated in European theaters.

Photograpic and theatrical lighting have always been used to elicit emotional responses. Designers in this medium are trained to reinforce intricately subtle human responses by the manipulation of light. Fear or happiness, suspense or relaxation, and naturalness or artificiality can all be expressed in the "languages" of color, shadow, contrast, and movement.

Photography and theater offer excellent steps in the study of all other lighting design applications for quite practical reasons. The flexible nature of theater lighting control and the portability of equipment allow the designer to alter and improve lighting effects "on the spot." The public yet temporary nature of the work allows the designer to publicize his or her successes while quietly burying the errors.

Theatrical or photographic lighting design concepts do not have universal applications. The "theatrical" statement is often too bold for day-to-day living. An impermanent medium does not lend itself to distinctly architectural problems of stability, practicality, long life, and maintenance. The subjective nature of theatrical lighting concepts does not coincide comfortably with the scientific "objectivity" that engineering interests apply to facilities supporting continued human work, safety, and relaxation. Yet,

333

because theatrical lighting offers so many chances to affect human response, its study offers clues to successful solutions of other lighting design problems.

McCANDLESS' THEATRICAL NATURALISM

A very popular approach to electric lighting for the stage was developed by Yale University's Stanley McCandless in his classic book, *A Method of Lighting the Stage*. Although not directly applicable to architecture, his simple theoretical divisions of the functions and qualities of lighting design offer an effective codification of light's potential as an active visual element.

The Use of Light

McCandless felt that light could be used to create a sense of visibility, naturalism, composition, and mood. These effects were to be approached through the qualities of brightness, color, form, and movement.

Functions

Visibility, according to William Nelson (a professor of lighting at Carnegie-Mellon University), is the most important function of theatrical practice. Unless the actor's body can be seen in all its expressive nuances, no other function has validity. That is not to say that clear levels of visibility are always necessary; the ability of lighting to obscure objects of secondary importance offers another measure of control.

Naturalism must not be confused with a single point of view. The viewer subconsciously orients himself to his environment through the acceptance of natural lighting and familiar motivational directives, but light application variations can lead him to the extremes of abstraction by violating naturalistic rules. McCandless' method is primarily concerned with the development of naturalistic viewing conditions that place the observer in a comfortable relationship to recognizable forms.

Composition, as used by McCandless, refers to pictorial aspects of form and balance. It has equal status with all other scenic techniques in its ability to depict human conditions.

Mood is defined as "that intangible dramatic essence"* developing a "feeling" or "atmosphere." McCandless suggested that this funcion of the

---

*Stanley McCandless, *A Method of Lighting the Stage*, Theatre Arts Books, p. 19.

viewer's psychology might be the primary contribution of lighting to any dramatic process.

Qualities

Brightness is defined as the visual radiation *entering* the eye. *Color* includes hue, value, and chroma. *Form* is defined as the ability of the viewer to perceive position, shape, and size. *Movement* is expressed in changes in any of the other qualities.

A Method

McCandless divides his lighting tasks into four categories. The *acting area* (where the actors appear) is separated from other scenic elements. If the area is large, it is further divided into small areas so that each one can be controlled for the purposes of composition and visibility.

To create a naturalistic resolution of shadows on the human face or body and to minimize stray illumination that might strike surrounding scenic elements, the light sources illuminating these areas are placed at an angle approximately 45° above the acting area.

In nature, form is partly revealed through an interplay of light and shadow. The sun illuminates an object from one side with major intensity while reflected light (from the sky or other environmental surfaces) fills in the shadow side with a lesser intensity. If this scheme were duplicated in the theater, the shadows would be too harsh, and the viewer on the shadow side would be placed at a disadvantage. A simple theatrical scheme is used to preserve naturalistic modeling of the human form, satisfy visibility requirements from all distances and viewing angles, and project a naturalistic effect. Two light sources are used to cover any one acting area. If an imaginary line is drawn directly from the actor to the audience, each source is placed on an angle 45° to either side of that line. Tints of color are then used to filter these lighting elements with a warm tint on one side and a cool tint on the other. The "warm" side is usually assumed to be the side from which the light source strikes the actor, and the "cool" side is normally associated with shadow. The actual warm tints (pink, straw, etc.) and cool tints (blue, sometimes lavender) are chosen to blend in with the specific action and setting of the play.

Background illumination is separated from the acting areas so that its special requirements may be properly balanced with the actor's visibility.

Blending and *toning* is achieved with lighting instruments that soften the transition between backgrounds and acting areas and the transitions between several acting areas. Three or four colors, on separately controlled circuits, are used (red, green, blue, and sometimes white) so that any tint or shade may be mixed in continuously variable intensities.

Special units usually provide the motivational light sources. In naturalistic portrayals, humans *expect* to know where the light is coming from, even when the functional illumination does not actually come from the expected source. On the stage, for example, no one expects a "practical" table lamp to provide all the lighting, and yet, if the lamp is illuminated, the audience will unconsciously accept it as the natural light source. Special light sources are often used to produce naturalistic effects such as sunlight, moonlight, and firelight as well as the illumination given off by chandeliers, sconces, table lamps, and lanterns. Also included in this special category are effects that are not indicative of naturalism.

OTHER THEATRICAL DESIGN TECHNIQUES

Jewel Lighting

In many older theaters, the mounting systems required for McCandless' technique of acting area lighting do not exist. It is not always possible to locate light sources above the actor at 45°. In these installations, the actors are primarily illuminated from a point directly in front of them (usually from the balcony edge). Since the light has only a slight vertical angle, it tends to wash out natural facial characteristics and cast shadows on the scenery. If footlights are used, their upward directed light further erases natural shadows. Some of the facial shadows can be restored through makeup.

The silhouettes cast on the scenery by front lighting can be removed by lighting it to a high intensity. Unfortunately, this process tends to blend the actor into the scenery. To minimize this phenomenon, strong back lighting and side lighting is used to "cartoon" the actor with a radiant glow on the hair, shoulders, and sides. This technique is sometimes called "jewel lighting" because it tends to make the actor shimmer with light.

Techniques for Encircled Staging

The McCandless method is principally stated for proscenium staging— where the actors appear behind a proscenium or "picture frame" and the audience views them from one side. However, modern staging may place the audience on three sides ("thrust" staging) or four sides ("theater in the round").

The McCandless method can be adapted to meet these conditions. If the audience sits on more than one side of the stage, additional light sources can be placed on several sides. Three or four sources may be used on any one acting area. If three sources are used, they may be tinted with warm, neutral, and cool colors (such as pale pink, lavender, and blue). If an acting area is illuminated with four sources, they may alternate with similar or different warm and cool colors (pale pink, blue, straw, and lavender are examples of different tints). Since "surrounded" theater cannot rely on massive vertical scenic elements (large "flats" will block the view of someone looking across the acting area), special motivational lighting may be used to emphasize three-dimensional props or the stage floor itself. Patterns are frequently projected on the floor, and all planes may be washed with comparatively vivid color.

It would be both impractical and unwise to attempt a description of all theatrical lighting practices in this architectural book. Only those design elements most related to our purpose have been included. There are a variety of other interesting approaches to lighting design for productions such as arena presentations (ice shows and pageants), exterior drama, and dance.

PHOTOGRAPHIC DESIGN APPROACHES

Lighting design for both television and photography (still and moving) is a modification of flat painting and theatrical techniques. The main problem in these areas, besides unusual technical requirements, is the resolution of three-dimensional objects in a two-dimensional medium.

In black-and-white photography, dimension is developed in a human portrait through the selective use of light intensity and direction. For naturalistic effects, two light sources are placed on either side and above the subject in a manner similar to theatrical area lighting. The brightest source gives the motivational impression of the light's direction. The second source, with lesser intensity, fills in the shadow. Back lighting may be placed above and behind the subject and aimed toward the camera (but not "seen" directly by the lens). Back-light sources make the hair and shoulders shine and, as in the theatre, tend to separate the subject from its surroundings. Patterns of illuminated background elements may be arranged to complement or contrast with the subject and, therefore, also help to give it dimensionality. A very small light source may be placed next to the camera lens so that it reflects in the subject's eyes and makes them sparkle.

In the theater, color on the actor may help the actor's expressions carry over comparatively great distances. However, when an individual's expressions are important in photography, a close-up is often used. For this reason, color schemes that might satisfy theatrical requirements would seem overstated in the photographic media. Colored light is sparingly applied, if it is used at all, when photographing a close-up of the human face. However, color may play a greater part in defining and molding the areas surrounding the individual.

SELECTED DESIGN ELEMENTS

Many design elements in theatrical and photographic lighting are used although there is no concrete scientific proof of their validity. They are rarely written down, but rather, passed from designer to designer through job experience. However, even if lighting design elements are not academically delineated, they often work with remarkable consistency.

Shadow

The presence or absence of shadow, as used in theatrical or photographic applications, can be described in terms of shape, angle, intensity, and definition ("soft" and "hard").

Deep (dark) and large shadows seem theatrically threatening or hostile and are often used to suggest power, dejection, distress, suspense, or solemnity. Small and light shadows are described as open and friendly and may indicate liveliness, excitement, safety, and joy. Soft shadows are associated with beauty, peacefulness, melancholy, or pensiveness.

Shadow quality is often related to the revelation of age and emotional condition. Aging stars do not appreciate the telltale shadows that clearly denote baggy eyes, crow's-feet, flabby cheeks, "turkey neck," arm imperfections or furrowed brows. Actors who portray age or character, however, depend on carefully developed shadows to reinforce prominent features. Emotional condition can be described through shadow-derived terms such as haggard, drawn, or lined.

Color

Color serves as a subjective language for the theatrical lighting designer. In the following discussion, an attempt has been made to connect theatrical impressions and folklore with researched phenomena. Only the simplest and typically used colors are described here in terms frequently applied to theatrical practice. Depending on circumstances and associations, the same color may have several effects. Although black and white are not technically colors, they are included because they are often considered as such in this connotation.

Black is the theatrical "color" for somberness. It is a coolish "color" and is often associated with despondent, dejected, and melancholy moods, although it can also create powerful attitudes.

Blue is theatrically associated with tragedy and spirituality. People tend to involuntarily withdraw from the lightweight and cool hue, even though it is one of the most universally appealing colors. Its low stimulation of muscular and circulatory activity associates it with leisurely moods that have also been described as comfortable, secure, serene, and tender. It is definitely a passive color.

Green is rarely used as a lighting color in the theater, and as a result, selections of green color media are very limited. Mixtures of green, such as "peacock" and "moonlight," do find application as accent colors. Psychological research indicates that exposure to the cool and passive qualities of green light decreases restlessness by relaxing muscular and circulatory activity.

Orange is often associated with comedy in the theater and develops the moods of warmth, excitement, and liveliness. On the other hand, it can also evoke distress, upset, and suffocation when used in related surroundings. Humans are subconsciously attracted to this active color, even though consciously it is one of the vivid lighting colors least preferred.

Red is theatrically associated with both comedy and activity. This medium-weight, warm color excites the nervous system in a striking and explosive manner. Particularly for the unconscious mind, red is both an attractive and dangerously fascinating color that produces moods described as stimulating and vigorous, while at the same time defiant, contrary, and hostile. Red is a most appealing and restless color.

Violet (lavender or purple) is connected to tragedy. It is a medium-temperature color creating moods that are both dignified or stately and melancholy or solemn—all with a subduing influence.

White is the theatrical "color" of awareness that also engenders the moods of peace and purity. It gives the feeling of being light in weight and cold or crisp.

Yellow is associated with comedy and warm and joyful emotion. It is a lightweight and medium-temperature color defining moods that are both cheerful and playful.

BIBLIOGRAPHY

Birren, Faber, *The Story of Color* (Connecticut, 1941).

Fere, Charles, *Sensation et Mouvement*, 2nd ed. (Paris, 1900).

Kimura, Toshiro, "Apparent Warmth and Heaviness of Colors," *Japanese Journal of Psychology* **20** (1950).

Luckiesh, *The Language of Color* (New York, 1918).

McCandless, Stanley, *A Method of Lighting the Stage* (New York, 1932).

Nuckolls, James L., Comments on the Affective Nature of Selected Light Colors, unpublished, 1969.

Odbert, H. S., Karowski, T. F., and Eckerson, A. B., "Studies in Synesthetic Thinking," *Journal of General Psychology* **26** (1942).

Pasto, Tarmo A., and Kivisto, P., "Group Difference in Color Choice and Rejection," *Journal of Clinical Psychology* **12** (1956).

Chapter Twenty-four

Architectural Lighting Design

<hr>

After many centuries, environmentalists learned how to develop structures that were illuminated only by daylight. Their success or failure could be measured by the way this medium was applied. When Edison and Swan introduced electric light as a new form with unique possibilities, environmentalists first treated it only as a direct substitute for candles, gas, or oil. As the technological revolution flourished, lighting was relegated to the technical crafts—it was treated with a grave respect remarkably free of inspiration.

Lighting design should be considered as an inseparable part of environmental design. It has an immeasurable effect on many of the environment's qualities, as do acoustics, air conditioning, and structural form.

Light cannot be seen until it strikes an object. That object is as much a part of the design as is the lighting that reveals it. In fact, lighting "designs" are usually and inaccurately judged on the effectiveness of the structure rather than on the lighting contribution.

It is imprecise to call the lighting authority a "designer." The term has too many applications in both technology and art. If the lighting practitioner is a successful aesthetician, he or she might be more accurately titled a "design consultant."

Tradition has bestowed the former name, although in practice the initiative for creative lighting must come from an environmentalist, for it is this authority who assumes responsibility for the total structure. Here, there is an interesting paradox in comparative experience. Because the lighting designer works on a small portion of a great many projects, he or she usually has made more mistakes and found more solutions than the person he or she serves. However, the environmentalist is the boss. His or her design conclusions often govern the success or failure of all contributions.

The lighting designer must work with many aspects of a project. In so doing, he or she must also learn to stay close to the authorities who recognize and respect his or her area of experience and expertise. Only then can the lighting concept be maintained, applied, and modified appropriately. The greatest gratification comes when collaborating with an environmental design authority who creatively applies what the lighting consultant has to offer.

Lighting designs are often most effective when they are the least noticeable. This subtlety of design expression often makes the field a difficult one in which to build a career. Occasionally, a powerful statement or personal eccentricity may be appropriate for a specific purpose, but personalized excesses should not be routine. A lighting designer must also avoid becoming infatuated with a particular style, or he/she will be unable to contribute to the wide range of problems typical in an average consulting practice.

Accidental and unexpectedly satisfactory effects often occur in lighting designs, despite the complex planning and consideraton given to any installation. Since the unusual incident cannot be avoided, it should be used as a source of inspiration. Unfortunately, some lighting consultants turn repetitive accidents into a career.

Lighting design is based on a mobile technology and art. It is precisely because of its constant evolution and expansion that lighting is one of the most exciting architectural design disciplines. Remember that the accepted "rules" of lighting design can always be broken, provided basic principles and valid application are clearly understood.

APPROACHES TO ARCHITECTURAL LIGHTING DESIGN

Quantitative Approach

With the higher light outputs and increased application that resulted from the introduction of fluorescent sources, quantitative prediction of illumination levels received primary emphasis. Technicians developed an approach toward lighting "design" that followed four simple steps:

1.   Determine the desired level of illumination.
2.   Select a luminaire that will produce this level.

3. Calculate the required number of luminaires.
4. Lay out the installation for uniformity of illumination.

Although this quantitative system neglects a complexity of factors governing the user's interrelations with a space, it is still accepted by an embarrassing number of authorities as the only criterion for lighting design. One reason for its continued application is its simplicity; simple numerical calculations can be used to explain away all the confusion inherent in this branch of environmental concern.

"Design" Approach

In July 1971, the inaugural issue of I.E.S.'s magazing *Lighting Design and Applicaton* contained an article that contrasted "engineering" and "design" approaches to lighting. The article underscored fundamental differences with the earlier model in four steps and suggested four alternative steps:

1. Determine the desired composition in the space through the parameters of line, form, hue, brightness, saturation, texture, function, and relation to other spaces.
2. Determine the desired appearance of objects through the established technologies of color rendition, visibility, and veiling reflections, in addition to the nonspecific aspects of sparkle, modeling, luster, line highlights, and shadows.
3. Select appropriate luminaires for various components of the lighting system using, if necessary, more than one technique for any space (e.g., general or accent lighting).
4. Lay out and evaluate the installation for visual comfort, veiling reflections, maintenance, and thermal control in relation to the objectives set up in Steps 1 and 2.

Before and during this reexamination of lighting design techniques, additional sophisticated computational methods of evaluation were emerging, including visual comfort probability and equivalent sphere illumination.

A Unified System

Shortly after the initial article appeared in *Lighting Design and Application*, Robert T. Dorsey, then president of the I.E.S., delivered a paper at the

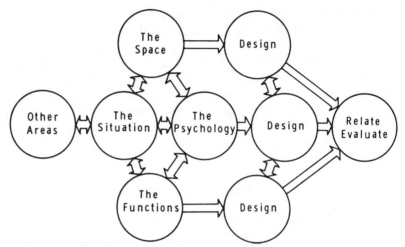

Figure 24.1.   Flow diagram of design procedure. [Reproduced, by permission, from *Lighting Design and Application* (September 1972): 24.]

Seventeenth World Congress of the International Commission on Illumination (C.I.E.) held in Barcelona, Spain, entitled, "A Unified System for the Esthetic and Engineering Approaches to Lighting." To illustrate his design network, Dorsey presented a flow diagram (see Figure 24.1). The diagram consisted of seven interrelated problems.

Transition

Dorsey suggested that transitional phenomena be considered when approaching the situation to be designed. These elements consisted of relative character, color, and brightness of adjoining spaces, as well as the time of day and certain other aspects.

Situation

Once within the situation under consideration, Dorsey evaluated the interaction between compositional (space), psychological, and functional criteria.

Space

The compositional or spatial criterion embraced the area of principal focus as well as the zones of secondary emphasis. At this point, Dorsey considered the elements of three-dimensional space, including brightness, area, color, texture, line, and form, in addition to the relationship of these elements between zones.

Psychological

In Dorsey's preliminary outline of psychological criteria (which he admitted was incomplete), the objectives related to the user's behavior were itemized in descriptive terms such as excitement, stimulation, quietness, warmth, and simplicity.

Function

Areas used for circulation, work, and rest were divisions of the functional statement. In the work division, color (and color rendition), plane of the task, sparkle, highlights, equivalent contrast, required luminance, and visual comfort were brought to bear.

Design

Design statements collected from all previous characteristics were inter-related to develop an approach based on existing lighting knowledge.

Relate/Evaluate

Finally, all criteria were evaluated in terms of economics (wages, behavioral benefits, added value, safety, available capital, and cost analysis) and integrated through energy criteria (thermal and acoustic).

Design Factors

In the April 1974 issue of *Lighting Design and Applicaton*, the I.E.S. Design Practice Commttee printed a preliminary outline of all factors that should be considered in developing a lighting design. The factors were based on the recommended practices of the society.

    I. Design objective (visual requirements—what is the visual activity?)
        A. Visual task, specific performance
           What is the task?
           Location and orientation
           Reflectance characteristics
           Critical visual details
           Variation in location
           Variation in time
           Area covered
           Three-dimensional perspective
           Observer orientation

B. Visual impressions
    Aesthetics
    Pleasantness
    Desirability
    Psychological import
    Modeling
    Shadows

II. Criteria
A. Visual tasks criteria
    Visual performance potential desired (illumination, ESI, and/or
      luminance)
    Spectral quality
    Color quality (CRI)
    Lighting directionality
    Disability glare
    Discomfort glare
    Transient adaptation (frequency)
    Polarization
B. Visual impression
    Psychological impressions
        a. Warm–cool
        b. Stimulating–soothing
        c. Active–passive
    Discomfort glare
    Lighting directionality
    Color quality
    Lighting variation
    Static–dynamic
    Strobing

III. Nonvisual specifications—area description
    Dimensional and structural character
    Reflectances
    Texture of surfaces
    Color of surfaces
    Orientation and location of task objective
    Ambient temperature
    Hazard conditions
    Ambient noise
    Surface transmittance
    Atmospheric conditions
    Geographic location

Operating period
Occupants
Life of structure
IV. Constraints
Life cycle costs
Energy consumption (kWh)
Resources
Modularity
Flexibility
Thermal input and extraction
Ambient temperature
Acoustical
Other engineering system
Personnel
Local codes
V. Design
  A. Fenestration
    Size
    Transmittance
    Reflection
    Refraction
    Thermal transmission and reflection
    Thermal conduction
    Color
    Controls
    Orientation
    Local surroundings
    Maintenance characteristics
    Location in space
    Luminance data
    Operating period
    Atmospheric conditions
    Appearance
    Stability
    Transparency
    Material strength
    Acoustical characteristics
    Operation characteristics
    Cost
  B. Electric lighting sources
    Lumens

Efficacy
Wattage
Cost
Operating temperature
Ambient temperature characteristic
Flicker
Durability
Color temperature
Color rendering index (CRI)
Spectral distribution
Maintenance
Physical size
Optical size
Life
Effect of operating cycle
Warm-up–restrike time
Luminance
Orientation
Candlepower distribution
Voltage and hertz
Reliability
Ballasting characteristics
Dimmability
Electromagnetic interference (EMI)
Acoustical
Source finish
Base
Failure mode
Shape
Filament
Auxiliary system requirement
C. Fixture
Candlepower distribution
Efficiency and coefficient of utilization
Cost
Luminance
Watts
Number of lamps
Appearance
Polarization characteristics

Size
Materials
Maintenance characteristics
Thermal characteristics
Acoustical
Durability
Weight
Component life
Mounting
Ballast characteristics
UL lighting codes
Special characteristics (hazard, enclosed and gasketed)
Air handling
Heat transfer
Thermal radiation

The British *I.E.S. Code for Interior Lighting*, published in January 1973, contains a slightly different approach to the basic factors involved in lighting design. Their listing is remarkable for both its clarity and brevity. Extracts are presented below:

General Requirements

1. Purpose of the interior (activities may be diverse, and more than one lighting scheme may be needed); probably layout of plant, furniture or equipment, where this is known.
2. Availability of daylight: the need to combine electric light and daylight.
3. Extent to which contrast rendering in the task is important: risk of veiling reflections.
4. Degree of modeling required and provision of directional lighting.
5. Color appearance and color rendering required.
6. Task and building illuminances; localized or general lighting; need for optical aids.
7. Requirements for glare control.
8. Statutory requirements for official recommendations.
9. Need for emergency lighting.

Environmental Conditions and Requirements

10. Presence or absence of hostile environment; need for special luminaires (e.g., flameproof, dust-tight, watertight.

11. Unusually high or low general temperatures (e.g., foundries, cold storage; effect on control equipment and luminaire components).

12. Possibility of high ambient temperature near luminaires (e.g., at ceiling level and in shop windows).

13. Possible effect of radiant heat from furnaces or other industrial equipment on luminaires and control equipment.

14. Effect of heat from luminaires on air temperature in interior; use of lighting heat for part of building heating.

Effect of Structural Features

15. Dimensions of interior: length, width, height.

16. Luminaire mounting height.

17. Luminaire spacing/mounting height ratio.

18. Reflectances of ceiling, walls and floor, including influence of furnishings, windows, and glazed partitions.

19. Coordination of lighting equipment with other building services.

20. Limitations on luminaire mounting position (e.g., roof structure, number of bays, modular construction of building, space available in ceiling void).

21. Effects of obstructions by parts of structure (e.g., beams) and other services (e.g., ventilation ducting, pipework).

Lamps

22. Lamp types which meet color appearance and color rendering requirements for interior activity.

23. Lamp light output related to source size and mounting height.

24. Rationalization of lamp type, color, and wattage, particularly with existing installations.

25. Heating up time to full light output and need for standby system to cover any interruptions of power supply.

26. Need to reduce flicker and stroboscopic effect.

27. Economics—capital and running costs.

Luminaires

28. Suitability for purpose.
29. Aesthetic appearance.
30. Luminous intensity distribution required.
31. Authenticated photometric data.
32. Need for special equipment.
33. Availability—present and future—of spare parts.
34. Weight; arrangements to hold the luminaire in place.
35. Use of supporting systems or lighting tracks.

Maintenance

36. Maintenance factors.
37. Accessibility of luminaires—need for special equipment.
38. Acceptability of proposed luminaires, lamps, etc. to client's maintenance staff.

Chapter Twenty-five

The Human Condition

In architectural lighting design practice, professionals are traditionally concerned with the functional aspects of light intensity, glare, brightness ratios, and so forth. However, if lighting practice is to fully satisfy human requirements, we must also consider aspects including human behavior, biology, and age.

BEHAVIOR

This section examines the qualitative aspects governing an observer's reaction to his environment and his sense of well being.

Studies of human behavior by perceptual scientists and behavioral psychologists have had fascinating results. It is not within the scope of this book to present all these findings, but those factors with direct application to lighting design will be summarized. Since many of the research findings examined here are new or tentative, the following comments must be cautiously interpreted as a preliminary to greater understanding.

Attraction

Reductions in lighting contrast that lead to diffuse environments tend to reduce visual control. Areas of visual interest, and the retained impressions of them, are more randomly selected. Circulation within diffusely illuminated spaces often appears to be casual and nondirected.

Taylor and Solov (1974), in their tests to evaluate light's involuntary attraction power, suggest that the intensity of attraction will vary with contrast. Flynn (1972), in his preliminary observations, offered the following chart:

	Focus-to-Background Brightness Ratio
Barely recognized contrast; negligible attraction power as a focal point.	2:1
Minimum meaningful contrast as a focal point; marginal attraction power.	10:1
Dominating contrast as a focal point; strong attraction power.	approaching 100:1

Flynn also suggested that attention is involuntarily directed to color areas that contrast with a neutral visual background. He concluded by stating that an observer who is unfamiliar with a space will move toward areas where color is predominant and toward areas of highest brightness.

Clutter

Prominant light and color patterns that are in opposition to spatial information may destroy orientation, confuse spatial comprehension, and distract attention. These patterns may lead to overload conditions evidenced by tenseness, frustration, and the inability to assimilate significant information clues.

Impression

The impressions associated with color have already been summarized as they are used in the theater to affect audience response. In architectural lighting studies, Flynn and others have linked color to conditions of light distribution and associated factors (see Table 25.1).

Meaning

Appropriate patterns of light contrast develop meaningful impressions. Flat contrasts tend to hide meaning and reduce interest. For example, normal light–dark patterns convey naturalistic meaning. When reversed, insensi-

Table 25.1.

Impression	Color	Condition of Light Distribution	Other Factors
Somberness	Cool tones	Diffuse	Higher light intensity
Gloom	Cool tones	Diffuse	Lower light intensity
Tension	Warm hues	Diffuse	Isolàtion from sound
Gaiety	Warm hues	Sparkle	Random light patterns
Enchantment	Warm hues	Sparkle	Rhythmic light and color patterns

tive or unusual contrast patterns confuse the viewer and develop feelings of mystery and fear.

A study was conducted by Barton, Spivack, and Powell (1972) to determine the effect of light angles on the recognition and evaluation of human faces. The authors noted that the fastest recognition of a face occurred when it was illuminated by a test spotlight placed at a horizontal angle of 45° to one side and between 0 and 35° down on the subject in the vertical plane. The more severe the shadows, the more difficult it was to recognize features. Words such as "hostile" and "threatening" were used to describe faces under heavy and sharp shadow conditions.

Personal Contact

As the intensity of illumination on people in moderately close proximity increases, communication (and the wish to communicate) improves. This increase is probably the result of a corresponding increase in ability to see facial expression and gestures at social distances.

As the intensity of illumination decreases between people and increases on areas surrounding them, feelings of anonymity and separation increase. Surround lighting places people in total or semi-silhouette, and therefore causes a reduction in facial perception.

Stimulation

Monotony, boredom, and other forms of sensory deprivation may result when tasks are uninteresting and there is no stimulation from spatial elements. Involvement can be improved when appropriate brightness variations (including such extremes as glitter and sparkle) and color patterns are sensitively introduced. There are indications, for example, that sparkle encourages conversation and enhances appetite.

Color Preferences for "White" General Lighting

The preference for a particular spectral balance of "white" general architectural lighting has been the subject of several studies. The results are inconclusive, because judgments were influenced by uncontrolled factors such as background, amount of color saturation, and adaptation. There is a strong indication that, in controlled conditions, a person can happily adapt to any one of the several apparently "white" spectral blends typically used in interior lighting practice if he or she is isolated without reference to other illuminants and if color evaluations are not critical. One response, however, seems fairly consistent. There is a preference for warmer tints of "white" light in the presence of lower illumination levels. Conversely, there is a preference for cooler tints with higher light levels.

THE AGING EYE

Research into architectural lighting and the standards proposed for task illumination have traditionally been related to observers between 20 and 30 years of age.

Until the nineteenth century, the normal life span was approximately equal to the age of today's "standard observer." However, by 1850 the average life span had increased to 40 years, by 1900 it was close to 50, and in 1950 the average U.S. citizen could expect to attain 70 years. Today, more than 10% of the population are over 65 and almost 25% are 50 and older.

Seeing ability follows the general process of senescence (aging). Although it is not a perfect test, the use of spectacle lenses can be selected as a rough indication of an age-related decline in seeing ability. Between 6 and 12 years of age, approximately 20% of the U.S. population require some correction; between 22 and 65 years, the figure is 60%; and over 66, nearly 100%. Most optometrists traditionally consider 40 year of age to be the demarcation between young and old eyes. Perhaps 50 to 55 years might be more accurate, since at that age the power of accommodation and its associated functions are no longer fully operable for the majority of the population.

Of course, all the senses normally deteriorate with age. The loss of taste and smell in healthy older persons has been documented. Senescent individuals are also more subject to a wide range of ailments, including those that specifically affect hearing and vision. For all aspects of the human condition, both physical and mental, the most pronounced difference between the youth and age is the degree of elasticity—the ability to bounce back.

Since a larger proportion of the population is living longer than in previous centuries, illumination designs must be developed with the understanding that what is satisfactory for the young observer may not apply to the aging observer. To study this phenomenon, it is necessary to review the effects of age on the observer's perception of his or her environment. This study is the province of the optometrist/ophthalmologist, and only those aspects most directly related to architectural lighting design will be outlined here.

Effects of Age on the Seeing System

In addition to specific ailments, such as glaucoma and corneal irregularities, that increase in statistical likelihood with advancing years, the eye is affected by the following normal aging processes.

Coloring of many eye structures develop a yellowish tint that is characteristic in persons of advanced years.

Fluid secretions and outflows decline, particularly after age 60. The eyeball shrinks, and clouding is often observed.

Iris openings become smaller, leading to reduction in the overall pupil opening, either when expanded or contracted.

Lens changes result in a loss of flexibility and certain opacities. The lens generally hardens, thereby losing its elasticity, so that it can no longer be changed to the more spherical shape needed to focus on nearby objects.

Muscle structures lose their characteristic partial contraction, overall muscle size is reduced, and coordination is impaired.

Psychological phenomena connected with aging can affect vision, since mental abilities and attitudes control much of what is observed. Several aspects directly affect seeing: movement and reaction time are slowed, fine motor coordination begins a gradual decline beginning at ages 30 to 35, and learning that requires the adoption of new associations grows more difficult (learning that requires reorganization of previous habit patterns does not decline as greatly). It is interesting to note that general intelligence seems not to decline markedly during mature years.

Retinal nerve fibers atrophy and join in the general deterioration of the seeing system.

Senescent Changes in Seeing Ability

The results of aging have predictable effects on the seeing process of healthy individuals.

Visual acuity decreases according to a predictable pattern as age increases. "Acuity" refers to the eye's ability to perceive small detail. Its decline begins by age 30 and continues at a slow rate until age 60, when the fall progresses rapidly.

Contrast sensitivity generally declines. Critical fusion frequency is also lowered (the rate of alternation, at which "flicker" disappears and the sensation of "steadiness" takes over).

Hue discrimination becomes less accurate. There is a marked reduction in the ability to discriminate finite hue differences at the blue end of the spectrum (due to the yellowing process), and there is a general loss affecting all parts of the spectrum. Based on a peak discrimination ability, attained when the observer is 20–30 years old, the scores of color matching tests show a 70% decline by age 60, and an additional 56% drop by the 80's.

Glare sensitivity increases, particularly the sensitivity to disability glare.

Refractive changes are rare between the ages of 25 and 45. After 45, there is a tendency toward hypermetropia (farsightedness—difficulty in seeing close objects clearly) caused by a decrease in refractive power. The most rapid change occurs between 50 and 60 years of age. After 65, there is a reverse trend toward myopia (nearsightedness—difficulty in seeing far objects clearly) or at least toward less hypermetropia. An increase in astigmatism is also noted. These changes are caused by one or more of the following phenomena: structural changes in the lens, depletion of accommodative power, and shrinkage of the eyeball.

Depth of focus increases for older persons in relation to diminishing visual acuity, resulting in decreasing hypermetropia and decreasing pupil diameter.

Adaptation starts to be limited at about 40 years in both rate and amount for dark and bright conditions.

Illumination level requirements are greater, especially at low light levels, as overall sensitivity declines and pupil size diminishes.

Accommodation begins to decline at an early age and continues at a regular rate until there is little or no focusing power at approximately age 60 (the condition of presbyopia).

Illumination for the Aging Eye

Present information dealing with aging people and their luminous environments is comparatively incomplete. However, certain concepts find general agreement.

Glare

The elderly have a reduced tolerance of extremes in light intensity and are sensitive to disability glare.

Direct glare should be eliminated through the careful baffling of all luminaires.

Indirect glare is of particular concern for older people. Highly polished floors, for example, may cause an impression that one's feet are slightly above floor level, create an illusion of depth beneath the feet, or evoke an undesirable impression of height. Specular walls and furnishings are sources of veiling glare, as are specular objects, such as magazine pages or chrome appliances.

Since most of the elderly wear spectacle lenses, they sometimes complain about glare reflecting from the rims of their glasses. This condition is caused by harsh down or side light.

Intensity

At the onset of presbyopia, individuals begin to seek better illumination. Therefore, illumination levels should be increased wherever detailed visual tasks, such as reading or sewing, are to be performed. Steps, doorsills, and all unexpected obstructions on the floor should be brightly lighted with adequate contrast. Exterior illumination should be generous and energized early in the evening. Accent lighting might be considered to provide additional illumination of keyholes, door latches, pay phones, building directories, or building numbers.

Changes in illumination level should be gradual. Since adaptation is a problem, it may be useful to provide unobtrusive illumination at all times in bedrooms, halls, bathrooms, and other darkened areas that may come into sudden use during evening hours.

Light Patterns

Lines or pools of light and certain forms of wall washing that give a false illusion of depth should be avoided when they are confusing; conversely, they can be used to advantage in the expansion of space around sedentary or confined individuals.

For reasons that have not been fully explained, some elderly people prefer to have light sources originate from a point near and slightly behind their heads. As an example, they often select table lamps in preference to overhead illumination.

Luminous Indicators

Lighting can be designed to guide the elderly and to warn them of impending danger. For example, light can call attention to passageways and doorways and indicate the presence of obstructions in walkways. Lighting systems can also be used to indicate the approach and height of steps, doorsills, ramps, and other changes in level that might otherwise be a surprise. Luminous switches and wall plates are especially helpful for the elderly.

Maintenance

If the elderly are to maintain their own lighting installations, each aspect of the system should be easily accessible. Pull-down luminaires or wall-mounted brackets that can be serviced from the floor are preferable to ceiling-mounted lighting that must be serviced by standing on a ladder or chair.

Fragile, complicated, or poorly balanced table and floor lamps, which may be upset and damaged during maintenance, should be avoided.

Operation

All aspects of the lighting system must be easy to operate without requiring difficult or dangerous movements.

Wall switches should be conveniently located in areas where they will be expected. They should have a simple, positive action such as is found with rocker-type plates that snap on.

Complex control systems should be avoided: A wall plate filled with dimmer and switch controls can be confusing even to the younger operator. Multiple switching should be located near all entrances and exits so that light is always instantly available within the space. Circuit breakers (preferred to socket or cartridge fuses) should be easy to locate and operate in case of emergency.

Convenience outlets should be numerous and placed in locations that do not require the user to bend down to reach them.

PHOTOBIOLOGY

Water, temperature, and light are the three most important environmental factors affecting man's physiological condition. Of these three factors, light is dominant.* The two aspects of light that receive the greatest study in terms of their biological ramifications are spectral composition and time variance. These aspects are thought to affect man both directly (by photochemical responses within the skin and subcutaneous tissues) and indirectly (through the receptor cells in the retina). In the latter case, the photopic input to the

*M. Evenari, in *Recent Progress in Photobiology*, E. J. Bowen, ed. (Academic Press, New York, 1965), p. 161.

retinal cells is transformed into nerve impulses that may terminate in brain regions that control glandular functions as well as regions controlling visual functions.

The intensity of light has an important effect on an individual's ability to see color and to visualize tasks with ease and accuracy. Low intensities of light may cause irritability and fatigue, but it is believed that eyestrain from insufficient illumination does not have a permanent effect. One of lighting's many myths is perpetuated when mothers complain, "You'll ruin your eyes unless you read with enough light." The other transient effects of low lighting levels are discussed in other topics.

Time and Color

The time sequence of light–dark cycles is thought to synchronize with many of our biological rhythms—in other words, to act as a biological time signal. Sleep–wakefulness cycles, 24-hour voluntary muscular activity, the eating cycle, ovulatory rhythm, and other biological rhythms are affected by light* The effect of complete darkness on lower animals has been extensively studied, but only limited experimentation has been done with human subjects (primarily blind people.)

The practical spectral range of human vision extends from approximately 370–770 nanometers. Since near-ultraviolet wavelengths are indirectly important to our visual environment, however, the range is often extended on the low end to 320 nanometers. Beyond these limits researchers find no practical role played by other radiations in the visual process.† Although the near-infrared portion of the spectrum vitally affects plant growth and other forms of life, the near-ultraviolet range between 290 and 320 nanometers has the greatest human biological significance. For this reason, research on the effects of radiation on humans has centered in both the harmful and beneficial aspects of this type of "light."

Beneficial Effects

The beneficial effects of illumination on human subjects usually occur at suberythemal levels—levels that do *not* result in a noticeable reddening of the skin. Several studies that attribute favorable results to near-ultraviolet wavelengths have been widely quoted.

*Richard J. Wurtman, "Biological Implications of Artificial Illumination," Illuminating Engineering Society Reprint #9-12 (September 1968).
†L. Thorington, L. Parascandola, and L. Cunningham, "Visual and Biological Aspects of an Artificial Sunlight Illuminant," *Journal of Illuminating Engineering Society* (October 1971): 34.

Infant Jaundice.   Phototherapy, using sources with an abundance of blue wavelengths, is successfully used to treat hyperbilirubinemia (infant jaundice).*

Calcium Absorption.   The aged have difficulty absorbing calcium from their diet if they are deprived of ultraviolet radiation. This absorption capacity improves after exposure to either full-spectrum artificial illuminants (those producing near-ultraviolet rays) or natural daylight.†

Rickets.   Near-ultraviolet radiation is necessary for the synthesis of a hormone that retards the incidence of rickets. In the smokey cities that developed during the industrial revolution, with their characteristically narrow and dark streets, rickets was prevalent because the near-ultraviolet radiation was limited.‡

Well-Being.   In a Russian study, school children were exposed to sub-erythemal dosages of ultraviolet light with the following results: (1) decreased incidence of eye fatigue, (2) shorter reaction times to light and sound stimuli, and (3) increased working ability.§ A similar study was conducted in a Russian machine shop. In this instance, the resistance to common colds was apparently increased with resulting reductions in absenteeism.**

These findings, together with other research, are not conclusive. They do suggest, however, that the physiological balance of the human system may be disturbed if it is not regularly exposed to direct or scattered solar radiation or to artificial sources emitting near-ultraviolet rays. These disturbances may include vitamin D deficiencies, certain functional disorders, and aggravation of chronic disorders, as well as a general weakening of the normal disease defenses.

Bactericidal Effects.   Ultraviolet radiation that peaks at 265 nanometers is lethal to certain types of virus, bacteria, yeast, and mold. For this reason, sources producing that wavelength have been used for part of a sterilization process and also to clean air in air-handling systems (see pages 106, 110, and 112.)

---

*R. Hodr, "Phototherapy of Hyperbilirubinemia in Premature Infants," *Ceskoslovenska Pediatrie* 26, (February 1971): 80–82.

†R. Neer, T. Davis, and L. Thorington, "Use of Environmental Lighting to Stimulate Calcium Absorption in Healthy Men," *Clinical Research* 18, (December 1970).

‡W. F. Loomis, "Rickets," *Scientific American*, 223, 6 (December 1970): 77–91.

§M. A. Zamkova, and E. I. Krivitskaya, "Effects of Irradiation by Ultraviolet Erythemia Lamps on the Working Ability of School Children," *Gigiena i Sanitariya*, 31, (April 1966): 41–44.

**N. V. Volkova, "Experience in the Use of Erythemic Ultraviolet Radiation in the General Lighting of a Machine Shop," *Gigiena i Sanitariya* 32 (October 1971): 109–11.

Harmful Effects

Timing. Travelers often experience adjustment difficulties after taking a jet flight across several time zones. This disruption of the normal day–night cycle can cause a general disorientation but it is usually transient.

In particularly receptive human subjects, flashing lights have been known to trigger epileptic seizure or upset a delicately balanced mind to the point of schizothymia or schizophrenia. When experiments with psychedelic drugs were popular, intense light rhythms (coordinated with sound stimuli, symbolism, and the drugs) were employed to loosen the conventionally restricted mind. The process was always dangerous, although its effects were sometimes impressive.

High Levels of Ultraviolet. An erythemal dosage of illumination manifests a noticeable reddening of human skin. Dosages of short duration may not be permanently harmful, but lengthy doses can cause dangerous physiological reactions, irreparable damage, or death. The harmful effects include loss of sight (caused by fixation on a source producing high levels of ultraviolet), sun-blindness, skin allergies, sunburn, sunstroke, tumors of the skin, premature aging of the skin, and skin cancer. In fact, the most frequent human cancer is skin cancer. It is directly caused by exposure to the spectral wavelengths between 290 and 320 nanometers.

A report by the American Medical Association's Committee on Cosmetics, reprinted in the booklet *The Medicine Show** states the followng:

There is indisputable evidence that continued exposure to the sun weathers and ages the skin. . . . Gradual inevitable changes take place in the superficial blood vessels of the exposed surfaces. The connective tissue of the skin undergoes degenerative changes that are reflected on the surface by wrinkles and a coarsening in the skin texture. The V of the neck becomes reddened, and spotted hyperpigmentation is noted over the exposed areas. This is somewhat reminiscent of freckling, but the dark spots are more irregular in shape and size than freckles. The lips become scaly, fissured, thickened, and eroded. Abnormalities of keratinization of different types and degrees develop. Some of these changes are pre-malignant. . . the end results of which can be skin cancer. . . . [The] effects of the sun are cumulative and at some point irreversible. Complete immunity to the effects of the sun is nonexistent.

The Medicine Show continues with an excellent description of the process, effects, and prevention of sun damage. In particular, it warns against the danger of sunlamps and cautions the user always to wear protective goggles.

*Consumer Union, *The Medicine Show* (Mount Vernon, N.Y., 1970), pp. 152–60.

Unfortunately, the human system does not immediately realize the harmful effects of ultraviolet radiation. Irreversible damage to the retina may happen without warning if an observer fixates too long on a strong, ultraviolet-producing source. The common sunlamp can cause retinal burns of the unprotected eye, and the user will be unaware that the damage is occurring. During each full or partial eclipse of the sun, many observers are blinded while attempting to look directly at the phenomenon.

BIBLIOGRAPHY

Barton, Melvin, Spivack, Mayer, and Powell, Peter, "The Effect of Angle of Light on the Recognition and Evaluation of Faces." NIMH Grant #MH15314-02, Environmental Analysis and Design, Laboratory of Community Psychiatry, Harvard Medical School, Boston, Mass., 1972.

Carmel, Kate, "The Aging Eye," unpublished research study, Parsons School of Design, New School for Social Research, New York City, 1973.

Corsini, Raymond J., and Fassett, Katherine K., "Intelligence and Aging," *Journal of Genetic Psychology,* **83,** 2 (1953): 249–64.

Flynn, John E., "The Psychology of Light," *Electrical Consultant,* eight articles published between December 1972 and August 1973.

Flynn, John E., Spencer, Terry J., Martyniuk, Osyp, and Hendrick, Clyde, "Interim Study of Procedures for Investigating the Effect of Light on Impression and Behavior," *Journal of the Illuminating Engineering Society* (October 1973):87–94.

Gilbert, Jeanne G., "Age Changes in Color Matching," *Journal of Gerontology,* **30,** 8 (1959): 561–62.

Hanes, Bernard, "Perceptual Learning and Age," *Journal of Consulting Psychology,* **17,** 3 (1953): 222–24.

Harper, W. J., "On the Interpretation of Preference Experiments in Illumination," *Journal of the Illuminating Engineering Society* (January 1974): 157–59.

Hirsch, Monroe J., "Changes in Refractive State After the Age of Forty-Five," *American Journal of Optometry,* **35,** 5 (1958) 229–37.

Hirsch, Monroe J., and Wick, Ralph E., eds., *Vision of the Aging Patient* (Philadelphia, 1960).

Illuminating Engineering Society, I.E.S. *Lighting Handbook,* 5th ed. (New York, 1972).

Kleiber, Douglas A., Muscik, Patricia L., Jayson, Jill K., et al., "Lamps—Their Effect on Social Interaction and Fatigue," *Lighting Design and Application* (January 1974): 51–53.

Pierson W. R., and Montoye, H. J., "Movement, Reaction Time and Age," *Journal of Gerontology,* **13,** 4 (1958): 418–21.

Taylor, Lyle H., and Sucov, Eugene W., "The Movement of People Toward Lights," *Journal of the Illuminating Engineering Society* (April 1974): 237–41.

United States Department of Health, Education and Welfare, *Patterns of Living and Housing of Middle-Aged and Older People* (Bethesda, Maryland, 1965).

Welford, Alan T., *Skill and Age: An Experimental Approach* (New York, 1950).

Chapter Twenty-six

Architectural Lighting and Associated Phenomena

========

The design approach to interior environments is frequently fragmented with specialists handling each individual system. However, there are significant interactions among systems that require design coordination. For the lighting specialist, several aspects of lighting design that can affect other systems come immediately to mind: conservation of lighting energy, heat production, effect on vegetation (phyto-illumination), contribution to safety, production of sound, and effects on surface deterioration.

THE CONSERVATION OF LIGHTING ENERGY

For the United States, 1973 was the year of the energy crisis. Shortages of several fuel types caused business people, building professionals, the general public, and politicians to express alarm at the wasteful application of limited resources. As a result, the users of lighting energy were asked to conserve available sources.

Although it is a conspicuous user of energy, lighting represents a small percentage of the total energy consumed in the United States. In a period of critical short supply, however, any intelligent saving is welcomed. Fortunately, short-term economic benefits are frequently achieved through conservation-oriented practices in the operation and maintenance of lighting. Conversely, long-range energy savings may suggest greater planning costs. Even when long-term economy is obvious, owners may not always be predisposed to expand already strained initial budgets.

Early in 1974, the U.S. Federal Power Commission estimated that approximately 25% of our available energy was used to generate electricity. The energy sources used to produce electricity were divided into the following categories: 45% from coal; 5% from hydroelectric power; 10% from geothermal, nuclear, and other sources; 20% from natural gas, and 20% from petroleum. Of the 25% of available energy used for electrical generation, only 5–6% was consumed for lighting. Therefore, it is easy to see that vast cutbacks in the consumption of lighting can never single-handedly solve the energy problem. An electrical energy saving of only 2–3% requires a reduction in lighting usage of over 50%. Such a reduction would not be feasible even considering the most conservative of today's lighting practices.

Many sensible power (and cost) savings are possible in lighting systems, but each one must be weighed against its possible negative ramifications. Unsatisfactory aspects, however, may not be clearly considered when the urge to economize is a popular theme. It would be a tragedy to lose the positive aspects of modern lighting practice through hastily considered "economies."

Now that the immediate need to cut back has been tempered by time and experience, it is possible to summarize and evaluate methods leading to a more efficient use of electrical power in lighting.

Daylight

Daylighting seems to be an ideal way to conserve energy. Daylight is abundant, it exists during most working hours, it does not deplete energy supplies, and it has traditionally been an integral part of architectural design.

Method

The techniques of daylighting are complex and extensive. They can only be summarized here. The successful use of natural illumination requires careful consideration of at least four factors in addition to those encountered in artificial lighting design: the desire for building occupants to see exterior views, uncontrollable changes in the amount or type of daylight, variations in the position of the sun, and the spectral composition of natural sources.

Caution

The inept use of daylight can result in problems such as disability glare, undesirable brightness contrasts, excessive variability, and unacceptable distractions. Solar lighting can also contribute excessive heat gain to a poorly designed space. The high ultraviolet component in natural light bleaches fabrics and causes materials to deteriorate.

Aesthetic and Practical Effectiveness

The most conservation-minded scheme will not be effective unless the inhabitants of the space find it pleasant. Similarly, plans for innovative illumination cannot be successful if they are not practical in relation to the other environmental factors. Lighting solutions based on generalizations or computational syntheses must always be weighed against specific human needs and design acceptability. Given a sympathetic approach, a compromise can be developed that leads to acceptable solutions that conserve electric power.

Economic Considerations

Many factors other than initial cost interrelate to determine the enviromental impact of a proposed lighting system.

Method

Full environmental cost should include an evaluation of light output and consumption in terms of effectiveness, energy use, purchase cost (including investment interest, taxes, and insurance), installation labor and materials, lamp replacement, normal maintenance labor and materials, depreciation with eventual replacement or repair labor and materials, and the system's impact on other aspects of the environment. Comparisons of alternative illumination methods should be used to determine the optimal system.

Electrical Control

Selective dimming and switching systems can help minimize energy consumption in unused spaces or in spaces where the intensity or pattern of use varies.

Method

Several methods of electrical control can be applied. (1) The connection of small groups of individual luminaires to manual switches allows unused luminaires to be de-energized at the occupant's discretion. Conventional wiring for numerous individual switches may prove to be expensive and inflexible. Advanced manual switching systems, not regularly used at present, may offer economy. Examples of these systems include low-voltage switching, sound-activated controls, carrier-current switching, and radio-frequency control. (2) Timed controls can be used to adjust the lighting of spaces with predictable traffic patterns. (3) Motion-detection switching can be used to activate lighting of spaces with continuously variable traffic patterns, such as stairways, stockrooms, or lavatories. (4) Photoelectric controls can vary the illumination according to either incident or reflected light levels. They can be used to switch luminaires on and off, or they can be adpated to continuously vary the artificial light level in response to graduated changes in the level of natural light or other light sources. (5) Multiple level ballasts for electric discharge lighting and three-way incandescent lamps offer multiple light output possibilities when coupled to any of the aforementioned controls. (6) Manual or automated dimming provides continuously variable light levels.

Examples

The examples listed here are just a few of the possible systems. (1) Photoelectric control for exterior lighting assures that it will be on when needed for comfort and safety and turned off when natural light is sufficient. (2) Security lighting can be activated by intruder detection devices in place of permanently energized illumination. (3) Switched or dimmed supplementary lighting can be incorporated into luminaires providing ambient light levels. When visual tasks of unusual difficulty are encountered, the illumination in specific areas can be increased. (4) Lighting programs for entire facilities can be developed to match business activities. For example, lighting levels might be reduced during noontime and before and after work. Override controls could be provided for unusual work schedules and cleaning. (5) Systems can be created to provide automatic adjustments in intensity, thereby easing the adaptation between naturally high and low light levels (e.g., for electric signs and in theater lobbies or tunnel entrances).

Caution

Lamp life will be shortened by increasing the number of starts. The actual reduction is governed by the amount of switching and the specific lamp type. However, dimming as a method of turning on and off light sources tends to extend incandescent lamp life. "Soft start" systems that reduce initial power surge are commercially offered for this purpose.

Electrical Power

Variations in standard electrical power may lead to more efficient lighting.

Method

Among the possible variations are the following: (1) High-frequency electric service (over 60 Hz) may improve the performance of electric discharge light sources by reducing watts of per lumen output, minimizing ballast heat loss, and increasing lamp life. (2) Low-voltage electric power (below 120 V) for incandescent lighting can accomplish more precise optical control (through smaller filament size), increase lumens per watt, and decrease heat per unit of light. (3) Higher-voltage power (over 120 V) for electric discharge lighting can mean smaller wire size and more efficient distribution of electric power.

Technical Caution

Both high-frequency and high-voltage power can be limiting. For example, standard incandescent sources cannot be simply installed in a building system limited to more than 120 volts unless a transformer is used. Low voltage can be expensive in wiring costs, since larger wire sizes and required for relative distances.

Environmental Control Systems

The approximate division of energy usage in industry shows 40% of the available total used for production, 40% for environmental control, and 20% for lighting. Since much of "environmental control" is air conditioning, control of the heat contribution of electric lighting also has an implication for energy consumption, as do reductions in simple lamp wattage. The size, orientation, and configuration of doors and windows affects both the contribution of natural light and the buildup of light-generated heat. Steps must therefore be taken to control the heat output of lamps, luminaires, and fenestration.

Method

Heat output can be controlled in several ways: (1) Lamps can be chosen that produce an increased amount of light per unit of heat. Incandescent lamps are the greatest heat producers. HID sources offer significant reductions as do fluorescent lamps, which produce the least heat. (2) Lamps and luminaires with dichroic or other heat barriers can prevent direct radiant energy from entering a space. (3) Luminaires that use air or water to remove (and store or reuse) heat can reduce air-conditioning requirements. (4) A study of a structure's fenestration will indicate the maximum natural contribution to lighting and the optimum contribution to heating. Effective louvering, tinted glass, and other architectural features (e.g., exterior reflectors at windows, awnings, and structural overhangs) all offer control possibilities.

Luminaire Efficiency

The selection of efficient luminaires increases the value of light output.

Method

Luminaire efficiency can be determined from simple calculations. (1) Overall efficiency for a luminaire can be determined by a ratio of the lumens emitted by the luminaire to the lumens emitted by the lamp(s) used in the luminaire. (2) The efficiency of alternative luminaires in illuminating a work plane can be derived by comparing coefficients of utilization for spaces of similar size and reflectance. (3) The maintained effectiveness of luminaires can be judged by comparing light loss factors for similar spaces.

Luminaire Light Controlling Elements

A luminaire's light controlling elements can distribute light in a manner that will enhance seeing ability and consume a minimal amount of energy.

Method

Several light distribution techniques can be used to advantage: (1) Oblique light distributions from general lighting sources reduce veiling glare when directed in from the sides of an observer. On the other hand, when sources are placed directly in front of or above the viewer, veiling glare may partially or entirely obliterate a view of the task. "Bat-wing" candlepower distributions provided by luminaire reflector or refractor designs have proven useful when an observer's orientation within a space is fixed. (2) Polarization can also be effective in the reduction of task glare. (3) As the visual surround approaches an even and diffusely reflective mass, it is increasingly less likely that the task will reflect source glare. Relative point or line sources create greater reflected glare problems than diffused sources. High contrasts between the light source and its surrounding surfaces can also create task-reflected glare. Equivalent sphere illumination formulations can also be used to determine maximum task visibility through reductions in glare.

Design Caution

Glare reduction techniques are not always completely effective. (1) For purposes of glare calculation, particularly with desk-top tasks, it is often assumed that the task lies flat on the test surface. In fact, the task (e.g., a bound book) is often not flat, but rather it is curved or tilted. Under these conditions, oblique light distributions may not eliminate glare on the task. (2) Translucent panels used in polarized lighting applications may appear cloudy or uneven in their light transmission.

Maintenance

Light output is improved by the effective cleaning of luminaires or other environmental surfaces and the replacement of lamps that have ceased to provide maximum light output.

Method

Lamps should be replaced at the end of their effective lives, not their average lives. All lamps suffer gradual light reduction throughout their lives—some types depreciate more than others, some depreciate faster. A 5% reduction occurs after roughly 400 hours for general-service incandescents, 2000 hours for tungsten–halogen incandescents, 3000 hours for F40 fluorescents, 2400 for mercury lamps, 1500 for metal halide lamps, and 5000 hours for high-pressure sodium sources. At the end of their average lives, general-service lamps lose 10 to 20% of their starting light output (after 1000 hours); tungsten–halogen incandescents, 5% (2000 hours); F40 fluorescents, 16% (20,000 hours); mercury, 25–30% (24,000 hours); metal halide, 26–32% (15,000 hours); and high-pressure sodium, 17–21% (20,000 hours). The actual point of light depreciation at which a lamp should be removed is governed by the maximum acceptable loss in light level as determined by a lumen maintenance chart (supplied by lamp manufacturers for specific lamp types). From the preceding figures, it can be determined that the relamping of luminaires may increase light output by over 20%.

Other maintenance procedures can lead to increased light output. If luminaire surfaces are cleaned, as much as 20% of the initial light level can be regained. If room surfaces are repainted, an estimated maximum gain in light level of 15% is possible.

Nonuniform Lighting Patterns

Energy can be conserved through effective light concentration at the task and reduction of lighting in unnecessary areas. When creatively handled, nonuniform illumination can also add important design interest.

Method

Several approaches will provide effective nonuniform lighting patterns. The layout of permanent architectural luminaires can be concentrated to emphasize the task, or supplementary lighting can be provided. The designer should also remember that spill lighting from major task areas will often adequately illuminate secondary tasks.

Caution

According to the I.E.S., general illumination should be at least 10% of supplementary illumination but not less than 20 footcandles. In addition, uniform illumination must be provided for task areas where shadows pose a safety problem (e.g., rotating machinery), may cause working errors (drafting areas, computer rooms, etc.), or lead to physiological problems (the aging eye responds poorly to strong contrast; vision abnormalities may require even values; arduous visual tasks often require close contrast tolerances).

Examples

Tasks can be illuminated with luminaires incorporated into furnishings. Overall and nonessential illumination can be minimized by accentuating selected features to give a feeling of higher ambience (accented plants, wall washing, etc.).

Operation of Lighting Systems

The development of an economical lighting system is only part of the battle in conserving energy used for lighting. The system must also be continuously operated with this goal in mind.

Method

Clear operating instructions should be issued to all persons who may operate the equipment. In addition to preparing operating manuals for maintenance personnel, specific instructions should be posted for lay users. It is also helpful to develop programming (switching and dimming) that automatically controls the use of light energy.

Task Orientation

The careful consideration of the nature of the task, its orientation within a space, its relationship to other tasks, and its flexibility will allow the introduction of several economies of lighting energy.

Method

Similar tasks should be grouped together for optimal lighting energy distribution. Variability in the intensity of general lighting and the positioning of supplementary lighting will accommodate changes in activity. "Landscaped" planning, because of its photometric reality as a large space, improves lighting efficiency when contrasted with partitioned smaller spaces.

Orientation of Light Sources in Relation to Tasks

Glare reduction, through the proper placement of luminaires, will lead to increased utility of illumination. Certain tasks require specific illumination orientations and are severely compromised by (or fail to respond effectively to) other placements.

Method

Several factors should be kept in mind when determining luminaire placement. (1) Know the task. For example, specular objects respond more to the shape of a light source and the number of light sources than to direction of the light or its intensity. Diffuse objects, on the other hand, respond more to the direction of light and its intensity. (2) To allow maximum visibility of a specular or spread surface (e.g., a glossy picture), place the angle of incidence so that the angle of reflection will be away from the viewer's line of vision. (3) Use ESI evaluations when glare-inducing criteria are complex. (4) Reduce direct glare by proper shielding of light sources.

Design Caution

Extreme reductions of contrast, when applied overall, may lead to psychologically dull installations where sparkle, sheen, or shine may have been more appropriate.

Source Efficiency and Appropriateness

The selection of efficient and appropriate light sources can reduce power consumption.

Method

Source efficiency can be determined by lumens per watt. In general, the lumen per watt ratings of standard artificial light sources are: 17–22 lumens per watt for incandescent, 56–63 for mercury, 67–83 for fluorescent, 85–100 for metal halide, and 105–130 for high-pressure sodium. Other factors include lamp cost, lamp maintenance, light quality, color, and the availability of appropriate luminaires and auxiliary equipment.

Design Caution

The preliminary results of recent studies indicate that the eye can see as well under lower levels of spectrally balanced light as under higher levels produced by spectrally deficient light sources. Studies of standard cool white and deluxe cool white fluorescent colors (and warm white with its deluxe counterpart), suggest that the balanced source (deluxe) may produce one-third more *useful* visual energy than the spectrally uneven source.

Generated light distribution should be appropriate. A diffuse source (e.g., a fluorescent lamp) may not be as satisfactory as a point source (incandescent) in the control of light, even though the diffuse source produces more lumens per watt. Conversely, a point source (metal halide) may not be as appropriate as a lower-efficiency diffuse source (fluorescent) for the production of shadowless illumination.

The participation of luminaires and auxilary equipment (ballasts, etc.) must always be considered when totaling the efficiency (lumens per watt) of light-producing units. See Table 26.1.

Technical Caution

Before substituting lamps, be sure that the luminaire and auxiliary equipment will accept the substitution in terms of heat output, structure, photometrics, and electrical requirements. And remember that initial dollar cost and maintenance of auxiliary equipment can overshadow lamp efficiencies.

Examples

A number of substitutions are possible; the following are only a few examples. (1) Standard-life incandescent lamps can be substituted for long-life lamps to improve the quantity of light output. (2) High-wattage reflector (R) lamps can be replaced by lower wattage PAR lamps. The

Table 26.1. Electrical Consumption of Typical Lamp and Ballast Combinations[a]

Lamp Code	Quantity of Lamps Attached to One Ballast	Lamp Rating in Watts[b]	Total Watts –ANSI Test	Comment
F30T12	1	30	46	
Fluorescent[c]	2	30	75	
F40T12	1	40	57	Standard
Fluorescent[c]	1	40	55	Quality
	1	40	50	Premium
	2	80	96	Standard
	2	80	94	Improved
	2	80	92	Quality
	2	80	86	Premium
Mercury	1	100	118	
Vapor[d]	1	175	200	
	1	250	285	
	1	400	454	
	2	400	880	
Metal[d]	1	175	210	
Halide	1	250	292	
	1	400	455	
HPI	1	250	300	
	1	400	465	

[a]All ballasts are High Power Factor unless otherwise noted. All ballasts manufactured by Advance Transformer Company, Chicago, Illinois. Other ballast types and manufacturers may carry slightly different ratings.

[b]Ratings apply for 120- or 277-volt electrical service.

[c]Fluorescent lamps are rated standard electromechanical ballasts (not electronic) tested to ANSI C82.2 methods and operate at 50°F minimum starting temperature.

[d]Mercury vapor and metal halide ballasts are enclosed and potted for interior use with Constant Wattage Autotransformer circuitry and will operate at −20°F starting temperature.

improved optics of the PAR lamp will produce as many useful lumens as the less efficient optics of the R source. (3) One 250-watt tungsten–halogen PAR (Q250PAR/FL) can replace two standard 150 PAR floods (150PAR38/FL) with an increase in light output and a reduction in total wattage used. Other power-saving reflector lamps are also available. (4) Tungsten–halogen and other special incandescent sources offer efficiency advantages over standard lamps. (5) Self-ballasted mercury lamps (the ballast is inside the bulb) can be used to replace incandescent sources in appropriate luminaires. (6) Certain HID sources can be interchanged within one ballast type for increased light output. (7) In fluorescent sources, the longer the lamp, the greater its efficiency (one 2-ft. U shape is also more efficient than two 2-ft. lamps). (8) With incandescent and HID sources, the higher wattages are usually more efficient.

Spatial Criteria

The size and orientation of spaces affect the efficiency with which light is used by the space. Proper configurations can lead to less light being used with the attendant conservation of energy.

Method

With a given ceiling height, it is a general rule that larger spaces use light more efficiently than smaller spaces. With a given length and width, a lower ceiling is usually more efficient than a higher ceiling.

Surface Reflectivity and Color

Careful consideration of the type and color of surfaces can lead to economy in the use of light and power.

Method

It is helpful to remember three simple rules: (1) The more reflective the surfaces of a space, the more efficient is the use of light. (2) Highly reflective matte surfaces are more efficient in their use of light than specular surfaces. (3) Color tints make more effective use of light than strongly saturated hues.

Task Optimization

The nature of the visual task itself affects the amount of energy required to illuminate it. In general, the following rules prevail: (1) The larger the task, the less light it takes to see it. (2) The brighter the task (in footlamberts, not necessarily, footcandles), the more acceptable it is. (3) High contrasts within the seeing task and between the image and its background are better than low contrasts. (4) Tasks that are not rushed are easier to see at lower light levels. (5) Specular tasks are more susceptible to veiling glare than diffuse tasks and may require greater illumination. (6) Color and texture can play important roles in maximizing visual acuity with reduced illumination.

Examples

The effect of task condition can be demonstrated with several everyday examples: (1) A book with shiny pages produces more glare than a book printed on matte stock. (2) Specular marble walls, a favorite element in lobby design, are more difficult to illuminate without veiling glare than are matte walls. (3) "Wet look" wall coverings, glass tabletops, chrome furnishings, and lacquered finishes all create severe glare problems. (4) Black print on a highly reflective matte page is easier to read than light gray print. (5) Images printed on yellow or green paper stocks are easier to see.

Design Caution

Although high task contrast is often beneficial for accurate seeing, contrasts in the areas surrounding the task must be carefully controlled or they will interfere with task visibility.

Removal or Reduction in the Output of Unneeded Light Sources

Savings can be achieved through lower illumination in areas that are not used, nonessential or overilluminated as a result of poor planning or altered use.

Method

Costs can be reduced by (1) removing all or some of the lamps in appropriate luminaires or (2) replacing high-output sources with low-output, energy-saving sources. Certain manufacturers produce electric discharge sources that can be interchanged within a given ballast type to reduce energy consumption and light output.

Design Caution

Uneven or dark apertures within any one visible space may be objectionable.

Technical Caution

False economies may result if the following factors are not considered: (1) Multiple-lamp fluorescent ballasts may be damaged if only one lamp is removed, and the remaining lamps may not operate. (2) Most electric discharge ballasts will continue to consume some electric power even when all or part of their connected lamp load is removed. (3) A single lamp may be removed from certain double-lamp HID units only if the ballast is not a series ballast. Under single-lamp operation, two-lamp HID ballasts may overheat thus shortening their lives. (4) Although mercury and metal-halide lamps may be removed from single-lamp ballasted luminaires without harm, high-pressure sodium lamps may only be removed for a short time. Unless the high-pressure sodium lamp is quickly replaced or the ballast is de-energized, the starting mechanism of the ballast will be harmed. (5) Lamp and ballast life will be severely shortened if lamps are arbitrarily substituted with ballasts designed to take only specific wattages. In particular, do not place energy-conserving lamps on ballasts that are not rated to support them.

LIGHT ENERGY AND THE PRODUCTION OF HEAT

Heating and cooling are traditionally the specialty of the air-conditioning engineer. Therefore, this chapter only outlines the criteria necessary to interface lighting design with this specialty. Further information can be obtained from the *Handbook of Fundamentals* published by the American Society of Heating, Refrigeration, and Air-Conditioning Engineers (ASHRAE).

Heat generated from lighting takes two principal forms: (1) Conduction and convection are generally discussed as one form of energy. Conduction is the process of heat transfer through a material. Convection describes the movement of heat resulting from gravitational action and differences in air density. The latter phenomenon is responsible for the upward motion of warm air. (2) Radiant energy refers to the parts of the electromagnetic spectrum including ultraviolet, visible color, and infrared wavelengths. Radiant energy sources do not heat air as do convection sources. Most of the heat developed by lamps is in the form of radiant energy. Light itself is heat and raises the temperature of any surface that absorbs it.

Every watt used in the production of electric light (including ballasts) generates 3.4 units of heat per hour called a British thermal unit (BTU). Although lamps are not 100% efficient as light sources, they *are* 100% efficient as heat sources.

Light Output in Relation to Operating Temperature

Ambient temperature does not affect the light output of incandescent lamps. If, however, the temperature surrounding an electric discharge source varies widely from design parameters, light output may decrease.

Generally, HID lamps are not affected by minor ambient temperature changes because of the insulating effect of the luminaire housings and the outer bulb wall surrounding the arc tube. Fluorescent lamps, on the other hand, are more exposed to changes in temperature because they are often used without auxiliary enclosures and the outer bulb wall also acts as the arc enclosure. Most fluorescent lamps are designed to operate in an ambient temperature of 77°F. Drafts on the bulb wall may be substantially below this temperature, while the temperature of fluorescent lamps inside unvented luminaire housings often exceeds 77°F. Therefore, if the ambient temperature is, say, 100°F, the light output of a rapid-start T-12 lamp may drop about 12%.

Variations in ambient temperature will also cause shifts in color.

The Lighting System as a Heat Source

All elements in the lighting system combine to produce the heat within any space.

Daylight

All the factors that describe natural light (see Chapter Five) affect the amount of heat that is contributed to an interior space. To review briefly, these include local terrain, land- or water-scaping, size and orientation of fenestration, and daylight control (blinds, etc.) as well as such variables as the sun's position, diffusion, timing, and intensity.

Artificial Light Sources

Incandescent lamps are inefficient producers of light in relation to the amount of heat they produce. The lower the Kelvin temperature of the lamp, the less light it produces in relation to its heating potential.

Electric discharge lamps produce more lumens per watt and therefore more light in relation to their production of heat. However, each watt of electricity used to power a fluorescent or HID light source (including ballast losses) still produces 3.4 British thermal units per hour.

Luminaire Heat Distribution

Three of the six C.I.E. classifications for light distribution can be applied to heat distribution: semidirect (60% of the heat projected downward and 40% upward), direct-indirect (equal amounts of heat projected up and down) and semi-indirect (60% up and 40% down).

Heat distribution is basically determined by the construction of the luminaire. In enclosed luminaires, much of the heat remains around the lamp(s) and ballast, which can affect performance. Luminaire materials vary in their ability to reflect or transmit selected wavelengths involved in the heating process. Recessed luminaires with transparent or translucent solid closures contribute less heat directly to a space and more to the area above the ceiling than luminaires without closures; lenses are better heat barriers than, for example, open louvers.

Luminaire Mounting.   The position of the luminaire in relation to room surfaces alters its heating ability. With pendant luminaires, the ceiling reflects or absorbs and then reradiates heat. Surface-mounted units involve radiation, conduction, and convection of heat directly into the space and through the ceiling or other surface; if the ceiling is a good insulator (as many of them are), temperatures within the luminaire will increase. Recessed luminaires release some portion of their heat above the ceiling line.

Luminaire Heat Controlling Elements.   "Static" lighting systems do not become involved in the lighting/heating process by special design. However, features can be designed into luminaires and associated structures that will control their air-conditioning performance.

Filters.   Both absorption and dichroic processes can be used to selectively filter out infrared radiation while passing most visible wavelengths. Transparency projectors, for example, may have a tinted glass in the optical system that removes unwanted wavelengths before they strike the film surface. Certain PAR lamps employ dichroic reflectors to selectively pass infrared radiation through the back of the lamp while projecting a relatively cool light beam containing most of the visible wavelengths.

Directed Heat Flows.   Air can be passed over the housing of a recessed luminaire, thereby removing the heat produced above the ceiling line. Slots can be introduced around the trim of air-handling luminaires to supply or exhaust air conditioning. If the air is exhausted across the lamps and/or ballasts, the luminaire is termed a "heat extraction" unit. Heat removal may also be affected by circulating water or other fluids next to the lamps and ballasts. The benefits of utilizing the heat produced by luminaires with these and other processes include: efficient handling of lighting heat, improved thermal performance for the space, and improved lamp performance of fluorescent sources. It must be noted that electric discharge lamp light output often relies of the heat of the bulb wall. In particular, light output can be lost by decreasing bulb wall temperature below the manufacturers' stated tolerances—as when a standard lamp is used in very low exterior temperatures during winter months or when lamps are situated in front of cold-air ducts.

Information Useful to the Air-Conditioning Specialist

The air-conditioning specialist must determine the thermal contribution of luminaires within a single space. To help in this task, the lighting designer should supply the total wattage (including ballasts) for each type of luminaire, as well as facts about luminaire heat distribution, mounting, and heat controlling elements.

PHYTO-ILLUMINATION

When indoor plantings fail to grow satisfactorily, the lighting is frequently blamed. This is not always justified, since other factors, such as disease control, humidity, nutrition, pest elimination, propagation, soil condition, and temperature, are also important to plant health. However, along with temperature and soil, light is considered a most vital element in plant health.

We restrict this discussion to illumination and examine the following contributory aspects: intensity, spectral composition and balance, light energy source, and time cycle (photoperiodism).

Lighting Factors

Light *intensity* requirements vary with the plant species. In most cases, 50 footcandles (a minimum) will produce a low-level response in plants; on the other hand, some plants need direct sunlight, which may reach 10,000 footcandles. However, most popular plantings require no more than 1500 footcandles of artificial light to prosper.

A by-product of high lighting intensity is temperature. Care must always be taken to avoid direct burning. Once below the burning level, most temperature requirements are stated in terms of "off" or night temperature. The "off" temperature is particularly important because proper cool night temperatures help vegetation to digest the food collected during "on" hours. General speaking, most plants will thrive in temperatures ranging between 50 and 70°F.

Spectral composition and *balance* of artificial illuminants must receive special consideration. Most authorities agree that the more important spectral wavelengths are 450, 650, and 730 nanometers. The blue spectrum encourages foliage growth, while the red range develops flowering. The importance of far-red radiation has received particular emphasis, since this part of the spectrum most directly affects phytochrome, the light-sensitive pigment found in all vegetation. Phytochrome, in turn, controls the timing of a plant's development.

More specifically, too much blue light will cause limited flowering or flowerless plants with stubby short growth. An excess of red leads to stringy ("leggy") and tall plants. Green and yellow have no influence on most plants, since the similar color of their foliage tends to reflect these radiations. The effects of ultraviolet are not fully understood, although excessive ultraviolet rays can lead to damage.

The *light energy source* is important in terms of its spectral and heat-producing qualities. In "phytotrons," elaborate growth control spaces, a mixture of fluorescent and incandescent light has traditionally been preferred. As the illumination increases, the desired ratio of incandescent to fluorescent sources seems to change slightly according to the ratios shown in Table 26.2. For example, if 120 watts of fluorescent light is producing the desired illumination on a plant's surface, this source should be balanced with 40 watts of incandescent light.

A base illumination from fluorescent lamps is suggested because it will not produce the excessive heat that would be generated by an all-incandescent system. As suggested by the recommended high illumination levels, 800 milliamperes (high output) or 1500 milliamperes (very high output, Power Groove, or super high output) lamps may be preferred to normal 430 milliamperes sources, and these lamps may be placed very close to the plants. A glass or plastic sheet is often placed between the lamp array and the plants for added protection. Forced ventilation and cooling of the resulting lamp and plant compartments is also common practice.

The cool white fluorescent lamp color has been most often used in professional nurseries, although recent studies indicate that warm white may be equally effective.

The listed ratio of incandescent lamps is recommended because of the far-red radiation requirement. Because incandescent sources produce excessive heat, many low-wattage lamps rather than a single high-wattage lamp should be used to supply the requisite balance.

Major lamp manufacturers have introduced several fluorescent sources that are advertised for use without an incandescent supplement. These

Table 26.2.

Footcandles on Plant	Wattage Ratio of Fluorescent to Incandescent	
to 1000	3	1
1001 to 2000	4	1
2000 and up	5	1

lamps bear such trade names as Plant Light (General Electric: indicated by the code, PL), Plant-Gro (Westinghouse, GRO), Gro-lux and Gro-lux Wide-Spectrum (Sylvania, GRO and GRO/WS), and Vita-Lite (Duro-Test). It should be noted that the fluorescent–incandescent combination is still preferred for use in professional and experimental installations. However, as a single-source solution, not under critical conditions, the aforementioned lamps may provide a better light source than a simple all-standard fluorescent or all-incandescent installation. The unusual color balance of these lamps may also have design importance: Plant-Gro has a yellowish cast, both Plant Light and Gro-lux are purplish, and Vita-Lite appears as a balanced white (Ra = 91 at 5500°K). Authorities vary in their recommendations for optimal artificial light levels for plant growth and maintenance in regards to specific plant types. A current reference should be used to determine acceptable levels.

The use of HID light sources for plant growth and maintenance has only recently been investigated. The importance of these sources is immediate, since the illumination of large public spaces containing plantings (offices, covered shopping malls, etc.) increasingly depends on them. No single type of HID lamp appears to provide optimum results. However, experimentation by Dr. R. J. Downs in the phytotron at North Carolina State University indicates that a one-to-one mixture (by wattage) of high-pressure sodium with either deluxe-white mercury vapor or simple metal halide lamps produces adequate results.

Time cycles, variations in the length of "on" or daylight and "off" or darkness, have a great effect on certain plants because of the phenomenon known as photoperiodism. Generally, plant species can be divided into three groups: (1) short-day plants (averaging approximately 10 on- and 14 off-hours), (2) long-day plants (18 on and 6 off), and (3) day-neutral plants (cycle not important). Certain plants are more sensitive to the light cycle at particular periods of their development.

SAFETY AND LIGHTING

Protective Illumination

Lighting patterns may be used to protect persons and objects from criminals. Continuously illuminated spaces help prevent unauthorized activities, and intruder-activated lighting may have additional surprise value. In both instances, the criminal may assume that a space is occupied if it is illuminated.

Lighting for Safety in Normal and Emergency Conditions

Inappropriate lighting can interfere with safety under certain conditions: (1) Light levels that are too low prevent the observer from comprehending the details of the environment. (2) Insufficient contrasts lead to visual confusion about the location and shape of objects. As an example, if the contrast between the riser and tread of a stair is not clear, the user may not be able to quickly determine the position or height of the stair. (3) Conversely, too great a contrast leads to distorted object appearance or, in the extreme, disability glare. (4) Sudden changes in light level prevent the eye from accurately discerning the environment for short or relatively long periods of time, depending on the extremes encountered. (5) Unexpected variations in the characteristics of a luminous environment have similarly serious effects. A fully and evenly illuminated room that is suddenly changed to sharp shafts of light may cause panic and confusion.

The I.E.S. is considering the recommendation of the following base lighting levels as absolute minimums for safety:

Condition	Activity Level	Footcandles
Low hazard	Low	½
Low hazard	High	1
High hazard	Low	2
High hazard	High	5

The standards that have been developed for safe lighting must be interpreted by licensed professionals in terms of their application to specific facilities in their localities. These standards may be existing or proposed, enforceable or recommended. Examples include the Life and Safety Code published by the National Fire Protection Association, the National Electric Code, and numerous local codes.

The selection of lighting equipment for emergency conditions is a specialty of architectural engineering consultants. Several equipment categories are typical: (1) Emergency generators are often located in larger buildings or in spaces that require power that may not be interrupted or must be available for long periods of time. (2) Battery-operated lighting can be centrally or separately located. In general, central systems are used in one-story structures of less than 10,000 square feet. Unit power packs are used to sense failures of normal lighting power within the area that they illuminate. The newest units are relatively maintenance free and can be integrated within functional or decorative luminaires. Most battery systems can only provide illumination for limited periods of time (measured in hours). (3) Phosphorescent sources have been used for signage. However, their light output is inherently weak, and they glow for only a limited time after normal light sources have been extinguished. (4) Tritium gas sources have enjoyed a limited popularity in emergency lighting (see Chapter Nine). (5) Flash tubes, fired in sequence, are occasionally used to lead occupants away from unsafe places in emergency conditions.

SOUND AND LIGHT

Because of the increased use of electric discharge light sources and lighting control systems, the generation of sound by lighting equipment requires special attention.

Sound Generated by Electric Discharge Ballasts

Both fluorescent and high-intensity discharge ballasts are basically electromagnetic in character. The alternating movement (ac) of electric power through their coils causes mechanical vibrations and electrical interference.

Radio Interference

A feedback of radio-frequency energy into the power lines can cause radio interference. Better quality ballasts contain radio interference suppressing capacitors that reduce excessive noise in nearby radios or sound systems.

Direct Ballast Sound

All electrical equipment produces some noise that can be heard with the unaided ear, but electric discharge ballasts are a particular problem. The problem manifests itself as a buzz or hum. Ballast hum will be noticeable only when it exceeds the ambient noise level. Ambient noise is comparable to ambient light: It is the surrounding or pervading level of sound. Therefore, it is obvious that a ballast made primarily for use in a factory would not be suitable for a library.

The presence of objectionable ballast noise depends on various factors. They include:

1. *Ambient sound level.*
2. *Luminaire design and construction.* Although the ballast is the source of the noise, luminaire parts that can be vibrated by the ballast may greatly amplify the original sound. Vibration-sensitive components such as louvers, shields, reflectors, and all sections of a metal housing should be securely held in position or even shock-mounted. There is no alternative

to superior luminaire construction, although initial cost may be greater. However, when attempting to insulate ballast noise in a luminaire, do not try to shock-mount the ballast within the luminaire body. Good ballast-to-metal contact is important for the conduction of normal heat away from the ballast (in effect, the luminaire body acts as a heat sink for the ballast).

3. *Supporting structures.* Be sure that the luminaire's mounting device does not transmit vibration to the supporting members of a building's structure. Sound-absorbent materials may have to be used to isolate luminaires from structural components.

4. *Type and purpose of the room.* If noise is expected (such as in a factory), ballast sound ratings can be less stringent.

5. *Acoustics of the room.* Hard surfaces or other sound-reflecting conditions will reinforce the ballast sound; soft, sound-absorbent surfaces will deaden noise.

6. *Number of ballasts.* As the number of ballasts in an area increases, the collective ballast sound rises accordingly.

Users should always specify a ballast "sound rating" when they recommend electric discharge luminaires. Many ballasts are sound-rated, with "A" as the most quiet, "B" as less quiet, and so on. Unfortunately, some lamps cannot be used with quiet ballasts. If the generated noise will be offensive, intrinsically noisy ballasts should be mounted in locations remote from the luminaires they serve.

Many acousticians believe that the ballast sound-rating program developed by manufacturers is imprecise. They point out that current testing and rating procedures are open to question. Accordingly, it may only be said that "A" sound-rated ballasts are apt to be quieter than "B" ballasts.

Sound Generated by Dimming Equipment

Solid-state dimming creates special sound problems. The problems are particularly severe in theatrical or television practice because large numbers of centrally located dimmers may be used. In architectural practice, dimming noise may be quantitatively less severe, but thoroughly annoying under certain conditions.

Lamp Filament Vibration

It may not be possible to remove all of the hum produced by a dimmed incandescent lamp even with the best system. Pear-shaped lamps in high wattages are especially subject to hum. Low-noise construction lamps feature short and solid filament supports constructed of nonmagnetic metals. Tungsten–halogen light sources often effectively lower lamp hum or buzz.

Since a luminaire reflector can project sound as well as light, the use of a lens can provide a mechanical block to sound passage.

Mechanical Vibration of the Dimmer

The filter choke, a device designed to minimize the buzz or hum that reaches the filament, will make noise itself. These devices, when used in quantity or in large sizes, should be properly isolated from spaces that should be sound-free. In large architectural installations, special rooms are built to house the offending equipment.

Electrical Noise Radiation

Electromagnetic interference (EMI) from dimmers can be heard on AM radios and, under certain conditions, in other audio circuits. The best way to combat this problem is to purchase high-quality dimming components. A good rule of thumb suggests that if the current rise time equals 350 milliamperes per second or less, objectionable EMI will be minimized. However, few wall-box dimmers meet these criteria. There are also other variables to this problem that allow one inexpensive wall-box dimmer to perform flawlessly while another of the same type and make will create objectionable interference.

Stray Magnetic Fields and Conducted Electrical Noise

Conducted electrical noise is a form of interference that is caused by the way dimmers affect the building transformer. The noise is conducted through the building wiring and into the equipment that powers it. Stray magnetic fields are developed when current flows in large loops of wire. Both problems, while of significant concern to television, radio, and theater installations, are infrequent architectural concerns.

SURFACE DETERIORATION

Light causes some deterioration of most materials. The amount of deterioration is determined by (1) the ability of the material to absorb and be affected by the light, (2) the intensity of exposure and its time period, and (3) the spectral composition of the illuminant. Of course, other factors such as corrosive atmosphere, temperature, and humidity may accelerate or retard photochemical change.

Ability of the Material to Absorb and Be Affected

For a material to be affected, the energy that it absorbs must exceed the limit that the material can withstand. Not only does any sensitive material have to be studied, but its relationship with other materials may be important. For example, a paint applied to paper may be more prone to deterioration than the same paint applied to canvas. Two forms of deterioration will interest the environmental designer: (1) discoloration (fading or changing color) and (2) mechanical changes (embrittlement, tear resistance, or crumbling).

Intensity of Exposure and Time Period

Obviously the longer an object is exposed to light, the greater is the potential danger of deterioration. Intensity is also important, and Table 26.3 can be used to determine the order of intensity.

Spectral Composition of the Illuminant

Although both visible and invisible spectral energy can cause photochemical deterioration, the shorter wavelengths present the greatest danger. Since the spectral transmittance of lamp glass stops at approximately 290 nanometers, the near region of ultraviolet is of principal concern.

Table 26.3. Light Intensities Causing Deterioration[a]

Object	Approximate Maximum Level[b] (in fc)
Metal, stone, glass, ceramics, jewelry, and enamel	Unlimited[c]
Oil and tempera painting, undyed leather, horn, bone, ivory, wood, and lacquer	15
Textiles, costumes, watercolors, tapestries, prints and drawings, stamps, manuscripts, paintings in distempered media, wallpapers, gouache, dyed leather	5

[a]Adapted from G. Thompson, "Conservation and Museum Lighting," *Museum Association Information Sheet* (May 1970). Illumination used for approximately 8 hours per day.

[b]Maintained levels taking into consideration higher initial light output.

[c]Subject to display and radiant heat considerations.

Table 26.4.[a]

Source	°K[b]	Percent Probable Rate of Damage	
		Bare Light Source	Window Glass
Zenith Sky Light[b]	11,000	100[a]	32.9
Overcast sky	6,400	31.7	14.0
Cool white deluxe[c]	4,300	11.5	6.1
Warm white deluxe[c]	2,900	9.2	4.4
Daylight[c]	6,500	8.4	7.5
Incandescent	2,854	2.8	2.2

[a]Adapted from Laurence S. Harrison, "An Investigation of the Damage Hazard in Spectral Energy," *Illuminating Engineering* (May 1954): 256.
[b]Zenith Sky Light is used as the base light source.
[c]Fluorescent sources in apparent degrees Kelvin.

By testing the spectral distribution of light sources, their percentage of probable damage can be estimated when used uncovered or behind ordinary window glass. Table 26.4 lists a few examples.

Glass or plastic transparent filters can be supplied for daylight, incandescent, and fluorescent light sources. They are designed to allow most of the visible spectrum to pass while preventing harmful radiations from being transmitted. Filter manufacturers (Corning, Rohm & Haas, Pittsburgh Glass, and others) should be contacted for latest developments and spectral performance.

BIBLIOGRAPHY

American Society of Heating, Refrigerating, and Air-Conditioning Engineers, *Ashrae Handbook of Fundamentals* (New York, 1967), Chapter 28.

Cusano, Arnold J., "What's Available," *Lighting Design and Application* 4, 5 (May 1974): 6–8.

Electrical Consultant, "H.I.D. Luminaire Sound." *Electrical Consultant Magazine* (July 1974): 32–35.

General Electric Company, *Electrical Space Conditioning*, TP-126 (Nela Park, Cleveland, August 1971).

Illuminating Engineering Society, "Electric Lamps as Heat Sources," *Illuminating Engineering*, **61**, 3 (1966): 124–25.

———, I.E.S. *Lighting Handbook*, 5th ed. (New York, 1972), Chapter 16.

———, "Lighting Systems as Heat Sources," *Illuminating Engineering*, **61**, 3 (1966): 130–34.

———, "Luminaires as Heat Sources, *Illuminating Engineering* **61**, 3 (1966): 126–29.

———, "Methods of Controlling Lighting Heat," *Illuminating Engineering* **61**, 3 (1966): 135–37.

————, "Systems for Controlling Lighting Heat," *Illuminating Engineering* **66**, 3 (1966): 138–44.

————, "Thermal Environment—Conservation of Light Heat Energy," *Journal of the Illuminating Engineering Society* (October 1973): 18–20.

Kaufman, John E., "Lighting for Safety," *Lighting Design and Application* **3**, 3 (March 1973): 6–8.

Kilkelly, Brian H., "A New Code—A New Ballgame," *Lighting Design and Application* **4**, 5 (May 1974): 4–5.

Loch, Charles H. "Octave Band Spectrum Criteria for Lighting-Generated Sound," *Journal of the Illuminating Engineering Society* (July 1973): 411–417.

Petersen, Warren, "The Unit Approach," *Lighting Design and Application* **4**, 5 (May 1974): 9–14.

Sanford, John L., "How to Pick a Thyristor Dimmer," *Lighting Design and Application* (December 1973): 40–55.

Silvers, J. J., "Visual Aspects of Life Safety Lighting," *Lighting Design and Application* **2**, 8 (October 1972): 17–25.

Index